# AMERICANS ABROAD

# AMERICANS ABROAD

## A Handbook for
## Living and Working Overseas

## John Z. Kepler
## Phyllis J. Kepler
## Orville D. Gaither
## Margaret L. Gaither

PRAEGER

PRAEGER SPECIAL STUDIES • PRAEGER SCIENTIFIC

New York • Philadelphia • Eastbourne, UK
Toronto • Hong Kong • Tokyo • Sydney

Library of Congress Cataloging in Publication Data
Main entry under title:

Americans abroad.

    Includes index.
    1. Americans—Employment—Foreign countries.
I. Kepler, John Z.
HF5549.5.E45A45       910′.2′02      82-630
ISBN 0-03-060598-9            AACR2
    0-03-000219-2 (pbk.)

Published in 1983 (hb) and 1984 (pb) by Praeger Publishers
CBS Educational and Professional Publishing
a Division of CBS Inc.
521 Fifth Avenue, New York, NY 10175 USA

456789    052    987654321

Printed in the United States of America
on acid-free paper

# Dedication

A MERICA'S EXPATRIATE TRADITION is not a new one. Since the country's founding, many of its citizens have gone abroad to live and to work. As diplomats and merchant tradesmen, scientists and physicians, agricultural consultants, soldiers, Peace Corps workers, missionaries, journalists, artists, and retirees, as well as corporate businessmen and women, they have played a significant part in making the world a safer, healthier, more caring, and more progressive place in which to live. They have been living advertisements of American ideals, but they have also brought back a much wider and better informed view of life in other countries.

Today, some two and a half million Americans (exclusive of diplomats and members of the military) live around the globe. They are the twentieth-century pioneers—the expatriates for whom this book has been written and to whom it is dedicated.

# Acknowledgments

THE AUTHORS RECEIVED enthusiastic cooperation, support, and assistance from many sources. Their appreciation goes to:

Dedicated government officials in the host countries visited and the diplomatic and information office staffs of these countries in the United States.

America's diplomats abroad and in Washington, particularly the efficient people in the family liaison departments.

Many private groups abroad, such as the American clubs and American women's clubs, international school administrators, English-speaking church groups, medical personnel, realtors and estate agents, international lawyers and public accountants, branches of U.S. banks, overseas hot lines, and the offices of many multinational companies.

Japan Air Lines and Pan American Airways, whose services went beyond merely providing efficient, comfortable transportation.

Arthur Young & Co., which has an excellent grasp of all the intricacies of expatriates' U.S. and foreign tax positions and provided the chapter on U.S. taxation.

Expatriates and repatriates by the hundreds who shared their experiences, joys, and frustrations freely and candidly.

Brigitte Domenjoz, whose expert knowledge of life in France provided invaluable background for the Paris chapter.

Canadian consulates and women's clubs, who graciously made available information they had collected.

Our tireless typists, who converted illegible notes into a readable manuscript.

# Preface

*F*OR MANY, A TRANSFER ABROAD becomes an opportunity to experience the excitement of new places, the pleasure of new friendships, the opportunity for new accomplishments, and the challenge of widening the horizons of life.

For some, these opportunities become twisted into stressful situations that can aggravate and magnify preexisting family problems. The consequences can range from simple anxiety to antisocial behavior, divorce, alcoholism, drug addiction, or other major problems that may require a termination of the overseas assignment.

Sociologists and psychologists have coined terms such as "transfer stress," "culture shock," and "counterculture shock" to identify and focus upon these mobility issues.

Corporate America, also, has recognized that personal expectations, as well as personal situations, can make or break a move abroad. It has learned that not all employees and employee families are good candidates for transfers abroad. Some individuals have an inborn sensitivity that makes them natural diplomats. Others impart and receive misconceptions that lead to poor public relations for their country and their company.

While there is no foolproof method to identify which individuals will be successful in an overseas situation, multinational executives are promoting selection based on self-confidence, practical judgment, ingenuity, language ability, friendliness, emotional and marital stability, adaptability, and social and cultural exposure at home. But good selection is not the whole answer. More and more, sponsoring organizations are aware of the importance of preparing these recruits through education in the culture, history, and practical aspects of living in the new country.

Unfortunately, most expatriates still bemoan the fact that not enough useful information and assistance is provided them when they need it.

This book, in its first thirteen general chapters and in its seven chapters of specific foreign cities, will introduce the potential expatriate to the things that must be considered in deciding upon an overseas position and then in accomplishing the move. It does not purport to solve all the problems of life abroad or to cover the world. But if it makes the experience abroad more enjoyable and worthwhile by reducing the uncertainties, the authors will have achieved their goal.

# Contents

# Introduction

WHEN THE GAITHERS SETTLED into a far northwest suburb of Chicago in the mid-1970s, they found that chatting with their next-door neighbors, the Keplers, meant more than discussing the local scene or the kids' activities. Both families were currently involved in the international field, and both were former expatriates. While coming back to the United States held many wonderful rewards, it also meant adjustments that often were far greater than those experienced on the first move abroad. The two families began to compare notes on the joys and problems of expatriates as they leave for and return from an assignment. They were well aware of the lack of basic information on living and working abroad from their own experiences. This book evolved in an effort to help others who might be facing the same problems.

John Kepler had been an international lawyer for 20 years, and as head of the international legal section of a Fortune 200 company, he traveled to every area of the world to handle the company's international business. His work also put him in touch with the personal legal problems experienced by the company's employees around the world. His wife, Phyllis, whose many-faceted career had included that of a teacher both here and abroad and a position as home furnishings editor on a major city newspaper, was now a free-lance journalist. Her research for articles that appeared in newspapers and magazines took her all over the world. As a student, Phyllis Kepler had spent some time in Europe. But when she returned many years later as a homemaker, she discovered life was not the carefree, simple existence she had experienced earlier. Not only was it difficult to figure out the various cuts of meat in the local market, just getting to and from the market was a problem. Stores did not provide parking lots nor bags in which to carry home the purchases. When the Keplers' car was stolen from the streets of a European capital, they learned about the local police system; when all their clothes were stolen, they additionally learned about coping with major shopping expeditions.

But still the Keplers developed a deep appreciation for the international life and were eager to discover new places and to experience new adventures. In the years that followed, they drove a car overland from Paris to New Delhi; traveled the Pan American Highway in a school bus converted into a camper; explored Europe's Communist bloc nations by car; and crossed portions of Saudi Arabia by train. They combed through the Orient not only to see the sites but to visit the people. Everywhere, they met Americans who were not just visiting the area but living there. They began to think about a book for and about these Americans abroad. More recently, the Keplers established an international consulting firm, Kepler Associates, based in Chicago, to handle all aspects of moves abroad.

When the Gaithers were transferred overseas in the late 1960s, they were given one month to report. This was normal procedure. Orville Gaither went ahead to assume his new position, but Margaret Gaither stayed behind to sell the house, make the purchases necessary for a life abroad, allow the children to finish the school semester, and terminate her employment.

As chief engineer of a large multinational corporation, Orville Gaither had traveled much of the world and was conversant with the problems of living overseas. At various times in Margaret Gaither's career as a psychiatric social worker, she had taught and interpreted human behavior. Theirs was a stable and secure marriage. All these components added up to the formula needed for success in an overseas assignment. But they soon discovered they were not pre-pared for the events that were to follow. Culture shock was a phrase that was just beginning to be tossed about, and there was little general understanding of this most maddening of maladies or of the problems that must be faced in establishing oneself in another culture.

The Gaithers must have served their apprenticeship well; for when they were transferred to another overseas operation nine months later (having survived a child's critical illness, and having lived through six frustrating months looking for a house, two months redecorating it, and one month selling it and packing to leave), there was no noticeable culture shock. Problems? Yes, but they had just been a part of a vivid demonstration that there is a solution to all dilemmas.

In their second overseas location, the Gaithers began to examine the difficulties of the incoming expatriates and to help them when possible to traverse the cross-cultural abyss. Sometimes they suc-ceeded; but on occasion families were quietly and sadly repatriated.

When Orville and Margaret Gaither returned to the United States in the mid-1970s, the economy was in the grips of spiraling inflation. Getting back into a stateside home took their overseas savings. Their children had difficulty breaking into peer groups at schools. Orville Gaither exchanged a five-minute automobile trip to the office for a two-hour commute. The Gaithers once again were in the throes of culture shock, but this time it was magnified by their inability to accept the fact that they should have such difficulties in their own country. Through interviews with every possible returning expatriate, they found stories similar to their own. In his position as Vice-President of International Production, and later as Vice-President of the Africa and Middle East Region, Orville Gaither was directly responsible for personnel planning for transfers abroad. He began to institute cross-cultural training and seminars for departing families, but still more was needed.

Concern for the plight of the expatriate was the catalyst that changed two families' ideas into a working project.

Together the Keplers and Gaithers studied every aspect that affected life abroad as well as on return. They talked with multinational executives here and abroad, hundreds of Americans who were living overseas, corporate physicians in international medical departments, businessmen and women who equip and move those going overseas to live, international school administrators and teachers, U.S. State Department delegations, and delegations from other countries stationed here in America. Collectively, they traveled over 200,000 miles on this project in order to conduct interviews, try the local transportation and communications, eat the local foods, live in local accommodations, and in general test the environments experienced by American expatriates in many major cities around the world. Relying on their own specialties and backgrounds, they examined each problem area. Yet, much of their work overlapped and their book became a joint endeavor.

It was, of course, impossible to cover the world. Instead, they tried to show life in several major European and Asian cities where many Americans reside. They also covered other cities that, because of space limitations, were not reported in this book. But for those heading to an international assignment not included within these pages, more information can be obtained by contacting the authors through Praeger Publishers in New York.

# PART ONE
# The Move

# 1

# Assignment Abroad— Should You or Shouldn't You?

SSIGNMENT ABROAD! The words conjure up visions of travel, intrigue, glamor, romance, forays into history, and the mysteries of the world. It can be this—and even more! However, it can also be the forerunner of incomparable anxiety, stress, frustration, and loneliness. Which it is depends, in no small part, on the expatriate and his family: their qualifications for and their preparations to be twentieth-century pioneers.

The decision to move abroad involves many factors that much too rarely are considered in depth. Some expatriates adjust immediately and happily to overseas life; others never do. There are many disadvantages, as well as the obvious advantages, that should be carefully weighed and balanced; no personnel manager or well-meaning friend can do this for you. And while it is difficult not to be swayed by the compliment implicit in selection for the overseas staff, it is well to remember that the decision that is made will have a long-lasting effect on family and self. In fact, it may well be the most important decision you will ever make.

If you are a candidate for an overseas assignment, there are six basic questions to ask yourself.

## What Will an Assignment Abroad
## Mean to Your Career?

If climbing the corporate ladder is your goal, take a look at those at the top. Did they have overseas experience? If so, that may be your answer as to whether the move is necessary to advance your career. But also consider if the corporation is firmly committed to overseas development, or if there are indications that they might withdraw their investments and their manpower. And what about others in positions similar to yours? Are they going abroad? Are they staying abroad? Or are they rotated back to the States on a regular basis? Are they able to build on their foreign experiences, or do they find that their stateside peers have left them far behind, careerwise?

For many individuals, of course, the opportunity to travel, to meet different people, and to experience different cultures is the primary goal. But no matter how you rate your priorities, there are certain practical considerations. You will want to assess whether:

Financial remuneration is sufficient to make disrupting your home and moving your family—perhaps halfway around the world—worthwhile;

Housing, cost of living, and educational allowances are included in the total financial package;

Annual company-paid physicals are included;

Needed stateside medical treatment is made available on a travel-paid basis;

There is allowable, paid-for travel in case of the critical illness or death of an immediate member of your stateside family;

Travel to point of origin and return is paid for in the annual home leave; and

Travel time is awarded and added to your annual vacation package.

Having considered these questions, you should then examine the most important one of all: Do you really want to go? Does there lurk within your soul a spirit of adventure and a desire and willingness to be a diplomat? Even with all answers indicating a "go," if there is no real wish for an overseas assignment, look again. The desire to go is implicit in the success of such a venture.

## What Will an Assignment Abroad Mean
## to Your Spouse's Career?

For those among the rapidly increasing two-career families, the consideration of an overseas move may well be like opening Pandora's box. With few exceptions a work permit is a prerequisite for employment abroad; for the accompanying husband or wife, that permit most likely will not be available. Only those with unusual skills or specializations in demand in the host country are customarily able to obtain the necessary permit for employment.

The American career woman who follows her husband overseas will find that job opportunities range from essentially nil in the Muslim world to very limited in the more industrialized nations. It is this commonly accepted lack of opportunity that led the international manager of a Fortune 500 corporation to comment, "If career development for the wife is considered on an equal par with that of her husband, the couple probably should not consider an overseas move."

In some instances, couples facing this dilemma have decided to live and work apart, giving rise to a new phenomenon—the long-distance marriage. However, the high cost of international phone calls and the expense of international travel and hotels for an occasional rendezvous make it much more difficult to maintain the contact and the stability that a similar marriage within the United States might have.

Some couples have attempted to solve the problem of divergent careers by agreeing to move if either has a significant promotional opportunity. Increasingly, women are being asked to take overseas positions. The young female MBA has made a significant impact upon the international banking scene; and more and more the foreign service officer is a woman. This can present an entirely new set of problems to these "shoe upon the other foot" couples. In one instance a young female banker who was transferred to Hong Kong found that her husband, an artist, eagerly accepted her transfer. It was not difficult for him to move his base of operations. But to their amazement, they found they were considered strange by old-timers of the Territory, who felt that husbands simply did not "follow" their wives.

Clearly, dual-career couples should carefully assess their career options and the long-range effects of an overseas assignment. If you are thinking of giving up a stateside position to accompany a husband or wife overseas, you should consider whether:

Your employer has an international division and offices abroad. Is there a possibility of obtaining a transfer to your spouse's proposed location?

Your spouse's corporation could utilize your talents and training. Would they consider sending a husband-wife team abroad?

You could train for a different job, obtain another degree, or do advanced research and studies while in residence abroad.

You have particular skills or training that is not generally available that you may be able to utilize abroad.

You would be willing to work on a volunteer basis to get international experience. Would this be a helpful addition to your résumé?

Your training and experience qualify you to teach on the university level or at a high school or trade school while abroad.

You could return to the same—or a similar level—job, in the same setting or perhaps in a new locale, after such an absence.

While there is little doubt that a time-out can delay the achievement of career goals, there is evidence within expatriate circles that for couples who are able to accept the difficulty, often the absolute inability, for both to work while abroad, an overseas assignment can become a special time. The opportunity is there to become experts on local culture, learn another language, travel, perfect hobbies, and spend extra time with families. Once back in the States, couples look with great longing and pleasure on this very special time in their lives.

## What Is the State of Your Marriage?

Of all the factors that affect success or failure in an overseas situation, none is more important than the state of a marriage. Expatriates' advice is explicit and to the point:

Unless your marriage is secure, don't even consider an overseas move.

Persons considering a transfer abroad should recognize that they may be sounding the death knell to their marriage unless it is strong and viable.

It is apparent that overseas transfers are often viewed as an opportunity to breathe new life into a marriage. Instead, the pressures can shake it apart. Does the overseas divorce rate exceed the national average? No one knows for sure but one thing seems certain:

divorce in an overseas situation is most traumatic and ego shattering, not only to the husband and wife but also to their children, who may suddenly find themselves thousands of miles from one of their parents.

Most veteran expatriates tend to agree that an assignment abroad may be more difficult for the noncareer person. Although the locale has changed, the businessman or woman will continue to speak English (the international language of business) and to do much the same work in a situation similar to the one he or she left behind. The spouse, on the other hand, must handle a new life for the family in a country in which neither the customs nor the language may be understood. Just the purchase of food for a day may seem an almost insurmountable obstacle at first. For them, as for their partners, the assignment abroad is doomed from the first if they do not wish to go.

Spouses who feel apprehensive about a proposed move should ask themselves these questions:

Are you very reluctant to leave your parents or other family members?

Do you feel insecure about going to a foreign country with only your spouse and children to depend on?

Do you dislike intensely having to pack up and move?

Are you agonized by the thought of having to learn the metric system, a new monetary system, and a new language?

Are you frightened by the thought of shopping in a native bazaar or shops where the shopkeeper and other customers are of another race?

Are you very concerned about the diseases with which you might come in contact?

Unless you can view a move as mutually beneficial, not only as a desired career experience for your partner but as a challenge and opportunity for new cultural exposure for yourself and your family and an opportunity to travel, to see new places, and to meet new people, an overseas assignment should be looked upon with great caution. It is crucial that persons considering such an assignment be candid—not only in assessing the strength of their marriage and in analyzing what such a transfer means to them but also in understanding what it means to their marriage partner. If that person is adaptable, self-reliant, self-confident, cooperative, and willing to be a diplomat for his or her country, it may be a green light all the way. On the other hand, if the partner expresses timidity, fear of change, and a reluctance to move, a transfer abroad would advisably be delayed until the two can obtain counseling from a skilled psycho-therapist who can help to examine and resolve the underlying fears related to such a move.

## What Effect Will an Assignment Abroad Have on Your Children?

"Daddy," cried a bewildered five-year-old girl as she listened to her family discuss their upcoming move to London, "we can't live there, we don't speak English."

The outcry (far wiser than the uninitiated might think) came at the end of a "worry list," one of the most effective techniques in revealing fears. Everyone old enough to participate either jots down or tells of his worries and concerns about the proposed move. They can then be analyzed and, if possible, resolved.

It is only fair to discuss both the positive and negative aspects of an overseas move with children and to give them some input into the final decision. Parents should recognize, however, that the prospect of leaving familiar faces, as well as places, may cause a child to be fearful and apprehensive. The attitude of the parents is extremely important. Excitement and anticipation are usually contagious, but children are also quick to detect feelings of despair, frustration, and bewilderment and to reflect them in their own unhappiness. A positive mental attitude and open lines of communication are extremely important at this time.

Just when is it best to move overseas? Seasoned expatriates advise that for most families that time comes during the "3-P" years—pablum, playschool, and PTA. It is then that the home is the central aspect of a child's life; if family relationships are strong and secure, the child generally will not have any major, that is, unresolvable, problems in adjusting to life overseas.

Sociologists and child guidance specialists who have studied the problems of the tumultuous teens are in agreement that youngsters have difficulty making the additional adjustment to a move during their high school years. Unfortunately, most corporate or foreign service families do not have the latitude of remaining in one area for four years. Usually the best they can do is to plan toward a two-year stint during their children's junior and senior years.

Overseas teenagers for whom a move is part of the format of life agree that they can adjust to a move during their high school years—as long as they are not asked to move during their senior year. They are quick to point out that the situation is somewhat different in an overseas school where mobility is a constant factor, and both students and faculty have experienced, firsthand, the trauma of culture shock.

If you are considering a move overseas and have school-age children, you should determine:

What type of grade schools are available—that is, host country schools, international schools, American schools;

If there is an established, accredited high school;

If there are special language curriculum classes, classes for slow learners, classes for gifted children, or other specialized instruction;

If sports, band, and other extracurricular activities are available.

On the whole, overseas students as well as their parents are enthusiastic about foreign schools. They cite the smaller classes, teachers (often expatriates like themselves) who are really interested in their students, opportunities made available by the schools for language and cultural studies, school-sponsored trips to nearby (and some not so nearby) areas, as well as the ready acceptance into U.S. and European colleges and universities. (See Chapter 5.)

## Can Your Health Needs Be Met Abroad?

Many Americans feel that they have never had better or more personalized medical care than they have had abroad. There are exceptions, of course. Expatriates living in the less-industrialized nations have sometimes found facilities to be "only fair" or "grossly inadequate," and have recommended returning to the States, or one of the area medical centers—Rome, London, and the like—for childbirth, surgery, and critical health care. If you are considering an overseas assignment, you should ascertain the following:

What medical facilities are available in the prospective overseas post?

Are they adequate for childbirth, severe illness, emergencies, and surgery?

Are there physicians and dentists with recognized training?

Are specialists available? Are they English speaking?

Does the expatriate medical care program include pretransfer physical examinations, supplemented by periodic stateside physicals?

Many of the large multinationals have gathered extensive information on the medical facilities near their foreign installations. Some even name company doctors to act as guardians of the health of their corporate workers in those areas.

The U.S. government is also concerned with the availability of health facilities for its citizens abroad. In the health and medical information report, which is prepared by each U.S. embassy and made available to residents within that area, reputable practitioners, along with their qualifications and the notation as to whether they speak English, are listed.

In most instances health care availability is not a reason for turning down an overseas assignment. But here again, the situation must be evaluated on an individual basis. Someone considering time abroad will want to assess personal health care needs and those of dependents, and may even find it desirable to refer questions to a medical expert. In exceptional cases, such as where a family member suffers from a moderate to severe illness, or is handicapped, a company physician or other medical authority should be consulted early in the decision process. Corporate officials stress that the advisability of moving such a person abroad, as well as the evaluation of medical care available in the host country, is too important an aspect for a layman to evaluate without expert medical advice.

Heretofore, as a general rule, it has not been recommended that a severely ill or handicapped person be moved abroad; but there have been notable exceptions. Depending on the nature of the illness or handicap involved, and type of treatment required, some expatriates have been able to work out satisfactory medical, hospital, and in-home nursing arrangements abroad, sometimes even at substantially lower costs. Others, by balancing out types of services available with length of stay, opportunity for career advancement, and other factors, have felt positive about accepting overseas duty. While the above is not to suggest that an overseas relocation is possible, or even desirable, in all medical situations, it is to suggest that it is worth the consultation and evaluation of informed medical personnel.

## Is Your Parents' Situation Stable?

A recent University of Chicago study revealed that a leading concern of middle-aged couples is the continued health and welfare of their own parents. The Chicago study highlights the worries of foreign residents who reportedly feel that no problem has been more difficult to contend with than that of aged and ailing parents from whom they may be many miles removed. The study further recommends that would-be expatriates anticipate and plan for the possibility of parental problems. Especially where other siblings are involved, it is important that satisfactory arrangements be worked out in advance. (It is well to recognize that the family member who remains at home may feel left alone to cope with new and increased obligations.) In some cases, of course, there are no close family members with whom to share responsibility. A parent's failing health might then be a flashing red light to an otherwise "go" situation.

Advancing parental age, though a very legitimate concern, need not rule out the possibility of time abroad. Nonetheless, it should be recognized that the process of aging may suddenly disrupt a previously stable situation. An expatriate who had to return many times to New York from Buenos Aires to care for an ailing mother soon found her finances and marriage in shreds. To avoid situations such as this, cooperative family planning and some knowledge of community resources are needed. If you are considering an assignment abroad, you should ask yourself, and you should discuss with your parents and other close family members, whether

Your parents can live independently, with full responsibility for themselves;

Their present health situation, both physically and mentally, is satisfactory;

They are covered under Medicare for both hospitalization (Part A) and medical (Part B);

They have a good supplemental medical policy;

There is someone who can act in your stead in case of a health crisis;

There are community resources they can utilize (are visiting nurses and physical therapists, homemakers, home health aides, and meals on wheels available in their area?);

There is a good local hospital, good nursing home, or nearby retirement home;

There is a senior center or other social service center, such as the Family Service Association, which could be a resource in planning;

They have made a will or indicated other final instructions; and

They will need your financial assistance.

The answers to these questions, though by no means definitive, should provide a basis on which to judge a parental situation and to assess whether it reinforces or contraindicates the acceptance of an overseas job offer.

## Other Considerations

Unless you are familiar with life in the proposed post, you should obtain all the information possible on it. Consulates, travel agencies, and libraries have a wealth of general tourist-type data; the State Department area handbooks, post reports, and American Women's Club booklets are usually factual and accurate. Many multinationals are adding cross-cultural seminars and premove familiarization trips to the descriptive literature or audiovisual documentaries they customarily present to an employee considering a move abroad. People who have lived in the area are also a great resource. Their information on schools, residential areas, and business and social customs may be more practical and up-to-date than any you will find elsewhere.

Some individuals cannot accept great differences in their living conditions. Rather than find out too late that your happiness is tied to the amenities of life in a community in which you feel comfortable and settled, consider the mode of living that you most enjoy. If you are turned on by the sophistication of opera, theater, and high-fashion establishments that you may not find at the overseas location, recognize it. But consider, too, whether you are willing to make the best of circumstances, to accept the bad with the good. If you are not, the international life may not be for you.

There is no foolproof method for determining who will be successful and happy in an overseas assignment. Psychologists are advocating stress tests prior to selection for overseas positions; personnel counselors are promoting selection based on such positive qualities as security, self-confidence, practical judgment, ingenuity, language ability, deep and kind friendliness, and social and cultural exposure at home. However, veteran expatriates tend to agree that

> the successful expatriates are a very special breed. They possess the ability to be flexible, to be adaptable, to maintain a sense of humor in the face of all odds, and the willingness to roll with the punches.

It is important to heed the recommendations of the professionals, but we must also look to that special insight gained through years of experience abroad. If your picture of yourself and your family fits theirs, then you are probably ready for an assignment abroad.

## Suggested Reading

Cleveland, Harlan; Mangone, Gerard J.; and Adams, John Clark. *The Overseas Americans*. New York: McGraw-Hill, 1960.

Schwartz, David. *The Magic of Thinking Big*. Hollywood: Wilshire, 1959.

Ziglar, Zig. *See You at the Top*. Gretna, Louisiana: Pelican, 1974.

# 2

# The Ideal
# Expatriate Businessman

*J*UST AS LIVING ABROAD is not for everyone, working overseas is also a selective process. Long before a new assignment is discussed with the potential expatriate, senior company officials or personnel committee members have made the decision that this person, more than any other, has the personal and business skills necessary to succeed in this particular foreign assignment. This chapter should assist that senior company official or group by looking at those special skills and attributes of the "ideal" expatriate businessman (hereinafter referred to as IEBM).

## Stateside Planning

Just as some individuals have discovered that living abroad is not for them, company management will find that not all of their best domestic personnel are uniquely qualified for working overseas. The best qualified, most highly valued domestic employee may be a complete failure in a comparable assignment in the international side of the business. The harsh fact is that living and working internationally requires special skills and attributes not necessarily required of the successful domestic worker.

Before looking in depth at some of those skills, the need for assigning the expatriate must be evaluated. The only real reason for a foreign assignment is that the company has a job to be filled and that there is no national employee available who meets all the company's requirements.

There may be a national employee qualified by education, prior experience, or training, but lacking the company experience required for the job. In short, the national may meet technical requirements but not be knowledgeable in the methods of operation and procedures used by the company. If a national employee had all the skills, including company experience, he would no doubt get the job, because he usually has more to offer than the expatriate with similar business acumen. His language proficiency and his acceptance by his countrymen can never be duplicated by an expatriate. No matter how well he speaks the language, or how "native" he becomes, the expatriate will always be a foreigner to the national populace. The company and the expatriate should accept this, and work from the strength of the situation—rather than trying to circumvent the fact that the expatriate serves a true need, fulfills it until it no longer exists, and then moves on to another assignment.

Aside from the unique position of the general manager, the nationalization of personnel should be orderly, carefully planned, and skillfully executed to be accomplished within a general time frame without excessive pressures to meet an inflexible deadline. In other words, do not wait until "nationalization" is forced to develop your national staff.

The selection of general manager or the top job in an overseas post deserves some special comment. Many times the interest of the company cannot best be served by a local; this depends upon the type of company and the sensitivity of the job. Many governments cater to American (or other nationalities) because they want and expect the particular business expertise of that country. They often feel cheated if a local is named to fill the very top post, and seem to resent the appointment. In highly nationalistic countries the appointment of a national can create severe problems for the individual, especially if he is forced to choose between the interests of his country and the interests of his company. If sensitive negotiations are required with the host government, he may be ineffective because of this inner conflict. In one case a general manager who was a national found himself negotiating against his former college professor (now a government minister), and the intimidation by his former teacher resulted in his ineffectiveness as a negotiator. An American company official had to be called in to finish the delicate negotiations.

In certain other cases a national in the top job may be many times more effective than the best expatriate. Careful study on the part of corporate planners is required in this especially sensitive area.

## The IEBM

An attempt to describe the "ideal" expatriate businessman will fail because such an individual probably does not exist; so we will have to settle for some of the characteristics, traits, and attributes that have been observed through the evaluation of individual expatriate performance. These special characteristics are considered in order of their relative importance.

### *Patience*

The first and most important virtue is patience. The IEBM must spot small errors without actually "seeing" them. National staff are very sensitive to the fact that a mistake can cause loss of face, not only with the boss but with their peers. The IEBM sent to teach and to supervise must be willing to settle for a little less than perfection. He should be willing to give a sincere pat on the back, along with a suggestion for improvement the next time. To demand stateside quality of a subordinate in a developing or emerging country is too much to ask or expect of inexperienced, untrained, or partially trained staff. Patience on the IEBM's part allows the national to learn in an atmosphere that lets him be comfortable without being over-confident. The patient IEBM will give the pat on the back and still make certain that the national could improve his performance if he would consider . . . et cetera. Next time the national will try especially hard to improve his job by giving consideration to that suggestion. This same process must be repeated until the national attains the highest level of effectiveness he is capable of achieving. For the IEBM this may take months or years, but to follow any other course will result in either failure to accomplish the goal, or abject frustration on the part of the IEBM.

The IEBM must never give way to the temptation to "do it himself" because he believes he could do the job faster and with more skill than the learning national. Giving in to this temptation is guaranteed to result in the national's losing face and never learning to do the job. Patience allows the IEBM to endure the difficult task of watching someone learn to do a job to which he has never been exposed.

Patience must be exercised continually, for one failure may permanently damage the effectiveness of the IEBM. Most nationals in less developed countries, and especially those in emerging nations, are seeking to develop their credibility and may be especially sensitive to even the slightest criticism. This leads to the second special skill for the IEBM.

## Sensitivity

The successful IEBM must be sensitive—sensitive to his surroundings, sensitive to the feelings of his hosts (the people and the country), sensitive to the needs of his expatriates. The hard-charging, aggressive, and successful stateside employee who uses any means to reach his carefully planned goals probably will have difficulty in developing the sensitivity to recognize danger signals within the ranks of his fellow expatriates and among his national staff. This attribute is particularly crucial in the nations of the Far East and Africa. Western European countries can better accept the aggressiveness of the typical stateside businessman because they have been exposed to this type of individual for a longer period of time.

The IEBM will become father confessor to his staff—in all matters from domestic problems to incompatibility with other employees—in a manner never contemplated or experienced in a domestic assignment. He must become an excellent listener, a skillful suggester of ways to enable expatriates to solve their own problems without becoming inextricably involved in them.

Sensitivity must not be confused with weakness, for the third basic requirement for the IEBM must be strength.

## Strength

The successful IEBM should have the strength of knowledge in his field of expertise, as well as the mental strength to train, test, retrain, and retest until his local staff has accomplished the transfer of technology to the expatriate's level of expectancy. He must be strong enough to resist lowering these standards or compromising his level of expectancy. Strength is closely aligned with patience in this scenario.

Mental strength and character are important characteristics in the IEBM because of the close association required in the expatriate community. Illness, deaths, and personal problems are shared and identified with to a degree much greater than in the United States business community. The strength to share problems and to respond in an appropriate manner is aligned with sensitivity.

The IEBM must have both physical and mental strength in order to deal effectively with foreign governments. The ability to take a position, hold it, and attain the required agreement in governmental negotiations for concessions, visas, work permits, import of goods, customs, and other areas, taxes the patience and requires great willpower to keep the IEBM from just giving in to the system. In this delicate area the IEBM must remain cool, patient, and stay as strong as Tabasco sauce; but he must also be as smooth as the finest scotch and as diplomatic as the bouquet of a fine French wine.

The IEBM must handle a myriad of problems with little outside input, even from the home office. A recent example involved the medical evacuation of an expatriate wife. After 11 hours of frustration over nonfunctioning telephones and failed attempts to confirm airline connections, the overseas manager finally got through to the States, where an associate was able to confirm all flights while the overseas manager held on the other line—less than ten minutes to accomplish a long day's effort. This requires patience, strength, and perseverance on the IEBM's part. The end of the story? Not quite. The patient's husband berated the overseas manager for not moving faster to get his wife out of the foreign country, so there were no thanks, just additional frustration. Only the manager's ability to understand the man's worry and concern for his wife and his strength of character not to "blow up" saved the day.

## Honesty

The IEBM must be completely honest and straightforward. Honesty follows patience, sensitivity, and strength only because something has to be first; but this attribute is one that will gain and maintain the respect of locals, both employees and government. These people are quick to see through the thin veil of facade and partial truths. An IEBM who has lost credibility with his fellow employees or the host government has lost his value to the company, and he may as well pack his bags and move on. The expatriate will generally live and work more closely with other employees and the host government than he would in the States. There is usually no way to separate the "office" from the "home." You usually play with the same people you work with, and therefore your circle of friends may be smaller than it would be in the States. Small discrepancies are noticed almost immediately; hence the need for complete honesty cannot be overemphasized. One manager put it this way: "If I tell you something, believe it, because it will be the absolute truth."

## Decision-Making Ability

The IEBM must be a decision maker. While decision making is important in any management function, for the IEBM indecision is failure. Many people are afraid to make decisions without a committee to back them up. Often the committee simply does not exist in the overseas location, and the IEBM finds himself having to make quick decisions on his own—often with incomplete and imperfect data. If he is unable to make the tough decisions because of technical weakness or simply because he is not mentally prepared to do so, the overseas employee will become frustrated and ineffective. He must prepare himself to make the best decision he can with the information available, and then he must put this behind him without becoming self-damning if everything doesn't go just as he anticipated. He must remember that his staff may not be capable of providing 100 percent accurate data on which to make his decision—not because of a desire to deceive him, but simply because the stage of their development does not permit them to analyze the data with absolute accuracy.

The top job in an overseas location can be a very lonely one. Often problems cannot be discussed with subordinates and there are no peers with whom to consult. In many places contact with the home office is restricted to telex or written communications, or to sleepy conversations in the middle of the night. The IEBM must be self-sufficient and strong enough technically, professionally, and personally to do what has to be done without constant guidance from above. A very successful team manager in a stateside job may be unable to handle the isolation of an overseas assignment.

## Realism

The IEBM must be a realist. He must realize that he is a guest in a foreign country whose culture and business practices may be vastly different from those found in the United States, and that he must act accordingly. He should evaluate realistically why he is in the foreign country, and what he expects to accomplish. Recognition of the fact that goals and timetables must be planned and accomplished using essentially the local resources may result in a completely different program than might otherwise be considered reasonable.

## *Teaching Skills*

A special trait that is more important in an overseas assignment than in a domestic post is the ability to teach skills to another who may or may not possess the same educational background. While the old axiom that "nothing is taught, and things or processes are only learned," may be technically correct, the IEBM must ultimately provide opportunities for learning to his national counterpart, employees, or potential replacement. A skillful expatriate can turn events that are essentially mistakes into vivid learning experiences. An even more skillful expatriate may create a learning experience by the use of the simple "guided discovery" approach in which the national is exposed to a situation that will force or create a real learning experience. Whatever methods are used, the end result must be the same; the required knowledge must be transferred.

Frequently the learning or transfer process will appear to be dishearteningly slow, and the IEBM must devise ways and means to constantly test the level of the learning experience. If the desired skills have not been learned, the IEBM must recycle or reteach the information until the national attains the desired level of competence. It will be of little value to the company to send a competent domestic expatriate into an overseas job that requires ultimate replacement with a competent national, unless the expatriate has the skill to transfer his knowledge. This skill may not be required by a successful employee or manager in a domestic environment. The IEBM should be a master at teaching and transfer of knowledge, and be willing to share this ability with his national employees.

## *Social Skills*

The IEBM, to a much larger extent than his stateside counterpart, must be a "social" person. He must truly enjoy people, and he must be prepared to sacrifice a considerable amount of his personal time to represent his company at social functions. As a matter of fact, in most overseas locations the IEBM of a large company can find himself on the "cocktail circuit" almost every evening. This in itself has led to the downfall of many expatriates, but that story will come later.

After so much social contact the IEBM may develop an antisocial syndrome that makes him wish to withdraw completely from the circuit. To do so may be fatal. The secret is to know when and how to say no, but to accept and to host with sufficient frequency that the company is represented satisfactorily. Some events are command performances, and they must be treated with special care to avoid embarrassment to the host or the invitee. Examples of this type of no-refusal would be a seated dinner with an ambassador on the occasion of a visiting state VIP, or any invitation from a high-ranking host government official.

### Team Skills

The special skills, attributes, and personal characteristics of the IEBM have been discussed at length, but there are other skills that require the cooperation of the family of the IEBM. The first of these is the husband-wife team.

This team must be strong, unflappable, and outgoing—especially if the male member is the company's top or near-top representative and frequent entertaining is required. In this setting the wife becomes an unpaid but essential company employee. Her ability to plan and effect a seated dinner for 50 or a cocktail buffet for 300 makes her an invaluable asset to the company's presence. Needless to say, this requires a great deal of willpower, resolve, and desire on the wife's part to be a team player in the performance of her husband's job.

Some wives may dislike this part of their husband's job, and as a result either will not participate or do so grudgingly. The latter attitude is easily perceived by persons in the host country, and is more detrimental than nonparticipation. The IEBM is seldom effective in this type of situation, and corporate planners should take this factor into consideration—especially for top and near-top executive positions in overseas subsidiaries.

Most corporate planners recognize the need for a strong husband-wife team in top overseas spots, but a good many fail to recognize the need for a strong marriage in virtually all overseas assignments. An unhappy wife leads very quickly to an unhappy expatriate, and an expensive repatriation is the inevitable result. At minimum moving costs of $50–100,000 (1982) for the repatriation, and a similar cost for a replacement, mistakes involving unhappy wives can become costly in a large organization.

## Special Problems for the IEBM's Wife

Corporate planners will do well to recognize the needs of the expatriate wife. While the expatriate can immerse himself in his work and find himself on familiar ground, no such tie to the past exists for the expatriate wife who finds herself alone in a new world. Proper corporate planning should include the preparation of the wife, as well as older children, for their new life abroad. Failure to consider these needs may result in premature repatriation or extreme difficulties for the family.

The problems for the wife overseas are manifold. The working wife will seldom be able to find employment in an overseas location, owing to the difficulty in obtaining a work permit from the host government. If the wife is required to work for economic reasons, or if she has her own profession and is either unable or unwilling to set her goals aside for the duration of the assignment, the family should definitely be directed away from an overseas assignment.

Many former working wives find that their husband's assignment abroad can provide a time for completion of a college education or for an advanced degree. This obviously is limited to those locations where such facilities are available, but courses in local culture and language are available nearly everywhere. Other wives find that they can substitute volunteer services that allow them to maintain their level of competence in their profession, even though no income is forthcoming from their efforts. This can be especially true for those trained in social service, counseling, education, or specialized education—such as foreign languages or slow learners.

In addition to being concerned about her career goals and her husband's, the IEBM wife (and her husband) expends a great deal of energy taking care of and worrying about her children. Teenagers that might become involved with drugs are a special worry. For youngsters, especially those moving into South or Central America or the Orient, a knowledge of drug traffic and the often harsh handling of Americans who participate should be mandatory. More than one expatriate family has been given 24 hours to leave the host country because a teenager smoked a little "pot" or sniffed a little "coke." In some cultures, mere possession may result in severe prison sentences; and dealing in narcotics may carry a death sentence. All too many expatriates feel that because they are Americans they are exempt from host country laws. Jails throughout the world are filled with such believers. The simple fact is that there is little the American government can do to help persons caught in this web. If a family has a record of teenagers involved in even minor drug abuse, this should be sufficient reason to keep them in a domestic environment.

The wife of the top expatriate in a foreign country may also discover that all manner of family and socioeconomic problems find their way to her. Just as her husband may become a "father" figure, she in turn may become a "mother" figure to the families of expatriates. She must be sensitive to such needs, but at the same time resist becoming involved in family problems that are not within her ability to correct. Frequently, all that is needed is a listening ear.

## The Problem of Alcohol

The IEBM should not have a problem with alcohol, nor should his wife. Nothing kills a corporation's image as quickly as a manager or his wife who becomes inebriated at every social function. Even minor problems in handling alcohol are magnified in an overseas environment. Job frustrations, such as failure to extract stateside performance from subordinates, as well as those associated with being in a new environment, may turn the casual or social drinker into a person who requires two martinis just to unwind after a hard day at the office. If the next event is a cocktail party and a late dinner, he may find himself becoming dependent on increasing amounts of alcohol, unless he is very careful.

A potential alcohol problem for the expatriate is magnified for the IEBM manager and his wife due to the additional exposure to top-level host country government personnel. Once the expatriate gets the name of being "a drunk" or an alcoholic, he has lost his usefulness to the company, even if his performance on the job is outstanding. The reason is simple. In the reduced sphere of work and play with the same people, his extracurricular image simply cannot be separated from his on-the-job performance. As credibility is lost, so goes his effectiveness as a manager and his recall is the next logical step.

The top expatriate manager and his wife will often find themselves at the top of the cocktail party circuit. Sometimes there may be as many as two or three "command performances" in a single evening. Ginger ale, Perrier water and lime, or Coke and bourbon (without the bourbon) may keep the two sober and out of danger of early recall by the home office. Many expatriates have learned to nurse one gin and tonic over a long, long evening.

It should be noted that an alcohol problem in a Muslim country is magnified, since many of the people with whom expatriates deal in their job are nondrinkers and their religion looks with disfavor on the use of alcohol.

# Summary

If you are a corporate planner, a potential expatriate, or a member of an expatriate family, you should leave this chapter with the following firm convictions:

IEBMs must possess special skills not required in a comparable domestic assignment.

IEBMs in top jobs face special problems and therefore require a high level of skills; they must be exceptionally well chosen.

IEBMs and their wives must function together as a team; the wife of the IEBM is absolutely essential to his success.

The wife of the IEBM faces very special problems; her qualifications are an important consideration in the selection of the IEBM.

Children are important team members.

Repatriation for the IEBM may be the result of the actions of any family member.

Drugs and alcohol problems are greatly magnified in the overseas environment, and can be a factor in recall.

The situation of the IEBM's stateside family must be taken into account; IEBM performance can be greatly affected by family problems on the home front.

# 3

# A Thousand and One Things To Do Before Departure

*A*FTER THE INITIAL EUPHORIA, cold reality sets in, innumerable aspects remain to be considered, and a myriad of seemingly unaccomplishable feats must be completed in a short amount of time. Now, as never before, it is important to *remain calm and retain your sense of humor!*

Policies related to overseas moves vary greatly—from corporation to corporation, country to country, and even classification to classification. While some transferees have six months to a year to prepare for a move abroad, other assignments are effective immediately. Some ship all their belongings; others air freight essentials and rent or buy furniture later. Be sure that you fully understand your corporate moving policy, the requirements for residence in the posted area, and the essential aspects of life in the host country.

## High Priority

This is the time for schedules and lists. Careful itemizing of things to be purchased and procedures to be completed is all-important.

## Physical Exams

You will want to schedule medical, eye, and dental exams at an early date so that potential health problems can be detected and treated or referred to physicians abroad for follow-up. As you do, you should request copies of your family members' medical and dental histories, X-rays, and prescriptions for both glasses and drugs.

Plan to take a six-month supply of drugs and solutions for contact lenses. Since pharmaceutical products may have different trade names abroad, medicines should be described in generic terms with strengths specified.

## Immunizations

If the examining physician does not have an update on inoculations needed for your assignment area, you should contact one of the following:

The nearest consular representative of the host country;

The local public health department;

The Division of Foreign Quarantine, Public Health Service, Department of Health and Welfare, Washington, D.C. 20201; or

The Center for Disease Control, Atlanta, Georgia 30333, for HEW Publication CDC 83-8280, "Health Information for International Travel."

You should also obtain an international vaccination certificate for each member of your family from either the passport office or the local public health department, and ask your family physician and pediatrician to list all previous inoculations.* All later inoculations should be carefully noted and then filed with your passport.

## Passports

Application may be made at a passport agency, before a clerk of a federal or state court authorized by law to accept applications, or at selected first-class post offices. All first-time passport applications must be executed in person and will require:

Proof of Citizenship—a certified copy of applicant's birth certificate, including the filing date and a raised seal.

---

*This certificate is the only internationally recognized record of immunizations; it will be an essential requirement for crossing many international borders.

Identification—a naturalization certificate, driver's license, or government, industrial, business, or academic identification if it contains signature and photograph of applicant.

Photographs—in duplicate, signed, taken within the previous six months. (Have at least 12 to 15 for use from time to time.)

Passport fees.

## Visas

Visas are considered a formal approval to proceed. They are usually applied for by the corporation; however, application may be made by the employee or an independent travel agency. Application forms and requirements for residence may be obtained by contacting the nearest appropriate consulate.

## Work Permits

Except in unusual circumstances, all persons who work abroad must have work permits. Corporations usually consider it their responsibility to obtain permits for their personnel; however, transferees should be fully aware of the requirements for work permits and for residence, and should be sure these requirements are met before departure. More than one incoming expatriate, having posted his landing card to show new residence, has been placed on the next plane out for failure to show a valid work permit.

## The Major Decisions

### Housing

Owing to the double-barreled effort of high interest rates and escalating real estate prices, most multinationals are recommending that their employees either keep their homes and rent them, or sell and reinvest the proceeds in other property. If your return will be to another area, you might wish to consider selling your present home and purchasing another in that city to keep up with the inflation level there. Some expatriates have bought condominiums or houses in resort areas where they can sublet easily and reserve a block of time for themselves each year. This plan has been a happy solution for the expatriate who wants to give his family a feeling of roots during the transient overseas period of their lives as well as afford them the opportunity to visit with, but not be totally dependent upon, relatives during home leave. A word of caution, however—check carefully with your tax adviser on condominiums and their use before a purchase.

## Automobiles

Expatriates have found that they enjoy having their own cars to drive when they are home on vacations. Whether you can afford the luxury of keeping a car back home for one month's use a year may depend upon whether you need the money to reinvest in a car overseas (figure the cost of a rent-a-car during vacation, however), the relative value of the automobile, the cost of insurance, and a place to keep the car in storage. Should you decide to keep a car, do have your mechanic advise you on long-term storage.

## Airplanes

Airplane owners quite often rent or lease their planes, reserving vacation usage for themselves. Some expatriates have moved their planes to their new locations abroad and have found conditions that were very favorable for the private flier. In South America, for example, maintenance costs are less, and the airways are not as crowded as in the States.

## Boats, Dune Buggies, and Other Vacation Vehicles

Expatriates who have been transferred from places like Chicago in the dead of winter have found that there is almost no out-of-season market for these items and that corporations usually look the other way when it comes to forced-sale losses. Unless you have a friend or relative who can provide storage, your best bet may be to rent storage space until the proper season when you can sell at a fair price or until you may have the opportunity and the money to buy a resort place where it could be used. A few expatriates transferred to places like Trinidad and the Philippines have brought their boats and enjoyed them immensely.

## Planning Ahead for a New Life

For the spouse lucky enough to be posted in an area where household help is inexpensive and readily available, there may be more free time than ever before experienced. There may also be an overwhelming postmove shock—unless this period is anticipated.

If you are in such a position, perhaps it is the time for you to reach back in your subconscious to childhood dreams. Did you dream of becoming a writer, an artist, a doctor? Did you ever want to master a sport, or to be a bridge player, or to become a cook of repute? This may be the time—the time to write that Great American Novel, study art in the great museums, become active in the local art colony. It may be the time to apply for admission to a host country medical school (the chances for admission are probably better than in the United States) or to complete an undergraduate degree. (If so, take your transcript of college credits with you.) It may be the time to learn to play tennis, golf, or bridge or to enroll in a Cordon Bleu cooking school. It may be the time to take a correspondence course or to learn music, tailoring, or weaving. It may be the time to throw yourself, full force, into voluntary activities with any of a number of service organizations.

But it will be the time only if you make it happen. Unless you wish to live vicariously through the lives of your family, you, too, must have goals that can be achieved within the circumstances of your new life. Decide what you would like to do and prepare yourself to do it by establishing a plan now.

## Books and Periodicals

If your goal is to read the great American classics, you will need to take them with you. If you plan to spend all the time possible with your children during their formative years, you may need storybooks, special games, and a how-to book, such as June Johnson's *838 Ways to Amuse a Child* (Macmillan, Riverside, New Jersey). You may also find helpful books on childhood development (perhaps Paul Hauck's *The Rational Management of Children* [Libra, New York], Sidney Werkman's *Bringing Up Children Overseas,* [Basic Books, New York], or *The Princeton Center for Infancy—Growing Up Years* [Doubleday, New York]).

If you are setting out to be a successful hostess, be sure to take along the cooking and serving equipment you will need, as well as a supply of cookbooks. There is a wealth of ideas in such books as Louise Montague Athern's *The Entertaining Woman's Cookbook* (Abelard-Schuman, New York and London) or just the very basic Better Homes and Gardens' *Guide to Entertaining* or *Betty Crocker's Hostess Cookbooks,* which are available in any bookstore.

You will want to take an extensive inventory of books. Television and radio programs broadcast in a foreign language may prove to be without appeal, while the newspapers in English will be more limited in scope than those you are accustomed to reading. Under these circumstances, books will become an important diversion. Some expatriates recommend subscribing to a book-of-the-month club. A firm with an international membership is the Doubleday Book Club (Customer Service Center, 501 Franklin Avenue, Garden City, New York 11530; telephone [516] 294-4000).

A quarterly journal that reviews a wide but choice selection of new English-language books is available by post from Braithwaite and Taylor (P.O. Box 28, London, SW 11). This internationally focused bookstore advertises "books by return mail at bookstore prices."

Although they may be delayed in arriving, magazines play a vital part in keeping the expatriate in tune with the situation back home or current with his professional field. Some expatriates budget for a magazine of personal choice for each member of the family, a couple of general interest magazines, and a professional journal for each of the parents.

## *Clothing*

In planning clothing for overseas residence, it is wise to consider your present wardrobe and then make additions based on the following.

### *Climate*

Will it be hot or cold, humid or arid; will there be seasonal changes or a year-round climate? Will homes be air-conditioned or cooled only in part? Will they be centrally heated? Is it adequate by American standards? Is gas turned on by calendar and not by need?

In a cooler climate, dress for both men and women will be more formal than stateside. Wool suits for day and warm flannel night wear are definitely in. With warmer climates, dress is looser, more casual, and cotton is a must. Men often wear short-sleeved sport shirts or shirt-jacs with casual trousers to work; and boys of all ages may wear short pants and short-sleeved sport shirts to school. Girls and women choose cool, comfortable dresses or slacks—which may not reflect the fashion trends elsewhere.

### *Culture*

As guests within the country, expatriates have a responsibility not to offend the sensitivities of its citizens. This may mean that women should refrain from wearing shorts or slacks in public places, or that they should remove their shoes or cover their heads before entering a temple. In the more orthodox Muslim countries, where women are still heavily veiled, expatriate wives are expected to keep their arms and legs covered. For example, in Saudi Arabia wives customarily have floor-length, long-sleeved dresses made on pattern 82031, which is printed by Burda-Moden (Offenburg Baden, West Germany).*

In general, however, expatriate residents are not expected to dress as the natives do but rather within a framework of propriety in which it is usually possible to follow their own sense of fashion.

### Positions within the Host Country

At top-level management positions, entertaining often is quite formal, with invitations specifying either "lounge" (business) suit or "black tie." Besides his tuxedo, the top-level executive will also need several "good suits" for calls on government officials. (In the tropics, this may be a short-sleeved version of the Safari suit.) Imported menswear, as well as fine custom tailoring, is available in most countries.

The executive wife should have some formal attire, either long dresses with jackets or long skirts with blouses—perhaps a hostess gown, caftan, or party pajamas. She should also have three or four daytime dresses, as well as several pairs of slacks and skirts with interchangeable blouses and sweaters, and the necessary accessories to go with them.

An engineer and his wife or a missionary couple assigned to remote, provincial areas will find their wardrobe needs much less sophisticated. Jeans and shirts, simple dresses, and a couple of "dress outfits" should suffice.

University students, as well as students attending American or international grade and high schools, dress much as they do in the States, unless there is a uniform regulation. Scoutleaders, and boys and girls of scouting age, should take their uniforms if there are plans to join scout troops abroad.

### Washability

Even in London, Amsterdam, and Rome, expatriates complain that they have had fine woolens shrunk by the dry-cleaning process.

---

*Similar to Simplicity Pattern #8827.

In Egypt, and many other countries as well, it is possible to have dry-cleaning done only at the major international hotels. And, as might be expected, it is quite expensive. Some expatriates become proficient in cleaning clothing in the backyard with benzine. Most agree it's best to choose clothing that is washable.

### Special Clothing Needs

Women who have tried to squeeze themselves into foundation garments made for the slight female figures found in much of the world are emphatic in advising that a good supply of bras and girdles, as well as swim suits, be included. If you plan to take advantage of a local tailor or seamstress, you should also take along material and patterns as well as a selection of basic sewing supplies.

Take shoes (American feet are longer and narrower than overseas norms)—everything that you might need until your next trip back to the States: sport, business, dress, and sturdy shoes with thick leather or rubber crepe soles for sightseeing. Expatriates suggest buying shoes for children at half-size intervals, and alternating wear between a sneaker and a leather shoe.

## Cosmetics and Skin-Care Products

Although American-brand cosmetics are available overseas, costs often are double, even quadruple, the stateside prices. It will save you money to take cosmetics to last until the first trip back to the States. Skin-care specialists suggest that cosmetic purchases be made with the climate in mind. For example, a hot, humid climate such as that in the Philippines causes a skin to be more oily than usual. Thus a moisturizer lighter than that normally used would be appropriate. Women living in this type climate should use a sun screen daily on all exposed areas as well as under their foundation. This is a protection against the ultraviolet sunrays that induce sunburn, aging, and skin cancer.

In a very dry, arid climate such as that of Saudi Arabia and Egypt, women should double up on skin protection by using a moisturizing emollient (for example, a collagen product), which helps the skin to retain moisture. Here again, a sun screen would be helpful. However, in both of these instances, a woman should consider purchasing two shades of cosmetics, one to use immediately and another a shade darker to use after she has become suntanned.

Skin care in a cold, dry climate should be the same as that in a hot, dry climate. If there is lengthy exposure to the sun, as there would be, for example, skiing in Switzerland, a sun screen is advisable, an extra moisturizer should be used on the lips, and heavy moisturizing cream applied at night. In a cold, humid climate such as London's, only a light moisturizing cream is necessary.

## *Holidays Ahead*

The traditions of home become even more important in an overseas setting. Expatriates who have carefully packed away their holiday decorations and sent them to storage have lamented this mistake more than all others. Their advice is to not only bring your Christmas tree ornaments, strings of lights, and replacement bulbs aplenty but also include your familiar decorations—perhaps table or door pieces—and a couple of rolls of ribbon to freshen them each year. Most important, bring a permanent-type Christmas tree, and a gift or gifts for each family member for that first Christmas away. Other seasonal or holiday decorations are also good to bring along.

## Everything But the Kitchen Sink

"No cabinets, no closets, no shelving, just rooms with four walls and in one, a sink with four legs." Descriptions of housing such as this are not unusual in some parts of the world, and it will take more than imagination and a sense of style to create a livable home. Whatever your destination, you can be almost certain storage will be inadequate. Bookshelves, shelf brackets, or the new open T-, L-, or X-shaped clips to fit various sizes of boards will be a big help. Cup and clothes hooks, dish racks, and fitted space extenders of any sort are helpful throughout the house but particularly in the kitchen.

In addition to your usual kitchen equipment, you may need special items such as a large pot for boiling drinking water (when the water is not potable), a pressure cooker and an extra gasket ring and safety valve in high elevations, and canisters and salt shakers with dehumidifying crystals in their tops, as well as additional tight-fitting plastic storage containers for humid areas.

Common sense dictates the elimination of duplicates or items that are generally not used in the day-to-day preparation of food. However, you will want to include items that you use and enjoy. Many expatriates take their fine flatware, glassware, and china, while others opt for the practical but pretty.

In some areas of the world you may also wish to take along foodstuffs. Company policy will dictate here. Regulations depending, you may wish to include a couple cans of shortening for party pies (to be used until you can adjust to the local product), a few boxes of cake mixes to see you through until you can adjust to "baking from scratch" (mixes are rapidly becoming available abroad but are still very expensive), a couple of cans of cranberries for the first Thanksgiving and Christmas away from home (usually not available overseas), vacuum-packed pecans for those holiday pies, and silver and brass cleaners, which are often not available regardless of where you reside.

If you have infants, you should inquire about the availability of formulas and baby foods. If there is a void in this area, you may decide to make blender food, but you may wish to pack a few cans for vacations.

The movement of personnel around the world has done much to internationalize the food market. Most items that you want will be available, but the cost probably will be higher than in the United States.

## Linens

On the subject of linens, expatriates are united—take them, even if the transfer is temporary and furniture is not included in the move. The quality available abroad usually does not compare with the wrinkle-free percale sheets and luxuriously soft towels at home, while the cost is customarily much higher. Bed sizes are not universal either. An American twin is 3'3" x 6'3"; the English twin, to be found in most Commonwealth countries, is 3'3" x 6'6".

Besides bed and bath linens (many overseas residents prefer bright colors, since bathrooms are often a sterile white), you may wish to include everyday place mats and stay-press napkins in place of paper napkins, which are usually expensive as well as of inferior quality; dishcloths and kitchen towels in quantity, if you anticipate having a maid, as they use them for many purposes; tablecloths—only if you have them. Save these purchases for an overseas splurge. There are many beautiful Irish linen, Belgian lace, embroidered Chinese, or hand-printed Egyptian cotton cloths awaiting your purchase.

## Furniture

Many expatriates agree with the American resident in Italy, who admonished, "If you can only take a limited amount, it should be your bed and your pillow." Under a policy that allows for the shipment of full household effects, most people eliminate duplicates, nonessentials, or furniture that may be affected by the climate to which they are moving. As a wife in Singapore put it, "Unless you can be sure you will have air-conditioned, temperature-controlled quarters, antiques, feather-filled divans, etc. should be left in storage."

Many expatriates advise against major furniture replacement before going overseas, as:

Furniture may be damaged in transit;

Shabby furniture can be revitalized; services are usually cheaper and workmen expert;

Voids in furniture can be filled in abroad; the exception is card tables and chairs, which, with round wooden tops, can effect a supper table for six or eight; the suggestion—take more than one set.

## Decorative Items

Weight allowances permitting, you may wish to consider the shipment of:

*Carpets.* In some countries carpeting is expensive and of poor quality. Large room-size rugs or rolls of carpet are sometimes suggested. Other areas may have beautiful hand-loomed rugs.

*Draperies.* A good drapery design book and drapery essentials— weights, hooks, interfacing, and traverse rods in different lengths— should be included. Costs and availability of fabrics vary widely, so some take along a bolt of inexpensive drapery fabric in a neutral shade.*

*Upholstery fabrics.* In some areas cloth is expensive and the selection is limited. Climate should be an influencing factor in the choice of materials. A gaily colored cotton might be right for the tropics, while a velour or other heavy fabric would be more appropriate for the Continent.

*Lamps, pictures, objects of art, and floral arrangements.* These are an individual choice, usually influenced by the mode of life of the expatriate family.

---

*The continuing use of the same drapery fabric throughout a house, as well as in subsequent residences, allows the addition of an extra width or another window of draperies and still permits the achievement of continuity and good looks.

## *Fix-It Kit*

Settling in to a different life-style—perhaps changing gas bottles, priming water pumps, and making emergency repairs (it may be you or else) as well as the routine jobs—necessitates a basic set of tools. Good tools, especially electric or power tools, sell for two to five times the cost of similar tools purchased in the United States. A minimum list should include:

Saber saw with spare blades;
Skill saw with extra blades;
Insulated electric drill—$3/8''$ with $50'$ extension cord;
Good quality twist drill bits—$1/16''$ to $1/2''$ by $1/10''$
   increments with neck-down shanks;
Down-shaft to fit drill;
Good tool marker;
Claw hammer;
Ball-peen hammer;
Wrenches—combination: $3/8''$, $7/16''$, $1/2''$, $9/16''$,
   $5/8''$, $11/16''$, $3/4''$, $13/16''$, $7/8''$, $15/16''$, and $1''$;
Metric set—if you are going to a metric country;
Crescent wrenches— $6''$, $8''$, $10''$;
Pipe wrenches— $10''$, $14''$, $24''$;
Tape measure—$12'$ or $16'$;
Small spirit level;
Pop rivet tool with $1/8''$ and $3/16''$ rivets; $1/4''$, $1/2''$, $3/4''$ in length;
1 set masonry drills—$1/8''$, $3/16''$, $1/4''$, $3/8''$, size;
Rawl-plugs or plastic plugs to fit masonry drills
   (for putting up pictures, and the like in masonry walls);
1 pair $12''$ to $14''$ water pump pliers;
1 pair electrical pliers—$8''$ or $10''$;
Electric tape (3M or equivalent)—UL approved;
Weatherstripping—$1/2'' \times 50'$ rolls; and
Mixed picture hangers, nails, sheet metal and wood screws.

## Letting the Rest of the World Know

Your current friendships are often a bridge to friendships abroad. Hardly a move is made that you do not find that someone has a cousin, business acquaintance, or long-ago friend near your new address. This commonality of interest frequently leads to new friendships abroad and helps to bridge the early period of culture shock and loneliness. Don't hesitate—ask if they'll advise the friend of your arrival date and favor you with a courtesy call.

Educational, social, and fraternal organizations to which you belong are further resources. Do advise their national or international offices of your new address (office) and ask for a computer printout of members in your new country. An expatriate transferred to London could hardly believe that an old college acquaintance lived only a few blocks from her new residence, or that there was a total of 150 alumni in London and the surrounding areas. Another expatriate found that her membership in a New Orleans chapter of a businesswomen's fraternity was only a backdrop for a more meaningful participation—and new friendships—among the 135 members she found in Brussels. University lists also provide the basis for many meaningful get-togethers and lasting relationships in remote centers of the world. The Texas Aggie alumni, for example, "meet and greet," whether they are in Texas, Turkey, or Trinidad.

As you resign from clubs or organizations, keep in mind that many have international affiliates—among them, the Elks Club, the Lions Club, the Rotary Club, the Kiwanis Club, the Press Club, the Petroleum Club, the American Chamber of Commerce, the Knights of Columbus, and the Masonic Lodge. The YMCA and YWCA also have organizations in many countries, as do the Red Cross, the Cancer Society, and the Boy Scouts and Girl Scouts. If you have been an active member, do not hesitate to ask that organizations write letters of referral to their sister groups in your new community. Making worldwide referrals is a coming practice, providing for the transfer of credentials (volunteer hours, training, expertise, and so forth).

Contacting your children's schools is also an early must. You should request that the principal have prepared for you a complete record of your children's academic (including standardized test scores) and extracurricular activities. Overseas counselors suggest that students transferring in midsemester bring copies of the books they are studying, so that the overseas teachers can determine what material they have covered. If this is not possible, names and authors of the texts should be included, along with a descriptive paragraph. Records should be hand carried by you, rather than entrusted to the overseas mail.

If you are affiliated with a church, you will want to ask your minister, priest, or rabbi to prepare a letter of transfer to a new congregation.

The U.S. Post Office will forward mail for one year within the United States or its territories. However, it does not forward any mail to addresses outside these areas. It is helpful if you can have mail forwarded to your local company address for inclusion in their company mail pouch or have letters readdressed and the more expensive overseas stamp attached. If this is not possible, your local U.S. postal service will put your new overseas address on first-class letters and return them to the sender for a period of one year. Magazines or other second- or third-class mail will be discarded if return postage is not guaranteed.

## Moving With Children

The logistics of an overseas move may seem to preclude a continuing in-depth study of the country to which you have been assigned. However, it is vitally important that your whole family have a feel for the country, its people and its heritage, before you arrive. Take the time to read and translate to the children everything that you can on your new homeland, including its politics, religions, and cultures. Delve into its heroes, its heroines. Get city and county maps and familiarize yourself with them. Make games with the children planning out routes to places, so that street names, park areas, and other major sites become familiar. Learn the international road signs. Obtain a set of currency from a bank or money exchange dealer and have the whole family learn the approximate values. Introduce the metric tables and then play shopping games with the children using both the metric system and the new money, until the entire family is competent and comfortable in both.

Help the children develop travel manners. Pull out your Emily Post, Amy Vanderbilt, or Letitia Baldrige book on etiquette and review with them the proper way to make an introduction or the how-tos of dining on a plane or in an elegant restaurant. If you are scheduled for residence on the Continent or in one of the Commonwealth countries, expect to come in contact with a more formal way of living and entertaining. Even children shake hands upon being introduced and upon departing.

Whatever the age of the child, it is helpful for him or her to talk with someone close in age who has lived or visited in the host country. The opportunity this affords to see a country through another's eyes—to learn firsthand about schools, things to do, and places to go—may do much to remove a lingering fear of uncertainty and to help a child to become comfortable, even excited, about the prospect of a new home in a new country.

## Adventure Enroute

Just getting to where you're going can be a memorable, part of your posting abroad. Those with some extra time, enthusiasm, and the spirit of adventure will want to investigate the many combinations of tickets available on a supplemental basis to their corporate airline tickets. Owing to the maximum permitted mileage policy in effect by the airlines, there are a number of "allowed stopovers" that permit ticket holders to set down in other places served by the carrier. With the cooperation of the airlines, opportunities more than exist to sightsee, explore, vacation, whatever—enroute. Because stopovers are limited to the regularly scheduled stops made by the carrier, expatriates who regularly travel back and forth between the same destinations often use other airlines for part of the trip in order to visit different locations along the way.

Supplemental ticketing also allows the traveler to realize substantial savings on trips made within the same year to nearby areas. For example, a return coupon, which is obtainable for a small additional fee, allows Philippine-bound travelers to stop in Taipei, Saigon, Bangkok, Singapore, Okinawa, Hong Kong, or Bali. What a way to gather steam or to unwind! Looking ahead to annual leave and company-paid-for returns, some foresighted expatriates opt to purchase an around-the-world ticket. The chance is theirs to visit the countries down under or sightsee in Europe to or from their point of departure.

## Suggested Reading

Winston, Stephanie. *Getting Organized*. New York: Warner Books, 1979.

Malloy, John T. *The Women's Dress for Success Book*. New York: Warner Books, 1978.

Guither, Harold D., and Thompson, W.N. *Mission Overseas*. Urbana, Illinois: University of Chicago Press, 1969.

# 4

# The Moving Affair

## Export Firms and International Shippers

YOUR INITIAL CONTACT with an export firm and international shipper inevitably brings the move into focus. If there have been lingering doubts, they now vanish rapidly. The move is about to happen!

The export firms you contact may be set forth by corporate policy, but do ask for references. If at all possible, get more than one estimate of charges. Having the services of reliable export and international shipping firms can be a real asset to an overseas move; such firms customarily have much up-to-date information.

Export firms should have current data—not only on type of appliances and transformers needed, but also on repair stations within the country; in addition, they should offer to mail—postage paid and free of charge—any parts needed during the time the product is under warranty. Before making any purchases, you should ask about the warranty period and how the firm handles repairs that may be needed during the time you are overseas.

You should also ask to see a list of authorized repair and part centers in the country to which you are being posted. Does it appear to be up-to-date? Which major supplier has a center closest to the area you will be living? General Electric states that they now have a center in every country in the world; and apparently Maytag and Westinghouse are beginning to establish overseas service centers. The clue to service may lie in purchasing the brand having the nearest service representative.

Most export firms cater to the mail order, as well as the drop-in, trade. Upon request, they will mail a catalog of overseas appliances, housewares, and transformers; upon receipt of a confirming order and payment, they will ship to a U.S. address or to an overseas location. If delivery is made directly to the international carrier, and you do not take possession in the States, you generally are not charged with a sales tax. For assistance with worldwide appliances, you may wish to contact:

Thor Export Sales
130 Madison Avenue
New York, New York 10016
Telephone (212) 679-0077

American International Exports, Inc.
1346 Connecticut Avenue, N.W.
Washington, D.C. 20036
Telephone (202) 294-4296

Irv Wolfson Co.
3221 West Irving Park Road
Chicago, Illinois 60618
Telephone (312) 267-7828

Sears and Roebuck also carries 220-volt washers, dryers, and refrigerators, which they can order from their central warehouse and have delivered to you in a three- to six-week period. They do not carry transformers. While all of their gas ranges carry the convertible orifice for butane gas, the range clock is designed for 60 cycles and will not function properly on 50 cycles. Parts for Sears appliances on a worldwide basis can be obtained by contacting:

Sears and Roebuck
4640 Roosevelt Boulevard
Department 157 Export
Philadelphia, Pennsylvania 10132
Telephone (215) 831-4000

## Worldwide Appliances

### *Major Appliances*

Your present large electrical appliances—washer, dryer, refrigerator, and freezer, all of which operate on a motor—will have a shorter life span if you take them overseas. The 220 voltage overseas versus the 110 voltage in this country is not such a great problem. This can be taken care of with a step-down transformer; but the constantly higher load imposed by the 50-cycle current coupled with the wide variations in the overseas voltage are the sources of most appliance motor failures. The constant voltage transformer will help with the sudden surges in electric power, but the overseas 50-cycle system means that your motor appliances will have to work harder, thus shortening their lives. In the case of a washer and dryer, both the motor and clock timer also run at a slower speed and take a longer time to complete their cycles. For this reason, it is better to purchase new equipment designed for 220 volt/50 cycle, unless you are absolutely certain that present machines are designed for 50-60-cycle current (see plate on reverse of machine) and that they are in excellent condition.

Since American ranges operate with a heating element rather than a motor, they do not present such a problem. Both electric and gas ranges work equally well abroad; however, the gas stove should be purchased with the convertible orifice for bottled gas. The clock and timer on your stove run on 60 cycles, so when you head into 50-cycle living, they will run slower. While you may opt to replace them with 50-cycle equipment, the observance of a simple rule will allow you to use the clock timer without replacement. Simply multiply the time allowed in your recipe for baking by the ratio 6/5 or use the handy scale in the figure below. Just remember that you will have to set the timer for a slightly longer period than that called for in the American recipe.

### *Cooking Time for Your U.S. Recipe, Overseas (50-cycle clock timer)*

| • | 12 | 24 | 36 | 48 | 60 | 72 | 84 | 96 |
|---|----|----|----|----|----|----|----|----|
| 0 | 10 | 20 | 30 | 40 | 50 | 60 | 70 | 80 |

There are a number of companies, among them Caloric, Magic Chef, and Crown, that make the electric or convertible orifice gas stove with the 50-cycle clocks.

While it is often possible to rent or buy appliances within a country, they are usually quite expensive—sometimes two to four times stateside prices—and often much smaller. Occasionally, it is possible to purchase appliances from departing residents, but this is not considered a reliable option by many expatriates who freely advise that unless your corporation warehouses appliances for issuance on arrival, you should take your own.

Since parts may be difficult, if not impossible, to obtain in many areas of the world, and repairmen trained to fix a sophisticated machine or a particular brand nonexistent, it is recommended that expatriates start out with new or fairly new major appliances in the simplest design of a leading brand. As a general rule, existing appliances should not be taken if they are more than four years old. It is helpful to know the type of appliances used by the expatriates in the area to which you are moving as well as the relative cost and reliability of gas versus electric use.

## Cooling and Heating Appliances

In some areas water heaters, space heaters, or room air-conditioners and electric fans are readily available from departing expatriates. However, you are usually advised to bring the equipment with you. Electric water heaters commonly used in the United States are 220 volts and will operate equally well on 50-60 cycles. Again, check gas versus electric costs overseas. If you purchase the water heater and space heater in gas, be sure to have the convertible orifice for bottled gas.

Air-conditioners are commonly used and readily available in 220 volts in the United States, but check that the motors are not split phase—that is, operate on 110 volt from one leg of a three-wire service. Some units may be equipped with a 220-volt compressor motor and 220-volt fan and blower motors and can be more readily used in the 220-volt countries. You may wish to obtain professional advice on whether to take the units.

If the units you now own are single-phase 110 volt that plug into a regular wall receptacle, you probably can use these overseas with a large (1,000 to 1,600 watts) step-down transformer. Since most of these units utilize sealed compressors similar to the refrigerator and freezer, the motors may not be designed for 50-cycle current (relevant information on back plate), and the life expectancy may be reduced. Again, it is probably best not to bring along appliances over four years old.

In many countries electricity costs have risen to such an extent that expatriates generally are air-conditioning only the bedrooms and perhaps a small living area. In these countries a fan can be very useful.

## Electronics

You will need both a step-down transformer and an adapter for most U.S. record players. The motor in stateside equipment is designed to turn 3,600 revolutions per minute on 60 cycles, but it will turn 3,000 revolutions per minute on 50 cycles. Usually, it is a very simple procedure to slip a small plastic rubber or steel sleeve over the capstan pulley that drives the machine, so that it will turn at the proper speed. Most original equipment suppliers can provide this very inexpensive adapter; some equipment, in fact, comes with the adapter in the cabinet in an inconspicuous spot. Occasionally, however, the pulley may need to be changed completely; in other instances, usually with the more sophisticated brands such as Garrard and Dual, it may be possible to convert the equipment to 220 by changing the wiring. Still other equipment, such as Saba, North American Phillips, and Norelco, has universal transformers. Owing to this variance, equipment should be taken to an authorized service representative or to an export firm (such as Irv Wolfson in Chicago) that has a specialized electronic department for overseas servicing. Many pieces of equipment manufactured for overseas sales have internal transformers that go from 110 to 220 volts at the flip of a switch.

## *Television*

For an American television set to be used in a host country, it must be compatible with the voltage, cycle, and system. If your television is not compatible, it is best to leave it in storage and plan to rent one, at least on a temporary basis, after your arrival. Purchase of a television should be made in the host country.

## *Miscellaneous Appliances*

### *Lamps*

Your stateside lamps should be brought with you. In a 220-volt/50-cycle country, they can easily be converted by using 220-volt bulbs and adapter plugs, which are always available in the host country.

## Clocks

Your electrical clocks will be of no value in the 220-volt/50-cycle countries. Exporters will have the 220-volt snooze alarm, or you can opt for yesterday's windup alarm.

## Sewing Machines

With a transformer, 110-volt/60-cycle machines can easily be used. For better service, take name brands. Singer, for example, now has retail and service stores throughout the world.

## Typewriters

Smith-Corona features a 220-volt machine, but most "leisure" writers take their 110-volt/60-cycle typewriter and use a transformer. (Include extra ribbons, some bond and carbon paper, envelopes, and erasers.)

## Dishwashers

Portable dishwashers are strictly an optional item. Water pressure may be a problem in some areas. Unlike the freezer or refrigerator that uses hermetically sealed motor compressor units, the dishwasher always has a separate belt-drive motor. The intermittent duty of the dishwasher allows it to be used with a transformer with little danger of burning out the motor, especially if the motor is designed for 50-60 cycle operation. When compared with the alternative of purchasing a special 220-volt dishwasher or the purchase overseas of a smaller, less efficient unit at a much higher cost, the decision to take your 110-volt portable will be one you won't regret. Even if the motor burns out, replacement fractional horsepower motors are usually available overseas, and any competent repairman can install a new motor. If you decide to take a dishwasher, you should also take faucets and adapters.

## Vacuum Cleaners

Some expatriates do take the 220-volt/50-cycle vacuum cleaners or even purchase them abroad; but many opt to go the transformer route. The vacuum cleaner motor, which is a little smaller than many other appliances, can be used with a transformer without any real difficulty. There may be a little less suction than usual, and it can be cumbersome using transformers unless you have one on wheels. A supply of vacuum cleaner bags is a must.

## Icemakers

Icemakers are generally not taken. However, some couples who entertain extensively (as company managers responsible for public relations) and who live in countries in which the water does not have to be boiled have found them very helpful.

## Coffee Makers

Almost everyone living overseas entertains, so a 26- to 40-cup party perk is a very basic part of any household.

## Pasteurizers

In the countries in which pasteurized milk is not available, this unit can literally be a lifesaver. It is available with automatic cutoff, in the two-gallon size, through Sears catalog department, farm catalog.

## Meat Grinders

In areas where corn-fed beef and aging are not part of the way of life, a meat grinder can help to make a tough piece of meat a little more edible.

## Small Appliances

Transferees usually take the small appliances that they enjoy using at home. Most small appliances that are used intermittently can be used with a transformer with relative success and fairly long life. However, nearly all of these appliances are available in the 220 volt, 50 cycle through export firms or at somewhat higher prices abroad. Only irons are in a somewhat different category. Expatriate advice, "Take two." Since the price of the 220-volt/50-cycle irons compares very favorably with the 110-volt 60-cycle, why not take the former along with your presently used 110?

## Transformers

If you are moving to a country that uses the 220-volt current, you will need a variety of step-down transformers that convert 220-440-volt current to 110 current, so that 110-volt appliances can be used. Transformers are available in a variety of sizes, ranging from 100 to 300 watts. There is, for example, a 1,600-watt Franz's converter, a small plug-in, which can be used with nonmotorized equipment and is ideal for bathroom appliances such as curling irons and electric toothbrushes. There is a special, large-size refrigerator transformer. And there is even a central transformer that can be installed at the source of power that will convert all the electricity in the building. However, this is very expensive and is not usually considered an option for the transient expatriate.

To determine the size you need, find your appliance that requires the greatest wattage, add 500 watts for safety, and buy a transformer that size or larger. For example, for a fry pan of 1,350 watts, add a 500-watt safety factor for 1,850 watts or a 2 kw (kilowatt) transformer. The big 2 kw transformer will handle almost anything you have in the house, even operating more than one appliance at once as long as the combined wattage does not exceed the transformer capacity.

No transformer larger than 1,600 volts should be used in an ungrounded socket or with an ungrounded plug. A transformer in use may be slightly warm, but it will never be hot. Should this occur, it probably means that the appliance to which it is attached is in trouble. It should be disconnected before the transformer is damaged.

Wattage and voltage are marked on a plate that is attached to the bottom of each appliance. In some instances, amperes may be used in place of watts. It then becomes necessary to multiply the number of amperes by the voltage of the appliance to determine wattage. For example, an appliance marked 5 amperes and 110 volts = 550 watts.

Transformers often can be purchased in the host country, new or secondhand from departing expatriates. They are also sometimes available on a stateside basis from those who have been repatriated, as well as from the export firms that specialize in worldwide appliances. They should be constant voltage transformers with no exposed wires, and they should conform to accepted safety standards having, for example, the Underwriters Laboratory Seal of Approval.

## International Movers

International movers seem to embody the philosophy of "relax and leave the moving to us." Not only are their international personnel reputed to be the best and most experienced on the payrolls, but they provide a bevy of allied services that can include selling 220-volt/50-cycle appliances to you; getting your pet to the kennel, vaccinated, and airshipped to you; or shipping a car or boat to your final destination. In addition, the data they have accumulated through previous moves can be most helpful:

Streets in Tokyo are so narrow that the Tokyo-bound should have household effects shipped in two 20-foot containers rather than one 40-foot container.

Houses in Hong Kong are scarce, and apartments are small—incoming residents usually find it advantageous to minimize their shipment.

Expatriates who have suffered extensive moving damage agree that much of it was caused by the rain, high humidity, mildew, and pilferage during the time the shipment sat outside on the docks waiting to be put on a boat, moved into the warehouse, or sent through customs. Both they and the multinational executives surveyed were in agreement that *only* the steel-framed ocean-land containers, which come in 20-foot, 35-foot, or 40-foot sizes, should be used for international moves, unless only a small shipment is being sent. They suggest that the carrier include—along with his written estimate—packing dates, moving-out dates, and written assurance that the steel container will be used. They also recommend that transferees who are limited to a certain number of pounds advise the carrier in writing of their authorized allowance and request that it not be exceeded without written consent. (See the Appendix.)

Contrary to domestic moves, which are subject to the regulations of the Interstate Commerce Commission and where interstate movers are held responsible for damages or losses up to 60 cents per pound per article, there are no regulations on international moves. While the domestic carrier may be responsible for a 60-cents-per-pound liability during the time the goods are in his hands, the forwarding company may only have a 10-cents-per-pound liability, and the ocean transfer company may limit its liability to $400 for a 40-foot container; but the foreign carrier may have no liability at all—depending upon the regulations in his country. Under these circumstances, it is very important that the shipment be covered by transit insurance.*

Upon request the Interstate Commerce Commission (Public Information Offices, Interstate Commerce Commission, 12th and Constitution Avenue N.W., Washington, D.C. 20423) will provide a free annual performance report of shippers. You will also find their booklets, "Summary of Information for Shippers of Household Goods" and "Loss and Damage Claims," informative.

---

*Your homeowner's insurance policy will not cover goods in transit to a foreign location.

## Inventory of Household Possessions

Most corporations provide transferees with inventory forms that list household possessions on a room-by-room, original-cost/replacement-value basis. While completing it is a time-consuming and frustrating task, it does provide an excellent insurance record, and it does expedite the task of deciding what to take and what to leave.

Based on your preliminary research (climate, probable temporary quarters, probable permanent housing, voltage, and the like) and your company regulations (full or partial shipment), you should have beginning answers to the following questions:

Will we need it? Have we used it in the last year? Does it fit? Is it broken? Depending upon your answers, you may wish to consider a garage sale or donation to an organization such as the Salvation Army.

Will we need it immediately? (See section on accompanied baggage.)

Will we need it in a temporary residence? (See section on survival kit, air freight style.)

Will we need it in permanent quarters?

Can it be used upon our return? Does it have such monetary or sentimental value that it should be left in a bank or fur vault, or with friends or relatives? Does it need temperature-controlled storage, or can it be kept safely in commercial storage without climatic control?

As you consider each item, you should list and, if possible, separate the items for accompanied baggage, air freight, ocean shipment, specialty (bank or fur vaults) or regular commercial storage, and giveaways. Except for donations, which will need only your estimate of value, each listing should include the purchase price, the replacement value, the date the article was bought, and a serial number, if there is one. On items that have high burglary value (radios, televisions, and the like), you should take the time to stencil your social security number with an engraving pen. Antiques, artifacts, or articles of unusual value should be set aside for professional appraisal. You will want to take along pictures of these, and you should also take pictures of your china, crystal, silver, and each piece of furniture. This is not only a good record in case of theft; the pictures of the furniture can be quite helpful to a repairman in the event of damage.

## *Preparations For Packing*

Settling in in a foreign location is much less complicated if everything is ready for immediate use. Since it is important to prevent bugs and mildew from causing damage while the goods are in transit, everything should be clean and dry. Special preparations should include:

*Linens, bedding, drapes, clothing.* Launder or dry-clean each item.

*Area rugs.* Professionally dry-clean and mothproof.

*Furniture.* Vacuum upholstered furniture and spot clean or professionally clean, if needed. Put a light protective coat of wax on all wooden furniture.

*Grandfather clock.* Tie chains and remove pendulum and weights for separate packing.

*Hi-fi components.* Pack in original box if possible. Secure (screw or tape) chassis to base plate. Secure pick-up arm and remove knobs (to prevent breakage or loss).

*Silver pieces and flatware.* Polish and wrap in tarnish-proof paper or cloth.

*Objects of art.* Clean and place in one area for special handling by movers.

*Photos, slides, and negatives.* Put in an air-conditioned atmosphere for 48 hours prior to packing to remove moisture. Pack in a plastic box with silica gel packets and seal tightly.

*Small appliances.* Clean and polish. To prepare iron for transit, set dial on steam and heat for an hour.

*Refrigerator and freezer.* Clean with soda water and let stand with the door open for two days prior to packing. A few charcoal briquets or coffee grounds will control odors and mildew (put one sock inside the other, add one-fourth pound of coffee or charcoal, and tie). Be sure the doors are taped shut.

*Cookstoves.* Clean thoroughly (old grease becomes rancid). Knobs, grates, and oven racks clean easily if they are soaked overnight in a presoak solution. Be sure these items are wrapped and packed separately to prevent damage.

*Portable dishwasher.* Clean and dry thoroughly, including the hose.

*Washers and dryers.* Disconnect, dry thoroughly, and stabilize tubs.

*Air-conditioners.* Fasten the compressor down (see the instructions in the pamphlet that came with the equipment).

Veterans of overseas moves have suggested the following moving procedures:

Pack air freight first, so that excess weight can be removed and repacked with the sea shipment. To avoid any possibility that the air freight might be packed with the sea shipment or put into storage, transport it to the warehouse for later transshipment immediately after it has been packed.

Pack sea cargo, and seal.

Pack items to be left in storage in the States. Be sure that the inventory is accurate, so that items needed later can be easily located.

They also recommend that small children and pets who may not easily understand what is happening during a move be cared for elsewhere if possible. This is a good time to call in the offers of help made by friends and relatives.

There are many demands for attention during a move, but you should be available to supervise the packing and to go over the inventory of furniture as it is prepared. You will want to be sure that the inventory clearly indicates the exact location of any scratches or worn places. If you cannot come to an agreement with the packer on his description of the furniture, write your own beside it. It is also a good idea to color code all boxes and furniture, using a different colored tape for each room. Non-English-speaking unloaders can easily understand that all items marked with one color go to a certain room.

As boxes are packed, they should be labeled, color-coded, and the contents listed on the inventory sheet in case of loss. All irreplaceable items, valuable documents, diplomas, photos, or other paper memorabilia that cannot be restored once damaged should be hand carried. However, some expatriates are now beginning to put articles of value, such as silver, with other items, noting only on their personal inventory sheet that, as an example, box 51 contains 14 sheets and two silver bowls. While the silver must be listed somewhere on the inventory, it is not so immediately obvious that box 51, which is listed as 14 linen sheets, contains other valuable items.

## Loading and Locking

While the moving company personnel may be expert at packing, sometimes they do not realize the incredible beating that distant port facilities can give a shipment. You will want to be sure that the items are protected against slippage, concussion, and friction and that the heaviest items are at the bottom of the van. If the container is headed for the tropics, you should ask that the carrier pack some silica gel packets in the container with the other items. Unless the shipment is not completely filled and has to be taken to the warehouse to be braced for the trip, you should watch the container being closed and sealed with a tamper-proof lock. Some expatriates then lock the van with one or two locks of their own and retain the keys.

If you are responsible for the moving charges, you should plan to be present at the weigh-in or have the carrier telephone you with the actual weight. You will want to arrange for a certified check or money order to reach the carrier before your departure, as the goods will not be transshipped without prepayment. You will also want to be sure that you are given the international bill of lading, the packer's inventory, and the insurance certificate.

## *Accompanied Baggage*

Deciding just what to include in your accompanied baggage may be among the most difficult of your decisions. As soon as your itinerary is set, you should check with your airline carrier, as your weight allowances, to some extent, are dependent upon your destination. Extra pounds can be carried on an overweight basis, but it is very expensive to do so.

The clothing and other essentials you pack should be influenced by the climate, activities for the first few weeks (sight-seeing, receptions, dinner invitations), and exactly where you will be staying (hotel with pool and/or formal dining room). Articles that can help to make your initial period in a new country more pleasant include:

Sports or other leisure-time equipment or books
Cosmetics and toiletries (including cleaning-fluid, shoeshine fluid, fingernail polish, remover, detergent, and towelettes in individual packages)
Soap in a plastic box and wash cloths
Small bathroom clothesline
Hot curlers or curling iron, shaver, hand steamer, with 220 adapter, if needed
Travel laundry bag or plastic bags
First-aid and medicine kits
Sewing kit (needles, threads, snaps, hooks, safety pins)
Cupsize electric immersion heater
Tang or lemonade mix (packets)

Small knife
Can opener
Screwdriver
Baby food and other small-child essentials
Flashlight with new or rechargeable batteries
Travel alarm clock
Door alarm

## *Travel Wardrobe*

Clothes to travel in rate special thought. Since you will probably be met by a company representative, you will want to arrive looking neat and pulled together. Tight clothing constricts veins and promotes problems on long flights; so in addition to being a wrinkle-free fabric, travel clothing should be comfortably loose. An all-weather coat with a zip-out lining, which makes it comfortable in almost any climate, is considered a good addition to a travel wardrobe.

## *Carry-On Bags*

Since luggage often is delayed or temporarily lost enroute, experienced travelers usually plan to take one carry-on bag that has a change of clothing (perhaps just a shirt for adults and a complete outfit for children), pajamas, cosmetics, toiletries, and a medical kit. Some travelers also carry perfumes, nail polish, remover, and other items that might be damaged by freezing or low air pressure.

A separate flight bag should contain everything that you would like for the trip—a warm sweater (it can get cool on airplanes at night), footlets, magazines, books (the stewardess will have stationery), small games, hard candy, gum, towelettes, and a collapsible cup or other items needed for the very young. Some travelers who have expensive jewelry, cameras, or silverware carry it in their flight bag to prevent pilferage. These items should be locked in the hotel safe immediately upon arrival.

## *Children's Flight Bag*

Each child will want to help select items to be included in his flight bag, but you may wish to suggest that his choices include some of these long-time favorites listed by expatriates and their well-traveled children:

Tissues

Wash and drys

Comb and brush

Snacks—for those long airport waits (cheese and crackers, juice, hard candy)

Small dolls—Barbie and Ken, G.I. Joe, Kiddle dolls, and the like

Color-form kits—stick-ons such as dolls, clothes, autos, houses

Coloring books, crayons

Puzzle books

Comic books

Paperback novels on a small-fry level

Simple model kits

Potholder looms, yarn, or other handicrafts

Small toys and cars

Puzzle boards and metal puzzle rings

Magnetic checkers, Scrabble, dice, and number games

Playing boards and cards

Merlin or other electronic games

Tape recorder with story tales and ear plugs

Paperpacks for tic-tac-toe, sink the battleship, and the like

Word games

Travel diary and pencils or pens

Instamatic-type camera (for older children) to record their impressions of the trip

Scrapbook for mementos of their travels

Pilot's log available at all private airports; enter child's name, date of trip, from—to (Los Angeles to Paris)

### *Important Papers*

In addition to the legal documents listed in Chapter 11, you will need to hand carry the following items. They should be packed in a briefcase or a small bag that can be kept locked and within your sight at all times. These items are essential to your survival abroad!

Passport for each family member

International certificate of vaccination for each family member

Visa

Work permit

Airline tickets

Travelers checks

International credit card

Travel instructions or itinerary with copy of hotel confirmation;
International driver's license

Directory of overseas telephone numbers (company officials)

International bill of lading, insurance certificates, and packer's
inventory

Airline waybill number and receipt for air freight

Keys to lock on steel ocean container

Car papers, record of car serial and motor numbers, and extra set
of car keys, for those taking cars

Luggage keys

Inventory of safe deposit box in the United States

Power of attorney

Copy of will

Extra passport pictures

Expense records

U.S. stamps (so that hand-carried letters can be mailed in the
United States)

## *Survival Kit, Air Freight Style*

Your air freight shipment will enable you to survive and to enjoy
that oftentimes nebulous period between your arrival in the host
country and the arrival of your household effects. Most corporations
have very specific regulations about air freight allowances. It is
important to be aware of these limitations and to strictly adhere to
them, as excess poundage can prove to be a very costly affair.
International carriers have scales for this purpose and upon request
will provide a weigh-in service.

Since air freight is usually flown in unpressurized, unheated
compartments, flammable or explosive products such as nail polish,
polish remover, matches, or lighter fluid should not be included.
Liquids should be in screw-top plastic bottles, enclosed in plastic
bags. As a final word of caution, do be sure that your international
carrier gives you a receipt for your air freight shipment and that he
obtains, and informs you of, the airline waybill number from the
airline carrier, as you will need this number for delivery in the host
country.

It may not be possible to predict in advance just what you will
need, but company policy should be an influencing factor. If your
company domiciles newcomers in a hotel or completely furnished
temporary flat, you may need very little in the way of extras. If, on

the other hand, they leave it to you to find a sparsely furnished "temp" or to rent beds and other basics so that you can go immediately into a permanent residence, a few extras to make it more homelike may be worthwhile. Whatever your situation, shipments should be personalized by your individual family requirements and preferences.

It is important to anticipate this period in your lives and to recognize, in advance, that you will probably have more free time and less to do with it than you have ever previously experienced. Take a wide range of activities for the children and plan to make it a learning period. Pack language and study aids and a host country guide book; as a family, continue a study of the new language, the currencies, the metric system, the transportation system, and the country in general. You will find this a good time to write letters to friends and relatives and to read the best-sellers and the latest magazines you've been laying aside. Adult games of your preference and craft and hobby kits are also good take-alongs.

The transportation of ocean freight from the United States to other parts of the world usually can be expedited in a six-week to three-month period; however, extenuating circumstances such as dock strikes, port congestion, or the unavailability of host country housing may delay reception. Although rare, there are instances where families have been transferred from the tropics to the cold north winds before their ocean freight reached them. So, plan for an indefinite period and unforeseen events, take a complete range of clothing for all occasions, but also include at least one outfit for a completely different climate.

You will want to be sure that clothing and linens are packed in waterproof containers. Footlockers with waterproof liners are excellent for these items. Usually packers can provide waterproof boxes for other items; however, small appliances suffer less damage if they can first be packed in their original factory cartons.

The following items are suggested for life in a sparsely furnished temporary residence:

*Baby equipment.* Cribs, playpens, vaporizers, and the like.
*Bed and baths.* Sheets, pillowcases, pillows, and blankets sufficient for family; windup alarm clock, bath towels, hand towels, washcloths.
*Children's equipment.* Children's phonograph and musical or story records, storybooks, favorite toys, surprise toys or books for a lonesome day, prizes for story on new homeland, and the like.

*Cleaning supplies.* Mop, broom, dust cloths, furniture polish, scouring powder, and sponges.

*Laundry aids.* Clothesline, clothespins, iron, and a few clothes hangers.

*Cosmetics and toiletries.* As needed for a three-month period.

*Kitchen.* Plastic dishes, plastic glasses (which can later be used in a picnic hamper), stainless or other inexpensive flatware, plastic mixing bowls, refrigerator dishes, water and juice containers, measuring cups (plastic) and spoons, skillet and cooking pans (limited number), meat forks, spatula, stirring spoons, kitchen knives (paring, cutting), egg beater, can opener (manual and corkscrew), baking pans, cookie sheets, cake and pie pans, plastic dishpan, dish rack (for draining dishes), rubber mat, rubber gloves, rubber sink stopper, dish towels, dish cloths or sponges, scouring pads, hot pads and potholders, place mats, napkins, cookbook, spices and condiments, salt and pepper shakers, small electric appliances (coffeemaker, blender, toaster or waffle iron, fiying pan or slow cooker), paper plates, paper napkins in assorted sizes, picnic hamper.

*Medicines.* As needed for three months.

*Miscellaneous.* Candleholders with candles, ashtrays, family pictures or other small items to personalize apartment, reading lamp, extension cords and plugs, transistor radio or small stereo, small tape recorder, tapes (to record first experiences and send tapes to relatives), step-down transformer (if needed), stationery and envelopes, address book.

*Optional.* Typewriter (portable), sewing machine (portable), sewing supplies and material, tennis rackets, golf clubs, scuba gear or other hobby equipment; seasonal items (Halloween, Thanksgiving, Christmas, birthday) for holidays that fall before the arrival of the ocean shipment; tax records, expense account reports, or other business papers that may be needed before the arrival of ocean freight; tool kit (small, assortment of small nails, screws, hammer, screwdriver, pliers, and crescent wrench).

## Pets by Jet

In considering whether to take your pet with you overseas, it can easily be argued that a beloved pet can help to stabilize a household and provide companionship and an element of security when all else is new and different. Moving a pet abroad, however, can be complicated, expensive; and for the pet, who may sense its owner's concern, the move can be frightening. It is important to consider all the aspects related to moving a pet to an overseas post.

Regulations regarding entry to a foreign country are usually quite explicit and rigidly enforced. They normally require a minimum of a certificate of good health—sometimes in triplicate and sometimes within the last 7 days—and a rabies vaccination at least 30 days old and not more than 180 days old. However, you should also ask your veterinarian to research the diseases and parasites native to the area to which you are moving to determine if other shots should be given or other precautions taken. The foreign consulate will be able to give you detailed information on entry requirements, which may include a veterinarian certificate endorsed by the Inspector in Charge, Bureau of Animal Husbandry, United States Department of Agriculture, and a permission to ship or an import license. Without meeting these requirements, the animal may be returned home on the next plane. In some instances, requirements may involve a period of quarantine, which can be a demoralizing aftermath to a frightening trip. If your pet is elderly or high-strung, you should consider whether it is kindness to subject it to this experience, or whether it might be happier in another stateside home.

If you have a very small pet, it may be able to fly with you in a crate that will slip under the seat or as baggage or excess baggage. However, most airlines will not accept a pet for cargo shipment if the temperature is below 40°F or above 80°F, taking into consideration both the origin and the destination. If your pet has had previous motion sickness or is quite high-strung, you may wish to request that your veterinarian give it a tranquilizer before departure. Dogs or cats should wear both a flea-tick collar and a collar with a firmly attached identification tag. The pet's leash should be removed and attached to the cage, along with a cloth bag of food, and a tag with your overseas address, and a telephone number where you can be reached.

In any case, airline regulations concerning the handling and transport of pets are highly restricted, both on travel within the continental United States as well as abroad. In arranging for overseas travel for your pet, you are advised to check early with the airlines you will be flying, both domestic and international, for their exact specifications.

If your pet is departing the United States at New York, having been transshipped from another United States city, you may wish to book it into the SPCA (Society for the Prevention of Cruelty to Animals) kennel there overnight. Similar accommodations are also available at Heathrow Airport in London, provided that the pet meets their stringent entry requirements. Although your employer may not pay the cost of transporting your household pets, it is considered a deductible moving expense by the Internal Revenue Service, and you should keep accurate records of all charges involved.

## Suggested Reading

Friedrich, Barbara, and Hultstrand, Sally. *Did Somebody Pack the Baby?* Englewood Cliffs, New Jersey: Prentice-Hall, 1978.

Kleeberg, Irene Cumming. *The Moving Book, How Not to Panic at the Thought.* New York: Butterick, 1978.

Phaltz, Marilyn. *Move Your Family Successfully.* Tucson, Arizona: H.P. Books, 1979.

PART TWO

# Home, Children, and Health

# 5

# Home Is Where
# The Heart Is

*T*HE RECENT RECOGNITION by corporations of stresses associated with an overseas move has led many to attempt to buffer the moves of their expatriate employees. The pretransfer cross-cultural orientation seminar has been a particularly effective means of introducing families to a new culture. "Adoption" by an overseas host employee with a similar family structure has also been helpful. This process involves letters—to congratulate and inform—prior to the move; this is followed after the move by get-acquainted visits designed to familiarize the newcomers with local customs and help in interpreting cultural differences.

Corporate orientation and general information briefings generally supplement these contacts. In some instances, however, this responsibility has been assumed by corporate wives' advisory groups with great success. Their efforts to inform and to orient the newcomer to a different life-style, their practical advice, and often their actual help in enrolling children in school and their parents in language courses, acquainting them with local shopping practices, and locating housing and medical practitioners provide the one thing a new expatriate needs most—a support system. Both the individual and the corporation benefit, as it enables the newly arrived to get down to the business of living and working in a minimum of time, without having to solve anew each problem associated with residence overseas.

The incoming expatriate who is the sole company representative may have to assume the primary responsibility for his family's orientation. Expatriates who have had this experience suggest that the newcomer make contact with a local resident who can advise on customs and procedures in establishing residence. In most instances, corporations retain legal counsel to advise them on host country regulations related to the establishment of new businesses. Some expatriates state that they, too, have relied on this counsel. Others immediately establish bank accounts and strive for a friendly and informative relationship with their banker. They emphasize that a foreign affiliate of their U.S. bank, or a branch with reciprocal banking arrangements, will usually simplify banking arrangements as well as be more responsive to the plight of the newcomer.

Newcomer's services, similar in composition to the corporate wives' advisory groups, have begun to emerge in countries where it has been possible to obtain work permits. For a modest fee, American wives will guide the newly arrived through the maze of permits, licenses, and registrations as well as dispense information on residential areas, schools, and leisure time activities. A call to the president or vice-president of the American Women's Club, whose name should be on file at the American embassy, will help to uncover such services. You should also be able to obtain information on activities within the American community in which you may wish to participate. American Women's clubs, historically, have a large membership of newcomers, as well as a wide range of activities. Their functions often include get-acquainted coffees, orientation lectures, sightseeing trips to nearby cultural centers, as well as relatively inexpensive charter flights to neighboring countries. In many areas they also publish handbooks on life in the host country.

Although some people do not consider themselves "joiners," the advice is to become one:

> This is no time to play the part of the reluctant dragon. Life without family is hard, but life without family or friends is a zero. Be a joiner—at least until you get to know people.

If you are a newly arrived expatriate, you may be surprised at the number of social, religious, and philanthropic groups within the host city. Many will be organizations with which you are familiar and perhaps some will be organizations to which you may have previously belonged. Don't hesitate to reestablish your membership in such groups as the Petroleum Wives, the Girl Scouts, the Cancer Society, and the Red Cross; in the case of men, the American Club, the American Chamber of Commerce, the Lions, Rotary, or Kiwanis International, and professional groups or special interest clubs. And look into the university clubs or associations for university graduates from the host country and their foreign residents. "Belonging" will make being an alien a little easier. In fact, it may make a big difference.

Overseas churches with large expatriate memberships are sensitive to the woes of the newcomer. In addition to fostering what many expatriates term "a truly meaningful religious experience," much of their ministry is directed toward meeting the particular needs of the expatriate. Notable among these ministries is that of the Union Church in Manila, with its newcomers' support group, Hospitality International, and the American churches in London and in Paris, whose support of the "Bloom Where You're Planted" series has helped newcomers to view with new understanding the cultural differences and the ways in which they can best handle life within that framework.

The prospect of residing in a hotel until your furniture arrives (a probable six weeks to six months) is not a pleasant one for most families, especially those with small children. The obvious answer is a temporary residence. If you are in this position, you should check bulletin boards of schools, clubs, and supermarkets as well as the classified sections of newspapers and with acquaintances about "leave" accommodations. These are residences that have been temporarily vacated by those on vacation. Occasionally, it is possible to rent short-lease furnished apartments or to rent an apartment and furniture separately.

## Finding a Home

With few exceptions the worldwide housing market is generally regarded as tight. Prices have escalated rapidly in the last decade, and overseas Americans quite commonly find themselves paying astronomical prices. Even "prime" rentals may have to be completely redecorated, modernized, or rewired and have closets, kitchen cabinets, or water pumps added. In some instances, the landlord will assume the responsibility for these additions. In others, the prospective tenant has no recourse but to do them himself and hope to recover a portion of it in "key money" from the next tenant. No matter how many improvements have been made, the landlord may choose to ignore them and concentrate on any visual evidence of damage when the tenant moves out. In some countries it is common practice for both the landlord and tenant to hire representatives to examine the house for damage at the time the tenant moves in and moves out. Regardless of local customs, a tour of the house and its premises should be made with the landlord or his representative and even the slightest damages noted in writing prior to moving in. This paper should be attached to the lease, along with a complete inventory of furniture and its condition in the instance of a furnished house.

It may be helpful to know that the rent asked by the landlord is not necessarily what he expects to get. Haggling over rental prices is common practice in many parts of the world. Be prepared to bargain. A landlord who asks for a year's rent in advance may expect to get only six months. Six months' rent in advance will often get a lower rent settlement. And be prepared to have an attorney or solicitor represent you. It's not only good business sense—it may be a prerequisite to concluding a rental transaction.

Do make an effort to inform yourself about the local housing market and customs, problems to which you should be alert (low water pressure in Gilarmi area), and desirable neighborhoods. If at all possible, make your own survey of neighborhood areas before you start to look at a residence. Consider the:

*Location.* Where is it in relation to schools, work, church, hospitals, and shopping?

*Proximity of public transportation.* This is an important amenity for household servants or school children.

*Traffic congestion.* Be on the alert for congested traffic and nearby high-traffic institutions (manufacturing plants, schools, and the like).

*Services.* Is there sufficient fire and police protection? Street lighting? Is there garbage pickup? How often?

Expatriates throughout the world agree that the grapevine is the best way to find housing. They suggest that if you can obtain accommodations that have been lived in by other Americans, you may find that many of the problems that you might normally expect to face, such as wiring and plumbing for washers and dryers, have already been solved. Talk to everyone you meet and make calls to the office of the American school, the churches generally frequented by Americans, and the American Club. If they have bulletin boards, post a notice of the housing desired; and, if possible, place an ad in their weekly or monthly newsletters. Some expatriates have had luck with advertisements in the city newspapers. Most suggest carefully scrutinizing the classified section of the weekend editions of the newspapers. Even the home appliances or home furnishings sales may provide a lead—ads prefaced by "American leaving" may mean that a home will soon be for rent.

While expatriates tend to believe that the best houses never reach the open market, they do recommend contacting rental agents. The fees are paid by the landlords, so there is no charge to a tenant. There is no multiple listing either, so you may wish to contact more than one agent. You may need to be persistent. Rental agents the world over are reported to be the same; they show the undesirables first.

A few firms are now employing international relocation specialists to assist their overseas employees in locating housing. If you have this option, utilize it by all means. Negotiating in French, German, or Japanese can be difficult for even the most fluent, let alone those attempting to get by on arrival-survival language.

Many expatriates recommend that newcomers ask an acquaintance with some tenure in the country to accompany them on a first house-hunting trip. They feel that the insight gained through the experience of living in an area can be invaluable to the newly arrived. They also suggest:

Note the address, name, and phone number of the owner, the rental fee, the terms of contract, the number of bedrooms, and the positive and negative features. As you look and compare houses, your ideas may change.

Check out every house suggested, even though it may not be within your housing budget or sound suitable for you. Descriptions are sometimes misleading.

Don't immediately disregard a house because of an undesirable location. The house's positive features may compensate for its location.

Furnished houses can sometimes be rented unfurnished or partially furnished, and vice versa. Discuss all possibilities, including an adjustment in the rent.

Unfinished houses may be potential rentals. Check with the foreman regarding availability and date of completion.

Look for "For Rent" or "For Sale" signs in desirable neighborhoods. Some landlords do not use realty agents for rentals; even those who wish to sell may settle for a desirable rental contract.

Talk with building superintendents in desirable apartment buildings regularly on the first and fifteenth. They are first to get word of a
move, and they may put you in touch with the present residents.

If all else fails, try knocking on the doors of the houses you
might like to live in. This has sometimes produced rentals.

Even in cities such as Cairo, where the influx of new residents
has limited the availability of housing, the expatriate communities
remain highly mobile; and housing, quite suddenly, does become
available. It is important to be flexible and to move rapidly if you
spot a house or apartment that you like. However, there are certain
aspects that should be considered in choosing a residence:

*Flooding.* Be sure that your building stands well above surrounding ground and that driveways and yards are adequately drained.

*Sanitation.* Sanitation will be affected by the surrounding area.
Rats, snakes, flies, and odors accompany nearby garbage-dumping
spots. Vacant lots may mean construction—noise, dirt, men, and
materials for months.

*Security.* Security is particularly important to consider in areas of
anti-American feelings or high instances of break-ins. Doors should
be tight fitting and either equipped or equippable with dead-bolt-
type locks and wide-angle lens. First-floor windows should have
wrought iron grills or shutters. Walls, fences, night lighting, and area
guards are definite positives.

*Utilities.* Utilities should be in working order *before* you sign the
lease. To determine if water pressure is adequate, you should turn on
the water in the kitchen and in the shower (preferably upstairs) at the
same time. Low water pressure and water routinely turned off for a
few hours a day may be problems that can be corrected only by an
electric pump and a storage tank. Would your landlord be willing to
supply it?

*Electricity.* Will there be a need for additional wiring or plumbing
for your washer and dryer? Will the electric water heater be provided, or are you expected to supply your own? Are there at least two
outlets in each room? Do the sockets and outlets work? A small plug-
in nightlight will facilitate this check. You should also determine
where the meter is and how you will be billed. Before occupancy you
should have an electrician check the wiring. This can be especially
important in an area infested with termites, as they can damage the
wire insulation and cause electrical fires.

*The heating and/or cooling system.* If the house is not centrally air-
conditioned, can parts of it be closed off and cooled? If a heating

system is used, you should ask them to fire it up for you, even in the summer. You should determine the age of the system, the fuel used, and whether the landlord will pay for any repairs needed.

*Telephones.* Consider the housing *only* if it has a telephone in working order and with an established number. Do not permit the phone to be removed with the promise of a new one. Waiting periods for a phone have sometimes extended to two years.

*Basic living space.* To determine whether your furniture will fit, take along a tape measure and a list of dimensions. Check closet size and the adequacy of kitchen or bath cabinets. If they are inadequate or nonexistent, will the landlord provide them?

*The garden.* The garden is usually considered the responsibility of the renter. But if the grounds are in poor condition, the owner should be asked to replant the grass and to do the necessary landscaping.

The lease should be comprehensive and should cover every aspect, including a penalty clause pertaining to repairs and painting. If the repairs and additions necessary for rental are not completed by a certain date, the tenant should reserve the right to have them done himself and to deduct the cost from the rent. If you can get the landlord to agree to the clause "Lessee pays for the repairs and deducts same from rent," you will probably be much happier for it.

Many landlords will require that you or your company sign a one- to two-year lease. However, you can protect yourself from difficulty in breaking the lease by the inclusion of a "diplomatic clause." This should ensure that if you are suddenly transferred out of the country, you will not have to pay a penalty or that it will be relatively small.

## The Delivery of Household Effects

The notification of the arrival of the household effects usually heralds the beginning of a holidaylike atmosphere. Being "at home" is about to begin.

In most overseas situations it is possible to make arrangements for the customs agent to examine a household shipment as it is being unloaded. This is a recommended procedure for many obvious reasons. However, if you are not able to do this, you will have to be present personally—or have a designated agent dockside—for the unloading and customs agent's search or else surrender your container key to the overseas mover and the customs agent who will make the search without you, then repack, and, if you are lucky, relock the container.

You should plan to have some outside help during the unloading procedure. High on your list of priorities should be someone to care for infants and toddlers (elsewhere if possible). One or two persons should watch the van being unloaded to be sure that passersby do not take mementos, as well as check items against your copy of the inventory sheet and make a note of damages. Another person should be positioned just inside the door to direct the placement of boxes and furniture. If you have posted a floor plan of the residence with furniture arrangements drawn in, and have placed color coding on the door to each room, the unloading process should be relatively smooth.

Most corporations contract for unpacking as well as packing. If you do not wish this service, if you wish to schedule it for a later date, or if the mover cannot or will not do it, you should so note on the bill of lading and the certificate of packing and unpacking that you will be asked to sign. *Any* damage should be noted on both your copy and the driver's copy of the inventory sheet. You should also add "subject to further inspection for concealed damage or loss."

The in-transit insurance coverage on your household effects will be terminated with its deposit within your residence. It is very important to have liability on your personal property and household goods ready to go into effect in case of fire, flood, or other forms of property damage. (Personal liability insurance is also considered important coverage. In some instances, a rider may cover servants for job-incurred accidents; but in other areas, such as Singapore, you may be legally required to take out a workman's compensation policy for workers whom you employ.)

## Help Wanted?

The decision to have help is usually influenced by the living conditions within the country and the seeming norms within the expatriate community. A servant may be necessary for security if break-ins are rampant, terrorist activities common, and anti-American sentiments strong. Many expatriates find their servants indispensable as "walking references" in their attempts to unravel a "foreign" society.

In some parts of the world, where the per capita annual income is very low and unemployment high, there is a subtle pressure to promote the economy by hiring native labor; but in continental Europe or Japan, where incomes have soared, many domestics have gone into more lucrative avenues of work. In London, for example, expatriates comment that without the emigrants from the British West Indies, Pakistan, Portugal, and Spain, it might be impossible to find help at all.

In keeping with European tradition, however, some expatriates living in the cultural centers of Europe have hired *au pair* (one of the family) girls. For the opportunity to learn the language or attend school part-time, "girls from the country"—often from other countries—will assume care of the children and minor household tasks. The pay is relatively low, and the value is dependent upon the girl and the family situation. Most of the larger cities on the Continent have *au pair* agencies as well as domestic employment agencies. These agencies are fully cognizant of wage scales, as well as the legal obligations of an employer.

Outside of the large cities, word of mouth is still considered the best way to find a servant. However, references should be carefully checked on each applicant. In areas where unemployment is high, references are often sold or passed around; many expatriates also require security checks through the local police and/or their corporation security officer. Preemployment and periodic physical examinations (including blood, urine, stool tests, and chest X-rays) should be required; however, the charges associated with them should be assumed by the employer.

Duties should be outlined and agreed upon during an initial interview. An expatriate who lived for many years in South America and the Middle East suggested, "Ask the applicants what they feel the job should entail. Their versions may be far more inclusive than yours." Salaries vary with the area, but they are influenced by the domestic's years of experience, recommendations, and the ability to speak English. It is customary to give a 15-to-30-day, and in some cases a 60-day, trial period, during which either party may terminate the contract without notice. Following this interval, it is expected that one pay period's notice be given. In the case of the employer, it is recommended that he give the servant the advance pay and discharge the employee immediately.

Under some circumstances a full-time maid may be indicated for the care and security of children (including teenagers); but do keep in mind that baby-sitting is basically an American institution, and outside the more cosmopolitan areas it may be neither feasible nor desirable.

The role of servants in rearing children abroad continues to be a subject for debate. It is true that servants can provide children with a close contact to a foreign culture. However, it is important to recognize that they may also bring with them a very different philosophy of childrearing, or even taboos and cultural practices, with which you may not wish your children acquainted. Additionally, servants have a tendency to feel that they are responsible for keeping their young charges happy and so may pamper and wait on them. The results, at times, have been less than favorable.

The expatriate employer should also be conscious of the impact that cultural and economic differences can have upon the behavior of their employees. This can be evidenced in the example of a Chinese housemaid who refuses to use a broom during the two official days of the Chinese New Year, lest she sweep the Happiness Spirits out of the house; or the West Indian domestics who believe that if they open a refrigerator door or get their hands wet on the day that they iron that they will get the "vapors." It is also evidenced in the confusion with which domestics regard the wide variety of cleaning agents and extensive range of electrical appliances customarily found in an American home. This confusion is understandable, of course, when you consider that they may be accustomed to far more simplified arrangements. Only with patience, understanding, and time can these cultural differences be overcome and good relationships established.

These suggestions from expatriates can facilitate the "saving of face" and what the Filipinos call *pakikisama,* which necessitates smooth, interpersonal relationships:

Be prepared to spend as much time as possible with household help at first.

Be explicit; give instructions slowly and distinctly; and be willing to repeat the instructions as often as necessary.

Establish good sanitation practices and then follow through to be sure that they are adhered to.

Color code appliances and their appropriate outlets. This is extremely important if you are using both 110 and 220 voltage. Be sure that employees understand any possible danger before they are allowed to use electrical equipment.

Put poisonous substances and medicines under lock and key.

Set up simple first-aid and fire prevention rules and simple procedures to follow in case of an emergency. Always have emergency money (taxi fare to a hospital) available.

Treat your help justly and kindly, but do not intrude in their personal lives.

Never scold a servant in front of an audience, but do not hesitate to show praise in front of one.

Except in cases of emergency, try not to loan money to servants, as paying it back always places a hardship on them. Try, instead, to teach them a little about finances and how to use normal banking procedures.

## Banking

There are many advantages to using a bank correspondent to that used in the United States. Among these advantages is the ability to get a "dollar check" readily cashed. Obtaining cash for everyday transactions can be a problem in areas where bills are customarily paid in cash and the charge account concept not prevalent. Rather than make regular trips to a central bank downtown, some expatriates set up additional "household" accounts at a national bank with neighborhood facilities. Expatriates in continental Europe can also open Eurocheque accounts. Under this system, anyone holding an account may (supposedly) write checks against it in any of 31 countries in Europe and North Africa (a real plus for those who love to travel). The Eurocheque card is considered excellent identification and will facilitate the cashing of checks whether or not that system is used; however, a bank identification card should be obtained for each person who writes checks on an account.

Many banks offer a service through which regular bills, such as rent, telephone, gas, electricity, and fuel oil, are paid automatically. In countries such as Belgium where there is only a five-day grace period between the receipt of the bill and its required payment, this can be a very convenient service to have.

Regulations for the issuing and cashing of checks vary, of course, but throughout Europe, and in many Commonwealth countries as well, a "crossed check" ( // —two diagonal lines drawn across the front of the check in ink) ensures that the check may *only* be deposited into the payee's account. A crossed check payable to "the bearer" can be paid into any account, however. To protect checks that are being posted, the words "account payee only" are often added inside the crossing to ensure that the check can only be deposited into the payee's account.

Many banks do not return canceled checks. Some, in fact, are prohibited by law from doing so. Further, it may not be their custom to send monthly statements, although some will do so for a fee or will allow you to pick up the statements. Under such circumstances it may not be easy to keep current with your banking accounts. However, it is important to do so to avoid the charges that are levied against accounts with inadequate funds and to pick up the errors that are occasionally made by the bank's bookkeeping department.

If you are domiciled in a country that allows you to take out only the amount of cash you brought in, you will also need to save the receipts for your dollars-foreign cash exchanges along with the *motif de paiement* or "nature of the transfer." In the instance of most expatriates, these transfers are referred to as "current salary" or "savings" accumulated in the United States.

## Money Sense

The pretransfer shopping binge—shoes for two years, linens for three, new appliances—is sufficient to leave both you and your budget in a depressed state. And just a week in your host country may be enough to convince you that the worst might be yet to come. *Inflation* is not just a word that Americans toss about; it is very much a fact of life throughout the world. In most instances, its upward swing has been so rapid that it has been impossible for cost-of-living allowances or housing subsidies to stay current with the actual costs. Expatriates in places such as London or Tokyo—the two most expensive cities in the world—report that they barely make ends meet unless they budget conscientiously and cost-of-living allowances are reviewed and revised regularly.

More and more, expatriates are moving toward zero-based budgeting—a concept in financial planning that requires them to look at each item to see if it represents the best use of their money. Some, in cities with good public transportation systems, are deciding to forego the luxury of a car. They may even decide to rent places further out, even though it means more time commuting, to keep housing costs down.

Whatever your financial plan, there will be a need for periodic reevaluation just to stay current with inflation. Food, some expatriates report, increases in price by the day—although its cost, in comparison with U.S. prices, is already high. This can come as a major shock to a newcomer who has failed to recognize that U.S. agriculture, which is by far the most productive in the world, allows Americans to spend a smaller proportion of their income on food than the citizens of any other major country.

It may take only a couple of shopping trips to convince you that your shopping habits have to change. If you're not sure how, study the market baskets of the nationals. What do they eat? How do they survive the high costs? Can you incorporate any of their ideas into your shopping routines?

The following suggestions may help to keep food costs down:

Avoid processed and convenience foods.

Eat locally grown fruits and vegetables but choose quality products. A national cookbook or a course dealing with the preparation of local foods may be a good investment, as well as fun, at this stage of the game.

Eat more dried beans, peas, and lentils; more whole grains, oats, corn, rice, wheat, and barley; and more nuts and seeds (locally grown, if possible).

Add protein extenders to prepared foods, thereby cutting protein requirements from about one-half pound to one-fourth pound. For example, in appetizers, salads, soups, sauces, and casseroles, add extra dry milk, cheese, hard-boiled eggs, or nuts. In baked goods, substitute whole wheat flour for part or all of the requirements; replace two tablespoons of white flour with soy flour; add two tablespoons of wheat germ for each cup of flour or add dry milk powder. In desserts, use eggs, milk, cottage cheese, or yogurt; add extra dry milk and nuts.

Buy foods in season. Watch price fluctuations carefully. Be prepared to substitute other foods of equal nutritive value.

In choosing a market, you should consider whether you or a servant will shop or whether you can order by telephone for home delivery. If a servant does the shopping, you may get lower prices, but you should expect to recompense with a small shopping fee. Telephone orders are also more expensive, but many expatriates feel that it is worth the price to avoid the hassle. In some areas "provisioners" who make a business of buying for expatriates will appear at your door soon after a move. Some overseas residents are convinced that they are one of the positive aspects associated with life abroad and regale their listeners with stories of hard-to-find objects— sometimes even American beef and iceberg lettuce—that their provisioners have located.

Regardless of where you live, you are almost certain to come into contact with that consuming pastime—bargaining. Except for art, antiques, or flea market sales, prices are fixed in most of Europe and in Japan. However, a trip or a transfer to the Mediterranean area, the Middle East, the Orient, or South America leaves little option: you either participate or pay the asking price.

# Communications

## *The Postal Service*

You may find the post office guide, which many countries publish, helpful in understanding regulations, services, and charges. Services vary around the world—post offices range from purveyors of stamps to providers of life insurance.

International postage is expensive. Many expatriates favor the air letter forms, which run somewhat less than an airmail stamp, and most become very adept at saying a lot in a little space. A typewriter can be a great aid in conserving letter space.

Until you are familiar with customs duties levied on incoming packages, you may wish to ask friends and relatives to avoid shipping articles to you by post. Almost all expatriates' repertoires include tales, which only become funny with the passing of time, of gifts received from well-meaning friends and relatives: $10 duty levied on a tin of Fritos; $35 for a pair of well-worn shoes. Unfortunately, there are also stories of pilferage. Books usually are duty free and are a favored suggestion to friends who wish to send gifts.

## *Radio and Television*

Television has not yet become the major force in the lives of those living outside the United States that it is for many U.S. residents. Some of the larger cities still have only a few channels, and the majority of the material, as might be expected in non-English-speaking countries, is in the national language. In addition to the problem of comprehension, the content may be questionable. In some areas, evening programs may be adult level. Expatriates suggest that parents either follow the local norms for children's bedtimes or carefully monitor the programs that their children watch.

Radio reception varies from country to country; however, the shortwave radio is universally popular with expatriate Americans. The Voice of America, the British Broadcasting Corporation, and other English-language broadcasts enable overseas residents not only to keep up with what is happening in the world but to get the "down home" view of American news. Billboard Publications (2160 Patterson Street, Cincinnati, Ohio 45214) has complete listings of wavelengths and schedules in their *Handbook for World Radio,* which is published annually.

## Newspapers and Periodicals

English-language newspapers, available by subscription or at your international newsstand, include the *International Herald Tribune,* the *Continental Daily Mail* (British), the European or Asian edition of the *Wall Street Journal,* and the U.S. military newspaper, *Stars and Stripes.* In many instances, there are also English-language newspapers that are published locally. Periodicals include the European (or Asian) *Time, Newsweek, Reader's Digest,* and, in some areas, the *Weekly Review* from the Sunday edition of the *New York Times.* There usually is also a good selection of other U.S. magazines that come by surface mail. Prices are considerably higher than in the United States, unless they are purchased on a subscription basis.

## Surviving the Experience

Perhaps *awareness* is the key word to surviving overseas. It is not enough to be cognizant of the political situation and its possible impact on your life; you must become an expert on all the pitfalls of life abroad. Are there certain areas to which you should not go? Expatriates state that in some countries university areas are a "hot bed" of unrest that you are advised to avoid. Are there certain things that you should not do, or particular precautions that you should observe? Do you need to be prepared for hurricanes, typhoons, or earthquakes? Does the water need to be boiled or vegetables given the Clorox scrub? Life in cities such as London, Paris, Singapore, or Tokyo can be deceptively cosmopolitan, and you can be lulled into an acceptance of the living conditions without investigating the pitfalls. Don't do it! Life in a "220 country" can be a "shocking" experience, and more than one expatriate has become a statistic by not being aware of the problems or disregarding the warnings.

In many areas the electrical wiring is placed directly into the masonry walls without being encased in a metal conduit. This can be a deadly trap for the unwary person who attempts picture hanging by using a masonry drill to install plastic or lead tamps. The masonry drill will cut quickly into the plastic sheeting of the 220-volt wire. In a wink the drill operator may be electrocuted or knocked from a ladder onto a concrete floor. Avoid this danger:

Use a double-insulated drill with plastic grips and no metal exposed. Look for the words "double-insulated" and for the Underwriter's Laboratory seal of approval.

Wear rubber electrician's gloves while drilling, wear rubber-soled shoes and use a wooden stepladder.

Kill all circuits to the room, if possible, and run your drill from another circuit.

Look carefully at the wall or ceiling for signs of chipped-out or repaired masonry and avoid drilling in those areas.

Electrical shock is caused by current flowing through the body from a point of high potential to one of low potential, as between a live wire and the ground. Usually the skin is sufficiently dry to resist the flow of a lethal amount of current at 110 volts; however, with 220 volts the danger is greater, and the addition of wet hands or feet reduces the resistance to a point where instead of an unpleasant shock, death may result. In areas where housing has tile floors that are frequently damp owing to humidity or mopping, everyone should exercise caution by wearing dry shoes whenever contact with an electrical appliance is possible.

Appliances using 220 voltage should be carefully checked from time to time to be sure that there are no worn cords or loose wires. In a rental situation it is good practice to have an electrician make at least the initial survey. Wherever any work is being done on electrical devices, even a simple bulb-changing process, the appliance should be disconnected from the wall or the main switch turned off. As an additional precaution, everyone in the household should know where the electrical switch box is located and how to turn it off.

All refrigerators and deep freezers should be solidly grounded by connecting a 14-gauge wire to a bright metal part of the appliance and to a good ground such as a cold water pipe. Occasionally, a lead-covered wire at the switch and appliance plug provides sufficient ground. If used, resistance between the lead sheath and ground should not be over 0.5 ohm.

Expatriates also advise preparation for power blackouts, which are so often a part of the power picture in the developing countries or which in even the most cosmopolitan of areas can be precipitated by a thunderstorm.

Always stock a plentiful supply of candles and flashlights. A gasoline lantern or a kerosene lamp (filled and ready to use) can also be a handy item to have.

Make sure that you have at least one battery-powered radio, so that you can keep abreast of possible local warnings.

If you use electricity to cook with, consider an alternate means such as a gas hot plate or a gas barbecue grill. If this is not possible in your household, keep a good supply of charcoal and a barbecue grill handy.

If you keep a food freezer, you may wish to contact a nearby supplier of dry ice and make arrangements for a supply in case of an extended blackout. However, if the door is kept closed, a *full* freezer can keep food frozen for a day, possibly two.

In some areas, housing may not have hot water heaters; or instead of a central unit, there may be individual units in each bathroom. If you have a voice in the selection of units, preference should be given to the electric unit. Gas water heaters in small bathrooms are considered potentially dangerous by expatriates who have used them. They suggest that the dangers can be minimized:

Do not rent housing in which a gas hot water heater is located in a room that cannot be ventilated. A window is a necessity.

Never keep the pilot light on when the heater is not in use.

Never bathe with the windows closed.

Obtain regular service from a competent service man on all units.

## Minding Your Manners

The need for manners that is evidenced in every culture never changes—it is simply the customs that do. Even within the continental United States there is wide variation in what is accepted as the "right" way to do things; and this, too, has been influenced by the passing of time and the change in life-style.

Etiquette experts are in agreement that "Doing the Right Thing"* is simply a matter of being courteous and thoughtful and treating others as you would like to be treated yourself. For expatriates and their families, this involves a conscious recognition that they are guests in a host country and a concerted effort to act with the decorum that might be expected of them if they were guests in someone's home. This, of course, covers a range of requisites, including:

---

*The name of a syndicated column on manners by Emily Post.

*Attitude.* Congeniality, compatibility, and an effort to be pleasant and agreeable are all important.

*Appearance.* Clothes should be in keeping with the prerequisites of the country and the standards of good taste. Too often the attitude is, "But no one knows me here," without the recognition that everyone knows you are an American.

*Respect for, and observance of, the customs and traditions of hosts.* Quite often this means the observance of protocol and formalities to which the casual American is not accustomed.

In general, outside the United States life is tinged with an air of formality. Invitations are often engraved or printed, and hostesses expect a written reply. In the instance of an invitation extended and accepted by telephone, an invitation "to remind" or *pour mémoire* often is sent later by the hostess. Invitations will usually designate the appropriate attire.

*Gala* (as at a first night at the theater, a concert, or the opera). Black tie, long dress.

*Formal.* Black tie or dinner jacket (also referred to as a smoking jacket), cocktail or dinner dress.

*Informal.* Dark suit (also referred to as a lounge suit or *tenu de ville),* cocktail or short dress.

Custom also dictates the behavior of the guest. It is usually appropriate to express appreciation to the hostess with some form of gift; however, gift-giving practices vary widely from country to country. It is important to be aware of the cultural implications that may be associated with a gift. For example, a gift of liquor should never be made in a Muslim country; and a timepiece, which in China is associated with death, should not be given to a Chinese. Throughout Europe, flowers sent preceding or immediately following a social event are a favored way to say thank you; but even with flowers, there are precautions. In Belgium, chrysanthemums, which are customarily used for funerals, would never be sent to a hostess; in Germany, a gift of red roses would be construed as a pledge of love. In some countries it is also customary to leave a tip for the help at a social event (do check local practices). A thank you note is always written to the hostess *immediately* following the event. It should go without saying that if you are entertained, you should return the courtesy within an acceptable period—this is often considered to be six weeks, but today's life-style indicates that it really could be longer.

Many corporations have backup people on their staffs who can brief their executive families on protocol and formalities. This is particularly important in countries such as England, where titles and forms of address vary but rules of behavior are very precise. While it is important to know what these rules are, and to practice them until they become natural and easy, it should not overshadow the need for expatriates to be themselves and to recognize that sincerity and genuine interest in others is the heart of good manners.

## Suggested Reading

Aslett, Don. *Is There Life After Housework?* Cincinnati, Ohio: Writer's Digest Books, 1981.

Baldrige, Letitia. *The Amy Vanderbilt Complete Book of Etiquette.* Garden City, New York: Doubleday, 1978. Revised edition.

Cassiday, Bruce. *The New Practical Home Repair for Women.* New York: Lancer, 1972.

DeCamp, Catherine Crook. *The Money Tree.* New York: New American Library, 1972.

Drake, George. *The Repair and Servicing of Small Appliances.* Reston, Virginia: Reston, 1977.

Family Handyman. *America's Handyman Book.* New York: Scribner's 1961. Revised edition.

Gross, Paul H. (ed.). *Successful Personal Money Management: A Practical Guide to Your Financial Planning.* New York: McGraw-Hill, 1977.

Liles, Marcia D., and Liles, Robert M.. *Good Housekeeping Guide to Fixing Things Around the House.* New York: Good Housekeeping Books, 1974.

Porter, Sylvia. *Sylvia Porter's Money Book.* Garden City, New York: Doubleday, 1976.

# 6

# Bringing Up
# Children Abroad

*B*RINGING UP CHILDREN ABROAD is a challenging and exciting experience. To date, however, it has been little researched, and the scarcity of material on childbirth and raising children overseas can leave the Spock-oriented with serious concerns. Until it is possible to reconcile a new situation, in a different culture, with a desire for a baby or with the needs of older children for more independent action, there may be total immobilization. A look at how other expatriates have handled these experiences may provide needed insight.

## Childbirth

Expatriates' ratings of prenatal care and delivery overseas ranged from fair to outstanding. Childbirth experiences ran the gamut from being totally pampered in a nursing unit with rooming-in privileges for the baby to giving birth via the Lamaze method in a doctor's office. In some instances, expectant mothers returned to the States for delivery, although airline regulations made it necessary for trips to be scheduled in advance of the scheduled delivery date (usually by about two months). Even expatriates residing in the so-called developing countries indicated that the problems generally associated with a pregnancy could be solved and should not override the decision to have a child while overseas.

## Infants and Toddlers

If parents are able to allay their fears about disease and adequate medical care for infants and other preschoolers, this can be an ideal time in which to have small children. Unlike their stateside acquaintances for whom the two-career situation is virtually a necessity, parents will have the latitude to really enjoy their youngsters. For those lucky enough to be posted to an area with available, readily affordable labor, there may even be the possibility of household help and occasional time alone and away from child-care responsibilities.

Insofar as infants and toddlers are concerned, the parents form an entire world; change slips by them as long as their life remains undisturbed. As they grow and develop, cultural differences and another language (which may be difficult for their parents to grasp) become norms. In fact, the histories of children who are brought up having day-to-day contact with parents who speak one language and another person—perhaps a maid—who speaks a different language, indicate that they achieve an early fluency in a second language and may even be genuinely bilingual. On the other hand, parents who give in to the temptation to turn the child rearing completely over to domestics who may have little or no formal education may be handicapping their offspring.

## Older Preschoolers

Ages 3 to 5 adjust to a move with greater difficulty than their infant brothers or sisters (or even those just older—6 to 11). A major environmental change tends to be upsetting to them[1], and they may need constant reassurances that their favorite toys are being sent ahead by air freight to await their arrival or that they will surely make new friends "just like Johnny." While they may be difficult to follow, routines and rituals are especially important when households and their normal activities are undergoing change. This is not the time to tackle major goals (like toilet training) nor to break bad habits. Instead, there may be the need for a little extra parental attention—cuddling, crooning lullabies, or reading favorite stories.

Temporary quarters in a hotel or flat may be a major challenge for both a parent and a child. There is a whole new set of rules and restrictions; even small children must understand that they are guests in this strange, new country and will have to act accordingly. Parents should not feel guilty about cramped quarters or hesitate to establish rules that prohibit playing on telephones, running down the halls, and the like.

Children possess an amazing resiliency, and they can bounce back from difficult situations or disappointments with an ease that astounds even their parents. In addition, they recognize, even as infants, the importance of a smile and seem to have an intuitive knowledge that a happy grin will get them across language or cultural barriers that might otherwise be impossible to penetrate. This point was emphasized by a four-year-old, whose first day at an international nursery prompted her comment, "You can smile in any language, Mommy."

Almost all countries now have some form of preschool. Many parents utilize nearby national or international nursery schools as a means of introducing their youngsters to those who live nearby, as well as for the opportunity to involve them in the culture of the country. In recent years, many American schools have added the five-year-old kindergarten program; some have also added the three- to four-year-old preschool.

## The Primary and Middle Schoolers

In an effort to determine how parents and educators handle it, and how youngsters themselves feel about the move, parents, educators, and students in a number of overseas schools were interviewed. It was the students' input, which later was confirmed by parents and educators, that led to these conclusions: youngsters in grades 1-9 move and adjust with relative ease to a first overseas location; to a transfer from one overseas school to another; and to a return to life and schooling within the United States. Most accept the move as a necessity of life. Survival is a matter of reintegration, and they tend to do it quickly, although it may not be painlessly. The loss of a peer group is never easy, and the simple process of enrolling in school can be a major obstacle to a child.

Overseas schools often elect to give incoming students a complete battery of tests, rather than relying solely on the report cards and achievement test scores that they present. When students are of all nationalities, from all parts of the world—as they are in many international schools—judging the level of their competence is an understandable prerequisite to class. However, it may be an unnerving and frustrating experience for a child who is confronting a situation in which everything, quite suddenly, is foreign. Overseas educators recognize this, and they recommend that parents be prepared to provide extra support and encouragement during the early days. Talking problems out is important, but emphasizing family rituals, serving favorite foods, and returning to a regular routine as soon as it is possible to do so are also considered helpful.

Parents who recognize that a new peer group is essential to the adjustment of their children, and who help this process along, further the establishment of firm new roots. The American Club, Little League, scouting, and excursions with other families can provide quick, new friendships and at the same time serve as a buffer in children's adjustment.

An extended period in a hotel or temporary flat can be a difficult time for the primary and middle school youngsters. They are too young to do many things on their own, yet they are already beginning to feel the pull away from their parents. Veterans of the experience say that it is smart to make a reconnaissance of the area early in the game and to spell out off-limits areas and what children can and can't do. (You may have a snack after school but not in the hotel bar.)

On the positive side, such changes in circumstances provide a natural background for the reaffirmation of acceptable and unacceptable behavior. Parents who have difficulty with this subject may wish to consult *The Executive Parent,* by S. P. Hersch, and *Youth and the Hazard of Affluence,* by Graham B. Blaine. Both authors are psychiatrists whose extensive experiences with troubled youth provide rare insight into the value of limit setting and discipline.

If youngsters are to make a safe and happy move into a new society, they must also have some understanding of safety rules (where traffic drives on the left, you must look right and not left before stepping off the curb—Commonwealth countries), customs (always queue—wait patiently in line—for buses, theater tickets, and the like—England and France), and traditions (be appropriately reverent when the host nationals fall prostrate on the ground in prayer—Middle East). In general, however, children reflect the feelings of those around them. If parents are able to project a positive attitude and take the adjustment to a new culture in their stride, their children usually adjust without major difficulty.

# The Teenage Years

Overseas teens are *pioneers* in the truest sense of the word. Living with a foot in one culture yet belonging to another, they are representative of a new international society in which national origin is of little importance. It is comprised of members who crisscross the world, moving from one foreign center of commerce and industry to another, gradually losing their national identity, and replacing it with the characteristics of the lands in which they have lived, the people they have met.

To outward appearances, these teens are sophisticated, assured. Most have eaten in fine restaurants, seen the best theater, traveled halfway around the world. Many have had firsthand exposure to leading museums and art centers; they are knowledgeable about world geography and international politics, and they discuss it with an ease fostered by association with schoolmates from different parts of the world. However, the usual facade of self-confidence that covers the insecurities of adolescence is highlighted by the fact that overseas teenagers are neither fish nor fowl. At a time when their stateside peers are exploring the values of their neighborhood groups, getting their first jobs, and learning to drive, these teenagers are thrust into contact with dozens of different value systems—usually unable to work, to drive, or to assert the normal manifestations of young adulthood. In some instances, they live under a cloak of protection, necessitated by the political situation within the country in which they reside. Their flexibility is strained by the necessity of adjustment to outside forces and to rules and regulations governing life in the host country.

Accepting the very liberal views on drugs, alcohol, and even teenage sexuality in cities such as London is one thing; but following it with exposure to the very stringent drug laws in countries such as Singapore or Turkey, or with the taboos on alcohol that are commonplace in Muslim countries, is quite another. The fact that teenagers survive as well as they do is a tribute to the strength of their parents and educators and to the positive role models they establish.

As yet there is no consensus—no recommended way—in which to raise teenagers and their younger brothers and sisters abroad. The overseas situation with the problems peculiar to it is too new; for each current philosophy, there are others to counter it. When visiting social scientists remind parents that rebellion and "acting out" are a natural part of adolescence, and that assuming the role of Mr./Ms. Nice American may be expecting too much responsibility from adolescents, parents are wont to advise them that the legal implications are very serious:

> Adolescents have to know; they have to be aware that as guests within the country, they are subject to the laws of the land, and if they get seriously involved with drugs or are involved in other infractions of the law, there may be nothing we can do to help them.

Instances in which adolescents have been in conflict with the law are embarrassing both to the host government and to the American community, neither of which is sure about the right way to handle the transgression. Where drugs have been involved, governments have on occasion shown leniency. Rather than subject the youngster to the laws of the land, they have sometimes given him and his family 24 hours to get out of the country. As hard as it is on the family, and as difficult as it is for the parent(s), whose overseas career(s) may be destroyed, usually it is even harder on the teenager who must assume the responsibility for these events.

In some instances where drugs are cheap, potent, and readily available and community concern high, experimental programs—utilizing seed money supplied by a drug abuse prevention grant from the Medical Division of the U.S. Department of State and financial contributions from the American community—have been instituted. In Kuala Lumpur, Malaysia, a successful community counseling program under the dynamic leadership of a husband-wife team of mental health professionals was begun in July 1977; in Singapore a similar and also highly laudable program under the sponsorship of the Singapore American Community Council (SACAD) provides counseling services, sports leagues, and a summer employment program.

In other American communities, extended day programs and enrichment courses during spring break, extensive league sports programs, scouting, and drama and music groups have been created. Teen centers are being organized, and some communities have even tackled the problem of summer employment for youth. Working with schools and American businesses, often in association with the American Chamber of Commerce, ambitious programs for summer and work-study programs for the school year are beginning to develop.

The normal traumas associated with the physical aspects of maturing, acceptance by peers, and defining a philosophy and goals for life must be contended with, regardless of location. There is little doubt, however, that on occasion teenage problems are compounded by residence abroad.

## Relationships with Peers

Just as I become really close to someone, either their dad is transferred or mine is. One day you have a really neat relationship going, and the next day—nothing. [Teenager—Cairo]

Making friends was complicated. People lived miles apart, and we weren't allowed to use public transportation. Because of Dad's position, and the unrest within the country, we had around-the-clock guards. This meant we stayed in our own house or yard unless Dad's chauffeur or Mom could drive us. [Repatriated teenager—third world country]

## Relationships with Parents

Mom and Dad spend so much time entertaining "visiting firemen," or working and traveling, that it sometimes seems they have no time for us. [Teenager—Singapore]

Moving to a developing country means a lot of different things, but for me it meant leaving Mom and Dad and coming back to the States to boarding school. I became so homesick that I ended up in the infirmary for a week. Now, I wouldn't trade for the experience; but then, I didn't think I was going to be able to handle it. [Repatriated college student—Trinidad]

## Alcohol

Anyone who is big enough to "belly up to a bar" can get it; but the fact that teenagers usually have to rely on public transportation makes it more difficult to get to, and less fun to use. [Parent—Belgium]

The legal age for drinking is 16 in the Netherlands; we got used to drinking there. When we moved to London we found much the same situation. From age 16 on, the kids were bringing bottles to parties. They had plenty of money, and no difficulty in buying a bottle from any beer and ale dealer. [Repatriated college student—United States]

## Drugs

Always available, but the penalties are so stiff that few dare to use them. [Teacher—Singapore]

A youngster accustomed to playing around with drugs can get into serious trouble. Drugs are not only cheap—they are so potent that an overdose can easily occur. [Principal—Philippines]

At the parent-student conference on drugs we were advised that marijuana was being laced with heroin to get the kids addicted. We were thoroughly frightened by the thought of it; and as a result, we tried even harder to stay on top of the situation with our kids. [Parent—Malaysia]

## *Teenage Sexuality*

The permissive attitudes within the United States are also influencing the overseas teen.

There is little talk about it. I assume that the sexually active girls are on the pill. [Parent—London]

Occasionally a teenage boy may visit a local brothel—there are so many here that it can't help but have an influence; or a pregnant teenager may have an abortion or return to the United States to have her baby. [Parent—Thailand]

In spite of the sometimes adverse influences, expatriates are inclined to echo the sentiments of a 12-year overseas veteran who stated, "Parents pass along the same moral and cultural values to their children, regardless of where they live. Raising kids overseas is little different from raising them in the States."

Many parents, in fact, are convinced that it is easier to raise children abroad. They note that youngsters have a way of assuming the characteristics of the land in which they live and the nationals with whom they associate. Since many cultures stress politeness as well as respect for elders, it is a positive influence. In addition, they note that the "special camaraderie" that the overseas teens often have with their parents has a snowballing effect on others.

Both the parents and the teenagers who were interviewed during our overseas survey were in agreement that teenagers are customarily happy overseas during adolescence. Interestingly, they also feel that most can handle an overseas move during their teenage years, as long as they are not asked to move during their senior year. The high mobility of student bodies overseas and the concern of educators for their incoming students are credited with the creation of an atmosphere in which newcomers can be readily admitted.

## The College Days

Although college is considered to be "the Great American Dream," our survey among expatriate parents and their college-age youngsters reveals otherwise when it corresponds with parents' transfers overseas. Many of the students left behind to begin advanced education experienced a marked sense of loss—a feeling of abandonment and worry over where and how their parents were living. Weekends and holidays, when their classmates rushed home, became times of acute loneliness for them. Some who sought to replace the void in their lives entered into premature marriages, joined the armed services, or quit school just to "bum around," while uncomprehending parents worried. These now-wiser parents advised:

> Even the older college kids need to know where and how their parents are living and to experience for themselves the cultural differences. However knowledgeable they may be, there is a tendency to feel that you may be living in a mud hut or some other primitive fashion.

> Give your youngster a year off from school—or even just a semester. Use their help in getting settled. Go with them to local museum exhibits; arrange for them to travel to nearby areas. If they become lonesome, let them enroll in a course at the high school or in a host country college—just to get acquainted. When they do go back to school, they can go, knowing that you are happy, and ready to be happy also.

The concept of higher education abroad has long been favored by Americans. It is understandable then that students whose parents live, or are moving, overseas quite often decide to study abroad. However, those who are interested in following this plan should investigate requirements early, as they often are quite different from those accepted by colleges and universities in the United States. Some universities may accept an outstanding student based on American College Test (ACT) assessment, Scholastic Aptitude Test (SAT) scores, Achievement Tests (ACH), and school record; but most foreign universities require the International Baccalaureate diploma or the completion of the thirteenth year and a "school-leaving" certificate. Students in residence in the host country who are fluent in the language sometimes take the thirteenth year and the school-leaving exams in a national school. However, the student should be relatively certain that he will be admitted to a host university before he undertakes this program. In many countries, the university system is so overcrowded that admittance is limited to the nationals. There are, however, a number of American-curriculum colleges scattered about the world with extensive programs for a semester or a year abroad as well as a degree program. Students interested in these programs may wish to obtain *The Whole World Handbook* (E. P. Dutton, New York) for a comprehensive listing of educational opportunities abroad; or write directly to:

Institute of European Studies
700 North Rush Street
Chicago, Illinois 60611
Telephone (312) 944-1750

Director of Admissions
American Institute for Foreign Study
102 Greenwich Avenue
Greenwich, Connecticut 06830
Telephone (203) 869-9090
                    or
37 Queens Gate
London, SW7, 5HR, England
Telephone 581-2733

Beaver Center for Education Abroad
c/o Beaver College
Glenside, Pennsylvania 19038
Telephone (215) 884-3500

For students who wish to pursue a summer or a semester of just plain travel, a handy reference book is *Let's Go—The Budget Guide to Europe* (Harvard Student Agencies, E. P. Dutton, New York) which supplies you with ideas for what to see, where to go, and inexpensive places to see and eat. The Eurorail youth pass, which must be purchased in the United States (available at travel offices), offers an inexpensive way for students to see Europe.

Another "must" for any Europe-bound student is the international student identity card, available from:

The Council on International Education Exchange
205 East 42nd Street
New York, New York 10017
Telephone (212) 661-1414

This entitles the applicant to discounts on tickets to theaters, museums, and historical attractions, as well as student hotels, university dormitories, and student charter flights.

Students interested in group touring may wish to consider a group camping trip—such as the 28-day trip through Western Europe sponsored by Sundowners and Contiki of London. There is also the possibility of combining touring with work. For information on these programs, students should contact the Council on International Education Exchange.

## College Preparation

For American parents who are subject to other international moves as well as the ultimate one back to the States, maintaining a continuity in their children's schooling and establishing a background for college board exams are the big considerations. When there is a change in the academic or emotional development of a child while overseas, testing may be indicated to determine the general level of achievement. Options open to parents include:

*General psychological evaluation.* Evaluation is available through the Testing and Guidance centers in major cities—often in conjunction with medical centers or universities. Testing covers a four-part series: achievement tests, aptitude tests, intelligence tests, and psychological tests. And it is designed not only to portray the level of accomplishment and what can be expected of the child but to pinpoint problem areas. This series of tests is indicated when a personality change accompanies a loss of interest in school.

*Secondary School Admissions Test (SSAT).* The SSAT may be given to grades 6 to 10, January and April, at designated test centers outside the United States. Arrangements for this test to be administered can be made in writing to the Educational Testing Service (Box 592, Princeton, New Jersey 08541). Although it is customarily used as an entrance exam for private schools, it provides a good evaluation of general achievement, including mathematical and reading comprehension.

Education specialists suggest that highly mobile parents accumulate files of educational material on each of their children—standardized test scores, professional evaluations, report cards, and a somewhat extensive sample of their written work. Over a period of time, a picture of their accomplishments, or lack of accomplishments, will begin to emerge. This can be very helpful to a new school as well as to a parent who is attempting to assess the voids in a child's education. In instances where families may be abruptly evacuated from a country, it may be the only record that the family will have to present to a new school.

Additionally, it is considered important for the highly mobile parent to know which tests should be taken during prep school years and to arrange for their youngsters to take them, regardless of where they might be.

## Preliminary Scholastic Aptitude Test

The Preliminary Scholastic Aptitude Test (PSAT) is customarily given on a trial basis in the fall of the tenth grade and for a final score in the fall of the eleventh grade. This is the qualifying exam for scholarships awarded by the National Merit Scholarship Corporation. Tests are given at worldwide centers, but special arrangements to take the test can be made by writing to the PSAT/NMSQT (Box 592, Princeton, New Jersey 08541).

## Scholastic Aptitude Test

The Scholastic Aptitude Test (SAT) is given by the College Entrance Examination Board (Box 592, Princeton, New Jersey 08541; telephone [609] 921-9000) on specified dates at test centers in the United States and many foreign countries. It is customarily taken by students in the spring of the eleventh grade on a trial basis and again in the fall of the twelfth grade. The highest score is the score used by colleges in the admission process.

## Achievement Tests

Achievement tests (ACH) compiled by the College Entrance Examination Board in English composition, Level I or II mathematics, languages, physics or chemistry, American or European history, and the like are given at specified dates worldwide. Usually, test dates are scheduled somewhat later than the SAT. Results are used along with the SAT in determining admission as well as course placement and exemptions.

## American College Test

The American College Test (ACT) assessment in English usage, mathematics usage, social studies, reading, and natural sciences is given by the American College Testing Program. It parallels the SAT, it is an admission requirement in many colleges and universities, and it is acceptable on an "either/or" basis with the SAT in many others. It is given on specified dates in test centers worldwide. Students taking the ACT customarily take a trial test during the eleventh grade and repeat it in the twelfth. Arrangements to take the test can be made by contacting the American College Testing Program (P.O. Box 414, Iowa City, Iowa 52243; telephone [319] 337-1000).

## *Advanced Placement Program (APP)*

Advanced-placement examinations in college-level courses taught on a high school basis are provided by the College Entrance Examination Board and administered to qualified students by their high schools. Some colleges give advanced placement, college credit, or both to students with satisfactory scores.

## *College-Level Examination Program (CLEP)*

College-level examinations test achievement in college-level courses. Tests are provided by the College Entrance Examination Board and are administered by the college. College credit is given for subjects where mastery is shown.

## *College  Choices*

For the student who has been raised abroad, the choice of a stateside university can be a formidable task. Most overseas schools, however, have guidance departments with extensive references and skilled counselors who are able to advise students. They usually recommend that families with high school students begin to make visits to prospective colleges during home leave following the freshman and sophomore years. The decision regarding which colleges to apply to should be made during the junior year or, at the latest, early in the senior year. All correspondence with the colleges should be sent airmail, and the schools should be requested to reply in the same manner. Students should be careful to note at the top of their application letter, "I am an American citizen attending _____School in _____" (supply city and country), so that their application will not be confused with those of foreign students who may also be applying.

## Choices in Education

It is evident that when parents make frequent international moves, they must assume more responsibility for the management of their children's education than if they had stayed within the continental United States.

Overseas schools usually present no real problems to the average child. In the small classes, with the individualized instruction that is available in many overseas institutions, innate abilities are often recognized and refined to a larger extent than might be possible in a U.S. school.

The child of exceptional intelligence also does well in the overseas situation. Many schools have accelerated classes; many more operate on the theory that children should move ahead at their own pace. At the American School in London, for example, it is not unusual to find a preteen studying high school calculus and supplementing his in-school study with large blocks of time spent in museums and art centers. Overseas education is further enriched by special cultural studies, extensive foreign language opportunities, and school-sponsored trips to nearby (and some not so nearby) historical places.

For more extensive information on schools available overseas, see the chapters on individual cities. In addition, you may wish to write the cultural affairs officer at the American embassy in your new location or contact a host country consulate for information on the education systems in their country. You may also wish to contact:

> The Office of Overseas Schools
> Department of State
> Washington, D.C. 20520
> Telephone (202) 235-9600

or

> The Office of Dependents Schools
> Department of Defense
> 2461 Eisenhower Avenue
> Alexandria, Virginia 22331
> Telephone (202) 325-0188

or obtain a copy of *Schools Abroad of Interest to Americans* (the most recent edition, published by Porter Sargent, Boston, is available in most libraries). Table 1 shows the type of schools available to the expatriate student.

In the instance of learning disabled, mentally retarded, or physically handicapped youngsters, the specialized facilities and edu-

**Table 1**

*Schools Available to the Expatriate Student*

| School | School Year | School Day | Uniform | Grade | Curriculum | Description |
|---|---|---|---|---|---|---|
| Host country | May vary with climate | Varies; may be extended (7:30-4:30) or split session (7-12 or 1-6) | Uniform or strict dress code usual | Varies; 1-10, 1-12, or 1-12 − 2 | Varies with sophistication of country; may be full diploma, International Baccalaureate program (for students seeking admittance to European colleges), or much less extensive | Courses different than United States; teaching more regimented and in host country language; enrichment facilities often limited in scope; U.S. children may be subject to anti-American sentiment |
| Third-country school (e.g., British Day School, French Lycees, and the like) | May vary; usually follows customs of sponsoring country | Usually follows customs of sponsoring country | Uniform or strict dress code | May be kindergarten, junior and middle and sometimes senior | Varies with country; may be preparatory for senior school with children returning to their own country for senior-age (13+) school or may include full International Baccalaureate program | Courses differ from United States; teaching more regimented and directed toward passing the next set of exams; classes in language of sponsoring country, with instruction usually excellent; enrichment facilities may be limited |
| Department of Defense schools (typical of this school type is London Central High at High Wycombe Air Station, 32 miles northwest of London) | August-May | Full day | Informal dress code | Kindergarten-12 | American college preparatory; probably approved member of the North Central Association of Colleges and Secondary Schools in the U.S. | Usually excellent physical plant, with extensive enrichment facilities and athletic program; excellent, well-paid teachers; may be both boarding and day |

| School type | Term | Schedule | Dress | Grade levels | Curriculum | Characteristics |
|---|---|---|---|---|---|---|
| American-sponsored international schools (typical of this school type is the International School, Manila) | August-May | Full day (or 7:15-12:45) with extended-day extracurricular informal activities | Dependent on country; may be uniform or informal | Kindergarten-12; sometimes pre- and nursery schools, too | American college preparatory and general academic; may also offer full diploma, International Baccalaureate program | Private, independent school, often established as the "American School" but changed to reflect the increasing international attendance; international faculty with high academic qualifications; usually large, modern plant and extensive enrichment facilities; small classes; excellent education |
| Church-sponsored, American-oriented boarding and day school (typical of this school type is Faith Academy, Rizal, Philippines) | August-May | Full day | Uniform or dress code | Varies; may be kindergarten-8, kindergarten-12, or kindergarten-12 + 2 | American college preparatory; in some instances freshman- or sophomore-level college courses | Private, independent schools; established for the children of missionaries; usually highly rated coeducational nonsectarian boarding school with local U.S. or host country residents admitted on space-available basis |
| International boarding school (typical of this school type is Marymount International School, London, or TASIS, Surrey, England) | Follows custom of country | Full day | Uniform or strict dress code | Varies; may be 1-12 or only 8-12 | May be both European and American preparatory | Private, independent schools noted for their excellence in education; small classes and individual attention; may not be coeducational as in the case of TASIS; may be church affiliated as well as affiliated with U.S. colleges |

| School | School Year | School Day | Uniform | Grade | Curriculum | Description |
|---|---|---|---|---|---|---|
| U.S. boarding school (typical of this school type is Incarnate Word Academy, San Antonio, Texas or Admiral Farragut Military Academy, St. Petersburg, Florida) | August–May | Full day | May be uniform or strict dress code | Varies; may be 1-12, 6-12, or 1-12 + 4 | American college preparatory; may have additional specialized curriculum as is the case with military school; may also have 1-4 years of college instruction | Private, independent schools; usually noted for small classes, individualized instruction, and high academic standards |
| Correspondence school (such as Correspondence Instruction Extension Division, University of Nebraska, Lincoln, Nebraska 63508 or Calvert Schools, Tuscany Road, Baltimore, Maryland 21210) | Your option | | | 1-12 + 4 | American college preparatory plus college courses | Self-study courses designed to be effective from primary grades through college; may be the only resource for children in isolated areas whose parents do not wish to place them in boarding schools |

cational specialists that are included in the U.S. school systems will not usually be a part of the American-oriented curriculum overseas. On occasion, however, parents have petitioned host governments for the privilege of placing their children in specialized host country facilities. If the medium of instruction is English, educators feel that students can make the transition, but they advise parents to be aware that the educational goals, as well as the curriculum itself, may be different in the overseas schools. They suggest that parents obtain as much information on host facilities as possible before making the final decision to place their children in host schools.

### *The Visually Impaired*

In the instance of the visually impaired, parents may wish to write the:

International Council for the Education of the
  Visually Handicapped
Christoffel Blinden Mission
Nikel Ungenstrass 124 D-6140
Bens Heim, 4 West Germany

for the *Directory of International Facilities for the Visually Handicapped*.

The Educational Director of Helen Keller, International
15 West 16th Street
New York, New York 10011
Telephone (212) 620-2100

may also have in-depth knowledge of host country facilities. This organization has been instrumental in planning and developing many foreign schools for the blind, as well as training national teachers to staff the schools. It is the extension of the:

American Foundation for the Blind
15 West 16th Street
New York, New York 10011
Telephone (212) 620-2000

Requests for information on U.S. schools for the visually handicapped should be addressed to the above address.

## Speech and Hearing Impaired

Some overseas schools do have speech pathologists. If the school in your host country does not have this resource, you may wish to contact the:

American Speech, Language and Hearing Association
10801 Rockville Pike
Rockville, Maryland 20895
Telephone (301) 897-5700

for recommendations. They suggest that parents may wish to have their child referred to a private speech pathologist in the host country for therapy outside of school. This assumes, of course, that the consultant speaks English and is able to communicate with the child.

Parents who are not able to work out effective programs for their speech- or hearing-impaired child may wish to consider private boarding schools. *The Registry of Private Schools for Children with Special Education Needs* has a complete listing of appropriate schools. This book is generally available from city libraries.

## Learning Disabilities

Parents of children with learning disabilities should contact a local chapter of the Association for Children with Learning Disabilities for general information or referral to diagnostic facilities, or they may wish to contact the:

American Association for Children with
  Learning Disabilities
4156 Library Road
Pittsburgh, Pennsylvania 15234
Telephone (412) 341-1515

The national organization can supply lists of diagnostic facilities throughout the United States as well as a *Directory of Educational Facilities for Children with Learning Disabilities.*

## Physical, Mental, or Emotional Handicaps

Parents may wish to contact the:

Information Center for Handicapped Individuals
6051 G Street, N.W.
Washington, D.C. 20001
Telephone (202) 347-4986

for information on special school programs, diagnostic facilities, clinics, and vocational guidance.

## Note

1. S. P. Hersch, *The Executive Parent,* New York: Sovereign Books, 1979, p, 105.

## Suggested Reading

Benton, Myron, *How to Survive Your Children's Rebellious Teens—New Solutions for Troubled Parents*. New York: J. B. Lippincott, 1979.

Blaine, Graham B. Jr. *Youth and the Hazards of Affluence*. New York: Harper & Row, 1966.

College Entrance Examination Board. "College Entrance Guide for American Students Overseas," 1975, College Board Publication Orders, Box 2815, Princeton, New Jersey, 08540. ($1.25)

*The College Handbook,* 1975, College Board Publication Orders, Box 2815, Princeton, New Jersey, 08540. Information on colleges in the U.S., Canada, Mexico, and France. (1280 pages, $6.95)

Dunbar, Flanders. *Your Pre-Teenager's Mind and Body*. New York: Hawthorn Books, 1962.

Gesell, Arnold; Ilg, Frances; and Ames, Louisa. *Youth—The Years from 10–16.* New York: Harper & Row, 1956.

Greenberg, Henry F. *Child Care*. Nutley, New Jersey: Rocom Press, Hoffman La Roche, 1973.

Hartley, Ruth E., and Goldenson, Robert M. *The Complete Book of Children's Play*. New York: Thomas Y. Crowell, 1963.

Hersch, S. P. *The Executive Parent*. New York: Sovereign Books, 1979.

Lamont, Lansing, *Campus Shock*. New York: Dutton, 1979.

National Institute of Mental Health. "Facts About College Mental Health." DHEW Publication No. (HDM) 77–72, 1977, 5600 Fisher's Lane, Rockville, Maryland 20857.

Spock, Benjamin. *Baby and Child Care*. New York: Pocket Books, 1968.

—————————. *A Teenager's Guide to Life and Love*. New York: Pocket Books, 1971.

Werkman, Sidney. *Bringing up Children Overseas: A Guide for Families*. New York: Basic Books, 1977.

# 7

# Health Care Overseas

*F*OR MOST EXPATRIATES, the assurance of health care abroad has long been one of the major concerns. What do you do if a medical emergency arises? Or if a family member is in need of regular or special care? Or even what is available in the way of routine medical or dental services? For American families used to large metropolitan hospitals, personal physicians, out-patient clinics, and corporate health plans, the unknowns surrounding health care are real and troubling. And a factor in this uncertainty has been the relative lack of an information network (aside from word of mouth from returning expatriates) on which to evaluate the total health care picture in a location abroad.

Fortunately, the picture is changing—in large part as companies themselves are assuming a more active role in researching and providing health care services for their expatriate staff. Some multinationals with corporate medical departments have made intensive studies of overseas medical facilities; some are even retaining qualified physicians and/or nurses to ensure appropriate medical care for expatriates and their dependents. If the area is isolated, they may also forward vaccines and health care bulletins on a regular basis.

Corporate readiness to take employees and their families to a recognized medical center abroad, or to bring them back to the States for critical medical care, has also been a positive factor in the total health care picture abroad. Some corporations have retained the services of medical emergency firms such as International SOS Assistance, Inc. (Two Neshaminy Interplex, Suite 208, Trevose, Pennsylvania 19047; telephone [800] 523-8930), which provides a variety of emergency services ranging from telephone consultation to transportation of the critically ill, by ambulance or airlift, to treatment centers or to their homes. This service is also available to individuals by the week, the month, or the year.

For those without the backup services of a large corporation, evaluating the professional competence of a doctor or dentist or the adequacy of emergency and hospital facilities can be a challenge. Both medical and dental programs tend to vary from U.S. norms. Students are customarily accepted into these schools at a younger age than their U.S. counterparts, often without the U.S. prerequisite of a university degree. The training itself also varies. Aside from a word-of-mouth reputation, the best basis for judgment of a professional's probable competence still seems to be the reputation of the university conferring his or her medical or dental degree, and the extensiveness of the person's postgraduate training. American physicians often recommend that expatriates seek the care of board-certified members of the Royal College of Surgeons, Pediatrics, and the like, from England or Canada, or diplomates of the American Board of Medical Specialties (American College of Surgeons, Pediatrics, Psychiatry, and so on) living abroad. Most U.S. physicians and libraries will have copies of the *Directory of Medical Specialists** listing U.S. board-certified physicians with overseas addresses.

In most countries the U.S. embassy provides information on local medical facilities. Doctors, dentists, and hospitals are listed, although not rated. However, the basis for inclusion on the list appears to be an ability to communicate in English and acceptable levels of professional competence.

In spite of the fact that there are now many highly qualified medical specialists and fine medical facilities abroad, medical expertise does vary from area to area. Expatriates' ratings of medical care overseas range from "superb, better, cheaper" (many are enthusiastic about the plastic surgery and orthodontia they have been able to afford) and "more personal," to "impossible, inadequate, and unsanitary."

---

*Published for the American Board of Medical Specialists by Marquis's Who's Who, Inc., 200 East Ohio, Chicago, Illinois 60611.

## Preventive Planning

There can be little doubt, however, that your goal, whether you are traveling or in residence abroad, should be to maintain the state of your health and avoid the use of all emergency services. This, of course, involves adherence to the precepts of preventive health care, which have so often been the message of family practitioners: "Lose weight, cut back on alcohol, stop smoking, eat better foods, and get more rest and exercise." It also involves a certain amount of planning to survive the experience of life away from accustomed medical care.

Some expatriates are insistent that training in first aid, cardiopulmonary resuscitation (CPR), and the Heimlich technique should be prerequisite for international transfers; they advise those being transferred to become proficient in these areas before departure. If time is limited, they suggest that you at least enroll in a CPR course (American Red Cross, American Heart Association, YMCA, or your nearest hospital or paramedic unit), which takes only six hours and plan to follow through with a first-aid course soon after arrival. The Red Cross, Red Crescent, and St. John's Ambulance Corps are among the organizations teaching first aid outside the United States; at least one of these organizations will be found almost everywhere. However, you should plan to take with you a good first-aid manual, as well as a comprehensive medical reference book* and a fairly complete medical kit.

The kit should contain both prescription medications and over the counter drugs used by family members. To prevent any questioning about drugs at customs, medicines should be clearly labeled and copies of the prescriptions should be included in the kit. The kit should also contain regularly used necessities (such as contact lens solution) in addition to items that might be needed in the course of traveling to, and getting settled in, a new location. The list of items and medications to be included in a medical first-aid kit varies, but the following basic list is suggested by international medical departments and medical reference guides:

Thermometer[†]
Tweezers

---

*See Suggested Reading for recommended titles.

[†]If you have been posted to an area using Celsius (centigrade) thermometers (Europe), it will be helpful to report body temperature to a physician in this way. The thermometer is placed in the armpit and will read one degree lower than if taken by mouth. To convert Fahrenheit readings to Celsius, subtract 32 and multiply by 5/9. Thus, 98.6°F = 37.0°C.

Scissors
Eye dropper
Tongue depressors
Dental floss
Adhesive tape
Moleskin corn plasters
Band-Aids
Bandages, 2″ × 2″, 3″ × 3″, 4″ × 4″ (sterile)
Vaseline gauze
Gauze bandage rolls, 1″ wide and 4″ wide
Triangle bandage
Ace bandages, 2″ and 4″
Disposable needles and syringes
Q-tips
Sterile cleanser such as hydrogen peroxide, 2 percent tincture of
    iodine, or povidone iodine (Betadine)
Foot powder, foot fungus ointment such as tolnaftate (Tinactin)
Aspirin, preferably buffered
Baby aspirin or liquid acetaminophen
Mild laxative such as a bisacodyl (Dulcolax)
Antacid for stomach such as Gelusil, Maalox
Motion sickness pills such as meclizine (Bonine)
Antidiarrhea medication such as diphenoxylate HCl (Lomotil)
Antibiotic, such as tetracycline*
Eye drops such as Visine AC for travel distress
Head cold, hay fever symptoms, such as chlorpheniramine
    (Chlor-Trimeton)
Cough medicine (adult), such as Robitussin DM
Nose spray, such as phenylephrine (Neo-synephrine 1/8–1/4 per-
    cent = pediatric strength)
Sleeping pills, such as flurazepam (Dalmane)
Ear drops, such as an analgesic with benzocaine (Auralgan)
Syrup of ipecac, to induce vomiting in case of poisoning
Calamine lotion for rash, insect bites
Insect repellent such as Repel, Cutters
Water purification tablets such as Halazone, or 2 percent tincture
    of iodine
Dry skin lotion
Sunscreen preparation

---

*Contraindications for use should be carefully observed.

# Emergency Medical Information

In recent years a number of nonprofit organizations have sprung up to assist the American who becomes ill in a foreign country and who, because of an inability to talk or to speak the language, cannot communicate important medical facts. One such organization, Medic-Alert, sells identification tags in the form of a gold, silver, or steel necklace or bracelet. The tags alert and inform as to specific problems of the wearer, such as serious allergies to medications, wearing of contacts, and the like. Medic-Alert will also inscribe the bracelet in a language other than English, if the purchaser supplies the inscription and if the inscription can be written in alphabetic letters. If this information is not known at the time of purchase or if the purchaser resides in a country where symbols are used, the information should be inscribed on the tag soon after arrival. Medic-Alert also maintains a 24-hour service that allows medical personnel to call a central registry for additional information on the tag wearer. It can be contacted at 840 North Lakeshore Drive, Chicago, Illinois 60611; telephone (312) 280-6366; or at 2323 Colorado Avenue, Turlock, California 95388; telephone (209) 668-3333.

Medic-Check (8320 Ballard Road, Niles, Illinois 60025; telephone [312] 724-8280) offers a similar service. It issues a tag and a metal wallet card that can hold up to eight lines of information about your health. Again, to be effective, this really should be inscribed in the language of the country in which you reside.

The American Medical Association or the Metropolitan Life Insurance Company will provide emergency medical ID cards free or for a nominal fee. American Express provides passport size medical information cards free on request to their card holders.

The "Medical Passport," a pocket-size personal health record, is used by the U.S. State Department for its overseas personnel and their families. Developed by an internist, Claude E. Forkner, it is marketed by the nonprofit Medical Passport Foundation, P.O. Box 820, Deland, Florida 32720; telephone (904) 734-0639.

The Medical Passport provides a concise history of illnesses (personal and family), surgery, medication, allergies, and hypersensitivities, medical and laboratory studies, immunizations, X-rays, dental treatment, and oculist prescriptions. For the highly mobile international family it is the basis for continuity in medical care. In a medical emergency the information it contains can be life saving.

## Dietary Precautions

_Prevention_ is synonymous with _precaution_ in an overseas situation. It begins with your pretrip immunizations and continues with a cautious entry into a foreign world. More than one newly arrived expatriate has been quickly forced to his bed by the ravages of "turista"—which may be known variously as Montezuma's revenge or the curse of the Pharoahs. His undoing—possibly only a meal in the hotel dining room. The safety of food and water is such an accepted fact everywhere in the United States that it is difficult to realize that the food or water served in the luxurious restaurant of a major hotel in another part of the world may not be safe. Worldwide variations in sanitation standards, the chemical treatment of water, and types and uses of fertilizer are among the reasons for exercising caution in consuming water and foodstuffs. Both at home and while traveling when abroad, there are a few simple rules and procedures that will see you through safely.

### _Water_

Unless you are absolutely certain that the water is potable, you should refrain from drinking it, brushing your teeth with it, or putting ice cubes in your drinks. A small electric coffeepot or a cup-size electric immersion heater can be a real boon to the hotel resident. Boil water steadily for five minutes before transferring it to a previously sterilized container with cover, or treat it with an iodine compound such as Lugol's solution, or 2 percent tincture of iodine. If you prefer, a chlorine product, Halazone tablets, may be used.

Tincture of iodine is readily available everywhere and is easily used in a restaurant—two drops to a glass; stir, and wait 15 minutes before drinking. Contrary to popular thinking, water is not "purified" by freezing it or mixing it with alcohol; nor is it safe to use hot water directly from a faucet for rinsing the mouth or brushing the teeth. Water filters only help with gross particulate matter, and they should not be relied on alone. Bottled water is considered safer than tap water; but it, too, is sometimes contaminated and, unless carbonated, may be plain tap water. Carbonated soft drinks are thought to be safer than noncarbonated; but, again, if you choose soft drinks, it is safer to choose a well-known brand. If you're a beer or wine drinker, you have it made. They are almost always safe, although the danger of alcoholism may arise if there is prolonged and constant use of these beverages. Hot tea or coffee (without cream), hot chocolate, and hot soup are also considered safe if they are boiled in the preparation.

## Milk

Milk and milk products are considered safe if they have been subjected to a high temperature to destroy the microorganisms and prevent bacterial growth (usually 161° F for 15 minutes for pasteurization). Canned evaporated, condensed, or dried milk may be used instead of whole milk, but only boiled or treated water should be mixed with them. A long-life (six weeks to several months, ultra-high temperature) milk is now being prepared and sold in some Common Market and Commonwealth countries. Milk products such as ice cream, cheese, and custards should be considered questionable unless they are prepared in a sanitary manner from products that have been ascertained to be safe.

## Fruits and Vegetables

Throughout continental Europe, life is virtually a vegetarian's delight. Fruits and vegetables are beautiful, fresh, and apparently safe. In more tropical or developing countries, there are differences in the farming of produce and in the types of fertilizers used, and you should make corresponding changes in your use of fresh produce. Particularly if you are traveling or have an extended stay in a hotel, you should be careful about eating fresh fruits or raw vegetable salads. The process of cooking destroys the dangerous parasitic organisms, and you may be assured that fruits or vegetables that are well cooked and served hot are safe.

If you are concerned about the lack of fresh fruits and vegetables in your diet, there are solutions. Take your favorite fruits or vegetables to the room with you, wash them carefully in water that you have boiled for a full five minutes, and put them to soak in your safe water in a sterile washbowl. Use 2 percent tincture of iodine until the water turns the color of weak tea; let soak for at least 30 minutes; and peel before eating.

If you become a resident of the area, you may find that it is sufficient to wash fruits or vegetables that are to be peeled in your boiled water; however, some expatriates feel more comfortable about using fresh produce if it has been scrubbed with a detergent or placed in a chlorine soak.

Leafy vegetables or stalks that cannot be peeled are a little more risky; however, medical experts advise that if the leaves are scrubbed with detergent and then given the iodine soak, much of the danger can be eliminated.

## Meat, Poultry, Fish, and Shellfish

Even though you may have a fondness for rare meat, or in the case of fish or shellfish, raw delicacies, you should avoid all foods that are prepared in this manner during your tour of overseas duty. Tight controls within the United States have greatly reduced the amount of infected meat sold here. While trichinosis is still a threat in pork, Americans are knowledgeable about its preparation. Internationally, there are fewer safeguards, and even undercooked beef can transmit intestinal tapeworms. Further, raw fish can be a source of liver disease and, in the case of raw oysters, clams, or mussels, infectious hepatitis.

## Everyday Health Care

Once past the initial health problems associated with the adjustment to a new climate and culture, it is important to incorporate good health care practices into your daily routine. Also, there may be precautions dictated by your locale. For example, in the tropics care should be taken to prevent sunburn and heat stroke, but you should also avoid contaminated beaches and nonchlorinated pools, stray dogs (because of the danger of rabies—advise children *never* to pet or befriend stray animals), and mosquitoes (because of the danger of malaria—do follow good "preventive" measures). Particularly if you have small children and domestic servants, you should take every precaution to prevent household accidents.

## Accidental Poisoning

Of the 1 million Americans who are accidentally poisoned each year, 90 percent are children under the age of five. In an overseas situation, where there may not be a poison control center, and where you may not be fluent in the language, a case of poisoning is potentially more lethal than in a stateside setting.

Poison control centers recommend that you keep syrup of ipecac and activated charcoal on hand. However, you should not use either until you have contacted the poison control center or, if there is not one, your doctor. Numbers should be posted near your phone. The Rush Presbyterian St. Luke's Poison Control Center in Chicago,

Illinois (telephone [312] 942-5969), will provide consultation to your overseas physician if needed.

Mr. Yuk, the green scowling face on stickers distributed by the U.S. Poison Control Center, has been particularly effective in warning children of dangerous products. You may wish to obtain some from your nearest poison control center or by sending a stamped, self-addressed envelope to the Rush Presbyterian St. Luke's Poison Control Center (1753 West Congress, Chicago, Illinois 60612). These labels should be placed on hazardous products. Poison control centers also recommend that you take the following precautions:

Store all hazardous substances in high cabinets, out of the reach of children.

Put child-protection locks on cabinets and medicine chests where potentially dangerous items are kept.

Keep poisonous substances in their original containers—they are familiar and clearly marked.

Be careful not to leave containers open and accessible to children.

Clean out medicine chests regularly. Flush any medication that is not being used down the toilet. Take special care to safeguard flavored medicines. Use child-proof caps.

Know the names of your house and garden plants. Many of them can be harmful.* It may be helpful to mark the names of houseplants on their pots and keep them out of the reach of toddlers.

Instruct children that something dangerous is a "NO, NO."

Know what is hazardous:

| | |
|---|---|
| Acids | Bubble bath |
| Ammonia | Camphorated oil with phenol |
| Antifreeze | Carbon tetrachloride |
| Antiseptics | Cigarettes |
| Aspirin | Cleaning fluids |
| Auto window wash solvent | Clinitest tablets |
| Benzene | Cologne |
| Bleach | Copper and brass cleaners |

---

*In Brussels, contact Centre Anti-Poisons (15, rue Joseph Stallaert, 1060 B; telephone 345.45.45).

For a listing of poisonous tropical plants, write to the Southeast Texas Poison Control Center (8th & Mechanics, Galveston, Texas 77550) for their documentation of *Poisonous Plants of Texas and the Gulf Coast,* or order *Plants Poisonous to People in Florida and Other Warm Areas* by Julia F. Morton (Morton Collectanea, University of Miami, Coral Gables, Florida 33124).

| | |
|---|---|
| Corn and wart remover | Nail polish |
| Dandruff shampoo | Nail polish remover |
| Dishwasher detergents | Narcotics |
| Disinfectants | Oven cleaner |
| Drain cleaners | Pain killers |
| Drugs | Paint |
| Epoxy glue | Paint thinner |
| Eye makeup | Permanent wave solution |
| Furniture polish | Pesticides |
| Garden sprays | Petroleum distillates |
| Gun cleaners | Pine oil |
| Hair dyes | Rodenticides |
| Herbicides | Rubbing alcohol |
| Insecticides | Shaving lotion |
| Iodine | Silver polish |
| Iron medicines | Strychnine |
| Kerosene | Toilet bowl cleaner |
| Mace | Turpentine |
| Model cement | Typewriter cleaner |
| | Vitamins |

## Vaccines

Monitoring the health of your family also includes careful planning for vaccinations. These should be given on a routine basis. A recommended schedule is:

| | |
|---|---|
| Typhoid booster | — every 3 years after age 6 |
| First and second oral polio booster (following initial series) | — generally age 1½ and 4 |
| Yellow fever booster | — every 10 years in certain countries |
| Tetanus (TD) | — every 10 years after age 6 |
| Gamma globulin (5cc) | — every 4-6 months after age 12 (in areas where infectious hepatitis is common) |
| Cholera booster | — every 6 months (only in certain countries) |
| Rabies (HDCV) | — every 2 years (only in areas where rabies is a problem) |

In the instance of infants born abroad, you may wish to follow the timetable commonly used by U.S. pediatricians:

| 2 months | — DPT (diphtheria, pertussis, tetanus), and OPV (oral polio virus trivalent) #1 |
| 4 months | — DPT/OPV #2 |
| 6 months | — DPT/OPV #3 |
| 15 months | — Measles, mumps, and rubella |
| 18 months | — DPT/OPV Booster #1 |
| 4–5 years | — DPT/OPV Booster #2 |

In some areas overseas the Bacillus Calmette-Guerin (BCG), an antituberculosis vaccine, is given at birth unless you specifically request that it not be given. A BCG vaccination voids the tine test to detect tuberculosis; persons so vaccinated always show a positive reaction.

Mumps and rubella vaccines may not be suggested abroad. In fact, these vaccines will not even be available in some areas. Public health departments are now recommending that mumps and rubella be given along with measles as a three-in-one vaccine at about 15 months, although each may be given as an individual immunization from 12 months to 18 years. If they are not available in your host city, you may wish to have your children receive these vaccines when you are in the States. Always have all vaccinations entered on your international certificate of vaccination.

If you have any unresolved questions about your child's immunizations or general development, they should be discussed with your stateside pediatrician when you are on home leave. It may be helpful to keep a chart of your children's height and weight and their motor and psychological development to discuss with their pediatrician each year.

## Dental Health

Many expatriates also suggest that you have your stateside dentist check your teeth and those of your children each year. Dental decay is reportedly the most prevalent of all diseases; in an overseas situation, where the water may not be fluoridated, it can become even more of a problem.

Some expatriates have found dentists whose techniques are commensurate with any of the more outstanding U.S. dentists; others have not fared so well. Randall Keller, a dentist in practice in a suburb of Chicago, suggests that you poll your overseas acquaintances for names of dentists whom they have used and about whom they have no complaints. He further suggests that you ask your stateside dentist to evaluate their initial fillings to see if they meet U.S. standards. Perhaps it will be possible to forego your stateside dental visits. On the other hand, your regular dentist may recommend that you carefully follow the principles of preventive dental care and see overseas dentists principally for emergencies.

## Orthodontia

While a dentist can complete almost any procedure in a month's time with concentrated effort, the orthodontist is locked into a certain time frame. If your child is currently in braces and you are planning an international move, you should ask your orthodontist to refer you to an affiliate in your host city who, if at all possible, uses the same techniques. Information concerning orthodontia abroad can be obtained from the *Orthodontic Directory of the World* (915 Broadway, Nashville, Tennessee 37203; telephone [615] 327-1804). Most orthodontists have office copies of this publication.

If your child has not yet started orthodontia but you anticipate a need for it while abroad, you should schedule a consultation with a reputable stateside orthodontist and discuss his recommendations as to need, starting time, and types of appliances. Again, you should ask him to refer you to a qualified affiliate in your host city. The orthodontic directory also notes whether a dentist's practice is exclusively orthodontia. If it is a nonexclusive practice, then that person may also be a candidate for your family dentist.

## Dental First Aid

Emergency first aid can be particularly important for the international traveler who may be enroute to, or recently arrived in, a foreign city. The ORx Dent-Aide Kit comes complete with dental mirror, tweezers, pain-deadening drops, goop to mix temporary fillings on the spot, and a 55-page manual to hold you until you can locate a dentist. It, or a similar kit, can be an important take-me-along. The ORx Dent-Aide Kit can be obtained from Dental Aide Products (Box 1164, Rahway, New Jersey 07065).

## On the Personal Side

Realistically, life abroad has many of the same traumas as does life back home. And being overseas is no cushion against the emotional responses that might ensue. Indeed, greatly distanced as it is from home and support systems, life abroad may accentuate feelings of helplessness and make problems seem all the more acute.

However, today's expatriate is much more fortunate than his predecessor in having access to help. The general recognition that life abroad can be fraught with problems has raised the social conscience in the expatriate community to such an extent that not only does it stand ready to lend a helping hand, it has turned its attention to the development of community resources to help the troubled.

In almost every community counseling services and sometimes even hot lines are in effect—an outstanding example is the volunteer-operated Life Line in Tokyo. Types of resources vary from community to community, however. In one community it may be a particularly gifted pastoral counselor who is tuned in to the needs of the expatriate community. In another it may be a community mental health center with an American psychologist or psychiatric social worker, in another a State Department-financed narcotics program with a counselor who is skilled in working with young addicts and their families. It may be an American-trained psychiatrist who is adept at communicating with Americans and understanding their viewpoints. It may be counselors at the American School or the International School whose concern for the "whole" student has led them into extended avenues of counseling.

How do you find out what resources your expatriate community has or what would be right for your problem? Contact the family liaison officer or the medical unit at the American embassy; talk to the pastor of your church or to your doctor or to a counselor at the American School.

Help may be available in the form of a newcomer's group or a self-help group, which, more and more, may be associated with churches catering to Americans, with American-oriented schools, or with American Women's clubs.

In some areas community counselors have held seminars on such timely subjects as adjusting to a new culture, the stresses and strains associated with life abroad, marriage under attack, and preparing for the return. They have also directed seminars toward the typical teenage dilemmas—alcohol and narcotics, teenage sexuality, philosophies of life, and decision making.

You may also find that help is available within your circle of acquaintances. An *expert,* after all, is simply a person who is knowledgeable about a given subject. While you should choose your confidants carefully (confidentiality is all-important), you may find someone who can provide real insight as well as innovative solutions to your problems.

Don't overlook the resources that may be available within your own family. Talking it out, sharing the burden, can be a real help; and you may find that two heads really are better than one.

If there seems to be no solution, what then? "Move cautiously," advised one wife who made the decision to pack the household goods and take her husband back to the United States for psychiatric treatment without requesting that their overseas medical officer do a thorough physical or consulting by telephone with their stateside physician. As it turned out, his simple depression following an acute but short-lived overseas illness could have been treated in a less drastic manner, and there would not have been an extended interlude in an otherwise brilliant career.

Of course, in some instances a return to the States may provide the only realistic solution. This is true in the instance of teenagers or adults who become addicted to narcotics. A speedy return may prevent their arrest and possibly long-term incarceration in a foreign prison. It will get them back to an area where they can get intensive therapy and away from their addict associates and their easy sources of narcotics.

It is also a good idea to come home when either member of an expatriate couple has such difficulty in handling the problems of overseas life that he or she turns to alcohol as a solution and quickly becomes a "problem drinker." A return to the States can bring relief of problems, the possibility of intensive therapy, and the support of groups like Alcoholics Anonymous as well as the support of stateside family members.

A return to the States is also indicated when a family develops an acute psychiatric or medical problem that cannot be treated effectively overseas. At that point the goals that brought the family into overseas service cease to matter. The prime concern must be with the welfare of the acutely ill member.

## Suggested Reading

American Medical Association. *The American Medical Association Handbook of First Aid and Emergency Care*. New York: Random House, 1972.

American National Red Cross. *Standard First Aid and Personal Safety*. New York: Doubleday, 1980.

Berkow, Robert. *The Merck Manual of Diagnosis and Therapy*. Rahway, New Jersey: Merck, Sharp, and Dohme Research Laboratories, 1977.

Carter, James P., and West, Eleanora de Antonia. *Keeping Your Family Healthy Overseas*. New York: Delacorte Press, 1971.

Clark, Randolph Lee, and Cumley, Russel W., eds. *The Book of Health: A Medical Encyclopedia for Everyone*. New York: Elsevier, 1973.

*Directory of the International Association of Medical Assistance to Travelers*. LAMAI, Suite 5620, Empire State Building, New York, New York, 10001.

Dupont, Herbert, and Dupont, Margaret W. *Travel with Health*. New York: Appleton-Century-Crofts, 1981.

Sehnert, Keith, and Eisenberg, Howard. *How to be Your Own Doctor—Sometimes*. New York: Grosset and Dunlap, 1977.

Vickery, Donald M., and Fries, James F. *Take Care of Yourself, a Consumer's Guide to Medical Care*. Reading, Massachusetts: Addison Wesley, 1976.

Wynder, Ernst, ed. *The Book of Health, A Complete Guide to Health to Last a Lifetime*. New York: Franklin Watts, 1981.

PART THREE

# Life in a New
## Culture

# 8

# Adapting to
# A New Culture

MOST PEOPLE BEGIN an overseas assignment with enthusiasm and fascination. Life is exciting and the differences strangely romantic. In fact, the initial period in a new culture may take on the aura of a honeymoon.

Gradually, however, the impact of the differences begins to be felt. There is the recognition that people not only look and speak differently; they act and react differently. There are new answers to old questions: good and bad, right and wrong, polite and impolite are all viewed from a different perspective. As social anthropologist Kalvero Oberg pointed out in his now-classic memorandum on culture shock:

> The signs or cues which include the thousand and one ways in which we orient ourselves to the situations of daily life—when to shake hands and what to say when we meet people, when and how to give tips, how to give orders to servants, how to make purchases, when to accept and when to refuse invitations, and when to take statements seriously and when not, are lost.[1]

Frustration and anxiety take hold, friends and family have been left behind, identity supports are nonexistent, the individual is alone in an alien society. There seems to be no way out. The glories of the United States are magnified, and the-streets-of-home-are-paved-with-gold syndrome may set in. Actual homesickness with stomach upsets or skin diseases, sleeplessness, apathy, depression, weeping, a distrust of nationals, and a fear of being robbed or cheated can follow, and may even be evidenced in the younger members of the family. Small children may regress to more infantile stages, interrupt toilet training, and exhibit antisocial behavior. Older youths and teenagers may find it difficult to study, to achieve, or to "belong." They may eat compulsively and, in extreme cases, may begin to experiment with alcohol, drugs, or sex.

Although it is almost never terminal, there is little doubt about the pain of culture shock. It is unlikely that a vaccine will be developed to prevent it, but there is growing recognition that immunity is influenced by:

An ability to adapt—sometimes referred to as "adaptive" energy that can be used to combat stress.

A desire for the experience—reflected in a desire to travel, or a consuming curiosity about the world.

A reason for being there—commitment to a goal, dedication to a job (the highly motivated may have almost no trouble in making the cross-cultural adjustment).

An effort to understand the differences—as evidenced by a willingness to look beneath customs and behavior to determine why people do the things they do.

As any expatriate can tell you, the problems of cross-cultural adjustment are very real. The process of becoming acclimatized, of adjusting to different foods and water, strange odors, and of dealing with shortages in housing, foodstuffs, and sometimes power, water, and telephones, as well as the "uncertainties presented by strange customs,"[2] is not easy. As might be expected, many expatriates react to the fight-or-flight instinct by packing their bags and heading for familiar shores.

No one seems to have accurate statistics on how many are thereafter listed as "repatriated prematurely," although in some industries attrition rates have soared in the 40 to 65 percent range;[3] but the fact that such a category exists is significant. Add to this the time, frustration, and anxiety involved in a "successful" cross-cultural adjustment, and there emerges a need not only for better cross-cultural training, but for greater understanding among expatriates of how to handle the stress associated with an international move.

## Stress and Cross-Cultural Adjustment

Perhaps the greatest contribution to the understanding of stress has come from the research of Hans Selye of the Institute of Experimental Medicine and Surgery at the University of Montreal. His definition of stress as the "non-specific response of the body to any demand made upon it" has been generally accepted.[4] This definition views stress as a reaction to almost any environmental circumstance or demand, pleasant or unpleasant, and it has led other therapists to describe stress, more simply, as all the pressures of life—the ordinary ones and the extraordinary ones.

Anxiety, on the other hand, is considered to be a typical stress reaction associated with distress, apprehension, and fear. It is anxiety combined with the loss of customary cultural props and support systems (friends and family) in the face of exposure to a new and possibly incomprehensible society that triggers the ills of culture shock.

The important thing to recognize is that stress and anxiety come from within. It is your perception of the situations of life that causes emotional trauma. Whether these events include a physical injury (such as a loss of mobility following a traumatic accident), or a psychological injury (such as a loss of confidence in your ability to meet the demands that life in a new society imposes upon you), the results can be equally devastating.

Responses to stress vary greatly. Just how you respond is influenced by your particular temperament—your early childhood experiences, as well as other experiences in similar circumstances, and your family or cultural background.

The successful handling of stress begins with self-knowledge. In a situation of great change, such as in an international move, it is important to assess the resources you have and those you may need to deal with the predicted stresses. A close and caring family unit can assist with this process, as well as provide a refuge in which to vent emotions and talk things out. Visualizing problems and maintaining a positive "I can" attitude are also important in minimizing the anxiety with which new situations are faced.

While there are no accepted barometers for measuring cultural adaptation, it is helpful to make a periodic progress analysis. If, for example, you find yourself or members of your family answering "yes" to the following questions, even after six months in a new situation, beware!

Do you have a basic inability or an adamant refusal to try to speak the local language?

Are your books on the history, art, and politics of the country gathering dust in the corner of the room?

Are the local attitudes unknown or incomprehensible to you?

When placed in a situation where you must participate in national customs and etiquette, do you feel insecure and cover it by talking about how things are done "better in the States"?

Do you have difficulty with servants? Are you frequently argumentative with them or with salespeople?

Does the unreliability, the "mañana" attitude of repairmen and others, threaten to drive you up a wall?

Does it make you feel better to tell all the newcomers, in front of the servants and, if possible, the boss's wife, what a lousy country it is and how many problems they will have?

Do you have a real reluctance to mix with the locals, or on the other side of the coin, to mix with Americans?

Do you find the thought of entertaining people foreboding?

Do you get excessively upset over red tape?

Are you constantly converting the local money into dollars?

Are you absorbed with the fear of being cheated at the market or robbed in your own home?

Does a less sophisticated environment for living (water and power shortages) or business (no electric pencil sharpener or access to computers) or a different pattern of life (three-hour noontime siestas, dinner at 10:00 p.m.) unduly frustrate you?

In assessing your answers to the above questions, you should be aware that the normal crises of life are doubly charged in an overseas situation. Consider the instance of Christmas, the most anticipated holiday of the year. It may not be possible to color the day happy when family is far away, gift selection is limited to expensive imports or the more inexpensive but nontraditional locally crafted items, and when Christmas trees may be nonexistent. If you have not been able to come to grips with the problems of settling into a different culture and remain primed for a fight-or-flight response, then the challenge of celebrating Christmas or any other holiday in this setting, or the addition of even one other life crisis, may seem overwhelming.

The extensive research of Thomas Holmes and Richard Rahe demonstrated a close relationship between life crises situations and subsequent illness or injury.[5] Our interviews with expatriates tended to substantiate their findings; but there were also indications that expatriates who were in the midst of other major life crises (divorce or serious marital difficulties, illness or death of a close family member, pregnancy or personal injury, son or daughter leaving home, and so forth) found that a cross-cultural adaptation was more difficult than it might otherwise have been.

## Coping Techniques

An expatriate should find positive ways to control the undesirable manifestations of stress. Unfortunately, many of the ways commonly used—tranquilizers, drugs, alcohol, even compulsive eating—only complicate the situation.

Just as responses to stress are very individual, techniques that enable one to cope with stress successfully must fit the individual. What works for one person may not work for another. Further, what works at one stage of life may not be as effective at a later date.

The research of Hans Selye recognized a very basic concept: you can handle stress better if you are in good health, get enough rest, and balance work and recreation. The search by other scientists for means to control the effects of stress led them back to the precept that activity is a biological necessity. In study after study, exercise has proven to be effective in disrupting the flow of adrenalin and normalizing body chemistry. Our grandparents may have called it "blowing off steam," but they wisely realized that beating a rug, gardening, or taking a walk alleviated the effects of stress. Allowing yourself a "fight outlet" by jogging, playing tennis or golf, or simply running in place is an invaluable technique in managing stress.

There are other techniques, of course. Progressive relaxation directs exercise toward muscle relaxation. By focusing attention on a certain muscle group and then systematically tensing and relaxing it, tension is released from the muscle fibers and relaxation achieved. (This therapy stems from the research of Edmund Jacobson, who was also a prolific writer on the how-tos of relaxation.[6]) As simple a technique as taking a long bath or sauna can also relax tense muscles. Biofeedback, acupressure, massage, diaphragmatic breathing, and yoga have many proponents. Thinking of positive things (which is often conceived to be redirected thinking), meditation, and daydreaming (focusing on a comfortable and relaxing scene) are favorites of many of the life science researchers. Prayer and communal worship have been the means used by countless individuals through the ages to handle the stress associated with life in an alien culture.

The redirection of energies, commonly referred to as "a change of pace" or "R and R" (rest and relaxation), and often a part of the package in "hardship posts," can do wonders for one's outlook on life. On a smaller scale, a change of activity—a night at the theater, a trip to a nearby beach, or a weekend of sightseeing—can provide temporary relief and, often, renewed vigor. This be-good-to-yourself technique involves practices that have been used effectively by many expatriates. It recognizes a basic premise: "If you can't beat them, you might as well join them." It may involve such simple solutions as hiring a maid to do the housework and enjoying a two-hour siesta along with everyone else. Often it involves a basic change in attitude, a decision to enjoy the mañana attitude found in much of the world, instead of fighting it; and with it comes, amazingly, increasing relief from stress. As you begin to savor life, instead of imposing impossible time schedules or a level of perfection that it may not be possible to attain in the part of the world to which you have been posted, you will have begun the successful navigation of the cross-cultural abyss.

It may be helpful to recognize that you have an innate adaptability, and that with a little effort on your part you can become a survivor. As a matter of fact, stress can be a very positive thing; it can be utilized to achieve even greater heights than might heretofore have been possible—witness the expatriates who "flower" in an overseas situation.

Such achievements do not occur overnight. As with most things, time is a factor. The solving of the initial problems and the adaption to a new set of values take from two to six months—sometimes even a year. If the problems and the stresses related to the initial adaption are not completely worked through, the individual may remain caught up in an emotional turmoil; or although they may seem to recover, the anxieties that have not been resolved may lie dormant, ready to erupt into the frustrations and psychosomatic ills of culture shock at a later point in the assignment.

## Eliminating the Source of Stress

Eliminating the stress associated with a cross-cultural adjustment must be a major goal. If the transfer is to an area where support and counseling services are either limited or nonexistent, self-help may be the only method for survival. It is simply sink or swim—a circumstance in which removing the external sources of stress must be a high priority.

Study your situation from every conceivable angle; analyze all possible means of rectifying the problems; and then make a sustained and determined effort to accomplish that goal. Be willing to temper your efforts with patience.

Greet those you meet with interest, kindness, courtesy, respect, and faith in their goodwill. Listen to their comments; be willing to accept advice that is positive and pertinent.

It may or may not be necessary to learn the language to handle the details of everyday life; but being able to communicate in the national language can open new vistas—the joys of a native pageant, the opportunities to converse on a more familiar basis with those you meet.

Get a feel for the area in which you are living. Review its history and politics. Research its art. Study its currency, the units of measurement, and the temperature gradient, and begin to think in those terms. Buy a map and a guidebook and get out into the fearsome traffic. It may not be as bad as it looks, and a knowledge of the surrounding area will give you a feeling of belonging. If time does not permit you to become an expert, at least become an informed guest.

Make a concerted effort to gain an understanding of the local customs, the differences in etiquette, and the underlying reasons for their observances. Don't give in to the temptation to disparage your host culture or to associate with those who do. Your overt disapproval or contempt of local customs can only undermine your positive participation in a new experience.

The old adage "When in Rome do as the Romans do" is one that cannot be overlooked. You are the guest in a host country. It is up to you to make the changes, although it may come as a shock to you that the ingrained values of Americanism are not always appreciated. Directness, openness, individualism, pride in punctuality, and self-sufficiency—all revered American traits—may have to be laid aside if you are to fulfill the reason for your presence in the country and be accepted by the people for whom you have come so far to live and work.

Some analysis of your own value system and a continuing ability to laugh at yourself and your mistakes are almost certain to be essential to the achievement of this goal. Remember that you are not the first, nor will you be the last, to traverse this pass. However difficult it may be, it must be even more difficult for the foreigner who attempts to permeate the American culture. A look into the "shoe on the other foot" situation provides real insight for the

American expatriate who is attempting life in another society. In their book *Making It in the United States,* Roger and Rosalina Morales Goulet noted:

> Americans seem to lack delicacy in their handling of personal relations. They sometimes come across as brusque and lacking in regard for their feelings. . . . [They] are accustomed to speaking their minds out to each other, and friends indulge in rough kidding . . . or loud, angry arguments without it affecting their friendships. To others who come from a culture that seems to stifle, sidestep, or divert conflict whenever possible and puts a high value on outwardly smooth personal relations among friends and associates, Americans sometimes seem as if they had learned their manners from watching old John Wayne movies.[7]

> The American preoccupation with punctuality is a long-running joke. Laugh about it all you want, but live by it just the same.[8]

> Americans . . . are generally cold, impersonal, and superficial. This claim is substantiated by such proof as Americans ask you how you are and don't wait for an answer [or say] "Come and see us sometime" [and never deliver a formal invitation].[9]

Don't allow yourself to become intimidated by differences. They will be the spice that sparks your sojourn abroad. Pick out a host national with whom you have empathy, and if you are not sure how to act or react in a certain situation, ask. People love to talk about their own culture, and they willingly forgive small indiscretions as long as you have regard for the precepts upon which their actions are based.

Reach out to the people around you; respond to the invitations of your associates; reestablish contacts with old friends or with the friends of your stateside acquaintances; and frequent places that the nationals enjoy. Make a real attempt to get to know the nationals; but also recognize that a close relationship may not be possible. As the Goulets noted:

> One reason for this is they do not usually invite foreigners to their homes, but instead entertain them in restaurants or stuff them at fiestas. The house is a status symbol, and unless he [the national] has one he considers fancy enough to show to foreigners, he would not entertain them at home. . . . [Unfortunately, many foreigners do not realize that] for Americans, intimacy rather than lavish entertainment is the true index of friendship.[10]

A recently repatriated corporate manager gave credence to this in the story of his relationship with a government minister whom he had periodically entertained during his three years in the country. On the eve of his return to the States, the minister had the manager and his wife to dinner amid many apologies. First, as he said, they had had to completely remodel the house, then they had to order new furniture, and then they had to hire a new servant; and so it had taken a "long while" to get ready for the dinner party.

The emphasis on "getting to know the nationals," as important as it is, has left many Americans with a feeling of failure that they have not been able to establish close and meaningful ties. They fail to realize that the high privacy fences or compound walls, and the extended-family relationships found in many countries, have been deterring factors. Of course, in some instances where there has been a shared interest in a sport, church, or volunteer activity, Americans have been able to evidence their interest in, and concern for, the nationals and have crossed over the barriers.

Participation is the name of the game; however, each person should establish a level of outreach with which he is comfortable. Just doing something to help others is a stress-reducing tactic, but individuals and the situations in which they find themselves vary. Undoubtedly, those with the adaptability and fortitude to stay and work problems through develop new coping skills, renewed confidence in their own abilities, and a gradual recognition that life abroad can be a truly enriching and rewarding experience.

# Notes

1. Kalvero Oberg, "Do you Suffer from Culture Shock?" (Brazil: International Cooperation Administration, United States Operations Mission to Brazil), p. 1.

2. Ibid., p.4.

3. Linda Edwards, "Present Shock and How to Avoid It," *Across the Board* 15 (February 1978): 37.

4. Hans Selye, *Stress Without Distress* (Philadelphia: J. B. Lippincott, 1974), p.27.

5. Thomas Holmes, and Richard Rahe, "The Social Readjustment Rating Scales," *Journal of Psychosomatic Research* 2 (1967):213–18.

6. Edmund Jacobson, *You Can Sleep Well: The ABC's of Restful Sleep for the Average Person* (New York: McGraw-Hill, 1938).

7. Roger Goulet and Rosalina Morales Goulet, *Making It in the United States* (Quezon City, Philippines: Phoenix Press, 1978), p.134.

8. Ibid., p.136.

9. Ibid.

10. Ibid., p.137.

# Suggested Reading

Benson, Herbert. *The Relaxation Response*. New York: Avon, 1976.

Brown, Barbara. *Stress and the Art of Biofeedback*. New York: Harper and Row, 1977.

Cooper, Kenneth H. *The Aerobics Way*. New York: Bantam, 1977.

Dychlwald, Ken. *Bodymind*. New York: Pantheon, 1977.

General Mills, Inc. *Family Health in an Era of Stress, 1978–79*. Minneapolis, Minnesota: General Mills, Inc. 1979. Available free of charge from General Mills, Inc., 9200 Wayzata Boulevard, Minneapolis, Minnesota 55440.

Goldberg, Phillip. *Executive Health*. New York: McGraw-Hill, 1978.

Holmes, Thomas H. and Holmes, T. Stephenson. *How Change Can Make Us Ill*. Chicago: Blue Cross Association, 1974.

Maultsby, Marie C. *Help Yourself to Happiness*. New York: Institute for Rational Living, 1976.

Pelletier, Kenneth R. *Mind as Healer, Mind as Slayer*. New York: Dell, 1977.

Schnert, Keith H. *Stress/Unstress*. Minneapolis, Minnesota: Augsburg, 1981.

Selye, Hans. *The Stress of Life*. New York: McGraw-Hill, 1976.

————————.*Stress Without Distress*. New York: J. B. Lippincott, 1976.

Shealy, Norman C. *90 Days to Self-Health*. New York: Dial Press, 1977.

Tubering, Donald A. *Kicking Your Stress Habits*. Dulbeth: Whole Person Associates, 1980.

# 9

# Safety and Security

*T*HE PIONEER PHILOSOPHY of open doors and open hearts, which is so basic to the American way of life, has made it difficult to accept the need to keep the drawbridge up and the garden gate locked.

Indeed, of the many Americans now living abroad, there are those who insist that they have never felt safer or more secure. But the fact of the matter is that crime and disaster are universal phenomena; crime statistics are on the rise the world over. Americans living abroad can no longer afford to consider themselves at a safe distance from threats to person or property; for they, too, sometimes become statistics. Unfortunately, as well, the worldwide reputation of affluence and influence that America has enjoyed has contributed to many mistaken notions about it as a country and its citizens as a people. As a result Americans have sometimes been set up as targets for robbery, even terrorism, just because they are Americans. Early recognition of this possibility, along with thoughtful efforts at prevention, are of utmost importance. Expatriate Americans can expect the cooperation of government and corporation in their efforts to maintain security abroad. But the first step is a security-conscious attitude and the cooperation and participation of all family members for the safety and protection of all.

## Security Abroad

For the American abroad, vigilance, which carries with it an awareness of the political and economic factors at work, a recognition of the need to keep a low profile, and a willingness to develop a security-conscious way of life may be the better part of valor. Attitude is the single-most important factor in increasing the protection of your home and family, according to Lloyd E. Singer, president of MTI Teleprograms, Inc. (4825 North Scott Street, Schiller Park, Illinois 60176). His firm, in conjunction with ten large multinational corporations, has developed a plan for executive protection abroad.[1] He suggests that as you develop security awareness, you are automatically taking the steps necessary to improve your security; and your family will follow your leadership. Although Singer stresses the utilization of all possible protective devices, his focus centers upon the positive participation of each member of the family unit. Awareness, not fear, is the keynote to the program.

Life in an overseas situation carries with it certain uncompromisable realities. You are the foreigner—your size, your coloring, your language or accent, your clothing, and the manner in which you conduct yourself are different and therefore visible. If, in addition, you live in such a way as to display your affluence, you are establishing high visibility and, perhaps, inviting disaster. The MTI Executive Protection Program stresses the maintenance of a low profile, as well as encouraging the development of good security habits. For the American abroad, this should include complying with the following precautions:

Develop the buddy system.

Don't trust strangers.

Never admit unexpected workers or other strangers into your home.

Get to know local police, firefighters, and other government officials.

Know your neighbors well enough to watch each other's homes during absences.

Be alert.

Don't make your family's routine obvious to outsiders. Some family member should know where the others are at all times. If any member is delayed in arriving at the destination (or anticipates a late arrival), the family should be notified at once.

Make sure all your family members know what to do if they suspect a security threat.

If you have servants, make sure they thoroughly understand their security responsibilities and duties.

Instruct your children and servants not to respond to requests for information from callers. Be vague about family members' absences.

Never accept packages unless they are expected and the deliverer shows identification.

Don't allow interviews of your family or permit anyone to photograph your family, your home, or its interior except for sound business reasons.

## Beat the Burglar

A successful game of "beat the burglar" begins prior to departure from the States—when you are purchasing equipment and inventorying household furnishings. At that time:

Make a detailed record and include photos of all valuables. Be sure that your listing includes the serial number as well as the date bought, purchase price (and receipt, if available), and replacement price. Mark all items likely to be stolen with your social security number stenciled with an engraving pen.

Verify the worth of valuable items with a certified appraiser, and obtain documentation of it. Consider the possibility of storage in a bank vault or of leaving such items with a trusted friend or relative.

Arrange for extra help to watch the packing, loading, and unloading to prevent the disappearance of articles.

Insist that goods be moved in heavy-duty, steel-framed, ocean-land containers and that they be sealed and opened in your presence.

Assess the company insurance coverage on your household effects while in transit. If it does not meet your estimation of value, consider the purchase of additional insurance.

Consider purchasing: (1) a simple battery-operated burglar alarm system, such as the proximity type, that will be effective during blackouts, that can be easily installed and operated, and that will emit a loud noise; (2) a mercury vapor lamp with at least one extra globe, which provides automatic dusk-to-dawn exterior lighting; if, later, they are found to be unnecessary they are easily resold; (3) automatic light timers—several to turn lights on and off in different rooms; (4) door-viewing ports (or "fish eyes") with a magnifying glass lens that allows you a view of the person outside without opening the door.

## At Home

Many expatriates follow the example of the local residents and hire household servants so that the house can be occupied at all times. However, this may be a disastrous move unless you first check servants' references carefully with all previous employers and their reputation with the police.

A loud and noisy dog and signs noting that you do have a "bad dog" and a professional protection system are considered excellent deterrents. Do take care to give your house an occupied look at all times. Good locks, lights, and possibly an alarm system will pay off in security and peace of mind. However, there are other security measures that you can take:

Insure your household effects with a reliable host country insurance agent upon their arrival.

Keep as few valuables at home as possible. Extra cash and a list of your valuables and expensive jewelry should be kept in a safe deposit box, preferably a branch American bank. You may also wish to keep a second list of valuables in an office safe.

Don't place valuable items such as stereos and televisions where they can be seen through open windows.

Do not leave bicycles or motorcycles on sidewalks, lawns, or easily accessible areas.

Lock cars and gas caps at all times.

Keep garage doors locked.

Keep the house locked at all times—even if you are working in the yard. Never put a house key on your ignition key ring or give a servant or child his own key. It is better to leave one with a friend or trusted neighbor.

Keep exterior fuse and switch boxes locked, and keep a couple of good flashlights around.

Keep ladders or other items that could help a second-story burglar locked in a storage area.

Keep shrubbery trimmed.

Keep your grass cut and snow cleared. They are giveaways that you are not home.

## When You Are Away

Many expatriates who are going to be away for an extended period arrange for someone to stay in their house. They advise that if this is not possible, you should make every effort to give the house an occupied look:

Set automatic light timers.

Put a radio on an automatic timer also. If you have a volume adjustment on your telephone bell, turn it to the lowest level. A prowler will be less likely to hear an unanswered call. Unplug other appliances except for the refrigerator and freezer. Shades and draperies should be drawn on all windows through which an intruder can easily look. However, on high or second-story windows that cannot be easily reached, the shade length should be varied, as total uniformity is a giveaway that no one is home.

Stop all deliveries, or have neighbors pick up newspapers and circulars; ask them to inspect the property periodically and to contact a company official and the police if anything is amiss.

Park your car in the driveway if possible.

### In Case You Meet the Burglar

If at all possible, avoid a direct encounter with a burglar. If you have determined that the intruder is in the house with you, put a locked door between the two of you and call the police. If this is not possible, turn on the stereo or make a loud noise that may frighten the intruder away. Some expatriates preplan disaster signals with their neighbors, such as the raising and lowering of blinds or flashlight or mirror signals. If you have such a plan, use it.

### After the Burglary

Once the burglar leaves, call the police and your company security officer. Be prepared to give them all possible information: the mode of getaway, a license number, and a personal description (race, sex, age, height, weight, facial features, and clothing). Any distinctive characteristics you can recall—a tattoo, speech differences—may help to pinpoint an identification. While you are waiting for the police to arrive, get your inventory of valuables. Begin to list the articles that you are sure have been stolen, but be careful not to move or touch anything.

You should contact your insurance agency as soon as possible after you have made your report to the police.

### Precautions for Pedestrians

Never carry large amounts of money or an assortment of credit cards. Pay all possible bills by check. Carry only one credit card, such as Barclay's or American Express, or cards used on a day-to-day basis as a backup. Keep a record of credit card numbers, as well as of other cards you may own, in a safe place. If you must carry a large sum of money with you, carry only a small part in your billfold and the rest elsewhere on your body—in a money belt or a body purse (which are available at most travel stores). A little emergency money is always a good precaution, particularly for a woman.

A woman should carry her purse close to her side with the clasp inward and her hand on the clasp. Shoulder bags are considered to be the safest; however, the large carryall, which is the favorite of so many expatriate wives, is much easier to grab than the smaller, more inconspicuous style. Women should be particularly cautious about setting their purses and parcels down in a subway or bus, in a grocery shopping car, or on the restroom floor or near the washbasins. An over-the-shoulder purse or camera is offered some protection by wearing it under a light coat or jacket.

Car and house keys should be carried on the body in preference to purses. If your purse is taken, you will at least have a place to go and a way to get there. A man's bulging wallet is an open invitation to a thief. It is considered safest tucked into an inside pocket of a coat; but men who insist upon carrying a wallet in a rear pocket should at least keep the pocket buttoned and, weather permitting, their coat pulled tightly over it. A small emergency fund elsewhere on the body is also a good resource.

You should be alert to the dangers lurking in the areas you frequent. Are there heavy shrubbery, shadowy doorways, or parked cars where criminals can hide? Establish areas of refuge—stores into which you can dash, police or fire stations. If you suspect someone is following you, change your route, take a taxi, go into any commercial establishment, or if you are in a residential area, pound on a door and shout for help.

If you are out alone, be sure someone knows where, as well as the estimated time of your return. If at all possible, follow the buddy plan or walk with the dog. There *is* safety in numbers.

## Precautions for Motorists

It is a good idea to have a first-aid kit, a fire extinguisher, an emergency tool kit, and emergency supplies such as flares and a flashlight always on hand in the car. Form the habit of giving your car the once-over before getting in. Does it appear to have been tampered with or damaged in any way? Are the tires intact and well aired? Is the tail pipe clear? Is anyone hiding around or in the car?

Once inside, buckle up—but first lock up. It is safest to use indirect ventilation, air conditioning, or heating so that windows may be kept raised. In any case, do not allow enough space above a lowered window for someone to reach in to grab packages or unlock a door.

Choose driving routes that are well lighted and well populated; be alert to areas of refuge. When parking, select an area as close to your destination as possible. Opt for areas that are well exposed and well lighted. Before leaving the car, be sure that all doors are securely locked and that all packages, as well as other items, are out of sight.

Finally, be aware that by such measures you are acting, defensively at least, to protect yourself against potential threat. Under certain circumstances, in certain countries, the game you play might suddenly switch to "outwit the terrorists."

## Terrorists and Terrorism

Although terrorists' operations have been observed to follow a general pattern, they do vary from country to country and from group to group. Some have used boycotts and hijackings and others sabotage (often bombings), and still other groups have raised large sums of money by kidnapping. However, terrorists' operations, to date, are focused in a relatively small number of countries.[2]

It is critical that expatriate executives gain a thorough understanding of terrorist activities in the country to which they are being assigned; and, moreover, that not only they, but their entire family, be willing to accept the risks involved. If this implies accepting the emotional impact of knowing that one may be singled out at any time, it should also carry with it the very positive assurance that the best of American technology and expertise is available for protection. Increasingly, this has involved the use of specially designed armored cars for top executives and chauffeurs trained in defensive driving techniques at schools such as Toni Scotti's School for Defensive Driving in Massachusetts or Bob Bondurant's School of High Performance Driving in Sonoma, California.[3] However, it is worth emphasizing once again that the protection afforded technologically is an adjunct to a program of self-protection designed for, and carried out by, all members of the top-level executive's family.

The problems of combating terrorism have been highlighted in the kidnap-hostage briefings that the Federal Bureau of Investigation has held throughout the United States; however, corporate strategies in the event of hijackings or kidnappings are among the more closely guarded corporate secrets. Nonetheless, most multinational executives freely admit that when isolated acts of terrorism lead to general unrest and civil strife, it is time to think of evacuation procedures.

## Operation Evacuation

Over the past ten years, in almost as many instances, Americans have fled their overseas homes seeking safety from terrorists' activities, civil unrest, and warfare. It has become increasingly apparent that the expatriate life-style is liable to threat and danger. Those who seek it must recognize that life abroad can, quite suddenly, become hazardous. Under such circumstances a realistic evacuation plan can become very important. Most multinational corporations anticipate such occurrences and, soon after the establishment of a branch plant or office in a new area, work out detailed plans for the evacuation of employees and their families and possessions.

Veterans of foreign evacuations maintain that expatriates should assume some responsibility for their own safety. If, overall, they recommend pursuing a calm, realistic approach to the problems that accompany a country in civil strife, they also stress being alert for changes in the political climate. They advise foreign residents to keep a supply of emergency foodstuffs, candles, and flashlights and to plan for an alternate way of cooking (charcoal grill, camp stove, and the like). An inventory of household effects should be kept up-to-date and instructions for packing attached. Upon the first indication that evacuation might be necessary, expatriates should begin to list and pack those items that they would like to take with them. Since luggage allowed is usually limited, it is necessary to be selective.

An expatriate who fled Iran during the massive evacuation of Americans in 1979 emphasized that persons going abroad should not take treasured or irreplaceable items. Americans there were evacuated on 24-hours notice and were allowed to take away only one suitcase each. Most people simply locked their doors and walked away, not knowing if they would ever see their life's accumulations again. Some corporations, at least, carried out effective evacuation plans. National supervisors made the rounds regularly, encouraging servants to stay on duty and to protect the homes and their contents. They paid the servants, assisted with emergencies, and finally supervised the packing of household effects. While everyone lost a few things, many received their possessions in surprisingly good shape.

For most expatriates, evacuation will continue to be something that they read about in the newspapers; but for those who learn firsthand the meaning of the word, preparedness will continue to be their best ally.

## Fight the Fire Before it Starts

It is sobering to realize that fire doesn't always happen to the other fellow and that the likelihood of its occurrence isn't changed by a move abroad. Fire prevention makes good sense, whatever the address. However, it is of particular importance in an overseas situation, where fire stations may be farther apart, as well as less sophisticated (particularly in the developing nations); and there may be other problems, such as the lack of water pressure.

The advice of the U. S. Fire Protection Administration may be lifesaving. It notes that 60 percent of all fatal home fires occur while the family is asleep; and that persons who lose their lives are usually victims of smoke inhalation rather than the fire itself—hence the importance of an early warning system that can detect smoke well before the average individual can smell or see it. For the best protection, its experts suggest putting an ionization-type detector for fast-burning open flames (such as fire in a wastebasket) in the hallway ceiling outside the bedrooms and at the top of major access stairways; and a photoelectric detector, which is most sensitive to a smoldering fire (such as fire in upholstery) near the family room area (installation should not be made in the kitchen, since smoke and vapor from cooking may trigger it).

Battery-operated units are preferable abroad, since they are not subject to power failure. The units should have the Underwriters Laboratory Seal of Approval, and they should be purchased in the States, since they may not be readily available abroad. The nine-volt batteries the units need are available worldwide. Installation is a simple screwdriver-type operation that can be completed in a few moments.

Like the detectors, the fire extinguisher should be selected on the basis of its ability to counteract the problems most likely to occur. There are three types of fire extinguishers; they may be marked "A," "B," "C," or combinations thereof. The letters refer to the three types of home fires:

Class A fires involve combustibles, such as wood, cloth, and paper;

Class B fires involve inflammable liquids, such as greases and gases; and

Class C fires involve electrical equipment.

Foam works well for class A and B fires, and a carbon dioxide extinguisher is effective against class B and C fires. However, the multipurpose dry chemical found in an ABC extinguisher will work equally well against all three types of fires. It is the extinguisher that is generally used in a 2.5-pound to 5-pound size.

All household members should be aware of the placement of, and the use of, a second-story escape ladder. This is a small folding ladder that hooks over the window and drops to the ground. It can be a good escape mechanism and is a recommended take-along for expatriates. They are available through many hardware stores or by mail order from Brookstore (127 Vose Farm Road, Peterborough, New Hampshire 03458; telephone [603] 924-7181).

Common sense dictates the conscientious adherence to preventive measures that stop a fire before it has a chance to get started. However, in the overseas household, which has added reason for following fire safety rules, this is often complicated by the addition of servants who have had no education in, or understanding of, fire prevention.

In these instances, home safety hinges on early instruction in safety prevention measures and conscientious follow-up to be sure that these regulations are constantly observed. Your check list for instructions should include the following:

Post your fire department number near your phone. Be sure that your children and your household servants know how to make a call for help and that they understand the danger of fire.

Don't smoke in bed or when you are likely to fall asleep in a chair. Negligent smoking is a cause of more than half of all home fires.

Cook with care. Keep an eye on the stove while boiling or frying. Never pour water on burning fat—it spreads the flame. Use a chemical fire extinguisher. However, in an emergency a wet towel can be used to smother the flames.

Check out the cords. Don't let electric cords of irons, lamps, and appliances get wet. Keep out kinks. Use heavy-duty cords for appliances that produce heat. Keep electrical items away from sinks, bathtubs, and washbasins.

Don't hide extension cords. Make sure that all extension cords are in good condition and out in the open, rather than under the rug, over hooks, or through door openings and partitions.

Don't overload circuits or sockets. Never use more than one high-wattage appliance on an outlet at a time. Check and be aware of all electrical hazards, such as appliance wires that overheat, fuses that blow repeatedly, or television pictures that contract when your refrigerator turns on.

Use approved appliances. Make sure your electrical appliances bear the Underwriters Laboratory Seal of Approval. Cut off the current when you are through using an appliance.

Keep proper fuses handy. Don't replace blown-out fuses with pennies, wire, or anything other than a new fuse. A 15-amp fuse is correct for most lighting circuits. Don't overload circuits. If you have any reason to suspect that your present wiring is inadequate or unsafe, you should have a qualified electrician go over the house. This is particularly true in areas such as the Philippines, where termites commonly eat through wiring, causing fires.

Inspect annually. Don't overload the furnace, hot water heater, chimney, or roof. Have them inspected yearly. Sooty or leaking flues can cause fires.

Use flammables outside. Don't use gasoline, kerosene, benzene, or other flammable liquids indoors.

Don't keep oily, greasy, or paint-smeared rags in the house or let old papers and trash gather in closets, attics, basements, or garages.

Use flashlights instead of flames. Never use matches or candles to light the way in the attic, closet, or basement.

There should be regular fire drills in which family and servants both participate and in which the escape exit and alternate routes are emphasized. Periodically, you should also make a survey of your home to assure yourself that you have followed all possible preventive measures.

## Notes

1. Jan Reber and Paul Shaw, *The Executive Protection Manual* (Schiller Park, Ill.: Motorola Teleprograms, 1976).

2. "Regional Risk Assessment" (Alexandria, Va.: Risks International, April 1979).

3. "Personal Memo: New Bodyguards for Executives," *Dun's Review* 106 (October 1976): 79.

## Suggested Reading

Guevara, Che. *Guerrilla Warfare*. New York: Vintage, 1961.

Jackson, Sir Geoffrey. *Surviving the Long Night*. New York: Vanguard Press, 1972.

Learner, Lawrence. *The Paper Revolutionaries: The Rise of the Underground Press*. New York: Simon and Schuster, 1972.

Marighella, Carlos. *For the Liberation of Brazil*. Harmondsworth: Penguin, 1971.

Moore, Brian. *The Revolution Script*. New York: Pocket Books, 1971.

# 10

# Parlez-Vous
# Anything but English?

*T*HE BIGGEST CHALLENGE, and also the biggest opportunity for prospective expatriates (man, wife and children), may well be learning the language of their new host country. Acquiring some degree of fluency in another language is a formidable task for most Americans. The United States just isn't oriented toward foreign-language study and use. While international investment of American companies has increased manifold, the percentage of our students in high school and college foreign language courses has dropped drastically. Only about 9 percent of college undergraduates are studying foreign languages. Even when there is some formal study, proficiency levels are low.

The Defense Language Institute requires 720 hours of instruction for the "easier" languages, whereas language majors in college have far less. "The deadliest sin of American provincialism," states Kurt Muller, assistant director, Foreign Language Programs, the Modern Language Association, is that "once we leave the language classroom we forget that English is not the only language spoken in our environment. We read current events in the English-language press, we even research foreign affairs using only English-language materials. Language use is often abandoned at the classroom door."

If our language background and capabilities are so poor, is learning another language worth the effort and expense? How often have you heard, "Everyone speaks English"? True, English is the leading commercial and, perhaps, diplomatic language. It is the principal second language in many foreign school systems. English accounts for the highest number of lessons given in the 61 Berlitz Schools of Languages in the United States and is one of the leaders abroad. According to Charles Berlitz in his fascinating new book on the world's languages, *Native Tongues,* English is second on the list of languages having at least 50 million speakers (it follows Chinese). English has achieved its strong position, in great part, because of its full vocabulary for the language of technology, science, and management.

The authors' own experiences have been that Spanish, and Portuguese in Brazil, are still the principal business languages in Latin America. Many of the other major and newly developing markets in the Asia/Pacific area, the Middle East, and Africa are still much more comfortable in their native languages.

There are many stories about marketing catastrophes due to language gaffes. When the Chevy Nova, marketed in Latin America, had the accent on the first syllable of *Nova,* it was the "new star" the name indicated. But by accenting the second syllable, as can happen in the Spanish market, it advertised a car that "No *va*"—that doesn't go!

Most companies and prospective expatriates concede the value of learning the host country language. For the wage earner, one of the leading foreign language educators has identified several advantages:

Business and cultural contacts are increasing with countries that have both a great pride in their own language and little previous need to learn another language.

Dependence on an interpreter creates several problems. First, it eliminates important inflections, emphases, and nuances of the original speaker. Second, it jeopardizes the chances of a "true" communication. (Remember the skits on the "Tonight Show" when a joke was passed on from one foreign language speaker to another in four different languages? By the fourth translation, the joke lost all humor and most of its sense.) Third, the time lag involved in utilizing an interpreter interrupts a spontaneous conversation and can alter the meaning. Fourth, it involves a third party in what might be a confidential discussion.

Ignorance of a language prevents acquiring or verifying facts firsthand.

The executive can select people around him from the entire labor pool, not just those who speak English. Being able to use monolingual people can save in salary costs.

Using the language of the host is a compliment that can help set the right tone for business.

In some respects, the need for language training is greater for the rest of the family than for the wage earner. The latter goes right to the office, associating with English-speaking people. The nonbusiness partner is thrown into contact with the general population in locating an apartment, shopping, and all other aspects of getting settled. The children may be the ones who ultimately learn the new language best, through lessons in school and social contacts. A very difficult adjustment can be facilitated by their ability to "mingle" directly in their new milieu.

Two other important reasons for learning at least something of the language are health and safety. Medical care can be quite different in foreign countries, so successful care demands the best communication possible. If you have a particular ongoing or recurring medical problem, say diabetes, it could be important to learn some of the vocabulary relating to that condition. So, too, with the ever-present specter of terrorism. However remote that might be, a little ability in the language might be crucial in avoiding injury or involvement.

The best reason for learning the local language may turn out to be your own self-satisfaction. The language is one of the important keys to understanding and appreciating the rich culture and personality of the people. It turns stifling English-ghetto living into an intellectual adventure.

Okay, you are convinced. What's the best way to learn a language? This depends upon the time you can devote and the money you can spend. Experts in the field say there are some general principles of which to be aware:

Try to start before you leave home. There are so many other demands when you are getting settled abroad.

Speaking is the first priority.

Take lessons from someone who is native to the language and who knows from personal experience what it takes to learn a second language.

An academic background in any other language will be helpful.

Mechanical aids, tapes, and records are helpful—but as adjuncts only.

Foreign language films and videotapes are helpful, if you can ignore subtitles.

There are a number of places offering language training: private tutors, evening or adult education classes in high schools or community colleges, formal language schools such as Berlitz, summer language institutes held at universities around the country, classes in religious institutions (such as Hebrew), and cultural institutes of the country in the United States. You can go all out with a "total immersion" course (hours and days of nothing but the language from several different teachers) or a less stringent commitment. Your company or organization may have its own program. A couple of places to check for programs are the Modern Language Association (62 Fifth Avenue, New York, New York 10011; telephone [212] 741-5592) and the nearest embassy, consulate, or tourist office of the country.

There are also several mechanical aids to supplement your classes on the market. Almost any record and bookstore will have a foreign language section. The Foreign Service Institute of the State Department sells some of its material through the Government Printing Office in Washington. An excellent resource is videotape—valuable because it can show the nonverbal body language as well.

Sophisticated electronics has permitted the development of hand calculator-size translators. After selecting key phrases by code number or spelling out words in English on the keyboard, a video readout of the equivalent foreign words appears. By changing small modules, the user has the choice of translations in several languages. At least one manufacturer is working on the next step—the addition of a voice, albeit mechanical, to pronounce the words.

These are fun gimmicks that can help break the tedium of learning a new language. But so far, automation has not replaced personal memorization of cases, declensions, and irregular verbs.

# PART FOUR
# Legal Matters

# 11

# Keep It Legal

## Know Your Rights and Obligations

WHEN YOU ARE ASSIGNED OVERSEAS, you will no doubt be provided with a letter, job description, or formal contract describing the new position and the terms of your transfer. This document is basic, so be sure that you understand every statement and nuance.

There are many other sources for matters that will govern or affect your new position and your life abroad. Written company personnel policies for international transfers should be read, understood, and even incorporated specifically into the document that covers your move. Do not rely on someone's characterization of what they provide—analyze them yourself. If there are points that are not covered that might apply to your situation, you should discuss them. Often, certain matters are discretionary with higher management. Try to get a reading on your management's attitude if any of these might crop up. Create scenarios and see how your company policies deal with them.

It's a truism to say that understanding your new position is essential, but this is still worth emphasizing. In addition to studying the job description or its equivalent, check to see if there are any restrictions or qualifications in the law of your new foreign country. There will be restrictions if you are a director or officer of a foreign subsidiary (see below). The practice of a profession often involves regulation and limitation.

Know the philosophy of your company or organization in doing business overseas. What does it think about "grease payments" (low-level payments to get someone to do his job faster or better), sales to Eastern Europe, high or low profile for its expatriates? Get a briefing from your company lawyers on U.S. laws with which you should be familiar. There are many laws applicable only to specific business situations or pursuits, but a few are likely to apply to anyone doing business abroad:

*The Foreign Corrupt Practices Act.* This act establishes standards for proper accounting and forbids certain bribes or other corrupt payments overseas.

*The export control regulations of the Department of Commerce.* These regulations govern the export of U.S. products and technology and establish rules for dealing with foreign boycotts such as the Arab boycott.

*Antitrust laws, especially the Sherman Act.* These laws prohibit monopolies, cartels, and certain unfair trade practices if U.S. commerce is affected.

*Tax laws.* Tax laws apply that relate to foreign transactions such as intercompany pricing.

*Equal opportunity laws.* U.S. civil rights statutes are being applied to international employment policies.

Before you leave the States, you should know about certain areas of the law in your new country that will apply to you, once you set foot inside its boundries. This can save you a lot of grief during the first days after arrival. You should research:

Visas, permits, and other entry documents for the family and any pets;

Foreign exchange regulations controlling the amount and type of currency you can take into the country;

Customs regulations with respect to articles prohibited from entry or allowed only with special documentation (firearms), dutiable and nondutiable personal effects, procedures and documents for unaccompanied baggage, and automobiles, if you bring one; and

Registration requirements after arrival.

Chapters that deal with specific locations provide much of this information. Nevertheless, it is advisable to check on the latest regulations with consulates, tourist offices, the U.S. State Department, or travel agents.

Both from a business and personal standpoint, some advance familiarity with the governmental and legal structure of your new country is worthwhile. Try to find time to look into:

Government organization
Political parties and leading politicians and leaders
The legal system: courts, attorneys, how justice is administered,
    particularly for expatriates
Banking, finance, and foreign exchange
Taxes: types, amounts, procedures
Accounting systems and practices
Trade associations
Labor laws
Internal travel restrictions
Law enforcement: the police, civil rights, practices

## Local Counsel

When you consider that you and your family are moving to a place where your business, home life, and everything you may do is governed by a different system of law and regulations, you can imagine that a local lawyer may play an important role in your life abroad.

If your company has a connection with local counsel in your new location, get to know him as soon as possible. He will be valuable in assisting you with any personal problems as well as business matters. Check with your internal company counsel for guidelines for utilizing foreign counsel for personal issues. What are his strengths and weaknesses? Does your company assume any of these fees? What is the billing rate?

There are several sources to aid you in finding local counsel if you do not have one.

Most public and certainly all law libraries will have the *Martindale-Hubbell Law Directory,* revised annually. It includes the names of lawyers or firms in most countries of the world who wish to indicate—by being listed in this publication—their interest and expertise in representing foreign clients. Usually, this book will list the leading international lawyers of any country.

A law library will have one or more specialized directories of foreign lawyers.

Many of the larger U.S. firms have offices or associated counsel in the larger world cities. *Martindale-Hubbell* will indicate this in its listings.

U.S. embassies customarily issue a list of lawyers and can provide some assistance in selection—short of an absolute recommendation.

You can check with local subsidiaries of U.S. banks or other well-established companies for the counsel they use.

Other expatriates may be your quickest and best source.

A few tips for dealing with local counsel are:

Get his home phone number right away. Emergencies have a way of happening after office hours.

Don't be too hesitant in getting help. Many people are reluctant to resort to legal proceedings; but in another country, with a different legal system, a delay in seeking advice may be costly.

If the matter could involve your business, or your relationship to your company, it is a good idea to use someone other than the company's local counsel to avoid embarrassing conflict-of-interest questions.

Don't expect counsel in another country to be very knowledgeable about U.S. laws—particularly the more complex areas like tax and estate planning. Even overseas U.S. lawyers may be out of touch to some extent.

Legal languages vary, so be careful that communication is accurate. One U.S. lawyer tells the story about writing to his counterpart abroad with a request that a deposition be taken of one of the important parties in a pending action. "Please depose the Minister of the Interior," he wrote. The foreign lawyer replied, shocked, "I will never be a party to putting the Minister out of office."

In every country you will find some differences in the legal profession. Knowing these will help you to understand the reaction of your foreign lawyer to a particular matter.

For the most part, present and former Commonwealth countries inherited their legal system from England, as we did. Still, there are local peculiarities. Literature and television have depicted the distinction between barristers and solicitors. And who is not familiar with the somber gowns and silver wigs that lend style and decorum to the courts of these countries? To dispel any remaining confusion, the barrister is the trial attorney and is the only one who can represent a client before the higher courts. The solicitor resembles a U.S. lawyer, working from an office and handling contracts and other matters not likely to involve litigation. But when a matter winds toward the court, the solicitor will brief the barrister. Very distinguished members of the legal profession will be designated "Queen's Counsel" (QC) and are sought after for particularly complex or important matters. If you are involved in an action with a QC on the other side, you had best get your own QC.

Much more different are the civil law countries. As a rule, lawyers are not as important in the general scheme of things, because the law does not depend so much on how the legal profession interprets law through deciding cases as on what is written in the statutes and regulations. Lawyers are not used in commercial transactions to the extent they are in the United States. Large firms and specialists are virtually unknown, although there is a slowly growing trend in this direction. Litigation is avoided and arbitration more common.

## Documents to Take

The volume of papers that an individual acquires and must maintain today keeps growing. Many of them will have to be taken when you go abroad. Here is a check list of the most important ones:

Birth certificates
Naturalization papers
Marriage license and divorce papers
Adoption records
Children's school records and test scores
Medical records (doctors, hospitals, prescriptions), dental charts and X-rays, and glasses prescriptions
Veterinary records
Tax records and supporting documents for the past year—and perhaps one previous year
Registration, title, and sales documents for any vehicle
U.S. customs registration papers to prove items are of U.S. origin and not purchased abroad
Inventories of: accompanied baggage, unaccompanied air freight, ocean shipment, and articles in storage

Insurance policies

Certificates of good standing from your local police: these are
    letters from your local police stating that you have not been
    convicted of a felony, are not currently charged with any
    violation, and are otherwise free to leave their jurisdiction.
    Often you will be required to submit such a certificate to
    obtain a visa

Any warranty document still in effect—be sure to check whether
    the manufacturer has a representative in the country who will
    honor the warranty

A supply of blank checks for any U.S. account; you will have to
    decide whether to have a U.S. address, a foreign address, or
    no address at all

Some documents can be taken with you or left behind, depending on your circumstances:

Stock certificates or bonds

Company stock option documents

Deed and other papers on your house or other real estate

Real estate tax records

Lease agreements

Installment purchase agreements

Older income tax records

Someone should have access to the documents you leave at
home. If they are kept in a safety deposit box, you can arrange with
the bank to give that person entry.

Two questions arise. The first is which documents should you
take with you, and which can be shipped with your other luggage
and personal effects? Second, should you bring originals or copies?

You should, of course, carry with you all those documents you
will need to enter the country. Remember that there can be a wait of
several weeks, perhaps even months, for your unaccompanied baggage to arrive and be delivered to your new residence. Then add a
safety margin in your mind for such things as customs problems and
dock strikes. Valuable documents should be hand carried. Documents that are shipped with furniture are subject to pilferage or
destruction (from moisture and even fire). To be extra cautious, leave
a copy in the United States of original documents you take with you.

This introduces the second question of originals versus copies.
There are a few documents—such as a will—that have legal value
only as originals. Copies would only be valuable for your own
information. Another group is those papers that will be required

officially in some matter before a government agency or court. For these you need true copies, notarized as such and then legalized by the consulate of the host country in the U.S. jurisdiction where the document is prepared. Legalization is a relatively easy two-step procedure. First, the county clerk, or a similar officer, attests to the validity of the notary's signature. Then, the consular officer acknowledges the document by stamping it or attaching a certificate. The cost is usually under $10.

## Estate Planning

Your move might just be the time to give some extra thought to your financial planning situation. Why? Because if you don't:

Someone who dies without a will in a foreign country runs the risk of extra expense and of having some of the assets disposed of under the laws of that foreign jurisdiction; this may create an exposure to estate or inheritance taxes in the foreign country;

The rules on distribution of the deceased's estate under the laws for intestate succession may not transfer property the way the deceased intended; and

If legal action is necessary for control over the estate, the assets may be tied up for years.

At the very least, then, your will should be reviewed, or prepared, if you have not previously done so. It is better if the new will, or codicil to the old one, is prepared and signed in the state where you will maintain your residence and where you will want the estate to be probated. If it is necessary to do this abroad, do it before a U.S. consular official.

Utilize the resources of your lawyer, accountant, insurance agent, and banker to help you plan a program that will take into account your move abroad and all that entails.

## Power of Attorney

To enable someone to sign documents or to handle any other business or legal matter on your behalf, you can give that person power of attorney, appointing him your attorney-in-fact. This is worthwhile in case of an emergency, even though you do not foresee any need. A power of attorney is particularly advisable if you have family members left at home. For example, someone should have the authority to okay emergency medical treatment for children remaining in school in the United States.

A power can be as wide or as narrow in scope as you desire—in other words, tailored exactly to your needs. The only problem could be the transfer of real estate. Other parties may object to a deed executed by an attorney-in-fact rather than by the owner; but usually this can be worked out in advance of sale.

## Banking

You will find it convenient to keep a checking account in the United States. In fact, you might consider retaining an account where you have been banking or establishing one in a United States bank with a branch in your new location. It is advisable to have someone in the United States as an authorized signatory on your accounts.

For many reasons, not the least of which are tax and foreign exchange considerations in your new location, you may want funds coming to you from U.S. sources deposited in your U.S. account. Please note, however, that mere deposit in the United States may not relieve you from the legal obligation to declare that income in your foreign country or even to remit the funds to it. This is one subject that should be clarified and understood completely before your departure.

Because of the vagaries of mail delivery in some countries, and the possibility in a few of inspection of mail from abroad, you may wish to have payments of certain debts made from your U.S. account. Both U.S. and foreign banks are beginning to offer the service of making payments of mortgage fees, utility bills, and other routine periodic payments. This service is particularly useful for expatriates. If the bank cannot do this, someone else with signing authority could receive and pay those bills. This will ensure prompt payment without having the transactions go through the mails or foreign exchange procedures of your new location.

You can have bank statements sent to you or to someone in the United States, depending upon your particular needs.

## Can You Be Sued?

Do not kid yourself that going abroad will insulate you from that nasty lawsuit someone may be planning to bring against you. If you have kept your residence in a particular state or jurisdiction in the

United States, most courts provide that process can be served on you by sending the papers to your residence or to someone who may be your agent. This is considered as lawful as if you were served personally by the sheriff. Someone should be checking your mail if a lawsuit is a possibility.

In most states, even though you have terminated your residence, you may still be sued and the papers validly served. The so-called long-arm statutes give a court jurisdiction over you if you have any property, if you are doing business, or if you have some other "minimum contact" with the area the court covers. Either you are served by publication (meaning that the appropriate legal document or notice is printed in a local newspaper for a specified time), or a letter is sent to your current foreign address.

## Residence

Your legal residence is important in many other aspects of life besides the jurisdiction of the courts. Some of the areas in which residency plays an important role are:

U.S. and foreign tax liability
Voting
Certain company benefits (your residence is the place from and to which your company will transport you)
Probate of estate
Eligibility for public office
Eligibility and tuition for schools and universities
Ability to remain qualified in certain professions

An assignment abroad will not change the residence you had before you left, no matter how long the stay overseas, if you have an intent to return ultimately to that residence and if you take no overt actions to change your residence. Note that some statutes in the United States do take into account actual physical presence—such as our tax laws. Any change in residence requires a physical presence in the new location and an intent to adopt it as the new home.

Under U.S. law you can have only one residence, although a husband and wife may maintain separate residences under certain circumstances. Also, U.S. law recognizes that citizens may acquire residence in another country without the necessity of becoming naturalized in the foreign country. The presumption is, however, that a person in a foreign country intends to keep his residence in his own country.

If you abandon your old residence (for example, sell your house) and have no intent to return—that is, you intend to reside in the foreign country, which is evidenced by some overt action or written statement—you probably have lost your U.S. residence. What actions indicate the intent to reside are questions of fact (that is, the facts or circumstances of a matter as distinguished from the law applicable to those facts).

It is possible to retain your U.S. residence under U.S. law but also to be considered a resident in another country under its laws. You may, for example, meet residence requirements of a foreign country for purposes of marriage or divorce. But the act of marrying or divorcing does not mean that you have relinquished your U.S. residency.

## Responsibilities of Officers and Directors

In corporate life a transfer overseas can mean assuming a position as an officer or director of your company's subsidiary. If this is your first exposure to formal corporate management, you should be aware that regardless of your responsibilities with your company you do assume some personal obligations, and even liability, in some countries by virtue of your new title. You are in a different position from your counterpart who may serve as a director from his office in the United States. You are right there in the country, subject to its laws. If you sign a false company tax return, there is a customs violation; if certain reports are not filed on time with government agencies, you could be subject to a fine, or your departure from the country might be delayed, or you might be prohibited from reentering in the future.

Do not be unduly alarmed about such possibilities. Expatriates have rarely been placed in active personal jeopardy. Just be aware of the responsibility—and act accordingly.

# 12

# You and the IRS

ANY FACTORS ARE INVOLVED in a decision to accept an overseas assignment. A significant and costly factor is the total worldwide taxes the expatriate will have to pay. This is especially true for U.S. citizens living or working abroad because their country is one of the few that taxes its citizens on their worldwide income while they are not in residence. Almost every country bases its taxes upon residency. For example, a French citizen is subject to French income tax laws while residing in France, but has no liability for French income tax after the last day of residency in France. However, if a U.S. citizen becomes an expatriate, he continues to be liable for U.S. income tax payments even though foreign income tax must also be paid. This is true whether compensation is paid in the United States or in the foreign country, in U.S. currency or in foreign currency, or by the U.S. employer or by the foreign employer.

Furthermore, the United States, as well as most foreign countries, requires that allowances such as housing, cost-of-living premiums, home leave, and the like be included in taxable income.

At first it might seem that combined U.S. and foreign income tax rates could easily reach 100 percent of income for a U.S. citizen working abroad. Of course, this is not the case. Rather, U.S. tax law contains several provisions designed to relieve or possibly eliminate double taxation. In addition, many foreign tax laws contain provi-

---

This chapter was written by John C. Staley and Robin Bowes of Arthur Young & Company.

sions that reduce income tax burdens and induce qualified expatriate labor and technical expertise to enter their countries. These foreign incentives vary from outright exemptions from tax to special deductions for "temporary" residents to modified rules during the first several years of residency in the foreign country.

## What Special U.S. Tax Rules Apply to Expatriates?

It should be understood that the U.S. tax rules governing expatriates are, in most cases, the identical rules that apply to citizens in the United States. For example, compensation, dividend and interest income, and capital gains and losses are taxed by the United States whether an individual is living abroad or at home.

However, expatriates are also subject to several special U.S. tax rules. In 1981 Congress, for the third time in five years, completely revised these provisions. The major changes include restoration of a foreign earned income exclusion, adoption of a housing exclusion, and elimination of the package of special deductions for living abroad. This new law is effective for tax years beginning after December 31, 1981. The provisions are quite complicated and in some cases provide for alternatives. The intention here is to provide only a general overview.

Simply stated, if the expatriate meets what is called a bona fide residence or physical presence test and has foreign earned income, he will then be entitled to elect to exclude certain amounts of foreign earned income.

### The First Requirement: Meeting the Residence Test

The expatriate must meet one of two tests to satisfy the first requirement.

The *bona fide residence test* requires that the expatriate be a bona fide resident of a foreign country or countries for an uninterrupted period that includes an entire calendar year. This is a subjective question regarding intent to reside in the foreign country, and intent is determined by all the facts and circumstances in each individual's situation. Some residence criteria are:

> What type of living quarters were occupied (hotel, rented quarters, purchased quarters, and the like)?
> How long during the year did the expatriate's family reside abroad?

Did the individual pay foreign taxes?

What were the conditions or limitations concerning the employment agreement and the type and term of visa?

Did the expatriate maintain a home in the United States? If so, what were the rental status and the tenant's relationship to the taxpayer?

The alternative test is the *physical presence test*. It requires that the expatriate be physically present in a foreign country or countries for 330 full days during any consecutive 12-month period. In contrast to the bona fide residence test, this test is purely objective. It requires only a specific number of qualifying days in a foreign country or countries. There is no reference to the expatriate's intentions regarding permanence or any of the other facts that determine bona fide residence qualification. A *qualifying day* means physical presence in a foreign country for a 24-hour period commencing at midnight.

## The Second Requirement: Source of Income

The expatriate must have *earned income* from foreign sources, which is defined as income received for the performance of personal services outside the United States in whatever form provided, be it salary, wages, overseas incentive premiums, moving expense reimbursements, housing allowance, home leave allowance, or other benefits.

## Earned Income Exclusion

Individuals who qualify under the bona fide foreign residence or physical presence test may elect to exclude in 1982 up to $75,000 of foreign earned income—that is, salary, bonuses, and the like. This exclusion increases by $5,000 annually until it reaches $95,000 in 1986.

## Housing Cost Amount

Such individuals would also qualify for an exclusion or deduction of reasonable housing costs in excess of $6,350 for 1982 (16 percent of the salary of a U.S. government employee, GS-14, Step 1). Housing costs attributable to amounts provided by an employer are excluded from income. Housing costs not attributable to an employer are deductible. Interest and real estate taxes are allowable as itemized deductions and are excluded from housing costs.

## Limitation on Total Earned Income Exclusion and Housing Cost Amount

The total of both items cannot exceed the foreign earned income of the individual. Housing costs not attributable to an employer—to the extent not deductible owing to this limitation—may be carried forward to the next taxable year and deducted, subject to the limitation in the next year. For example, an employee who qualifies as a bona fide resident works in a foreign country all of 1982 and receives the following compensation:

|  |  | Compensation (dollars) |
|---|---|---|
| Salary and other allowances | | 100,000 |
| Housing cost reimbursement | | 12,000 |
| Total compensation | | 112,000 |
| Less: | | |
| Earned income exclusion | 75,000 | |
| plus | | |
| Actual housing cost amount | | |
| (15,000 less 6,350) | 8,650 | (83,650) |
| Taxable compensation income | | 28,350 |

## Liberalized Camp Provisions

The provision in the pre-1982 law that certain foreign camps are considered part of the employer's business premises for purposes of excluding from income the value of employer-provided meals and lodging has been liberalized. Such camps will no longer have to be located in a hardship area or constitute substandard lodging. Expatriates living in camps are entitled to exclude their meals and lodging fully with or without electing the new earned income exclusion.

## Impact of Exclusion on Other Income

Taxable income remaining after the exclusion is subject to tax at the applicable income tax rate. Therefore, the earned income exclusion can have the effect of reducing the tax rates applicable to investment and long-term capital gain income.

## *Election of Exclusions*

The foreign earned income and housing exclusions are separately elective. This flexibility is provided because in certain circumstances the U.S. tax will be lower where excludable income is subject to tax and expenses and foreign tax credits can be claimed in their entirety.

Once made, an exclusion election remains in effect for future years. Expatriates may revoke an exclusion election at any time but may not reelect for five years without consent of the Internal Revenue Service.

## *The Foreign Tax Credit*

The foreign tax credit applies not only to expatriates but also to U.S. residents. However, it can offer significant tax relief to expatriates. The underlying concept is that U.S. taxpayers may elect to claim foreign income taxes paid as a direct credit against their U.S. tax on foreign source income subject to various limitations and special rules.

Entire books are devoted solely to the technical aspects of the foreign tax credit. Some of the more significant considerations are:

Only foreign income taxes qualify as a credit. Thus, foreign customs duties and value-added taxes are not creditable (nor are they deductible).

Qualifying taxes paid or accrued during the year may either be claimed as a credit or as an itemized deduction for the year. (It is normally more advantageous to utilize such taxes as a direct credit against the U.S. tax.)

The foreign tax credit is subject to a limitation. It limits the credit to the portion of the U.S. tax on income earned overseas. The formula used to determine the limitation is:

Foreign Source Taxable Income ÷ Total Taxable Income before Exemptions × U.S. Income Tax before Credits = Foreign Tax Credit Limitation

Note from the limitation formula that the numerator is only foreign source income: thus, U.S. tax cannot be completely offset unless virtually all income in the year was from foreign sources. When the limitation restricts use of some foreign income taxes as credits in a tax year, the excess may by carried back for two tax years or carried forward for five tax years.

## Moving Expenses

Expatriates, like other U.S. citizens, may claim a deduction for moving expenses associated with job relocation. To qualify, the relocation must meet specific requirements as to distance and duration of employment. Some moving expenses are deductible without limitation, while others are subject to statutory dollar limits. It should be remembered that all employer-paid moving expenses and reimbursements are income to the employee.

## Table 2

### Dollar Limitations on Moving Expenses—Here and Abroad (dollars)

| Expense | Move to or in the United States | Move to Foreign Country |
|---|---|---|
| a. Shipment of household goods and transportation of self and family | No limit | No limit |
| b. Storage of personal effects | Not deductible | No limit while abroad |
| c. Premove house-hunting trip and temporary living expenses at new location before permanent quarters are ready | $1,500 within a 30-day period | $4,500 within a 90-day period |
| d. Incidental expenses for sale, purchase, or lease of quarters at new or old location | $3,000 less lower of amount or limit used in "c." | $6,000 less lower of amount or limit used in "c." |

As demonstrated in Table 2, the dollar limitations are generally more liberal for moves to a foreign country than for moves to or within the United States.

### Expenses and Foreign Taxes Attributable to Excluded Amounts

It should be noted that expenses—including moving expenses—and foreign tax credits attributable to excluded amounts will not be deductible or creditable. Therefore, a disallowance or scale-down computation of these amounts must be prepared.

## Sale of Personal Residence

Any U.S. taxpayer who sells a principal residence at a gain may defer paying tax on the gain if the proceeds are reinvested in a replacement principal residence within two years.

The typical expatriate would not benefit from this provision because the foreign assignment would probably end after the reinvestment period. Therefore, for expatriates the reinvestment period is suspended while the expatriate is overseas. However, the total period before reinvestment may not exceed four years from the sale date of the U.S. residence.

## State Income Taxes

Whether an expatriate will owe state income taxes while overseas depends upon the tax rules of the state in which the expatriate is resident prior to transfer. Some states do not tax expatriates during their foreign assignment (except for certain rental income and the like derived from within the state). Other states tax expatriates as full-year residents in the year of transfer; others maintain that expatriates are taxable as residents even during years abroad.

## Reimbursement of Income Taxes by the Employer

Expatriates find that overseas gross income bears little relationship to at-home gross income, principally because they are receiving various overseas allowances, premiums, and reimbursements from the employer under an expatriate compensation policy. Likewise, many find that overall income tax burdens (both U.S. and foreign) are substantially in excess of at-home burdens. *At-home tax* is the U.S. tax the expatriate would have paid on income (without the overseas allowances) had he remained in the United States.

Many employers reimburse the expatriate to compensate for additional taxes resulting from an overseas assignment. The amount of reimbursement will depend on the employer's reimbursement policy: laissez-faire, tax protection, or tax equalization.

The laissez-faire approach is the easiest to understand. It simply provides that the total taxes imposed on the expatriate are solely the expatriate's burden. In most cases, it is the least desirable from an employee's perspective. For example, the cost-of-living allowance compensating the expatriate for excess living costs at the foreign post may be largely consumed by U.S. and foreign income taxes because the cost-of-living allowance is taxed as additional income. Therefore, it is not compensatory as was intended.

Under a tax protection plan, the employer reimburses the expatriate to the extent foreign and U.S. income taxes on all income for the year (including allowances, reimbursements, and the like) exceed the at-home tax. However, if the combined U.S. and foreign taxes are less than the at-home tax, the expatriate retains the difference—it is not returned to the employer. Thus, the expatriate may gain if actual taxes are lower than the at-home tax and is protected if actual taxes are higher than the at-home tax. As one can imagine, a tax protection plan is favored by expatriates. In low effective tax rate situations, it means they might have a hidden bonus to the extent that actual taxes are less than their at-home tax.

With a tax equalization plan, the expatriate will neither gain nor lose with regard to taxes. The employer reimburses the expatriate to the extent foreign and U.S. income taxes on all income for the year exceed the at-home tax. However, if the combined U.S. and foreign taxes are less than the at-home tax, the expatriate returns the difference to the employer. Thus, under tax equalization the expatriate always bears a tax cost equal to the at-home tax.

Calculating the at-home tax is important in determining whether an expatriate should receive a reimbursement. Many variables are considered in determining an at-home tax, and each employer's reimbursement policy differs. Some of the variables are the following:

Does the at-home tax calculation include the tax attributable to personal income such as interest, dividends, capital gains, and the like? Stated another way, does the policy provide for reimbursement on nonemployer-source income?

What amount will be assumed for itemized deductions? When an individual becomes an expatriate, itemized deductions usually decrease; for example, U.S. sales taxes paid were deductible while living in the United States, but foreign sales taxes are not deductible for the expatriate. Because the at-home tax should represent the amount of tax the individual would have paid if he stayed home, itemized deductions are a percentage—usually 12 to 22 percent of base income when a company calculates the at-home tax.

Are U.S. state income taxes considered? If not, the expatriate will benefit by the amount of state income taxes previously paid while home but not paid while living abroad.

### How Do These Reimbursement Policies Apply?

As an illustration we present an example employing these assumptions. An expatriate is employed in country X in 1982. He is married and has two dependent children (exemptions are $4,000). His base salary is $55,000, and his miscellaneous income is $1,300. He receives $30,000 for foreign allowances and reimbursements.

The company policy is that the at-home tax is calculated on base salary (excluding allowances) and personal income (the two totaling $56,300). Itemized deductions will be 16 percent of base salary and personal income, or $9,008 reduced by the $3,400 zero-bracket amount.

Given these facts, the calculation of the at-home tax using 1982 rates would be:

|  | Amount (dollars) |
|---|---|
| Base salary | 55,000 |
| Personal income | 1,300 |
| Total income | 56,300 |
| Itemized deductions (16 percent) | (9,008) |
| Zero-bracket amount | 3,400 |
| Exemptions | (4,000) |
| Taxable income | 46,692 |
| 1982 at-home tax (rounded) | 11,850 |

Assume the expatriate is residing in a low-tax country and pays combined actual U.S. and foreign income taxes of $11,000. (See Table 3.) Under laissez-faire, the at-home tax is not considered; therefore, the expatriate benefits because actual taxes are less than U.S. taxes would have been. Under tax protection, the actual taxes are less than the at-home tax, and the expatriate also benefits by the difference. Such benefits are sometimes referred to as a "disguised bonus." However, under tax equalization the expatriate would repay the employer for the amount by which the actual taxes are less than the at-home tax.

## Table 3

### *Actual Taxes Lower Than At-Home Taxes*

|  | Laissez-faire | Tax Protection | Tax Equalization |
|---|---|---|---|
| Salary | 55,000 | 55,000 | 55,000 |
| Allowances | 30,000 | 30,000 | 30,000 |
| Interest income | 1,300 | 1,300 | 1,300 |
| Gross income | 86,300 | 86,300 | 86,300 |
| Actual U.S. and foreign taxes | 11,000 | 11,000 | 11,000 |
| Less at-home tax | n.a. | (11,850) | (11,850) |
| Reimbursement to employer | None | None | (850) |
| Expatriate net income* | 75,300 | 75,300 | 74,450 |

*Gross income less actual taxes and reimbursement to the employer.
n.a. = not applicable

## Table 4

### *Actual Taxes Higher Than At-Home Taxes*

|  | Laissez-faire | Tax Protection | Tax Equalization |
|---|---|---|---|
| Salary | 55,000 | 55,000 | 55,000 |
| Allowances | 30,000 | 30,000 | 30,000 |
| Interest income | 1,300 | 1,300 | 1,300 |
| Gross income | 86,300 | 86,300 | 86,300 |
| Actual taxes | 20,000 | 20,000 | 20,000 |
| Less at-home tax | n.a. | (11,850) | (11,850) |
| Reimbursement to expatriate | None | 8,150 | 8,150 |
| Expatriate net income* | 66,300 | 74,450 | 74,450 |

*Gross income less actual taxes plus reimbursement to the expatriate.
n.a. = not available

Next, assume instead that the expatriate is residing in a higher-tax country and that the combined actual U.S. and foreign income taxes of $20,000 exceed the calculated at-home tax. (See Table 4.) Under laissez-faire, the expatriate pays all taxes. On the other hand, under both the tax protection and tax equalization policies, the expatriate would be reimbursed by the employer for the amount by which actual taxes exceeded the at-home tax. Under many tax equalization policies, the employer accomplishes the reimbursement by reducing base salary by the at-home tax and then paying all actual taxes.

## What Does This Mean to the Expatriate?

The U.S. and foreign income tax rules will have a significant effect on the expatriate's net overseas earnings. To understand their implications is not enough. Their real impact on compensation can be determined only within the framework of the employer's tax reimbursement policy. It is unlikely that a particular company's policy will be exactly as assumed in our examples.

In view of the complexities of the tax laws, the differing circumstances of each expatriate, and the variety of employer tax reimbursement techniques, each expatriate should review the particulars of an overseas assignment with a tax adviser.

PART FIVE

# Departure and Readjustment

# 13

# Coming Home

COMING HOME—a major event in the life of every expatriate—should be a joyful occasion. Lest you feel that your life abroad and your return to your home country is one continuous stream of problems, put your mind at ease. The major setbacks, culture shock and its counterpart, reverse culture shock, can be overcome. The key lies in knowing what to expect, and planning ahead either to accept or circumvent these obstacles to a happy life abroad and a happy return when your overseas duty is complete.

## Long-Range Planning

According to those who have traveled the return road, reverse culture shock can be more acute than the initial adjustment to an overseas location. Expatriates expect culture shock as they move from country to country abroad; and the more experienced feel that their extended service qualifies them to accept, and to fit into, the new way of life in a host country. But most expatriates are unprepared for the culture shock that awaits them when they finally return home. What most of them do not envision are the changes that have taken place in their homeland—changes certain to affect their own life-styles—since their expatriation.

Anticipating the problems you may face upon return should rate equally with understanding the problems you may face in a new culture. This may not seem important when you are in the midst of planning, purchasing, and packing for a move abroad, but this *is* the time to give thought to the future. Some important questions to ask yourself are:

*Breadwinner's Probable Return Assignment.* Will it be with the same corporation, missionary group, or institution of learning for which you now work? If the overseas assignment is for a specific position, will a return mean obtaining a new job with a new employer, perhaps in a new location? Will a return involve retirement?

*Probable Place of Return.* If you are returning to the same area, will your present home accommodate your family? If you have been assured that your return will be to another area, or you plan to retire on your return, should you consider selling your present home and buying one in the area of reassignment or retirement so as to stay current with the inflationary trends there?

*Probable Return Date.* Will the length of your overseas stay influence a decision to close up a house and leave it vacant, or to seek an interim renter, to lease it on a long-term basis, or to sell it? Will it influence the decision of a career woman to ask for a leave of absence or to resign, or the decision of a college student to take a year off to accompany the parents abroad, or to attend an overseas university on a temporary basis?

*Spouse's Probable Career Plans.* Will it be possible to return to the same or a similar job with the same employer? If this is not an option, it may be worthwhile to interview other potential employers or to make personal contact with successful employment agencies. Such a tactic may get your foot in the door and your résumé in the files; with a little luck it may even land you a job on your return.

*Probable School Plans.* If you have children who will be entering college while you are abroad or immediately following your return, or if you intend to return for additional education yourself, you should ascertain admittance requirements so that they can be complied with during your absence.

### Setting Financial Goals

Once the initial problems associated with an overseas move are solved, and you are comfortable in a new culture, life can be almost idyllic. There are new sights to see and new pleasures to explore. A return to the United States, however, is inevitable. Financial goals should be made with that in mind, but living costs are high and there are countless unexpected expenses. Some expatriates posted to "choice locations" find a steady stream of friends and relatives moving through their homes. A couple posted in London commented that they could have sent a child to college for what it had cost to feed and entertain stateside visitors.

The essence of financial planning is setting goals. Whether it is a college education for the children, a larger home on your return, investments, a retirement nest egg, or money for travel while you are abroad—these should be goals upon which you all agree, and toward which the whole family is willing to work. The underlying theme here is commitment and purpose. Without it you may face the same problems as a young couple who were recently repatriated to the Los Angeles area:

> Our three years abroad were marvelous. We simply threw our budget out the window and spent what we wanted on what we wanted. We traveled extensively, and we loved trying out all the different ethnic foods and attending theater and opera in each country. But . . . this didn't prepare us for a return to the United States. We had sold our small starter cottage when we were transferred because we thought we would like to come back to something larger. With the median price of housing standing at well above $100,000 in the Los Angeles area, we soon determined that we not only couldn't afford a larger house, we couldn't afford a house. And, even with our European conditioning, we found rents to be exorbitant. Talk about the ravages of the damned—we suffered it all—dismay, disappointment, disillusionment, frustration, panic! We loved our "time out," but looking back, we wish we had handled it differently.

The comment so often heard among the recently repatriated sums up the situation: "Why didn't someone tell us?"

## The Investment Future

One of the things that hits hardest at expatriates is their inability to stay current with the inflationary spiral in the United States. Real property, in the form of single-family dwellings, has probably taken the most significant increase of any commodity in the past few years. Unless the expatriate stayed in the real estate market, he can expect to buy back at a very dear price. The $5^3/4$ percent government loans to veterans, and the $6^1/4$ percent conventional housing loans of the

1960s, had been replaced by 12 to 13 percent loans by the end of the 1970s, and by 13 to 16 percent loans in the early 1980s. An expatriate who sold property with a 5¼ percent loan on it in 1970 found that it had doubled in price in three years. By the time he was transferred back to the States in 1982, it had quadrupled in price; and the country club membership he had sold for $3,000 was going for $11,000, with a year's dues to be paid in advance.

Problems precipitated by inflated prices have become so acute for returning expatriates that many international companies have set up property management programs. They have suggested to overseas employees that if they have not kept, or do not wish to keep, their residential property, that they invest in other income-producing property that will stay current with the inflationary trends and allow them to reenter the home market on their return.

Some expatriates have purchased recreational property, but others have bought apartment units, condominiums, business offices, residential lots, or ranch and farm land. Some have chosen to go into collectibles and have become expert in antiques, oriental carpets, rare books, coins, prints, or other memorabilia. Others have done very well in the gold and silver futures, and in purchasing precious and semiprecious gems.

Financial counselors advise that the crux of the matter lies with the development of a financial planning program based on projected cash flow and future tax liabilities. Its effectiveness lies in its early implementation. When one returns is too late to make the investments that will help to hedge against the inflationary spiral.

## Deciding to Return

While some people go overseas for two to three years and others go for the duration of a project, some people "hire on" for an indefinite period of time. As consultants to governments, as independent agents, or as manufacturers' representatives, such individuals may be posted abroad until they decide it is time to go home; just when that is may come without warning. A chance remark or event may remind them of how much they miss home; and a decision to return may slowly begin to build. There may be discontent with their present job or its future, or there may be concern about children or the unhappiness of a spouse.

For some expatriates the time to return comes when adult children marry and start families of their own. Missing out on this stage of their children's lives or the lives of their grandchildren can push an overseas assignment from the positive side to the negative side of the ledger.

> Our daughter and her husband were traveling in the Colorado Rockies when an approaching car suddenly slid into the car ahead of them, knocking it into the ravine far below. When they called us later—in shock and almost hysterical, the phone connection was so bad the sound kept coming and going. We could hardly understand each other. It was then that we decided to request early retirement. We realized that we could not minister to our children half a world away.

If you should find yourself in this position, do check your underlying thinking for less obvious motives—whatever the verbalized reason. Are there concerns, uncertainties, insecurities that can be worked through to allow your original enthusiasm for the job and the host country to surface? If you cannot rekindle your interest, at least _move slowly_.

Investigate the job market and the possibilities for a position in your field of expertise. Consider modifications based on your overseas experience and changed career interests. If living abroad has altered your concept of what you would like to do with your life, where you want to live, or how you want to spend your spare time, examine new alternatives.

Expatriates who have abruptly terminated overseas jobs suggest that individuals in this situation delay a decision to quit until they have had an opportunity to make a trip home to test the waters personally. Some expatriates who have resigned in haste have taken up to 18 months to find another suitable position, and have used up much of their overseas savings in the process. All too often, there are other problems.

## Changes in Life-style

The term _culture shock_ has been used to describe the difficulty in adapting to an unfamiliar or changed culture. Perhaps more than any other single thing, reverse culture shock signals the inability to adjust to a new set of circumstances. That a returning family should have difficulty adjusting to their own culture after adapting to a completely different culture abroad comes as a shock; the underlying reasons are so insidious and, at times, so inapparent that the experience can, as one repatriate put it, "leave you feeling as though you have been hit by a double whammy."

For one thing, returning home can mean a loss of status.

Americans who live abroad generally occupy a position of prestige. The posture, influence, and technological strength of the United States are respected; even the smallest child knows that "we" put the first man on the moon. Added to this are the benefits of being a well-regarded executive, specialist, or staff member of a successful American firm, as well as the positive self-image generated by being a twentieth-century pioneer. Out of this emerges an expatriate (and family) with a mission that is generally respected.

There are opportunities overseas to make contributions to the community, to meet visiting dignitaries, even occasionally to climb upon the diplomatic party circuit. The result can be a civic and social whirl that is breathtaking. The pace accelerates with a scheduled departure. The round of farewell parties can leave the whole family feeling like celebrities, and greater than justifiable expectations may develop regarding the manner in which they will be welcomed on their triumphant return. Happy anticipation fades into chagrin as it becomes obvious that life has gone on without them, and is little changed by their return. Further, there is likely to be little interest in their successes abroad, the places they've been, and the sights they've seen. There is even relatively little interest in international events. With a now broadened scope and greater understanding of foreign affairs, these attitudes can seem almost inexcusable until, as one repatriate put it, "It suddenly dawns on you that they don't know, and they are not interested in learning."

Reinvolvement with family can also mean difficulties. Family get-togethers are not the momentous occasions imagined, but rather opportunities to be updated on sister Sue's divorce, brother Bob's financial woes, Aunt Martha's treatment for cancer, cousin Dickie's bout with alcoholism, and Mother and Dad's failing health. For children particularly, who don't really know or have never had a relationship with relatives, it may be impossible to respond to admonitions to "come give me a hug and kiss."

All manner of problems are dropped in returnees' laps—often before they've recovered from jet lag. The attitude, which may even be verbalized, comes across as, "You've had your vacation abroad, now it's time to shoulder some of the family responsibilities."

In addition to the financial difficulties of getting resettled, there are all manner of household problems to be solved. If furniture was sold abroad and has to be replaced, this can mean a period of six months to a year with no furniture. It can also be months from order to installation of custom-made bedspreads and draperies. Cars, appliances, clothing, and hobby equipment—worn by use and repeated international moves—may need to be replaced.

Lawn mowers, snow blowers, and the like have to be assembled by the purchaser; appliance installers or service and repair people can keep one waiting for hours—even days—for their arrival. Domestic help is almost unavailable. The returning expatriate family who has lived in areas with large manpower pools and few jobs may have had several specialized servants—a chauffeur, yard boy, cook, maid, and nursemaid. They are shocked to find that one-day-a-week cleaning service costs as much as a whole month of similar services abroad.

The tendency of expatriates to remember things "the way they were" does not prepare them for a return to the United States. The population explosion, along with the influx of people from the rural areas and the increasing number of aliens, has turned villages into municipalities, and cities into metropolises. The resultant traffic on freeways and streets is seen as a major problem by many of the newly returned. One repatriated wife, unperplexed by driving in the tangle of Trinidad and the crashes of Colombia, returned to her home in Houston and was completely aghast at the high-speed driving on the Texas freeways. After attempting to drive in Houston traffic for several weeks, she finally gave up and said, "I just can't face it."

Individually, there are other problems. For the wife or house husband, repatriation means a return to duty as chief cook and bottle washer, housecleaner, chauffeur, and community contact. It means doing the washing and the sewing; being the provisioner and the gardener. It can also mean the resumption of a career or education laid to rest when the overseas jaunt began. Unless the expatriate has kept up with the changing conditions in his home town, home state, and country, he will be shocked to find that the changes observed and accepted in an overseas location are also happening back home.

While some people look forward to the return to conveniences and to the greater privacy of a household without servants, others lament the loss of help and have great difficulty pulling together the tasks of getting settled (with spiraling inflation this may mean assuming the paint-up, fix-up jobs associated with moving into a previous home, or a just-purchased older house), resuming responsibilities to their extended families, completing the many housekeeping chores, entertaining, and getting back into community service.

For some, the experience is so traumatic that they are quickly ready to return to a less-developed country. After having household help for several years, the mother of four small children—two of whom were twins—found that she was unable to cope with all the responsibilities of keeping a house and caring for her children. She encouraged her husband to seek another overseas assignment as soon as possible.

More than anything else, returning spouses miss the close friends and the depth of the relationships they formed abroad with others in similar circumstances. In their new stateside communities they may find that most wives, as well as husbands, work. There may be little time or interest for a newcomer. If they have returned to an old neighborhood, they may find that next-door neighbors have moved, that old friends have found new friends, that the spots they used to have in the bridge groups have long since been filled. They are strangers in their own peer group and must feel their way slowly. According to one woman, getting through this period is similar to walking a rail fence:

> If you mention the servants you had, or how life was easier overseas, people who may have little sense of country or patriotic fervor are insulted that you seem to be criticizing the United States. If you talk of places you have been, the sights you have seen, or the people you have met, they think you are being a braggart and a name dropper. There is little left that you can say.

## The Crisis for Children

According to one youngster, the hardest part of living overseas was leaving—leaving her friends and the servants. People to share family life with, and to depend upon when a parent is away, become especially important when everything about one is new and different. As a consequence, the attachments that children form with friends and the servants who care for them are unusually strong. Leaving them can be like leaving a cherished member of the family.

Making new friends in a stateside situation can also be tough, especially if the child speaks with an accent and looks or acts a little differently. Talk about where they have lived or traveled can bring initial rebuffs and comments such as "He thinks he's so smart."

Children are resilient, however, and with a little time and support they can rise above these first encounters and establish a firm place for themselves in their new neighborhoods.

## A Teenager's Return

Talk about lonely and left out, the kids who really have a rough time are those who return during the later part of their high school years. The peer groups have formed, and the high school romances are in full swing. Even in instances where parents have moved back to previous neighborhoods, returning students have had difficulty being accepted into the groups that have formed in their absence.

Even if they are successful in breaking into a peer group, returning students may have little in common with the other kids. The expatriate teenager is far more mature than his domestic counterparts. He is more mundane and more realistic. He is more political in that his interest in international relations far exceeds his interest in local sports or local politics.

A student-to-teacher ratio of eight to one is not uncommon in American schools overseas; whereas in the United States a ratio of 30-40 to one is normal. Overseas high schools may have only 200 to 500 students; in the States it may be 2,000 to 5,000. This return to being just a face in the crowd instead of an individual student can have a far-reaching and negative effect.

## A Repatriating Boarding School or College Student

All the aforementioned problems of the repatriating teenager are multiplied for the repatriating boarding school or college student whose parents are still overseas. Not only does he have reverse culture shock to contend with, there is the new experience of being "on his own"—often with no relative within 3,000 to 6,000 miles.

> I felt intimidated by the huge assortment of snack machines, and the masses of students.

> I could hardly wait to have a car of my own, but learning to drive was awesome. We had always had a chauffeur.

> I didn't understand American football. I felt totally "out of it."

> My accent was so different from the Southern drawl of most students that everyone thought I was a foreigner.

Some assume the accent, dress, and attitudes of their classmates as quickly as possible and try to merge into the crowds. Others discover previous classmates or American students who have attended overseas schools, or foreign students from countries in which they have lived, and they are drawn together by the similarity of their experiences.

> My daughter was raised in South America, and she speaks fluent Spanish. Somehow I had thought her four years in a U.S. college would Americanize her, but she found a group of students from South America, and was with them constantly, speaking Spanish.

In general, however, the sons and daughters of expatriates, like "army brats," seem to adjust better than the average child. Perhaps this is because they not only face the reality that they have little, if any, alternative, but also because the adjust-adapt-adopt philosophy has been a basic part of their upbringing.

## An Executive's Return to the Workplace

While the whole family struggles with becoming climatized and Americanized, the breadwinner faces a particular professional and organizational reorientation. Individuals who have gone overseas as technical specialists, engineers, or advisers to governmental or business projects often discover that they have fallen behind in their field of expertise and in some instances may find themselves passed over for stateside promotions. Scientists, professors, and even some businesspeople may find that they have been working or teaching at lower levels, and have consequently developed specialized leadership styles in order to reach the students or native work force. Both groups must update and refine their skills.

Many expatriates, however, return with specialized knowledge and finely honed skills. Medical personnel attached to missionary units in developing countries gain an understanding of certain diseases that would be unattainable in this country. Agronomists, biologists, and educators become world expert as they study, research, and develop findings into programs of pertinence for governmental, educational, and research institutions. Journalists, economists, and sociologists develop international reputations as they observe and record—firsthand—events that may change the course of our relationships with other nations, and, indeed, civilization itself.

International businesspeople become expert managers of far-flung corporations—which may operate with little, if any, technical expertise or trained labor. Out of necessity such managers become accomplished teachers, economists, and psychologists, as well as specialists in governmental affairs. In many instances they develop innovative ways to get things done that might not be permitted in a stateside organization.

For some individuals, one international assignment follows another. They become expert at starting up or expanding research programs, news bureaus, or corporate businesses abroad. Others accept stateside assignments, having packed incredible amounts of overseas experience into short amounts of time. They are primed to climb even higher mountains—assuming increasingly important assignments—and some do. (James Lee, now Chairman of the Board of Gulf Oil Corporation, gained his expertise in international business while he was assigned to Gulf's North Sea project in London in the late 1960s and early 1970s.)

Many repatriated men and women never again quite meet the challenge or realize the satisfaction their overseas assignments provided. In fact, the theme that has run through many of our interviews with these returning experts has been one of frustration and disappointment. There has been frustration that they were not more completely debriefed upon their return, and given the opportunity to make more extensive observations and recommendations; disappointment that the expertise and governmental contacts they worked so hard to develop were not being more completely utilized in their present job.

The following interview summary depicts the frustration of a newly repatriated executive:

> As manager for a large concern in Indonesia, this returning executive had run the company operation with virtually no direct help from the home office, handling policy, day-to-day personnel and operating problems on his own, and, except in unusual events, seldom mentioning these in his twice-weekly calls to his boss in the States. As president and general manager, his actions were essentially without review by his stateside superiors. His was, in effect, an autonomous organization with only loose ties, and a line on an organization chart to link him with a vice president of the parent company.

> Repatriated, with a sizable promotion, this manager soon found out that the staff job in the home office bore little resemblance to the action-oriented job he had left. Gone were the top-man concepts; gone were the social events; gone were the servants and company automobile; gone were the decisions made with snap and aplomb. In the place of these were endless committee meetings, seemingly unworkable procedures, and frustrations of everything passing through a dozen hands before a decision could or would be made. Social events became few and far between, and two to four hours of commuting each day replaced the convenience of a chauffeur-driven car at his beck and call.

> Perhaps hardest of all, the expertise that he had gained was completely unused in his new assignment. As a staff person, his input to line supervisors went through a screening process so arduous as to frustrate even the most dogmatic person. He became convinced that his eight-year stint overseas had really been a waste of time. He confided that if he had known what awaited him at home, he would have stayed overseas. In one final, bitter statement he questioned the entire value of his overseas service in terms of professional develop-

ment, and said that he felt he might have been better off to have remained in the home office without going overseas. His view was strengthened, in his own mind, by an observation that none of the top jobs in his organization were filled with persons having overseas experience.

After this candid interview and self-appraisal, one has to wonder if this manager realized that he was in the grip of a severe case of reverse culture shock. In this case, his own former security blanket—his job—had caused the greatest frustration of his repatriation. The situation he found himself in had left him without the strength and mental preparedness needed to effectively deal with his new situation.

## Some Steps Toward Readjustment

Options that allow the breadwinner or a career couple to keep current with technological advances in the United States and to advance toward career goals in an orderly fashion should be capitalized upon.

Efforts should be made to stay abreast of social and economic changes. Understanding the changing mores can make a return to the United States less traumatic. Developing a sound financial plan can offset spiraling inflation and provide for a secure future.

The responsibilities of parenthood are little changed by the addition of servants. Love, attention, and values are best provided by parents. Self-care, independence, and habits of sharing household tasks will be greatly appreciated upon a return back home.

Developing hobbies that are enjoyable and that can be shared as a family, as well as hobbies that can be pursued individually, has long-range benefits. It not only assists with the character-building process, it provides a valuable diversion during the lonely periods of readaption.

Keeping in touch with stateside friends and relatives makes for an easier return. Staying on top of family problems—expressing interest and concern with regular correspondence, telephone calls, or self-recorded cassettes, and visits at vacation time—keeps relationships strong.

## Home—At Last

Coming home is something every expatriate American thinks about and fantasizes about. The moment of touchdown with aircraft brakes screeching, the first steps back on American soil, the first sight of Old Glory flying in the breeze are images to capture in your mind and to hold forever. You are back—and it is impossible to believe that it will not be utopia.

Home is different things to different people. For some it is a paradise filled with juicy hamburgers and thick malts; for others, an air-conditioned shopping mall stocked with every conceivable product. For still others, home is a return to those all-consuming national pastimes: football, baseball, and basketball on wide screen television in their own living rooms, or firsthand at their nearby domed stadium; or to telephones that work and can put them instantly in touch with those that they hold dear.

For some individuals these things may be enough—enough to make the problems of homecoming seem inconsequential. Others are able to accentuate the positive and glide through the difficulties that accompany every major change. For still others, the loss associated with leaving close friends and a comfortable way of life, the loss of free time (no household servants), the loss of prestige and status, is so acute that their very reason for existence may seem threatened.

The many problems of living overseas—the horrendous traffic, narrow cobblestone streets, difficulties in finding houses, the occasional shortages of food and the necessity of shopping in a dozen different places to assemble a grocery order, the unfortunate incidents that can accompany an automobile accident, infringement of the law, or disagreement with a native—are forgotten as reverse culture shock sets in.

At this stage of the process, survival may depend on stepping back from the situation and looking at it in an analytical fashion. Rather than giving in to stress and anxiety, it may be better to change perspectives, reduce external pressures, make transitions more slowly, and accept what cannot be changed.

According to those who have been repatriated, the process of readaption involves many of the same techniques used in adjusting to life abroad.

You are in a sense a newcomer to your own country, and you need to refamiliarize yourself and your family with the current way of life. If you have children who have spent an extended period of time overseas, helping them to become Americanized should be a top priority.

Teach them how to play, or at least to understand, baseball, basketball, football (and, if possible, hockey and soccer). This should include a crash course in the "name" college and professional teams and their star players, and the old-time greats who have earned a seat in the heroes' hall of fame.

Encourage their exposure to the "in" musical groups, the latest movies, the popular television programs. Help them to become familiar with the names of musicians, as well as television and movie actors.

Introduce them to their new community. Take time to explore its parks and recreation areas, and visit the history and art museums and scientific expositions.

Visit the surrounding areas; develop a familiarity with the way people live and the things they do, as well as the areas of scenic beauty.

Plan vacations to emphasize the great moments in American history, the current government, and the unrivaled beauty of our country. Help them not only to become Americanized, but to be proud and enthusiastic Americans.

Family "rap sessions" in which enthusiasm, as well as mutual appreciation, encouragement, and help—including a division of household tasks—are stressed are an essential factor in acclimation. It also may be helpful to discuss techniques for success, positive thinking, or making friends. Be sure also that your children understand your views on drugs, alcohol, and dating (including sexuality); anticipate the problems (including indifference) your children may face and the alternatives for handling them. If they function more comfortably with small groups of people, you may wish to consider enrolling them in a small private school, rather than a large public school. The *Handbook of Private Schools* (Porter Sargent, 11 Beacon Street, Boston, Massachusetts 02108), now in its 62d edition, provides a comprehensive listing of private schools.

It is helpful to recognize that you are returning as different people than you were when you began your around-the-world jaunt. It would be impossible to leave the American way of life and live in another culture without changing in some fashion. You are probably more sophisticated and worldly, but also more sensitive to the needs of others. As a result, old answers do not solve new problems.

When neighbors do not come to call, it may be up to you to knock on doors and introduce yourself (almost everyone responds to a request for information about a neighborhood nursery school, dry cleaners, dentist, or to a ball in their back yard).

When teenagers feel left out, it may be up to you to suggest that they organize a high school newcomers club to meet other new people who also need a niche in which to fit.

When you can find no outlet for your own interest in international affairs, it may be up to you to contact the international student center at your local university or city-sponsored international centers that attempt to provide information and friendly assistance to transient and resident foreigners, and offer to help. One returning wife, who joined a newcomers club in a large Eastern city, found that 75 of the newcomers had either lived abroad or were natives of other countries. The international branch they organized kept them so busy with tasting luncheons featuring foreign foods, discussions, and book reviews on international affairs, and plans to help newcomers returning from life abroad, that she had no time to get lonely.

The problems associated with readaption, like the problems involved in an initial overseas assignment, may take from 6 to 12 months—and sometimes longer—to solve. If there are signs of overstress, professional help should be considered. Most communities have psychiatrists, psychologists, and psychotherapists in private practice, as well as in association with such agencies as the Family Service Association, Catholic Charities, and Jewish Community Centers. In some highly mobile areas these organizations have ongoing group sessions dealing with mobility and culture shock.

## And What Then?

Most individuals who are repatriated are content to settle down and let their homing instincts take over. There are, of course, some who are never quite ready to return:

> It was with real sadness that I realized we had made it back to the home office, and that the chances of other corporate transfers were relatively slim.
>
> Our family had thrived, and derived a great deal from both our domestic and international moves. We had grown close through our dependence on each other; yet it had been exciting for us to meet new and different peoples and to widen our horizons through travel.
>
> At their still relatively young ages, our children had picnicked on the shores of Loch Lomond in Scotland, examined Stonehenge in England, and the treasures in the Louvre in Paris. They had climbed to the tops of the tallest peaks of Machu Picchu in Peru, and marvelled at the remnants of this lost culture. They had skied down Austria's snow-laden slopes; skin-dived in the cool, placid waters of Tobago; and "jumped-up" with the natives of the Isle of Trinidad during their

all-consuming, unbelievably beautiful carnival. They had attended American schools in England, and English schools in Trinidad, but their knowledge of geography and love of history were inspired by a personal exposure they could never have had without our corporate moves.

Some husband and wife teams go on to become the VIPs who periodically visit overseas locations. Their overseas apprenticeships have prepared them to zero in on problems (such as schooling, medical, family, and volunteer service, etc.) and to discuss difficulties sensitively but positively; it has equipped them to entertain well on short notice in unfamiliar places, and to keep accurate expense account records. The positive image that these VIPs portray appears to be a source of inspiration and encouragement for the expatriate families they meet.

For many of those who have returned, being an American abroad was the ultimate experience. They have been soldiers in service to their country, as well as to the corporate enterprises, news bureaus, or missionary groups for whom they worked. They have been ambassadors of goodwill, promoting the idea of a safe, healthy, and productive life for all. Their exposure to the life-styles, artistic genius, political values, and intellectual systems of others may influence their own ideologies. Without realizing it, they may become members of a "third culture" of international citizens who find meaning in shared interests rather than a shared neighborhood. Their appreciation for the American way of life may be greater than ever, but their interests are more global, and, their *Bayanihan* spirit (in Pilipino, sense of community) is more international. They become citizens of the world.

Some of those who have lived abroad would go again, given the opportunity.

> Gosh, it was fun! And, gosh, it was not easy. If I had it to do over again, would I go? YES! But it would have been easier for me if I had known What To Expect.

This book has been written for *you*—the Twentieth-Century Pioneers who leave your homeland and go abroad to live and work—in hopes that it will enable you to know *What to Expect!*

# Suggested Reading

Berman, Eleanor. *The Co-operating Family: How Your Children Can Help Manage the Household—For Their Good as Well as Yours.* Englewod Cliffs, New Jersey: Prentice-Hall, 1977.

Cooke, Alistair. *Alistair Cooke's America.* New York: Alfred A. Knopf, 1973.

——————————. *Talk About America.* New York: Alfred A. Knopf, 1969.

Kaltman, Mary. *Keeping Up With Keeping House: A Practical Guide for the Harried Housewife.* Garden City, New York: Doubleday, 1971.

Kelsey, Alice. *The Working Mother's Guide to Her Home, Her Family and Herself.* New York: Random House, 1970.

Koberg, Don, and Jim Bagnall. *The Universal Traveler: A Soft Systems Guide to Creativity, Problem Solving and the Process of Reaching Goals.* Los Altos, California: William Kaufmann, 1974.

Landi, Val. *The Great American Countryside.* New York: Collier, 1982.

Rifenbark, Richard K. and Johnson, David. *How to Beat the Salary Trap.* New York: Avon, 1979.

Rolo, Charles J. *Gaining on the Market, Your Complete Guide to Investment Strategy.* Boston: Little, Brown, 1982.

Ruff, Howard J. *Survive and Win in the Inflationary Eighties.* New York: Times Books, 1981.

Uris, Auren. *Executive Housekeeping—The Business of Managing Your Home.* New York: Morrow, 1976.

# PART SIX
# Destinations Abroad

# 14

# Assignment London

HE 2,000-YEAR-OLD LADY by the Thames will entice, beguile, frustrate, and charm you; and just as you begin to pack for home, the tour completed, she will wrap her fingers around your soul, tear at your loyalties, and convert you into a confirmed Anglophile.

London is not just one of the world's biggest cities; she's a conglomerate of villages. It started with the Roman town of Londinium, but through the centuries it stretched, swallowed, and enmeshed scores of other hamlets until London today has become a fascinating swirl of serendipity that spreads over some 600 square miles of once-rolling English countryside.

It is difficult to tell where one village—today referred to as a *borough*—ends and another begins, but a subtle, enigmatic charm sweeps through each section, shrouding the city in a delightful mantle of surprise. Don't call London "the City." That—with a capital "C"—simply refers to the central financial district. And don't go in search of the "downtown." There is none. London is a patchwork quilt of shopping areas where you can buy anything from an old master to spangled jeans. The boroughs, all 32 of them, and their even smaller precincts have their small town centers squeezed along a main street usually referred to as *High*. But these boroughs are far removed from the small towns found elsewhere in the world. London is sophisticated and culturally supreme!

An assignment to London long has been considered a plum. "When a man is tired of London, he is tired of life, for there is in London all that life can afford," said Samuel Johnson. Even today, in spite of spiraling inflation, it tops the list as one of the most desirable spots for overseas living.

Londoners are tolerant of the thousands of Americans who have settled in their midst. After all, they reason, not everyone is lucky enough to be born a Briton. But do not expect them to overwhelm you with a royal welcome, literally or otherwise. The 46 million permanent residents of England admire privacy, individuality, and dogs—not necessarily in that order—and being accepted as one of them does not come easily.

"If you really want to know us, go where we go," advised a Londoner. "Take your children to the park. Walk your dog. Join special interest groups." And as any astute observer will add, "Above all, go to the pub!"

The neighborhood bar—tavern or whatever euphemism you might wish to bestow on it—is more than a spot to guzzle booze. It often is a good and relatively inexpensive place to eat. But more important, it is an enclave where the people meet their friends and neighbors, gossip, debate, play games, and sing. It ranks somewhere between an American clubhouse and a neighborhood community center with a bar thrown in.

The natives will probably be more confused by you than you by them. Said one local gentleman to an expatriate;

> You Americans have a fixation about balls. You absolutely love them, all shapes and sizes. American fathers are always taking their children out to play with them. It's pure madness! Why, someone in our neighborhood—I am certain it was an American—petitioned the authorities to allow ball playing in our local garden [park]. Thank God, the petition went nowhere. The garden is for reading and relaxing, not ball playing.

"But," he added, "I do like Americans. Really, they are my favorite people."

Outwardly the Britons may scorn American customs or, at best, reluctantly accept them. But beneath this surface protest, they often embrace them with the fervor of a dedicated cult member. American fast-food chains proliferate, and just try to make your way to the counter of a McDonald's or a Burger King on a weekday lunch hour. It takes infinite time and patience.

Probably no other city in the world offers you such a chance to be yourself. If you want to wear red shoes with purple laces, go ahead and do it. (Not at the office, please!) Chalk it all up to the Londoner's admiration for individuality or a strong sense of personal laissez-faire. But then, maybe you should blame it on local smugness. Londoners simply are too self-assured to be threatened by any oddities among them.

Mother country to the States, England provides an undisputed attraction to many Americans heading for her shores. But she also provides some problems. Just as mothers and daughters don't always see eye to eye, so it is with the people of these two nations. Americans find themselves asking how someone so like them can be so different; and yet these same Americans cross the channel to the Continent and simply smile over differences in views found there.

It is the attitude toward women and children that often baffles the Americans the most. One American woman whose husband had left the house hunting up to her was met with stalls and put-offs by estate agents (realtors) who felt that her husband should be present to set the allowance for housing and make the final decisions.

As for the kids, they are best ignored or relegated to an unobtrusive position in society. If these interpretations of local attitudes by the expatriates are rather harsh, the facts are that children do not enjoy the same degree of acceptance that their counterparts in the States do. You cannot expect restaurants (except those of the fast-food variety) to cater to children. One American family was refused a flat because their young children lived at home. Proper families who lived in flats of this caliber packed their youngsters off to boarding school.

The pace in London can be irritatingly slow for the newly arrived, especially since England has been exacerbated by strikes, here more politely referred to as *industrial actions*.

"Just keep in mind," a university professor said in addressing a group of newly arrived American women, "that when you apply for your telephone, you will not be met with the same sense of urgency that you experience back in the States. We are an old nation, and it seems that the older the country, the longer it takes to get things done. If you think it is bad here, take a look at Italy and Greece. They are much worse."

There *is* a different sense of historical scale here. Nothing is really old until it has been around 400 or 500 years, and newcomers in the neighborhood are those people who moved in 50 or so years ago. You, who will be there only a few years, are merely transients.

What may baffle you even more is the insular attitude of Britons. Granted, the nation is an island, but in this day of electronic communications and jet travel, geography should mean little. You can expect headlines in English newspapers to read something like this: "Volcanic Eruption in Italy. No Britons Dead." There is the now-infamous headline that appeared sometime back in the staid *London Times* that declared, "Fog in Channel, Continent Islolated." Despite this distorted geographical perception, the English have produced world-class leaders in about every field and endeavor.

The little nuances in life can sometimes be perplexing. Americans, for example, are noted for their frankness and candor. If they think you are not being honest with them, they most likely will tell you so. According to George Mikes in his humorous book *How to Be An Alien: A Handbook for Beginners and Advanced Pupils* (Penguin Books, New York), an Englishman will look at you rather perplexed and then slowly comment, "Is that so? Quite unusual, isn't it?" What he actually means is that you are a bloody liar. (And speaking of *bloody,* it is best to avoid the word. On this side of the Atlantic, it is considered obscene.)

All the little subtleties of the English way of life are studied, dissected, and explained to newcomers in a marvelous orientation class called "Bloom Where You're Planted" at the American Church (Tottenham Court Road, W 1—across from Heal's Store, near Goodge Street tube station) each fall. The course is both entertaining and packed with relevant information for the newly arrived expatriate. Call the church (637-4858) for more information.

Don't expect Londoners to hurry, overwhelm you with efficiency, quickly wait on you in shops, or take to any of your new innovations with any degree of excitement. They have been a long time accepting the idea that tea can be poured over ice. But do expect them to be polite, kind, and helpful if you really need a friend in an emergency. The newly arrived will constantly be amused, and at times frustrated, by the ambivalence in London life.

Here's betting you will struggle through it all, sometimes laughing, other times crying, and finally deciding you really love this country and its people. The local people have a saying for it all. Whenever they are faced with adversity, they simply tell each other, "Not to worry." You will be hearing it said time and again during your stay here. It may just be the best advice of all.

## Practical Pointers

Don't be surprised if strangers are seated at your table in a restaurant, and don't expect them to talk to you. Respect each other's privacy. You, too, can go up to an already occupied table with an empty chair and ask if you might join them.

Don't send your children next door to play with native youngsters nor expect the neighbor's youngsters to run over to meet yours. Write a note inviting Susan or Johnny to tea on Wednesday next.

When meeting the local people, do not as a way of a conversational opener ask about their jobs, families, homes, or even where they live. Instead, keep the subject completely impersonal. Discuss theater, current events, books, or museums you have visited. The best way to open a conversation is to comment on the weather. Personal questions are considered an invasion of privacy.

Be prompt. When the English set a time for a party, they expect you to be there.

It is customary to take an impersonal gift such as flowers or candy to the hostess at a dinner party.

Do not be put off by the elaborate array of flatware surrounding your dinner plate. The general rule there, as here, is to start at the outside and work inward with each course. The dessert spoon is often at the top, and the English frequently use a spoon for dessert where we would use a fork.

If you are likely to do some formal entertaining and will have contact with those of title, you should pick up locally *Debrett's Correct Form* and *Debrett's Peerage and Baronetage,* both edited by Montague Smith and published by Debrett's Peerage Ltd., London. There are several other guides and directories to the titled and elite of business and the clergy available in bookstores.

Do not forget to queue. The local people pride themselves on waiting patiently in line at bus stops, cinemas, and theaters, but they forget about it for trains and drinks at the bar during intermission at the theaters.

Do not expect to meet your next-door neighbor. You might want to knock on the door to introduce yourself, but do not be disappointed if the friendship goes no further. Again, it is the privacy bit.

*Pardon* means I did not understand you more often than it means an apology.

Public houses, or "pubs," have an odd assortment of hours. Generally, the bar hours are 11 a.m. to 3 p.m. and 5:30 p.m. to

11 p.m. The restaurant side may close a little earlier. Some pubs remain open on weekends; other close. It is best to check if you are not a frequent patron.

Never smoke at a formal dinner party until the Queen has been toasted. You can, however, smoke in the underground (subway), movies, some theaters, and trains unless there is a "no smoking" sign posted.

If port is served at a formal dinner party, only pass the bottle to the left, never to the right. A lady should wait for a gentleman to pour.

To telephone someone is to "ring" them. To "call" is actually to appear in person. It is best to avoid the word *sick*. Simply say that you are ill.

For answers to all types of questions, contact the Daily Telegraph and Morning Post Information Service at 135 Fleet Street, EC4; telephone 353 4242.

There is no definite rule in tipping, but generally you give hairdressers a small gratuity of 30p to 40p and another 20p to 30p to the one who washes your hair. Taxi drivers usually get 10 to 15 percent of the fare, and porters who carry your bags receive 25p a suitcase (more if the distance carried is rather far). You do not tip theater ushers nor hotel staff if there is a service charge on your bill. If there is not, it is customary to tip 10 to 12 percent of the total bill, divided among the help who have been of good service.

In these times of nationalism, do not lump all the people together as Britons. Refer to them as Scots, Welsh, Irish, and English and expect to hear the dialect and brogues change as you travel from one area to another. To muddle the language even more, there is a definite class accent with "cockney" at the bottom of the scale and the "Queen's English" or "Standard English" at the top.

For its size, England is incredibly varied not only in terrain but people. Each area maintains a strong regional identity. As one Englishman put it, "We are a mosaic, not a melting pot."

As you travel from the south to the north, you find a noticeable difference not only in geography but in the aforementioned accents and attitudes as well. The southeast is dominated by London with its old-school ties, clubbiness, and privileged elite. But in the north, you discover self-made millionaires. The Industrial Revolution took place here, and it is here that the individual appears to have more of a chance based on his initiative and brain power.

Traditionally, more people leave Britain each year than enter it as immigrants. During the late 1950s and early 1960s this changed for a few years. Then, there was a great influx of Commonwealth citizens, particularly from the West Indies, India, and Pakistan, who poured into the Island, raising the immigration number above the score of those who emigrated. Actually, the WOGs—western oriental gentlemen, as some of these darker-skinned Commonwealth newcomers are called—were encouraged to come to Britain during this period to help fill jobs not wanted by the local people. Today, sadly, some racial tensions exist in this country, which long prided itself on tolerance. The country has tightened its restrictions on immigration; and as one local history professor pointed out, anyone taking a close look at these new rules will note that they have a tinge of color discrimination associated with them.

For environmental reasons, it is now against the law to burn wood in your fireplace. Smokeless fuel is available.

While England is often plagued with drizzles that are relieved only by what the weather forecasters lovingly refer to as "sunny intervals," fewer inches of rain fall in London each year than in New York City. But the amounts of rainfall increase as you head into the higher regions of the north and west.

The climate in the United Kingdom is too varied to categorize, although it is not so well known that England has a riviera to rival the more famous ones along the Mediterranean. Tempered by warm Gulf Stream waters, the Cornish coast makes a delightful and relatively inexpensive retreat.

## To Bring or Not to Bring

### *Automobiles*

Leave them at home. A left-hand drive car in a left-hand drive country can be very inconvenient and even unsafe.

### *Clothing*

Almost everything is available locally but is expensive. Bring heavy coats with zip-in linings and liners for women's slacks, as locally purchased slacks are usually not lined.

Women should include skirts, sweaters, suits, and dresses for daytime—rarely slacks. Large-size clothing (above size 12) for women is difficult to find locally.

Men wear dark, conservative suits for the office and sport coats for sporting events or very casual free time. Also purchase extra socks beforehand, as locally made socks have short tops.

Children's clothes are very expensive here—double the U.S. price.

## Household

Bring fabric for upholstery; local labor is good and cheaper than labor in the States, but fabric is more expensive. Also include extra cots, trundle beds, or sleeping bags. Chances are good you will have many out-of-town guests.

## Appliances

The electric current in England is the same as that in most other European countries, 220-250 volts, 50 cycle. While your U.S. appliances are nice to have, they require bulky transformers, and timers, dependent on the cycle rate, will be ineffective. Another problem is that you may not have room in your kitchen for the larger American versions. If you still decide you want U.S. models you may be able to buy some secondhand in London from departing families. There are transformers available and a few U.S. trained servicemen in London.

English appliances are more costly, on the average, than their American counterparts, but the chief difference is the smaller size of the local units. Large American roasting pans and cookie sheets may not fit into a standard British oven. You need to get the connecting line and plug separately, as most appliances in England come without them. England is trying to standardize plug types but there still are several different versions in use. All plugs have built-in fuses for safety.

## Miscellaneous

Convenience drinks in packets are a very useful item. And peanut butter *is* available locally.

In the baking department, double-acting baking powder is a must for most American kitchens; only single-acting is available here. Angel food cake mix is hard to find.

# Housing

## *The Realities*

In London, probably more than in any other foreign post, you will want to weigh renting versus buying housing. Over 75 percent of American families do lease. Rentals, however, are extremely scarce, reportedly less than 10 percent of the total housing market. Many property owners think twice before leasing their units. Legislation permits the establishment of "fair rent" and provides the tenant some "security of tenure" for all accommodations except luxury class. This causes owners to consider selling rather than continue renting, thus compounding the rental shortage.

Most rental accommodations are furnished, many being those of Londoners who are abroad.

Prospective buyers can often get mortgages through American banks in London or from local building societies. The interest on these loans is one of the few allowable deductions from English income tax. With the lifting of all foreign exchange restrictions, there is no problem taking out the proceeds of a sale later. But be careful! The purchase of a home in England can affect your residency status for tax purposes and may act to increase your income tax liability. Clearly, the proposed purchase of housing calls for sound local legal advice on all aspects.

Houses are often priced "in excess of X amount of pounds," and it is a contest to see who bids the highest. It is extremely difficult for an *estate agent* to place a fair price on the house or flat. There is no multiple listing system, and, consequently, there are no records of previous sales in the neighborhood with which to compare. The square footage is never considered. When you turn around to sell it, expect to pay a commission rate of 3 percent.

There are no usury laws and no fixed interest rates; so the interest you pay at the time of purchase may be higher or lower in the following year. If you can obtain what locally is referred to as a "comfort letter" from your employer saying you are a good employee, financially responsible, and so on, you can probably obtain between a 70 to 90 percent mortgage. If your company guarantees the mortgage, it is possible to get a 100 percent mortgage. Otherwise, expect to come up with a 35 to 45 percent down payment.

If you decide either to buy or to rent, be prepared for being *gazumped.* This is a process that cuts you out of an apartment or house after you have agreed on terms (just a day or so before you are to move) because someone else has come in with a higher bid. It is a common practice.

Even a simple rental agreement must be referred to a solicitor (see Chapter 11) for laborious consideration and preparation of a lengthy contract. No amount of cajoling seems to speed up the minimal six weeks for this process.

Locating an address can be extremely difficult. There are 60 different ways of saying *street;* so you must know exactly whether the house is on Smith Street, Crescent, Avenue, Terrace, or one of the other innumerable designations. And you cannot assume that just because Smith Avenue is located in one area, Smith Street will be nearby. It may be on the other side of London. Sometimes house numbers go up one side of the street and down the other, making number 15 across the street from number 7. In newer areas, you probably will find the odd–even form of addresses. You may also discover that the house or apartment building has no number but simply a name such as Grove End Gardens on Grove End Road.

No matter where you live, the chances of having a home like the one you left in the States are practically zero. Kitchens may be too small, bathrooms may be antiquated by stateside standards (cabinets under the washbasin are almost unheard of), and heat probably will be insufficient in spite of a central heating system. In some older homes, you will have a geyser (hot water heater) above the kitchen sink and another in the bathroom that you must light every time you want hot water.

Exactly where you settle may also depend on just where your office will be in relation to transportation. If you head into the suburbs, you might want to consider the location of the London station for your particular train. Trains from the south come into both Victoria and Waterloo stations, from the north into Euston and Kings Cross, and from the west into Paddington and Marylebone. But since connections with subway and buses are excellent, this should not be the determining factor in deciding on location. However, there are apt to be more train disruptions on the lines to the south.

## Desirable Locations

Among the many areas in which Americans live in or near London, some of the most popular have been:

*St. Johns Wood.* Home of the American School in London and Lord's Cricket Grounds. It is 10 minutes to the West End by underground; 20 minutes to the City. Good High Street shopping. Considered to be a "foreign neighborhood" by native Londoners, and they are probably right. It is extremely popular with expatriates.

*Marylebone Road-Regents Park area.* Within walking distance to the West End theater and shopping areas; 10 minutes by underground to the City. Near Madam Tussaud's and the very lovely Regents Park. Location of the Cordon Bleu School of Cooking, the Royal Academy of Music, the famous London Clinic, and the equally famous Harley Street medical specialists.

*Mayfair.* An exclusive and expensive area that took its name from the commoners who held raucous fairs there each spring centuries ago. Bounded by Hyde Park with its famous Marble Arch and Speaker's Corner on one side and the Green Park and St. James Palace on the other. Its location and shopping are unrivaled, although it is becoming increasingly commercial. The American embassy is located here.

*Belgravia-Sloane Square area.* An area of distinguished addresses bordering the Buckingham Palace Gardens on one side and trendy Chelsea on the other. Belgravia's Eaton Square was the scene of the "Upstairs, Downstairs" television series. Excellent shopping. Minutes by taxi or underground to theaters and other West End shopping.

*Chelsea.* A jolly jumble of artists and style-setting boutiques. It was here that the mini- and micromini skirts burst upon the world. Hippies and coffee houses as well as poodles and prams. A popular residential area, its Kings Road draws all Americans if only for a glance at the swinging life-style and the Embankment where people happily reside on houseboats.

*Knightsbridge-Kensington areas.* Across from Hyde Park and the Kensington Gardens with the Kensington Palace, home of Princess Margaret and other members of the Royal Family. Outstanding shopping. A 10-to-15 minute underground ride to West End shopping and theaters. A culturally stimulating area, as it is the home of Royal Albert Hall as well as the Victoria and Albert Museum, Natural History Museum, Science Museum, City Guild College, and the Royal College of Art and the Royal College of Music. Americans seeking an "international atmosphere" for their children often place them in the Lycee Francais.

*Bayswater-Paddington-Maida Vale area.* Across from Hyde Park, Kensington Gardens on one side and the Marylebone, St. Johns Wood area on the other. A super location. Close to the Oxford Street shopping (West End), theaters, and business section. Near the American School in London. Excellent commuting to all of London.

*Hampstead.* Near the beautiful Hampstead Heath (park). Country living close in. Many lovely estate-type homes and gardens, some turned into elegant flats. Good High Street shopping with excellent restaurants where costs are often below those found in more central eateries. Near the American School in London. About 20 minutes to the central business district, but in many ways the best of many worlds.

*Wimbledon.* Pleasant country living. Has an international reputation as the tennis tournament center. Good shopping. Located on the southwest side of the metropolitan area.

*Hampstead Garden.* A planned community of the early 1900s that has been copied in many places around the world. Lovely private gardens and an attractive but sometimes perplexing maze of streets. Probably as close as you can come to the typical American suburban living where children can ride their bicycles around the culs-de-sac. Home to former King Constantine of Greece and his family. About 10 minutes farther out than Hampstead.

The suburbs to the northwest are extremely popular with expatriates. Many have located in a cluster of suburbs that include Pinner, Northwood, Ruislip, and Moor Park. These towns are still within the underground commuting system (Metropolitan Line).

*Moor Park.* A favorite area of Americans desiring country living. Two-story prestige-type homes built on and near Moor Park Golf Course. In the past, many Americans have bought here, but inflation has pushed prices quite high. Some rentals available. Good British day school; commute to the American School in London. A 30-to-60 minute drive into central London, depending on exact location and traffic.

*Ruislip area.* Owing to the proximity of the Ruislip Air Force Base and the High Wycombe Air Station, Americans settling in this area are usually air force personnel. Pleasant country living. West Ruislip Grade School. Village shopping. Good commute to city.

There are many delightful suburban areas to the west of London, too. Two popular ones are:

*Gerrard's Cross.* An area of fashionable country homes, beautiful gardens, and swimming pools. The distance from London is such that commuting is difficult for small children. Village shopping. Transportation to city.

*Beaconsfield.* A charming town, slightly farther out than Gerrard's Cross but similar to this town in types of beautiful homes and in price range.

To the south of London are the suburbs located in the area of Surrey. Two that have been popular with the expatriates are Walton-on-Thames and Weybridge. They are similar to Gerrard's Cross to the west with large, very expensive, luxury class homes. There is good High Street shopping. Walton-on-Thames has a delightful village center that resulted from a planned development scheme where the contrast between old and new is extremely pleasant. Many of the expatriate children in these areas attend the American Community School in Cobham. A school bus transports the children to and from home.

For a general idea of property values, the *Times, Telegraph, Guardian, Observer, Evening Standard,* and *London Evening News* as well as *Daltons Weekly,* the monthly magazine *Country Life,* the *Field,* and *New Home* may be of help. Also, check local area newspapers such as the *Hampstead and Highgate Express* or place an ad yourself, stating the type of accommodations you are seeking.

## Estate Agents

A complete listing of estate agents for a particular area can be found in the yellow pages printed for that particular district. (There are no general, all-encompassing yellow pages for the entire London area.) The following are agents who handle housing in the London area and have been helpful to other Americans. They will make arrangements for someone to meet you on the premises and show you the flat or house.

A C S Realty Service
Heywood
Portsmouth Road
Cobham, Surrey
Telephone Cobham 266 7251
Service sponsored by the American Community School primarily for families with students at that school, but it is glad to help other families. Very knowledgeable about the current housing situation for Americans in the areas around the school.

George Trollope & Sons
13 Hobart Place
Eaton Square SW1
Telephone 235 8099
Very good for houses and apartments in the Belgravia area.

Marler and Marler—King Wood & Company
6 Sloane Street SW1
Telephone 235 1727
Furnished and unfurnished properties.

Harrods Estate Offices
1 Hans Road SW3
Telephone 589 1490
Large range of properties in country areas and also town houses.

London at Home
2A Milner Street SW3
Telephone 584 5650
Have located accommodations for Americans whom they find "delightfully different" in Knightsbridge, Kensington, and Belgravia areas. Also arrange service flats.

Beckett, Son & Company
The Moor Park Estate Office by Moor Park
    Station, Northwood
Telephone Northwood 24131
Good for houses by Moor Park Golf Course.

Benham & Reeves
56 Heath Street, Hampstead NW3
Telephone 435 9822
For properties in the Hampstead and Highgate areas.

Crouch & Lee
45 New Bond Street W1
Telephone 499 6157
An estate firm in central London.

## Common Real Estate Terms

Some knowledge of common real estate terms used in England will be helpful to you.

*Freehold.* The owner of property has title to the land as well as to improvements or buildings on it.

*Leasehold*. The owner has no title to the land, only to the buildings. He leases the land for a period that can be months or years in duration, and he may pay ground rent for this privilege.

*C H W*. Constant hot water. Central hot water is supplied.

*CH* Central Heating. Usually turned on only from October to April or May.

*WC* Water Closet. Separate area for a toilet that is not located in the bathroom. Also called the *loo*.

*Key Money*. A premium a new tenant may be required to pay to the outgoing tenant to take over the latter's unexpired portion of the lease. The amount varies with the length of the term, the current rent, and other circumstances. This payment may be disguised as part of "fittings and fixtures."

*Fittings and Fixtures*. Commonly known as "F and F." Unfurnished accommodations, and even some very sparsely furnished, will not be equipped with such things as lighting fixtures, carpets, drapes, cupboards, closets, and other accessories. The tenant has them installed and then sells them to the next tenant, and so on. This is an additional charge required to take over a residence and should be roughly commensurate with the present value of the fittings and fixtures acquired.

*Flat*. The English name for an apartment, so called because it usually is "flat out" rather than two or more levels.

*Detached house*. A house standing in its own yard.

*Semidetached*. Two houses joined side by side and sharing the same lot.

*Terrace houses*. Row houses, usually three to five floors with two rooms per floor.

*Maisonette*. An apartment on two or more floors.

*Reception rooms*. The living rooms, dining rooms, and studies.

*American kitchen*. A kitchen with fitted cupboards.

## Utilities

Utility bills arrive only quarterly, so don't think they have forgotten you. If you have any complaints about your utilities, follow these procedures. For gas, complain to your local gas board (where you pay your bill); if that does not result in satisfaction, then contact the Gas Consultative Council (28 Charing Cross Road WC2). For electric, complain to your local electricity board; if this does not produce results, contact the Electricity Consultative Council (46 New Bond Street EC2).

## Education

Educational opportunities, either in the British system or in the international schools, are many and varied. Expatriate parents should understand and review the alternatives before making a hasty decision. Information on education in Britain can be obtained by writing the British embassy (3100 Massachusetts Avenue, N.W., Washington, D.C. 20008) for "Notes for the Guidance of Parents Wishing to Place Their Children in School in Britain." Private schools are still very strong here. Data are available on these schools and can be obtained from Independent Schools Information Service (ISIS) (26 Caxton Street, London SW1; telephone 222 0065). Their comprehensive reference booklet shows locations (maps) and gives factual data and fees covering more than 1,400 schools in the London area. A special office, ISIS International (telephone 222 6535) has been established specifically to assist parents living abroad. It is located at 3 Vandon Street, SW1.

The Gabhitas-Thring Educational Trust is an educational consulting firm that advises parents on the choice of private schools for children, taking into consideration their individual backgrounds and interests. No fee is charged for this service, and they can be contacted at Broughton House (6, 7, and 8 Sackville Street, Piccadilly; telephone 734 0161).

Private schools in England, those completely free of any financial aid from the government, are referred to as *independent schools*. There are about 2,300 of these schools, attended by roughly 6 per cent of the school-age population. Within this group of independents are public schools; while no exact definition is given to this latter group, they usually are those boys' and girls' schools whose headmasters are members of the Headmasters' Conference. Many of the boys' schools date back to the sixteenth century, some even earlier.

The traditional pattern for children attending independent schools has been attendance at a preparatory school beginning at age 7 or 8, passage of the Common Entrance exam taken at 13, and then admission to independent senior schools. Some American students have gained admittance, but entrance requirements are tough and waiting lists are long at such top schools for boys as Eton, Harrow, and Winchester, and Roedean for girls.

State schools, attended by the remaining 94 percent of school children, are free and most are coeducational. Most state schools are organized into a two-tier system: primary schools for ages 5-11 and secondary schools for ages 11-18. The primary schools emphasize the basic skills supplemented by art, music, and projects involving history, geography, and sciences. A few teach French. The secondary program prepares students for a series of exams all-important to their future careers.

The state also provides special schools for children with physical or mental disabilities. Expatriate youngsters may attend these special schools.

Compulsory education begins at the age of 5 in Britain. In actuality, however, many British children begin a full day of school at the age of 2 or 3 and are proficient in reading, writing, and arithmetic by the time most American children are starting kindergarten. There usually is a long waiting list for London nursery schools; however, the experience is thought to be well worth the wait.

If you are a resident in England three months or longer, your child is entitled to a place in a state school.

Parents of older children who wish to enroll them in British schools should be aware that the system of education has changed radically during the past ten years and is still in a state of flux. Therefore, it is essential to be advised properly by someone knowledgeable about British education.

While the American system is directed toward preparing the students for the American College Entrance Exams, the British system leads toward the GCE (General Certificate of Education) "O" (ordinary) level subject exams at the tenth or eleventh year and "A" (advanced) levels two or three years later. Subjects are taught in a different order and at different levels of intensity as compared with the American system. Additionally, after the "0" levels, each student must make the decision to study either arts or sciences and then limit himself to fewer subjects studied in depth. Some students completing this curriculum have had their English credentials accepted by Amer-

**Table 5**
**Schools Commonly Used by American Expatriates in Great Britain**

| School | Type | Plant | Students (S) and Faculty (F) | Curriculum | Accreditation |
|---|---|---|---|---|---|
| American School in London 2-8 Loudoun Rd. London, NW8 Tel. 722 0101 | Coed; day; ages 5–18 | Modern complex of 75 classrooms; 2 theaters; 3 gyms; 2 libraries | 1,600 (S) primarily U.S. and Canada, 132 (F) | U.S. college preparatory; open class plan | Middle States Assn. of Colleges and Secondary Schools; only school so accredited in London |
| International School of London Crowndale Rd. London, NW1 Tel. 388 0450 | Coed; day; ages 10–18 | On premises of Workingmen's College; 30 classrooms; 3 labs; auditorium; library; gym and sports field | 250 (S) 30% Britain; 15%, U.S.; 30 (F) | Preparatory for English O level, international baccalaureate, and U.S. college boards; field trips | |
| American Community School Heywood Portsmouth Rd. Cobham, Surrey Tel. (266) 7251 | Coed; day; ages 5–18 | Modern facilities on two campuses in Cobham and Middlesex | 1500 (S); 70% U.S.; 30% from 33 other nationalities | U.S. college prep; traditional American program | |
| Marymount International School George Rd. Kensington on Thames Surrey Tel. 942 8126 | Girls; boarding; ages 7–12 | On 7½-acre site 12 miles southwest of London; library; gym; labs; outdoor recreation | 180 (S); 22 (F) | International baccalaureate; U.S. college boards, selected O and A exams | Affiliated with Marymount College, New York; order of the Sacred Heart of Mary |

| | | | | |
|---|---|---|---|---|
| TASIS England<br>Coldharbour Lane<br>Thorp, Surrey<br>Tel. (09328) 65252 | Coed; boarding; ages 5-18 | 35-acre campus 18 miles from center of London | 380 (S); 85% U.S.; 38 (F) | U.S. college preparatory |
| *Other American Schools in Great Britain* | | | | |
| American School in Aberdeen<br>Craighton Rd. Cults<br>Aberdeen, Scotland<br>0224 868927 | Coed; day; ages 5-18 | On two nearby campuses in rural setting; upper school has new jr. high building; library; gym. Lower school situated on old private estate | 300 (S), primarily U.S.; 39 (F) | U.S. college preparatory and vocational |
| American School of Edinburgh<br>29 Chester St.<br>Edinburgh, Scotland<br>Tel. 031 225 9888 | Coed; day and boarding; ages 14-18 | | | U.S. college preparatory |

ican universities; but most parents fear that a transfer back to the United States or to other locations away from the British system would leave their high school-level students unable to meet the present stringent university requirements. As a result, they look for American-type schooling.

Some of the international schools have a program qualifying students for the International Baccalaureate diploma, which is generally accepted around the world by universities.

Table 5 lists schools commonly used by American residents in England and Scotland.

In addition to the schools listed in Table 5, there are several schools for other nationalities. The French sponsor a large Lycee Francais, but you must have good French-language ability to be admitted. The Germans, Japanese, Swedes, and Spaniards have their schools. Further information can be obtained from the European Council of International Schools, Inc., 18 Lavant Street, Petersfield, Hants (telephone 0730 68244). The U.S. military operates several schools for its personnel near London, and they may take a nonmilitary child on an exceptional basis.

Expatriates can conclude that education at the university level for their children need not require leaving England. Besides the justly famous English schools, there are several U.S. affiliated institutions. Some, such as Richmond College—a liberal arts college originally part of the University of London—and Schiller College—with branches in Paris and Madrid—have full programs leading to bachelor's degrees. Others are overseas branches of U.S. universities: Ithaca College's London Center and the program of the University of Maryland.

Continuing education for adults is provided by many institutions. Marymount College of Tarrytown, New York, has a London Center for women 25 years and older. Boston University and the University of Southern California have popular business administration courses.

Every conceivable educational course is offered in London, and many are available to expatriates. There are close to 100 courses on London alone at any given time. To find out where and what courses you can take, pick up a copy of *Floodlight* magazine on a newsstand, and it will give you a rundown on all that is available at educational centers within the jurisdiction of the Inner London Education Authority.

# Shopping

"It's almost pound for dollar," expatriates moan when describing shopping in London.

Sometimes a favorable exchange rate diminishes the bite, but London does merit its reputation as one of Europe's most expensive cities. It is also one of Europe's great shopping marts. With a little determination, you can uncover bargains available nowhere else.

When expatriates are asked what they cannot find or what they recommend bringing from home, the lists vary widely, yet they are always short.

As stated at the beginning of this chapter, there is no "downtown," but there are several primary shopping areas in London. The West End includes the average man's shopping street, Oxford, with the giant Selfridge's department store; the bargain hunter's Marks and Spencer; and the John Lewis department store, which boasts no one will undersell them, particularly in the appliance department. There is also posh shopping in the West End; and if you have lots of time, strong feet, and love to walk, you can cover it all in a leisurely day. Start at the Marble Arch and head east on Oxford Street to Oxford Circus. Here you turn south down Regent Street, one of the country's finest thoroughfares. Travel offices, all types of shops from one of the city's best toy stores to the famous Liberty's (antiques, elegant fabrics, exotic items from everywhere) front on Regent Street; and it is here that the city's most elaborate Christmas decorations arch across the thoroughfare during the holiday season.

Regent Street sweeps into Piccadilly Circus and then extends for a couple of blocks. You can walk its length or turn west at the Circus and head down Piccadilly, a street that earned its name from the piccadills (high collars) worn by the citizenry in the early Stuart period. Here are Simpson's, great for sweaters and famous for men's clothing, and Fortnum and Mason's, an emporium brimming with tradition, exclusiveness, and quality merchandise along with a superb food department. Among the other spots of interest along this street are the Piccadilly and Burlington arcades with lovely shops and Hatchards Bookshop, where well-informed clerks can come up with answers to just about any questions you might have pertaining to the literary world. Paralleling Piccadilly on the south is Jermyn Street with more top quality stores. Head back to Oxford Street with a tour along Old and New Bond Streets, both dedicated to exclusiveness, and branch onto Molton Street—classy, chic, and trendy with lovely boutiques. A few shops in this area close on Saturday afternoon, but many are open late on Thursday.

Approximately 10 minutes away from the West End by tube is the Knightsbridge shopping district, surrounded by one of London's most elegant neighborhoods and graced by Europe's largest department store, Harrod's. Situated on Brompton Road and stretching across one city block, Harrod's was started by a grocer, Henry Harroad, in 1849. Today, it has one of the most exotic (practical as well) grocery departments to be found in London. You can count over 400 different varieties of cheese in the food halls. But Harrod's has expanded so that it can claim to take care of its customers from cradle to grave. That's right—they even have a consultant on hand to arrange your funeral. Wednesday is the late night for shopping in this area.

In the neighborhood surrounding Sloane Square, 15 minutes by foot from Knightsbridge, are more shops, a theater, and the famed Peter Jones department store. Kings Road, known for both antiques and trendy, with-it clothes for the young at heart, enters the square on the west. Kings Road in recent years has overshadowed Carnaby Street, once the center for "mod" clothes and now rather scruffy.

The fourth—but in our opinion, not quite as desirable—major shopping area is Kensington. Stores here remain open late on Thursday.

In addition, there are certain areas within London that are famous for one particular item. Charing Cross, for example, is known for its many bookstores, although they are by no means confined strictly to this district.

There are large department stores elsewhere in London, and while the neighborhoods around them contain shops and restaurants, they do not qualify as primary or major shopping districts of the city. Along the boroughs' High Streets, shops close for a half day each week, usually on a Wednesday or Thursday. You will also find clusters of shops scattered everywhere, some with parking areas at their front doors, and one American-type shopping center, covered, massive, and with ample parking space; Brent Cross, as it is called, is to the northwest, about 10 minutes by car west of Hampstead.

There are several excellent books on shopping in London:

*London Shopping Guide* (Penguin Books, London), compiled by an American, Elsie Burch Donald, who has been living in London for a number of years. The fourth edition, 1981, is available in local bookstores and can lead you to just about any item you want to find.

*Village London, the Observer's Guide to the Real London,* edited by Peter Crookston (Arrow Books, London, 1978), is an excellent guide to High Street shopping. While it does not cover every High Street in London, it does give you a rundown on many areas that are popular with expatriates.

*London Guide A-Z.* (Geographers A-Z Map Company, Ltd., London, 1982). An invaluable pocket guide that not only has maps and lists places of interest for tourists, but also includes practical information for residents. Its shopping section has route maps for major shopping streets, showing each store on those streets.

Be prepared for a different approach to merchandising and customer service. Many shops are small and parking is often a problem, whether it is in the neighborhood or central London. Expatriates say that everything seems always to be "on order"; and when they do find certain items, they buy in large quantities.

"Believe it or not," said one absolutely bewildered American woman, "the favorite expression of salespeople when they are out of a popular items is, 'We have had so many calls for that, we are not going to restock it.' "

If there are only a few items left in a particular line of merchandise, the clerk may refuse to sell it to you on the grounds that there will be nothing left. And do not expect these clerks to overwhelm you with assistance or pleasant attitudes.

Generally, there is no problem exchanging merchandise or returning for credit. This particularly holds true for the large, reputable department stores. Stores have their individual charge account systems, and accept credit cards such as American Express.

Be sure to shop around, as prices vary from one store to another. It does not always follow that the more deluxe stores charge more for items. Some merchandise may actually be cheaper than in a so-called moderately priced establishment.

Sales are held twice yearly—after Christmas and in July. These are good times to buy linens.

For those who like the colorful excitement, the chance for a serendipitous discovery, and the sheer entertainment of outdoor markets, London is a paradise. Some of the most popular are:

Petticoat Lane. Sunday 9 a.m.-2 p.m. only. The biggest and best known. You may find virtually anything.

Camden Locke. Saturday and Sunday 9 a.m.-6 p.m. A general market for arts and crafts items, old clothes, and high class junk.

New Caledonian Market. Friday 5 a.m.-4 p.m. Specializing in antiques.

## *Services*

### *Appliance Repair*

There are numerous services now that repair and install American appliances. Check the telephone yellow pages for listings.

### *Plumbing*

Peter M. Linpower (8 Micklethwaite Road SW6; telephone 385 2349) specializes in plumbing problems and installations for American appliances as well as all general plumbing needs. You will find that his rates usually run slightly lower than plumber's fees in the major U.S. cities.

## Grocery Shopping and Food Preparation

### *Places to Go*

You will not find all the convenience foods you had at home, names will be different, cuts of meat will be a mystery, and you'll have to buy bags of sugar, flour, and the like in smaller quantities. There are no parking lots around most stores, so you'll have to walk your groceries home. However, the Waitrose Supermarket in Brent Cross Shopping Centre does have parking available. In many markets you'll find the baskets are much smaller than at home because the average woman shops daily, or at least several times a week. And while supermarkets have really caught on since the War, many of the older women, particularly, still prefer to shop in the smaller stores.

"Why should I save a pound a week shopping at a supermarket, only to have to give out two pounds to a doctor to repair my back," one Londoner indignantly told us. "I always injure my back having to wait in line so long for the cashier."

But in London supermarkets are here to stay, and they are becoming more Americanized as the years roll by. They now furnish bags (they are usually plastic and very small and you often must pay for them) and carry cleaning products—two unknowns not many years ago. At the Waitrose Store in Brent Cross, ask for brown bags. They have them, but they only dispense the paper variety when requested; otherwise, it's plastic.

There are several different types of groceries in London. Lining the High Streets are meat markets, green grocers for fruits and vegetables, bakeries, and grocery shops that are small and carry canned goods, cereals, cooked meats, cookies, and dairy products. Scattered around the city are chains of supermarkets: Tesco's, Sainsbury's, Macfisheries, Safeway, Fine Fare, Waitrose, and Pricerite. Safeway meats are favored by many Americans. The Europa chain has stores that stay open later and on Sundays. Many of the large departments stores have elegant food emporiums, especially Harrod's and Fortnum and Mason.

Many Indians living in London have opened small shops that keep much longer hours and fill the place of the U.S. 7-11-type stores.

Particularly popular with Americans because of its "back home" products is a small store by the name of Panzer's (15 Circus Road, London NW8; telephone 722 8162), close to the American School.

In the northwest suburban area try M. Chistians, Green Lane, Northwood, for many familiar U.S. products, such as cake mixes and baking chocolate.

For those who want the freshest food, good bargains, or both, and who can get out of bed very early in the morning, there are the wholesale markets like Smithfield for meat and Spitalfields for fruit and vegetables. Billingsgate, the fish market with a 1,000-year history, recently moved to a new modern facility.

Before you really begin to attack the food problems, you might like to pick up a local cookbook. Two we recommend are:

*British Cookery* (Croom Helm Ltd., London). This is a complete guide to culinary practice in the British Isles, based on research undertaken for the British Farm Produce Council and British Tourist Authority by the University of Strathclyde (Scotland). It is an excellent encyclopedia-type book that not only gives you recipes but tells you all you need to know about British foods from their history to the regional dishes of today.

*The Cookery Year* (Reader's Digest Assn. Ltd., London). This cookbook includes best buys for each month and recipes and background information.

For a top-notch reference source as to which stores specialize in which foods and where to buy the best, pick up the *Guide to Good Food Shops* (Macmillan, London).

## Tips for the Kitchen

### American-English Kitchen Equivalents

| American | English |
|---|---|
| Waxed paper | Greaseproof paper |
| Plastic wrap | Polythene, cling film |
| Mineral oil | Paraffin oil |
| Any dessert | Pudding, sweet |
| Farina | Semolina |
| Pie shell | Flan case, open plate tart |
| Spatula, turner | fish slice |
| Tomato ketchup—in some but not all cases | Tomato sauce |
| Tabasco sauce—when drops or 3/4 teaspoon is called for | Chili pepper sauce |
| Coleman's dry English mustard (very hot) | Mustard powder |

### Baking Hints

As we all quickly discover, using recipes from one country with products from another can result in some terrible flops. Here are a few suggestions that might minimize the disasters.

Try Allisons or Country Life *strong* bread flour. Frequently, extra flour is necessary to get the proper consistency.

McDougal's Extra Fine Flour is considered to be the nearest in texture to our cake and pastry flour.

Use English recipes for cake baking, as cakes seem to be particularly elusive with American recipes.

Cookeen is a good substitute for shortening such as Crisco.

Brown sugar in boxes is often *very* hard. Try buying it in plastic bags, either in Sainsbury's or in the Health Food Shop.

### Weights and Measures

*Liquid Measure.* The American pint is 16 fluid ounces, as opposed to the British pint, which is 20 fluid ounces. The American one-half pint measuring cup is, therefore, actually equivalent to two-fifths of a British pint.

*Solid Measure.*

| American | English |
|----------|---------|
| 2 cups | 1 pound butter or other fat |
| 4 cups | 1 pound flour |
| 2 cups | 1 pound granulated or castor sugar |
| 3 cups | 1 pound icing sugar |
| 2¹/₂ cups | 1 pound brown sugar |
| 2 cups | 1 pound rice |
| 1 level tablespoon | ¹/₂ ounce flour |
| 1 heaped tablespoon | 1 ounce flour |
| 1 level tablespoon | ¹/₂ ounce butter |

*Weight.* The unit of weight—called a *stone*—equals 14 pounds.

*Oven Temperatures*

| Degrees Fahrenheit | Degrees Centigrade | Gas Mark |
|--------------------|--------------------|----------|
| 475 | 250—very hot | 9 |
| 450 | 225 | 8 |
| 425 | Hot | 7 |
| 400 | 200 | 6 |
| 375 | Moderate to moderately hot | 5 |
| 350 | 175 | 4 |
| 325 | Moderately slow | 3 |
| 300 | 150 | 2 |
| 275 | Slow | 1 |
| 250 | 130 | ¹/₂ |
| 225 | 100—very slow | ¹/₄ |

## Transportation

Public transportation is excellent. Buses, subways (known as the underground or tube), trains, and even the airports interconnect. Anyone capable of reading a simple map can find his way on the underground, which runs from 5:30 a.m. to midnight. These maps can be picked up at the major underground stations; there also are giant-sized diagrams of the routings on station walls.

Taking the double-decker bus is delightful but more difficult. It takes some study of the bus routings posted on signposts at the various stops or a review of your map. Red buses crisscross the central area and extend far into the suburbs, where the green buses take over for travel into the country. You also can catch a Green Line coach for an express trip between the country and the city. The single-deck Red Arrow buses in central London provide a semiexpress service between major railroad stations with a minimum of stops.

If you are a commuter by tube or bus or if you use them on a regular basis, you might like to take advantage of some of the bargain fares. Ask about an underground season ticket, a London bus pass, a suburban bus pass, a monthly bus pass, an annual bus pass, add-on tickets, go-as-you-please tickets, cheap day return, red bus rover, Sunday tube fares, off-peak maximum bus fares, elderly persons' travel permit, and children's cheap travel.

There are also special fares for Green Line buses. Buy an outback off-peak cheap day return ticket or try a golden rover, which offers unlimited travel for a day.

A few all-night buses run in central London. Buses also travel throughout England; for information on this service contact National Travel (NBC) Ltd. (National Express Service, Victoria Coach Station, 184 Buckingham Palace Road, SW1; telephone 730 0202).

London taxis are probably the most comfortable in the world and the drivers are the most knowledgeable. Interior head space must be high enough to accommodate a gentleman's top hat. It's doubtful you'll ever be able to give the driver an address he won't know. An extra charge is made for each additional passenger, for each piece of luggage carried on the driver's platform, and for trips between midnight and 6 a.m. There is no bargaining on fares unless you want the driver to take you outside London.

Years ago when the railways were first built, the city fathers ruled that no tracks would cross the city center. Today, you find no central train station but rather a series of them: Liverpool, Kings Cross, St. Pancras, Euston, Marylebone, Paddington, Victoria, Charing Cross, and Waterloo. They delineate the limits of central London, and they are connected with the subway system.

Air transportation from London is excellent and you will be able to reach just about any place in the world. There are two international airports: Heathrow, which can be reached by both bus and underground, and Gatwick, which is connected to the city by a train that runs from Victoria Station.

If you have a spark of adventure in your soul, driving a car in England, particularly London, may be a delightful challenge. Remembering to keep the car on the left side of the road is not so difficult, but the little habits accumulated from years of driving on the other side are hard to break—glimpsing into the mirror on the opposite side or going in the right direction at a roundabout (traffic circle). The British sense of fair play does not always prevail on the highways, and you may catch someone passing on a curve or hill. Also, the hedgerows along the country roads are high and sometimes make visibility poor. Road signs are a puzzle. At country intersections you will find directions to all the little villages along your route rather than just the name of the largest town ahead.

If you are in a hurry, there are motorways linking the major towns. Join the Automobile Association (AA) (Fanum House, 5 New Coventry Street, London, WC2; telephone 954 7355) or the Royal Automobile Club (RAC) (83 Pall Mall, London, SW1; telephone 839 7050).

When driving, watch for bus lanes. These are marked by broad white lines, and private cars must keep out of them during certain hours. On some main streets, bus lanes are closed permanently to cars.

If you decide to buy a car, you might think about a secondhand one, since chances are good you won't want to bring the left-hand drive back to the States. Check with the family you are replacing to see if they have one for sale or check out such publications as the London evening papers, *Motor, Autocar,* and the *Motorist's Guide to New and Used Car Prices* for automobile listings. The auto clubs check and value secondhand cars for members.

Attend a class or two at the local driving school before you tackle the driver's test. Would-be drivers have been known to fail simply because they did not place their hands correctly on the steering wheel. One expatriate who has lived in many foreign cities says this is the toughest test of all. When it's time for the driving test, apply for an appointment on Form DL26 (M), obtainable from any post office. If you have any questions, contact the Metropolitan Traffic Area Office (Driving Tests, Post Office Box 643, Bromyard Avenue, The Vale, Acton). Application for the license itself is made on Form DL1, also obtainable at the post office.

To find your way around London, be sure to purchase the *London Deluxe A-Z Street Atlas and Index* (Geographer's A-Z Map Co., Ltd., London).

At night, keep your parking lights on if you are more than 25 feet away from a street light; a car parked along a bus route at night must always have the parking lights on. You'll find parking meters in effect from 8:30 a.m. to 6:30 p.m. throughout central London, and they vary in price and time limits. Only card holders have the right to park in certain areas.

You'll love to walk in London, but remember to look *right* when crossing the street. At a zebra crossing where you find not only the black and white stripes on the street but also flashing orange lights, the pedestrian has the right-of-way, but still be cautious. Two lines of studs and traffic lights to stop traffic is called a pelican crossing. Here, you must push a button to stop traffic to make it safely across the street.

## Communications

Remember the good old days when American newsstands were crowded with fiercely competitive newspapers? You will find it all again in London. There are 24 daily newspapers, including communist, Indian, Polish, and Arab papers. Eight major morning and two evening papers are published. On Sundays you will discover seven papers. Depending on your personal taste, you can select anything from flashy tabloids to conservative, reactionary, pompous journals.

There is one weekly newspaper published for Americans in Britain called *The American*. It covers news of interest to the expatriate community, current events, features on many topics, the arts, business, travel, and contains a handy guide to American organizations on the last page.

Each area of London and the suburbs has its own newspaper, some of them quite good. They will tell you what is going on locally, and they often are a good source of real estate information. For example, three good weekly publications—*Time Out, What's on in London,* and *Where to Go*—will keep you informed of local happenings, and a trendy, monthly publication called *London Index* carries some interesting features along with a lot of fashion and shopping news. *Which* is a consumer's guide. The *Illustrated London News* is very English but fun to read for anyone who wants to know all current culture available—lectures, concerts, art exhibits, and the like, as well as fascinating articles and many photos.

Viewers of public television channels in major U.S. cities have appreciated many high quality British television productions. There are two networks in England, the British Broadcasting Corporation (BBC)—the government network with no commercials—and the Independent Television Authority (ITV)—a private network with advertising.

Both the BBC and ITV have two channels. The second ITV channel just came on the air in November 1982 and is the first new station in two decades. It has sparked considerable controversy about its programming, which includes American pro football, extended evening newscasts, and avant-garde drama. Both networks have introduced another innovation: morning shows with news, weather, features and interviews.

Britons have become avid purchasers of videotape recording machines, as have other Europeans with bland national television programming. Cable service is still in the experimental stage.

Each network has several radio stations of varying programming—from light music to university level courses. Britons depend upon the "pirate" stations broadcasting from offshore for more adventurous radio fare.

Listings of BBC programs are in its publication, *Radio Times.* ITV programs are covered in *TV Times.*

The telephone system is good but expensive, and you rent your phone from the post office. Remember that you pay for all local calls. It is customary to offer 10p if you use a phone in a shop. Also, it is polite to offer to pay 5p or 10p if for some reason you have to use the phone of a neighbor. The English people do this. When using a pay phone, read the instructions carefully, as the system is quite different from that in the States.

The post office also issues licenses for automobiles, pets, televisions, hunting and driving; and hands out lists of neighborhood doctors who participate in the National Health Service. It will wake you up in the morning (191), advise you of children's activities (246 8007), give you business news (248 8026), food price news (248 8035), weather (836 4311), road conditions (246 8021), events for tourists (246 8041), and still more services listed in the telephone book. The office at 21 King William Street, Trafalgar Square, WC2, very obligingly keeps its doors open 24 hours a day.

It takes about three days for an airmail letter to reach the States. Cablegrams between the nations arrive within 24 hours. Telegrams can be sent from the post office or phoned. Dial 829 2345 for inland telegrams and 836 1222 for international telegrams. You can dial directly to the United States.

## Free Time

### *Tours*

You can discover London on your own by climbing aboard a city bus for a two-hour circle trip (from Piccadilly Circus, Marble Arch, and Victoria); boarding a boat along the Thames (at the Tower,

Richmond, Putney, Kew, Hampton Court, Greenwich, or Charing Cross bridges from April to October); or exploring on foot. There are dozens of tours that will take you everywhere from backstage at the theaters through London pubs or into the areas of high life and scandal. There are museums for every interest, and the lecturers are superb. Don't miss a talk at the Tate. Good books to guide you through your free time are:

*Michelin London* (Michelin, London). Not only does this give you detailed information about what to see, it also gives you background information on all the sites. At the front of the book is information on the history of the city, the government of London, the architecture and architects, and famous people.

*Nicholson's London Guide* (Nicholson, London). A rundown on everything from sightseeing to theater, shopping, and transportation. It's one of the best.

*London: Your Sightseeing Guide* (British Tourist Authority, London). There are pictures as well as information. It is not as detailed as others but still good.

*Nicholson's Guide to American's London* (Nicholson, London). While definitely slanted toward the American tourist, it is of interest to those who stay on for a while. In addition to sightseeing tips, it lists American airline offices, has a section on American history in London, and explains some very British sports such as rugby and cricket.

*Village London, the Observer's Guide to the Real London* (Arrow Books, London). This is one of our favorites. It is not the usual sightseeing manual, but it does tell you all about certain London villages, what to see and do there, where to eat, and what to buy. Tips that you would not get in the standard guidebook are included.

*The Penguin Guide to London* (Penguin, London). Details! Details! This is more than a guide book; it is almost encyclopedic in the background it gives on each site. It is a good reference source.

*London Walks* (Thames and Hudson, London). London is presented through a series of walks. There are excellent details with fascinating tidbits and personal comments by the author.

*Country Walks* (London Transport, London). This book definitely is designed for those who have more than a few days to spend in London. It is an excellent choice for the expatriate who has time to explore a particular area away from the usual tourist haunts. Most of the recommended walks are within reach of the London transport system. Some are just beyond but can be reached by the Green Line coaches from London. One walk, for example, called "American

Origins," takes you on a tour through Chorleywood, Sarratt, King's Langley, and Watford.

## Theater

The first permanent theater opened in London 400 years ago and today the theater scene is many faceted: the West End, comparable with Broadway, and fringe and outer London theaters, innovative and unique. On any given evening you can select from close to 100 productions. Some are American hits exported to London, some English successes destined for Broadway. Ticket prices in London are rising sharply, but they are still less than in New York.

## Music

Jazz, rock, recitals, chamber music, symphonic concerts, opera—every conceivable musical form of the Western world (and some beyond) is available in London. Check the newspapers and entertainment magazines for listings of musical events. Dance in every form is also to be found.

## Movies

Films in England are rated much as they are in the States but with a slightly different letter code. An X-rated film is just about the same as it is on the other side of the Atlantic with no one under 18 allowed into the theater. Anyone 14 or over can attend A films, while a U movie is for the general public, but with some material possibly not suitable for children under 14.

You can buy tickets in advance for a movie playing in the West End theaters, and sometimes this is a very wise move, particularly if it is a popular film. Theaters just a short distance from the West End or in the suburbs will charge much lower rates.

## Entertainment Centers

London has several halls and centers that are entertaining in themselves because of their historical grandeur or modern adaptability. The newest is the nine-level arts extravaganza, Barbicon Centre, with a total floor area of over 20 acres. It is the new home of the London Symphony Orchestra and the Royal Shakespeare Company. In addition to halls for these performers, the Centre has three cinemas, an art gallery, library, several restaurants, and facilities for meetings and conferences. It has been acclaimed for its acoustical excellence.

Another impressive complex is the South Bank Arts Centre—incorporating Royal Festival Hall—where almost 300 patrons can enjoy acoustically superior concerts and the newer National Theater. There are two smaller concert halls, a film theater, an art gallery, numerous restaurants, bars, and cafes. All are linked by attractive walkways and enhanced by beautiful landscaping and sculpture.

Other famous houses are Royal Albert Hall, Queen Elizabeth Hall, and the Royal Opera House.

## Sports

Yes, there is baseball in Britain, and any other sport from badminton to rugby union. London is the location for many international competitions that will enthrall spectators. Participants on an amateur basis can find organizations and facilities for their recreation. There is a British Amateur Baseball and Softball Federation. Guidebooks, such as the *London Guide A-Z,* list all of these. Another good reference is the annual *Sports Directory* issued by the Greater London Council for Sport and Recreation, 160 Great Portland Street, W1; telephone 580 9092.

Take golf, for example. The Automobile Association publishes a *Guide to Golf in Great Britain* listing over 1,500 courses. (It also publishes a similar guide on angling.) The clubs near London have waiting lists. Some are particularly popular with Americans. One is the Moor Park Golf Club, Rickmansworth, Hertfordshire, with two 18-hole courses open to the public on weekdays.

Even water skiing is available close by. While this sport usually takes place on the south and southwest coasts, there are facilities in Kent. Check with the British Water Ski Federation (16 Upper Woburn Place, WC1; telephone 387 9371).

Who knows? You may even become a fan of those esoteric British sports rugby and cricket.

## London on a Sunday

At first glance, London may appear to be shuttered on Sunday. Many museums are open, but legitimate theaters, stores, and many restaurants, particularly in the central part of the city, are closed. Even in the outer boroughs where you will find some eating places open, don't expect to drop in at any time for a meal. They probably will have a definite luncheon time, close for a while, and then reopen for dinner. There are a few exceptions such as the Milk Pail in Hampstead, which stays open throughout Sunday afternoon and serves a delicious bowl of hot chili along with herb bread and a good salad at very reasonable prices.

Sunday is a good time to stop in for tea at one of the posh hotels. Try the Ritz Hotel on Piccadilly or perhaps the Dorchester Hotel on Park Lane.

Here are a few places that expatriates favor on a Sunday.

Dickens Inn by the Tower
St. Katherine's Way, E1
488 2208
Traditional tavern in an historic setting.
English and continental fare.

Spaniard's Inn
Spaniard's Road, Hampstead NW3
This inn dates from 1580 and is full of tradition and atmosphere and a fascinating group of people on a Sunday afternoon. Lunches are served.

Louis of Hampstead
32 Heath Street NW3
The crowds line up outside the door on a Sunday afternoon for a spot of tea and some of the delicious Hungarian and continental pastries. You also can take the pastries home.

The Coach and Horses
8 The Green, Kew
This large pub, which dates back to 1580, is a great place to stop after a Sunday visit to the nearby Royal Botanical Gardens.

Wander through the open-air art exhibit on Bayswater Road on Sunday and take a look at pottery, prints, paintings, and jewelry for sale. Stop at the Speaker's Corner in Hyde Park and listen to orators vent their emotions or browse through Petticoat Lane Market on Middlesex Street in the morning.

## Organizations

Many of the posh clubs are grouped around Pall Mall and St. James Street in Westminster. If you happen to be in the area and see scores of gentlemen dressed in conservative dark suits heading toward the doors of stately, elegant buildings, keep in mind that they are not heading for a wake. They are simply on their way to a luncheon or dinner engagement at their club.

Here are some organizations for expatriates:

The American Club
95 Piccadilly W1
499 2303
Primarily a men's luncheon club.

The American Women's Club
1 Cadogan Gardens off Sloane Square SW3
730 2033
This is a club for American women and British women married to Americans. Its facilities include a beautiful old mansion with many meeting rooms, offices, and a restaurant and bar.

The English Speaking Union
37 Charles Street, Berkeley Square W1
629 0104
A lovely old mansion is once again headquarters for an organization. This club promotes a better understanding between the English and American people.

For a complete listing of these organizations, see the last page of *The American* weekly.

## Children's London

London is brimming with children's treasures. The list is endless, and for more details than space allows here, we suggest a number of publications. Available at the Tourist Information Centre (64 St. James Street SW1; 629 9191):

*Britain: Children on Holiday* (British Tourist Authority, London). This book covers what to do with the children while on vacation. It leads you to places not only in London but all over England, Scotland, Wales, and Ireland as well. It tells you which hotels have special facilities for children, which parks in London have activities designed strictly for youngsters, where to get baby-sitters or send your little ones to nursery school, sites to visit in all the above countries that are of particular interest to children, and special places where you can send the kids when you don't want to go along. It is an excellent reference source.

*Activity and Hobby Holidays* (English Tourist Board, London). You will turn the pages of this book constantly muttering to yourself, "unbelievable." The list of vacation spots where you can pursue a hobby, learn a new sport, or simply improve upon an old one is incredible. The book will be of interest to children about 10 or 11 and up and adults as well.

Available at bookstores throughout London:

*Village London: The Observer's Guide to the Real London* (Arrow Books, London). This book covers the best-known villages of London and not only tells you what they are like but also what to see and do there. At the end of each chapter is a special heading, "Good for Kids," and it leads the youngsters to some rather unique activities around London.

*Parent's Guide to Children's London* (Nicholson, London). As are other Nicholson guidebooks, this is a good one. It tells you what is going on for youngsters both in the cultural area and in the strictly amusement field. It also gives you a rundown on various organizations in the city that pertain to children's interests.

*Kids London* (Piccolo Pan, London). From active to passive activities, from the esoteric to the practical, this book covers bits of everything. It not only will tell you where your children can learn to ride, it also will direct you to horse shows. Interested in theater? Haunted houses? Sightseeing? Sports? Nature? This publication will tell you how and where to see and do it all. Excellent.

*Daily Telegraph Children's Guide to London* (Collins, London). An absolutely superb book for teenagers who want to do London on their own. It also has some excellent advice on how to take care of yourself when your parents are not along. In addition to what to see and do, this book also gives you places to eat as well as to buy clothes, books, and hobbies.

Before setting out to buy any of these books, we suggest you call your local bookstore or the tourist authority to make certain books are in. They are often fast sellers, and sometimes stores are out of stock. During holiday times (Christmas, Easter, and summer), check the *Daily Telegraph* for a listing of all current activities for children.

In addition to concerts, theater, puppet shows, museums, art classes, and even a bookstore for children (Children's Book Centre,

299 Kensington High Street W8; telephone 937 6314), there is a unique organization called the Molecule Club, which presents fascinating musical plays that explain science to the kids. There are even walking tours for the youngsters—try Junior Jaunts (13a Harriet Walk SW1; 235 4750).

## Churches

Churches of all denominations can be found throughout London. One of particular interest to the expatriate community is the American Whitfield Memorial Church (Tottenham Court Road; 580-6433).

The Saturday edition of the *Times* carries a detailed listing of church services in London, noting the preacher and the music to be sung.

## Health Care

If you are a resident, permanent or temporary, for at least three months, you are eligible for National Health Service. It is free—or almost. You will have to make a partial payment on medicines, prescription glasses, dentures, and dental treatment (except for examination). Hospital care, which includes bed, surgery, treatment, nursing, and medicines, is free.

You might like to choose private medical care. Here you will have control over both the doctor and time of treatment. Under National Health Service care, there is a long waiting list for the hospitals, even surgery that is considered nonessential, and you will be placed in a large open ward. As a private patient, you will have a single room. The British United Providence Association (BUPA) provides insurance for private medical care.

There are many private doctors and dentists, including orthodontists and periodontists. Check with a friend or neighbor or ask for the lists of doctors and dentists at the American consulate.

Here are pharmacies that are open all night:

Boots
Piccadilly Circus, London W1
This pharmacy has shops all over London.

John Bell and Croydon
50 Wigmore Street, London W1
Will deliver in some areas.

H. D. Bliss
50 Willesden Lane, London NW6

Don't be surprised if your physician makes a house call!

## Doing Business in London

Sir Winston Churchill's comment during World War II—to the effect that America and the United Kingdom were two countries divided by a common language—should be taken seriously by the American businessman about to take up an assignment in Britain. The differences in the common language are manifold and manifest every day. The everyday usage of common terms will soon assure the neophyte that there are far more serious errors than just calling the boot a trunk or the bonnet a hood in one's automobile (oops, that should be "carriage").

Business in Britain can be either very formal or disarmingly informal. Business in the City with your banker friend will be formal and very correct. Appointments will be made well in advance and kept with the precision of a well-oiled watch—10 a.m. means 10 a.m., not 10:03 a.m. or 9:57 a.m.; but be prepared and allow time for that avenging angel who guards the front reception desk and the equally protective private secretary who will gather your credentials and, after proper scrutiny and presentation of your calling card, announce your presence to her boss. It pays to bring a flower bud, a bit of candy, or a little business gift to the secretary occasionally. You can save yourself hours of waiting while she "puts you through" to her boss when you ring in for a chat. Don't bother trying to get your party on the telephone before you are "put through"; you will never win this, so just give up and accept it as the way one does business in Britain.

A pitfall for Americans can be the business lunch. Some words of caution are worthwile. You will soon learn that lunch with an English colleague can be anything from a kidney pie and a pint at the nearby pub to a marathon all-afternoon event from which most Englishmen will go straight home and never return to work (not that they would be in much shape to work anyway, after six or seven gin and tonics). Avoid this lunch when you can!

If informality is the keynote, take your business guest to your local golf club. These courses are very nice, relatively inexpensive, and a good place to discuss your business problems away from the telephone and secretarial intrusions—but please, not on the greens or on the fairway. Wait until you are safely in the nineteenth hole for discussion, as you both cool down from the round with a soothing drink.

If you are friendly with a top executive, you can be invited to a shoot or duck flighting by a business associate. It is likely to be a very formal affair with engraved invitations, "proper" shooting clothes (tweed jackets, plus fours, ties, and the like), and face masks (to avoid the ducks' seeing your face), and they often extend into an eight-course meal and the wee hours of the morning. You will be expected to furnish your own firearms, shells (cartridges), and so forth, but don't expect to bring any game home, other than a brace of birds. Your host considers the harvesting of his game as the harvesting of any other money crop. His gamekeeper, his kennel keeper, and his dog handlers must be paid; and his wild game is a valuable asset.

For information on how to conduct yourself in the field, discuss this fully with either an English colleague whom you trust or with another American who has experience. If you are invited on a "hunt," get your saddle-sore lotion ready and make sure that you do not confuse the *hunt, shoot, stalking,* or *flighting* terms.

In London, dress is important—whether you are in the City, in the West End, on the golf course, in the field shooting, on a duck flight, or at the cricket field. There are proper clothes for every occasion. The normal businessman will rely on the "lounge" suit, which is referred to as a business suit in America. Dark blue or black pinstripes are suitable for most business wear. Formal attire may be full dress tails or conventional tuxedo. There are suitable rental agencies located throughout the City and the West End that offer proper consultations on correct attire for any formal occasion.

The most important thing for an American businessman to remember is to use his English staff as resources on the way to conduct business in Britain. It is well to consider that English business is different and that if change is to occur, it must be the American who adapts to the way the host country operates. As with every rule, there is an exception. Here the exception is first, last, and always—do not compromise your American business standards. American business acumen is respected worldwide.

Most businessmen overseas are not prepared to live their businesses 24 hours a day, as do Americans, preferring to keep their private lives private and to conduct their business during specified business hours. It is well to learn and to respect other ways of doing business. You will, in turn, gain a reputation for being a good guest in the host country.

Being an American businessman in London can be fun and very rewarding. There are few places in the world that equal London as a business city, and the access to living within a very few minutes of your office can be downright habitforming. Most executives dread to see the day when a return to New York or a similar stateside post will come. The excitement of the city, the excellent entertainment, and the safe and friendly surroundings make it one of the top assignments (if not the very best) abroad. Regardless of how long you stay, you will have tears in your eyes when you leave London.

## Legal Matters

### *Currency*

The mind-boggling English currency system of pounds, shillings, and pence gave way to a decimal system several years ago. The unit is still the pound sterling, now divided into 100 new pence. Twopence coins are especially handy for public telephones.

### *Exchange Control*

Once a bastion of restrictions, regulations, and red tape, England now has no foreign exchange control.

### *Visas and Registration*

Most people going to England for employment require a work permit, which is issued by the Department of Employment on application of the prospective employer for work requiring professional qualifications, skills, or experience that a British national cannot provide. The permit holder is usually admitted for up to 12 months, but extensions may be granted. After four years an expatriate can apply for removal of any further time limit. If granted, the expatriate is free to take any employment without further approval. The spouse and children of a permit holder are admitted for the same period. Ministers, doctors and dentists, European Economic Community (EEC) nationals, and a few other categories do not need work permits.

Foreign Nationals with work permits have to register after three months with the Aliens Registration Office (10 Lambs Conduit Street, WC1; telephone 725 2458). Two photos are required.

## Personal Effects

You, or your agent, are responsible for making certain declarations to customs when your goods arrive. If you are present, the declarations are made orally. If not, then you must have an agent and have completed the form "Declaration by Importers of Effects Other Than Motor Vehicles." Don't forget to give your agent the keys to any locked cases.

## Pets

England enforces a very strict rabies control program. All pets entering the country (dogs, including blind guide dogs, cats, and other animals) must be quarantined at the owner's expense in an approved kennel for six months. An authorized agent must pick up the animal at the airport and carry it to the kennel. Lists of agents and kennels and an application for an import license can be obtained from the British Information Services, 845 Third Avenue, New York, N.Y. 10022; telephone (212) 752-8400.

## Automobiles

If you are going to be in England for 12 months or more, one automobile or motorcycle may be imported without duty and tax. The vehicle must have been owned and used abroad for at least a year before arrival, it must be for personal use, and it cannot be offered for sale or hire or otherwise disposed of for a period of two years from the date of import. Incidentally, this same one-year use-and-ownership requirement applies to photographic equipment, major appliances, hi-fi equipment, and some other items.

## Operating an Automobile

An expatriate may drive under a valid overseas or international driver's license for three months. After this he must take out a provisional license and display "L" (learner) plates. Holders of a provisional license must be accompanied while driving by someone with a valid Great Britain permit until he passes the driving test—and that is no snap. The test has the reputation of being complete and difficult. It is advisable to make an appointment to take the test, as there may be a delay of up to six months before one can be arranged. Driving offenses involving drinking are very serious. People convicted of drunken driving are almost always disqualified from driving for at least one year, and they may be heavily fined or sent to prison. The minimum driving age is 17.

Third-party liability insurance is compulsory in England. Litigation from automobile accidents is increasing, but it has not yet reached U.S. levels. Nevertheless, a typical case in England may require a year or more before trial.

## Guns

Anyone in England wishing to possess a rifle, shotgun, or handgun must have a certificate issued by the police. Such certificates are issued only for good cause, and personal protection is not regarded as good cause. Apply for a certificate before importing the gun at the Import Licensing Branch of the Department of Trade (16-20 Great Smith Street, London SW1).

## Marriage

Anyone 18 or over may marry in England. Young people between 16 and 18 need their parents' written consent. A license is required but not a blood test.

## Divorce

In general, a divorce is a rather simple procedure in England. The one cause is "irretrievable breakdown of the marriage," but the facts to prove such breakdown are the usual offenses of desertion, adultery, cruelty, or neglect. The simplest way to proceed is to have an agreed separation, which is recognized at law. After a two-year separation, an agreed decree can be granted for divorce with minimal cost and formality. Once an English court has jurisdiction and has granted a divorce, it maintains that jurisdiction forever, and either of the parties can return to the court for modification of the terms.

## Women's Rights

Most of the facets of the women's movement have been recognized officially by various laws in England. A wife has a right to retain in her own name any property she possesses at the time of marriage or acquires later and to take what belongs to her if the marriage is dissolved. A woman can obtain charge accounts and credit status in her own right. British women comprise one of the highest proportions of the workforce of any EEC country.

## Housing — Purchase and Renting

Houses are located through estate agents who do not operate through multiple listings. Each agent has his own listings. He generally is more interested in representing the seller of the property, since it is the seller who pays the sales commission. Mortgages are available for long terms (20 to 30 years) from building societies or life insurance companies. There are several important tax implications of a home purchase for an expatriate (see the section on taxes below). One nice feature is that there is no capital gains tax on the sale of one's personal residence.

The typical English rental agreement is much like that found in the United States, although subletting is generally prohibited. In some cases, the lessor may be willing to accept a reassignment clause to allow the lessee to break the lease term upon involuntary transfer. Typically, the lessee will be responsible for payment of all utilities and the real estate taxes or "rates."

## Death

On the death of a foreign national in England, any property that the deceased owns located in the country will be subject to English inheritance provisions. A solicitor should be consulted for specific details.

## Children

The drinking age is 18 for any beverage containing alcohol. Serving alcohol in private, as in your home, to a child below 18 is not a violation of law. Children of expatriates are not liable for military service. Adoption is almost impossible for foreign nationals.

## Drugs

Drugs, including marijuana, are rigidly controlled. There is a sharp distinction made, however, between offenses of trafficking—carrying very severe penalties—and offenses of possession. But even penalties for possession can run up to seven years in prison. Police have the power to search any person or vehicle without a warrant if they have reasonable grounds to suspect that a person has an illegal drug. Treatment of drug dependence is regarded primarily as a medical and social responsibility and, therefore, is provided through the National Health Service.

## Taxes

The Queen's English may be sacred in the United Kingdom, but Inland Revenue (their Internal Revenue) has some ingenious definitions for the term _resident_ when applied to taxation. For example, it is possible to work in England for portions of two years without being considered a resident and without any tax liability. Here's how it goes.

The length of time you spend in England is the principal determining factor, but other situations helping to establish residency are the purchase of a residence—from where your remuneration comes—and intent. You are not even considered a resident if you work in the United Kingdom for less than a year in total and spend less than six months in the country in any one tax year. As a "visitor" you are still subject to tax on your British income. The British/U.S. tax treaty may knock out that liability if you are not present in the United Kingdom for more than 183 days in any tax year and if your remuneration is paid by a non-British entity. This provides the tax-free situation first mentioned.

If you came to stay for up to three years and do not buy a residence, you are taxed on your total British earnings and on one-half of earnings in the United Kingdom paid by an overseas employer but not on remuneration for services outside England. Expatriates in this category are "resident but not ordinarily resident."

You are considered "ordinarily resident" when you have worked in the United Kingdom, or intend to stay, for over three years or you buy a residence. As such, you are taxed the same as the shorter-term resident in the preceding paragraph, except that the exemption for services outside the United Kingdom is reduced or eliminated. After nine working years, the liability for remuneration from an overseas employer is increased.

Your taxable remuneration includes reimbursed business expenses, foreign service allowances, and tax obligations paid by your employer (which amount is used to gross-up your British taxable income). Everyone except short-term visitors are subject to taxation of capital gains. The one interesting exception is that gain on the sale of a principal residence is not taxed.

Deductions are less generous than in the United States. Medical expenses, real estate taxes, charitable contributions, and value-added taxes are not deductible.

England has the PAYE—pay-as-you-earn—system similar to U.S. withholding. The return filing date is April 5. No calculation or payment of tax accompanies the return. You will be assessed, and then you must pay within 14 days unless an appeal is filed.

# 15

# Assignment Brussels

THE PROBLEM WITH AN ASSIGNMENT in Brussels is that you may never want to come home again. She is the best of many worlds—past, present, and future. To the expatriate she offers a special bonus: some of the best living conditions to be found anywhere in Europe.

To begin with, Brussels is beautiful. Her broad avenues lead past bubbling fountains surrounded by colorful summer flower beds and on through fairyland forests. Elegant, old town homes and luxurious apartments line her streets. Hidden in parklike gardens are grand old chateaus.

Modern office buildings mix serenely with Gothic structures, and narrow, medieval, cobblestone streets—one so narrow that two people cannot walk side by side—twist past century-old buildings just a short distance away from some of Europe's most efficient city expressways. It is a fantasyland and a modern, brisk, functional city all rolled into one magnificent package.

Brussels' old quarter with its breathtaking Grand Place, best viewed for the first time at night when lights shine on the fifteenth-century Gothic Hotel de Ville and the surrounding guild halls, is picture-postcard perfect. It is the Europe that tourists often want to see but can't find in the postwar steel and concrete towers. "The Grand Place," says Donald Cowie in *Belgium, the Land and the People* (A. S. Barnes, New York, 1977), "should be treated as a love affair."

Just as Brussels is symbolic of Europe's past splendors, she is singularly important as a city of today. Nearly 2,000 companies from around the world have established their European headquarters there right along with many Belgian firms. Her opulent shops, modern homes, transportation systems, and multinational organizations reflect a spirit of twentieth-century efficiency. Brussels calls herself "the capital of Europe"; and whether other European cities are willing to concede to the claim, Brussels at least can boast of having the European Economic Community (EEC) and the North Atlantic Treaty Organization (NATO) within her boundaries. NATO is designed to preserve Europe as part of the free world, and the EEC is the nucleus for a dream many have had for a united Europe.

Traditionalists may scoff at the giant Atomium that stands on the grounds that hosted the city's World's Fair in 1958. From a distance it looks like a tinker toy. But its nine massive silver globes—each 18 meters in diameter and the top globe 100 meters from the ground—linked together by tubular spokes, represents a molecule of iron magnified 200 billion times and is an appropriate symbol of the scientific leap into the atomic age made by a city that in 1979 celebrated its 1,000th birthday. Brussels and Belgium, while important historically, do not live in the past.

It is amazing that Belgium, just slightly bigger than the state of Maryland and with limited natural resources, is one of the top industrial and exporting nations of the world. Until the 1970s, this tiny country (together with its postage stamp neighbor Luxembourg) was the second largest exporter of steel in the world after Japan.

This industrial might was nurtured in a spirit of free enterprise that allowed some very strong manufacturers to develop—such as the famous photographic supply house Gevaert-Agfa—yet prevented the excesses of monopolization and cartels. The small shopkeeper gets more support and is healthier in Belgium than in most other developed countries. There are rigid laws on unfair competition. Pricing, sales campaigns, and advertising are policed to ensure honest commercial use. Government subsidies and interference are minimal. The result is a well-balanced mix of large and small entrepreneurs that produce and sell high-quality products ranging from synthetic billiard balls and surgical instruments to weaving machines and locomotives.

Throughout history, Belgium was developing craftsmanship while its neighbors were fighting wars. If her industry was destroyed in the process, she just rebuilt with the newest machinery and processes. Today Belgium's dominant position in the EEC has helped her prosper through her exports to fellow members. Besides steel, Belgium's strengths are organic chemicals and plastics, textiles, glass making, and cement.

Belgium exports more than just manufactured products. She produces 80 percent of her own food supplies and ships abroad billions of francs' worth of dairy produce, sugar, chocolate, processed cereals, canned fruit, and luxury products. Belgian farms are relatively small but are very modern and specialized. Who has not relished brussels sprouts, Belgian endive, asparagus, and even azaleas?

"Not many of our friends back home knew much about Brussels and Belgium," said one American now living in the city. "They asked us all kinds of silly questions when we went back. Someone wanted to know if they spoke Belgian there."

The Belgians, of course, do not speak Belgian, and therein lies a mountain of trouble. Some speak Dutch (Flemish), others French; and as the saying goes, "Never the twain shall meet," let alone merge. Anyone planning to live in the country must understand the story behind the deep schism that divides the people of Belgium.

The problem began thousands of years ago when the bloody, warring tribes of Celts poured out of southwestern Europe and spread through other parts of the Continent. What today is known as Belgium became the heartland of their somewhat nebulous confederation. They were stubborn rascals. Even Caesar had difficulty bringing them under control, for the "Belgae," as he called them, "were the bravest of all the tribes of Gaul."

The Roman Empire managed to instill a few principles of government into the Belgae. It also left them with the know-how to collect taxes and a unique knowledge for growing grapevines and turning the fruit into a delectable beverage. The Belgae picked up the language and religion of their conquerors. But in the third century the Franks, a Germanic people, came pouring into the area. They were never able to subdue the Celts and their way of life completely, but they did plant permanent roots in the same area. This resulted in two distinct groups of people in a tiny plot not quite large enough to accommodate the nationalism and jealousy that began to ferment.

Although both languages are official, there is a distinct barrier between the Dutch-speaking Flemish—descendants of the early Franks, living in the area called Flanders in the northern portion of the country—and the French-speaking Walloons—whose ancestors were the stubborn Celts or Belgae, who settled in Wallonia, the southern part of the country. To complicate matters even more, there is a small German-speaking section in a corner near the German border. Flemish has little international popularity, except in a few spots such as South Africa and parts of the West Indies. French, on the other hand, is the language of international diplomacy. With Brussels a diplomatic center, many of the best positions tend to be held by the Flemish. This may seem inconsistent, but the Flemish have been forced to learn French and are bilingual. The Walloons have stuck to their primary language. Another curiosity of this language situation is that Belgium has never developed a strong literary heritage.

The territory that today is Belgium has had meddling neighbors throughout her history. Spain, Austria, and France have all had their turn at ruling her. If Americans know nothing else about Belgium, they usually can come up with the name of the town Waterloo, where Napoleon met his defeat at the hands of the British in 1815. To Americans who live in Belgium, Waterloo, just a few miles south of Brussels, has a special significance as it is one of the favorite residential communities for expatriates.

After Napoleon's defeat, the Congress of Vienna decided that Belgium should belong to the Netherlands. The Flemish and the Walloons, both strongly Catholic, could not abide the Dutch Protestants. In 1830 they fought and won their freedom from the Netherlands and became an independent nation.

Ironically, the Flemish and the Walloons have remained formidable, if not warring, antagonists in a nation bent on uniting all of Europe. In an attempt to appease the two groups, the government declared Brussels, which actually lies within the Flemish sector, a bilingual city. Today everything from government documents to restaurant menus is printed in both languages.

It is natural to want to stereotype the two groups—to say that the Flemish tend to be more reserved, deliberate, and serious while the Walloons are extroverted and full of spirit, gaiety, and wit. But just as you do, you think of the Flemish painter Pieter Brueghel, whose masterpieces of peasants and their lives show what art historian Erwin Panofsky calls a "simple, strong and uninhibited veracity." Expatriates will find a great variety of personalities among the Belgians, for their country has also been a melting pot of Europe in many respects.

It is just as difficult to stereotype Brussels. There is a cosmopolitan facade that has been created by her international role as the capital of Europe. Close to 200 ambassadors and thousands of deputies glut Brussels, not to mention the bureaucracy that sustains them. This has brought skyscrapers, expensive restaurants, and limousines into the narrow streets. Yet everywhere one sees evidence of both the antiquity of this city—which celebrated her 1,000th anniversary in 1979—and of the many artists who have enriched her.

Brussels usually accepts foreigners with gracious hospitality, but she is not always prepared for Americans, and especially their children. Some expatriates told the story of how their youngsters decided to go caroling one Christmas, candles in hand, through the streets of their neighborhood. The Belgians were terrified. They turned out the lights in their houses, ran for the second floors, and hid. "What," they wondered, "could all these children be doing with lighted candles?" Later, the expatriates learned that many of the local people were afraid the children were going to burn down their houses. Another group of children equally shocked their neighbors by going door to door in the American hard sell manner to peddle some hand-drawn pictures to earn money.

Still, foreign workers, and there are hundreds of thousands, are considered "family." They cannot be deported for economic reasons. In Brussels, foreigners constitute 10 percent of the population.

## Practical Pointers

Handshaking among both sexes, even children, is the accepted practice. After becoming better known, this may be replaced by the three kisses on the cheeks. Usually, two men will only shake hands.

A special tax is levied on restaurants that serve liquor, so the majority limit their alcohol to beer and wine. Spirits are sold in private clubs *(cercle prive),* where you simply sign a membership form.

Most hotel bars are private clubs. But relief may be coming. The government is expected to introduce a new licensing procedure to permit Belgium's 52,000 bars and restaurants to serve liquor.

In a city with a strong haute cuisine tradition, you will be surprised to learn that the two favorite gastronomical treats are *frites* (french fried potatoes) and *gaufres* (waffles). Frite shops serving bags of freshly fried potatoes dipped in mayonnaise or other sauces are still quite prevalent in Brussels, but are beginning to close down. Collectors fight to preserve these ubiquitous stands and the small two- or three-pronged forks served with the potatoes as folk art. The waffles, baked in cast iron molds and served sprinkled with sugar, are the inspiration for the Belgian waffles served at fairs and carnivals in the United States.

Bring warm clothing as summers are cool and winters cold, often below freezing. Dampness is a way of life in Brussels, with some precipitation on an average of 200 days a year.

Pigeons are not a nuisance in Brussels. They are, in fact, a very important part of the local sporting scene with pigeon racing being extremely popular. Champions bring high prices in the bird market at the Grand Place on Sunday mornings.

If you want to keep your insurance on your residence in effect, you must have all chimneys swept once a year and get a certificate to prove compliance.

Foreigners can participate in local government in Belgium. A few are elected or appointed to foreigners' councils, which serve as a liaison between the foreign community and the town government.

When invited to a Belgian home for dinner, even by a close friend, bringing a gift of flowers or chocolates is customary.

You are sure to notice the incredible omnipresence of dogs in Brussels.

Expatriates are unanimous in saying that the biggest single factor in being comfortable in Brussels is some knowledge of French. The Belgians will be very tolerant of your errors.

## Housing

Finding a place to live in Brussels can be downright enjoyable. There is a wide selection of beautiful, big houses with spacious yards and gardens, as well as many lovely apartments near the city. For one American family, home became the entire top floor of a modern apartment building that overlooked a fourteenth-century monastery. Housing often combines charm and a sense of history with the practicalities of modern life.

If you do not wish to stay in a hotel while house hunting, you will find dozens of smaller residences, pensions, and studio apartments. Here are a few for you to consider.

The Continental Flatel
33 rue Defacqz
Telephone 538.29.57

Residence les Tourelles
135 avenue Winston Churchill
Uccle
Telephone 344.95.73

Residence New Yorker
401 avenue Louise
Telephone 649.34.31

With so much rental housing of all types available in and around the city, Brussels is more of a tenant's market than other European cities. Owners advertise frequently and a number of realtors cater to expatriates. The _Bulletin,_ an excellent news weekly in English, the French-language papers, and the _International Herald Tribune_ all have classified ads for housing in Brussels. Bulletin boards at expatriate organizations always are a good source. The realtors who specialize in housing for foreigners usually have a sizable inventory from which to select despite no multiple listing. Owners pay the commission. Some well-known realtors are:

Office des Proprietaires
80 rue de Namur
Brussels
Telephone 513.84.20

Immo Boulanger
60 avenue Marie Louise
Waterloo
Telephone 354.94.12
Particularly knowledgeable and helpful for Americans.

Perin Real Estate
54 avenue Reine Astrid
Waterloo
Telephone 354.19.19

If you scout an area yourself, watch for signs reading _A Louer_ or _Te Huur_ ("For Rent" in French and Flemish). A good pocket atlas, such as _Bruxelles Complet_ (Girault Gilbert, Brussels) will give you an alphabetical street index, addresses of important locations, and public transportation routes.

Brussels resembles a heart with the Grand Place at its center. It is divided into 19 communes or boroughs. The most desirable locations for expatriates have been in the communes in the south and southwest, the historic central area, and the southern suburbs surrounding the Soignes Forest.

## *Where To Look*

The popular southern communes of Brussels are Uccle, Ixelles, Woluwe-St-Lambert, and Woluwe-St-Pierre. Residents in the boroughs have access to good public transportation, the international schools, and sports complexes. The *maison communal,* equivalent to a city hall, is the governmental and social center. Each will have English-speaking staff to assist new foreign residents. They sponsor an adult education program, plan cultural and sports events, provide advice and assistance to youths, publish informative brochures, and oversee other communal activities that make life more enjoyable for Belgians and expatriates alike. The latter can participate in planning these activities through the foreigners' councils.

Going farther south through the ancient, towering trees of the Soignes Forest, you come to several suburban towns that have become popular with Americans looking for a setting similar to suburbs in the United States. One favorite is Waterloo. About 20 percent of the population of 27,000 is foreign, half being Americans. It is the main shopping center for the surrounding area and the shopkeepers try to satisfy American needs. The Waterloo commune provides the same services and assistance as the Brussels communes. It publishes a communal guide listing all the municipal and public services, businesses and professional offices, schools, sports activities, and public transportation services. It is not an American ghetto, however; the ambience is still that of a Belgian town.

Other suburbs where Americans can be found are Rhode-St-Genese, Overijse, Tervuren, Ohain, and Kraaienem. If furnished, a residence can be complete except for linens. Unfurnished units contain the barest minimum of furnishings and will be without fixtures, appliances, and cupboards. The tenant must furnish these or purchase them from the preceding tenant.

There are several types of housing from which to choose: completely detached homes, apartments, town homes, three- or four-story attached houses with enclosed gardens in the rear, and semidetached houses with a yard or garden on three sides. You may find any of these either furnished or unfurnished.

Rents in Brussels are high, but not much more than in New York or other major U.S. metropolitan areas. A residence in central Brussels will run about 20 percent higher than a comparable place in one of the suburbs. A furnished unit adds about 30 to 50 percent more to the monthly rent.

Leases, generally, are written for a term of three years renewable for two further terms, a 3-6-9 lease. Furnished units sometimes can be rented for shorter periods. Notice of termination must be given three months prior to the end of each three-year term or else the lease is considered renewed. You should negotiate to get a "diplomatic" clause, which allows termination at any time after giving the specified notice in the event the lessee is transferred. This feature may entail a premium on the rental or an indemnity of one to three months' rent.

It is customary that a very complete inventory be taken on beginning occupation and on leaving. This enumerates everything in the house or apartment and its condition. Frequently, an appraisal of the condition of the premises itself will be made by an architect or other expert. Try to negotiate so that this cost will be split between the parties.

Normal wear and tear is not recognized; unless otherwise specified in the lease, painted surfaces and damaged walls must be repaired. A guarantee against damage of three months' rent is usually required. This can be a blocked account, a bank guarantee, or cash. A blocked account is a special frozen account that accumulates interest credited to the tenant and is released and distributed by agreement of the parties at the end of the lease. The bank guarantee is a letter of credit provided by the bank, for a small percentage of the face amount, if the lessee is known to the bank and is reliable financially. If a guarantee is cash, the landlord must pay interest, but only if the tenant requests it. Don't forget to cover this point in the lease.

Tenants are expected to pay the utilities and property tax, and these are high. But both are subject to negotiation.

Rents are fixed on a monthly basis. They used to be tied to the increase in the cost of living. Now, at the end of the year, the government publishes the official percentage for increases.

Apartment dwellers will have additional charges for central hot water, the salary of the concierge, elevator service, and similar service fees.

## Domestic Help

Good live-in and part-time help is available but expensive. Foreign help from Italy or Spain may be a little cheaper, but they must have registered with the authorities and have an identity card (no work permit is required for EEC nationals). Apartments usually do not have servants' quarters; houses are big enough that live-in accommodations can be arranged. The *Bulletin*, Brussels' newspapers, and bulletin boards are sources for locating help. The best, however, is a personal recommendation.

Full-time help are entitled to receive one free afternoon and evening a week as well as Sunday and all holidays. After one year of employment, an annual two-week vacation is customary.

Certain formalities for taxes and social security are required by law. You, as the employer, are responsible for these. The schedule for taxes to be withheld can be obtained from the Service de Documentation des Contributions Directes, 45 rue Belliard; telephone 513.62.66. If you employ help for more than four consecutive hours a day, six days a week, you must register for social security purposes at the Office National de Sécurite Sociale, 76 boulevard de Waterloo; telephone 513.85.20. Accident insurance is compulsory for your help.

Au pair girls are often employed. Regulations concerning them can be obtained at the Ministere de l'Emploi et du Travail, Service Aides Familiales, 51-53 rue Belliard; telephone 230.90.10. Denmark is a popular source for these girls. Advertising in a Copenhagen paper usually brings many replies.

Baby-sitters can be found through many of the same sources as other help. In addition, check the bulletin board at the International School.

## Utilities

### Electricity

Most of Brussels has 220-volt/50-cycle, three-phase alternating current. Electric companies are government owned and operated, as are other utilities. Thus, you will encounter some bureaucratic problems when trying to get service. The maison communale can tell you which service your residence has if you cannot get this information from the landlord, realtor, or other tenant. Be sure to locate your fuse box and have a supply of *fusibles* on hand when you start turning on your lights and appliances.

### Gas

Gas is supplied by some of the same companies as electricity. Most of Brussels uses natural gas. Gas appliances from the United States probably can be used if the orifices are adjusted.

### Water

Water is provided in Brussels by the Compagnie Intercommunale Bruxelloise des Eaux, 70 rue aux Laines; telephone 513.87.81. It is very hard water, but softeners are available.

*Billing*

All utility bills should be paid promptly, within five days of receipt, or your service will be turned off. If you are going to be away, arrange for your bank to pay.

# Education

There is an excellent selection of schools and programs from which to choose. This is one country where a true choice between the local system and international schools can be made. The English-speaking international schools are:

The International School of Brussels (ISB)
Château des Fougères 19
Kattenberg, Boitsfort
Brussels
Telephone 673.60.50

A fully accredited, private, nonprofit, day school from kindergarten through high school with a typical U.S. curriculum leading to a general academic or international baccalaureate diploma. Located on a 45-acre wooded campus, the facilities are excellent. The enrollment is about 1,200 students, 60 percent from the United States, the remainder from over 40 other countries. The faculty numbers 70, many at ISB for over 10 years. There is a competitive program for boys and girls in 13 major sports. Recently, a nursery school program was introduced for 2-year-olds and older using the Montessori method.

St John's International School
Dreve Richelle 146
Waterloo
354.11.38 or 39

A coeducational Catholic school with an ecumenical approach for both day and boarding students. It takes children from age 3 through high school, but boarding is only for secondary school students. The fully accredited curriculum meets the requirements of U.S. advanced placement, British O level, and the International Baccalaureate. Enrollment is about 700 with a majority American.

Antwerp has one international school accredited by the European Council of International Schools:

The Antwerp International School
Veltwijcklaan 180
Antwerp
Telephone (031) 41.60.47

A private, coeducational day school for 275 students from prekindergarten through twelfth grade. It consists of four buildings located on a 34-acre campus. The program includes the International Baccalaureate.

Another school is located in Liège:

International School of Liège
Bd Léon Philippet 7 Xhovémont
Liège
Telephone (041) 26.84.83

This is a smaller school of about 65 students, also primarily American or English. The curriculum contains elements of both the U.S. and British systems.

The U.S. Department of Defense has a school for military, NATO, and diplomatic personnel. There are German, French, Japanese, and Swedish schools as well as a few other smaller schools with English as a principal language.

All of these international schools have several things in common: high tuition, limited capability to handle exceptional children, strong extracurricular activities, and field trips so students can absorb the beauty, history, language, and culture of Europe.

A complete list of these schools and other valuable information on the education system in Belgium is found in an excellent guide, *Living in Belgium and Luxembourg, 82* (Insight Publications, S.A., Brussels), available in bookstores and at some magazine stands.

The Belgian school system offers a dual path, public or private, both with high standards and capabilities. Free public schools (*ecoles officielles*) in communes and provinces and the private institutions, primarily Catholic (*ecoles livres*), meet the same state academic standards and receive state financial support. As in most European countries, there is a national curriculum. Children can attend any public or private school to which they are admitted, not necessarily in their neighborhood.

Belgian children begin in nursery school at age 2 or 3, but are not required to enter school until age 6. From ages 6 to 12, they attend a primary school. At 12 they enter one of the four types of secondary schools: general (highly academic with stress on languages), technical (more practical emphasis on technical subjects), artistic, and professional or vocational for those students going into specific trades.

A revised system was introduced in 1978 that permits more initiative and specialization in the secondary level. Any one can lead to advanced schools, technical colleges, or universities.

Foreign children are welcome in the Belgian schools. Special language classes are provided for the principal language in the school. Dutch is required in all Brussels primary schools, but a foreign student can be excused from these classes.

For further information about Belgian schools, contact the Ministere de l'Education Nationale, Service d'Enseignement Primaire (or Secondaire), Cite Administrative de l'Etat, Quartier Arcades, Bloc D, Brussels.

Several American universities, particularly the University of Maryland, have programs at the undergraduate and graduate levels.

## Shopping

The diversity of shopping sources in Brussels is seemingly endless. You may buy from street vendors, small shops, outdoor markets, enclosed galleries, boutiques, factory outlets, modern department stores, thrift shops, or even an auction. Add to this discounting, sales of "seconds," trading stamps, and buying clubs. The result is a shopping atmosphere in which the U.S. expatriate can feel at home but which has just enough novelty to interest even the most jaded buyer.

Belgium has tried to protect and maintain the small, independent shopkeeper. All retail establishments are required by law to close at a uniform time (8 p.m. daily and 9 p.m. on Friday) and close completely one day a week. As a result, Belgium has more small shops per capita than any other EEC country.

But shopping habits are changing. New shopping malls are popping up in the suburbs. Modern, multistory galleries with shops, restaurants, and entertainment vie with the traditional department stores in the center.

There are at least eight department store chains in Brussels with main stores in the downtown area along rue Neuve and boulevard Anspach and branches in the suburbs. They carry almost everything you would find in a U.S. store.

Brussels originated the shopping gallery in Europe with the Galeries Royales St Hubert in 1846. This opulent shopping palace, with its vaulted glass roof, smart boutiques, and restaurants, was the inspiration for today's downtown malls. One of its newest offspring, City 2, is nearby. It is truly a shopping city of several floors with bright colors, lights, music, and convenience stands throughout the many levels to bring gallery shopping into the twentieth century.

Both *Hints For Living in Brussels* and *Living '82* provide valuable information on shopping. A new book on shopping and services is about to be published, *Seleciones,* by Du Parc and Tibbaut. Watch for it in Belgian bookstores.

## *Clothing*

The one great influence on what is worn in Brussels is not the closeness of the neighboring French couturiers or the international aspect of the city's population. It is, unfortunately, the prevalence of water as rain, mist, or simply humidity. Rainwear and other clothing to defend against a wet, clammy, and occasionally steamy atmosphere is the center around which a wardrobe is planned. You will, of course, occasionally have a pretty day that will allow you to dry your rainwear.

Every woman used to have her own dressmaker or, on a higher plane, haute couture. Today, ready-to-wear apparel is the rule, the inexpensive dressmaker the exception (with identities considered top secret). Once you establish your Belgian equivalent size, you can find almost anything you need. Clothing, however, is comparatively expensive in Belgium.

Men will have to do some looking to find clothing not cut along the continental style of very well fitting jackets and shirts. American-brand shirts and other accessories are available. Sizes for tall men are hard to find.

The haute couture shops can be located under the name of the designer in the phone book; for example, Valentino is at 261 avenue Louise; telephone 647.36.44. Most of these shops are along avenue Louise.

The major department stores have a wide selection for the whole family. Inventories are often limited, so it is best to buy when you see something you anticipate needing. Shoes in narrow widths are hard to find. One store that tries to stock them is Bally.

The other principal central city shopping area is the uptown area known as "Deux Portes," roughly the area along the avenue de la Toison d'Or between porte de Namur and place Louise. Here you will find many modern, exclusive shops with beautiful, sophisticated displays of quality merchandise.

Fashionable jewelry and other accessory shops can be found in all shopping areas. Don't forget that Antwerp is one of the world's leading centers for the processing of diamonds. Certain products, such as beaded bags and leather goods, are well-known Belgian specialties.

## Home Furnishings

A wide variety in both the style and the price range of furniture is available. Belgian furniture makers specialize in expensive, top-of-the-line period reproductions and very utilitarian cheap furniture. Well-made medium quality furniture is hard to find.

Brussels is a good city for the antique hunter. There are many shops around the place du Grand Sablon and outdoor markets are held in this area on weekends. At the other end of the scale is the Salvation Army store at 55 rue du Poincon.

If you wish to rent furniture, the best known rental service is Otten-Wynants, just across from SHAPE headquarters at chaussee de Bruxelles, Maisières; telephone (065) 72.90.98. This store can furnish the whole house, from dishes to appliances.

Decorating your residence in Brussels can be fun. Almost every neighborhood will have a small decorator's shop. There are many beautiful fabrics, wallpapers, and carpets with skilled artisans to upholster your furniture or paper your walls. Oriental rugs have been a good buy in Brussels for years and still are. Belgian linens and laces are world famous. You should have some expertise yourself or seek help from someone knowledgeable to get the top quality.

Selecting appliances for Brussels involves the same trade-offs as in other European cities with 220 volts, 50 cycles: the size and convenience of American imports versus the practicality of the smaller local makes that are easier to repair and need no transformers. A few American manufacturers distribute in Belgium and are listed in the phone book.

Most department stores, particularly Galeries Anspach, have large hardware and do-it-yourself (*bricolage*) departments. Cleaning supplies, toilet articles, paper goods, water softeners, brushes, and other household items are sold in *drogueries*. Stores that specialize in kitchen supplies and household hardware are called *quincailleries*. Check the phone book.

## Discount Stores and Sales

Take advantage of discount stores and the sales usually held in January, July, or August. Major reductions in clothing, furniture, household goods, and appliances are offered by department and specialty stores.

## Books

English-language books, magazines, and paperbacks are available in major department stores, some newsstands, and especially at the Brussels branch of the well-known British firm, W. H. Smith, 7 Adolph Max; telephone 217.67.22 and the House of Paperbacks, 813 chaussee de Waterloo; telephone 343.11.22.

## Services

Both barbers and hairdressers run the gamut from expensive, famous-name establishments in hotels and shopping centers to the cheaper neighborhood shops. A 15 to 20 percent tip may be included in the bill; if not, you can leave it with the cashier.

Self-service laundries are found in almost every neighborhood. Some have only washing facilities (*wasserette*); others (*lavoirs*) have an attendant who will wash and dry your clothes and sometimes fold them for a small extra fee.

Dry cleaners (*teintureries*) offer regular and deluxe service, but tend to be a bit harsh on clothes and relatively expensive. Old-timers say to avoid the one-day service that some shops offer. Regular laundries (*blanchisseries*) will take all types of washing and ironing. Some will pick up and deliver.

Shoe repair can be done at most department stores. There is also Mister Minute in some of the galleries.

## Grocery Shopping

Foreign nationals of almost any country report that they can find their food as easily in Brussels as in any other location outside their country. Certainly, Americans have very little difficulty in getting U.S. brands, although at times at a premium. Veal, pork, and lamb are plentiful. Beef tastes somewhat different from that in the United States owing to leaner meat and less marbling. Of course, the cuts vary from U.S. and British practices.

There are a number of supermarket chains. Delhaize has stores throughout Brussels. Sarma (affiliated with J. C. Penney) handles food, clothing, and other housewares. Super Bazaar (G.B.) is a "super" supermarket chain, which means its stores are about the same size as U.S. stores. They stock household items, appliances, and other merchandise as well as food. Rob is a luxury food supermarket featuring exotic and imported foods.

In Waterloo, for example, there are three large supermarkets. One is a huge "hypermarket" carrying clothes, household goods, and hardware in addition to food. When you see the reserved parking spaces for handicapped, the aisle of generic foods and paper goods, and the choice of products, you may think you are in your favorite store back home.

The other sources for food are the many small neighborhood shops (where prices may be slightly higher but service more personal), the outdoor markets, the food sections of major department stores, and discount groceries.

Here are some of the smaller shops catering to expatriates.

Eddys Meat Market
64 rue de l'Elan
Watermael
Specializes in U.S. and English cuts.

Chez Louis
74 chaussee de Bruxelles
Waterloo
Telephone 354.76.29

Maison Ide
322 avenue de la Forêt de Soignes
1640 Rhode-st-Genese
Known as "Sams," this store has many American products not found elsewhere and is open Sundays.

The principal outdoor markets are usually open in the mornings on weekdays, some on Sundays. They feature fresh produce, fish, meats, and dairy products.

The department stores have large food sections that carry a variety of high quality merchandise, particularly hard-to-find American products.

Shops for foreign foods and specialties of almost every country are found in Brussels.

There are several discount chains that specialize in large quantity purchases. These are good for bulk purchases of beer and soft drinks, canned goods, paper products, and frozen foods. The principal chains are Colruyt and Makro. Check the phone book for the nearest store.

Remember, bread is sold at a *boulangerie,* pastry at a *pàtisserie.* Bread is baked fresh daily with no preservatives, so it should be eaten soon after purchase. The bakery will slice it for you if you request it. Packaged bread is found in the supermarkets.

Fresh fruits and vegetables are seasonal, but frozen is available year-round.

The variety of cheese is spectacular. French, Dutch, Italian, English, and Greek cheeses are available. There are several good shops around the Grand Place.

Milk can be purchased pasteurized and sterilized. The supermarkets carry pasteurized in dated cartons, and many dairies deliver to the door, although the milk trucks are not refrigerated. Sterilized milk does not need refrigeration, but it tastes different. Many expatriates consider the dairy products richer and better than their U.S. counterparts.

Frozen foods include not only the usual fruits, vegetables, meats, and fish but also gourmet and foreign items such as dessert crepes in Grand Marnier. American turkeys can be found in supermarkets.

Ice cream lovers received a boost when Baskin-Robbins came to Brussels. There are several stores in expatriate areas.

Belgium produces little wine, most is imported from surrounding countries. Beer is still the number one drink. Alcoholic beverages are available in liquor stores, supermarkets, and department stores.

Health food stores can be found in Belgium's major cities.

## Transportation

Belgians have always been aware of the value of quick, efficient transportation because of their country's location at the crossroads between its rich neighbors. The lines of transportation have been well developed and well used. By the sixteenth century, Antwerp was the richest and largest port in the world, and today is still one of the world's top five ports. Inland waterways such as the Rhine and Meuse have been developed through an extensive canal system. The railway network is among the densest in Europe. Thanks to rich coal and iron ore deposits and the technical skills of its workers, Belgian industry supplies many of the locomotives and cars that contribute to the efficiency and comfort of trains all over Europe. It is no wonder, therefore, that public transportation throughout Belgium is the envy of any expatriate who remembers the antiquated systems found in most U.S. cities.

The Brussels Metro has been under construction since 1965. A portion is completed with modern, clean cars and stations. Other underground portions have been constructed but are used by the tram lines for now and are called the "pre-metro."

The Societe des Transports Intercommunaux de Bruxelles (STIB) operates the Metro as well as the surface bus and tram lines. It publishes a good map of the entire system, which is available at the public relations office, 15 avenue de la Toison d'Or; telephone 511.49.18.

Tickets are good for all three forms, and free transfers can be made between lines at junctions (but no stopovers). You can purchase single tickets, books of five or ten rides, or a weekly, monthly, or yearly *carte d'abonnement* entitling you to travel anywhere in the city limits. These are obtained at the Bureau des Abonnements in the porte de Namur Metro Station. You will need a photograph. Children under 6 years travel free, under 12 years at a reduced rate. You must keep your ticket or transfer slip throughout your trip to show inspectors if you are asked. Service to outlying towns and suburbs is provided by the Societe National de Chemins de Fer Vicinaux (SNCV) through a network of red and cream colored buses. Fares are based on distance traveled.

Taxis customarily do not cruise in Brussels. They are hired by engaging them at taxi stands or by telephoning. The fare includes the tip. The driver can add a charge for return to the city limits if you take him outside Brussels.

## Cars and Driving

Cars imported from outside Belgium must have a Certificate of Conformity before license plates can be obtained. This certificate is issued after two technical inspections: the first to make minor modifications to conform to Belgian requirements (such as changing speedometer markings to kilometers) and the second to check the car's mechanical condition.

One car, possibly two if customs can be convinced you need two, will enter Belgium duty-free provided you have evidence of ownership for more than six months.

## Registration and Licenses

An expatriate can drive in Belgium for six months on his old valid plates. Application for new Belgian plates should be made fairly soon after arrival, however, because it may take some time (six to nine weeks) to complete the formalities. You apply at the Office de la Circulation Routiere, 12 Cantersteen; telephone 512.82.62. You will be issued one plate that is permanently in your name and may be transferred to another car. But you must have two plates on the car at all times. The second, duplicate plate is obtained from a garage or auto supply store. The registration card (*immatriculation*) must be carried in the car.

A bill for road tax based on the horsepower of the car should be sent to you within one month after your plates are issued. Thereafter, you will get an annual bill. For questions, contact the Bureau de la Taxe de Roulage, 56 rue de la Loi; telephone 513.82.06. There is also a tax on car radios.

You may drive in Belgium if you are 18 years old and have one of the following licenses:

*Nonresident license.* A nonresident living temporarily in Belgium can drive on a valid license from his own country. But once residence papers are issued, a Belgian license is needed. Most people file for this license when they apply for their identity card.

*Belgian license.* If you have a valid EEC or U.S. license, you will be issued a Belgian license without taking a test. Otherwise, you must pass the written test, with the help of an official translator if necessary. If the applicant never has had a license, a driving test or attendance at a driver's school is required. A Belgian license is good throughout Europe.

*International license.* This license must be obtained in a country other than Belgium. The international licenses are never valid in the country where issued.

### What Must be in the Car

Registration card
Insurance "green" card
Road tax receipt
Driver's license
Receipt for inspection (for cars over four years old)
Accident report form
An emergency sign, usually the standard triangle reflector

First aid kit
Fire extinguisher
Safety belts that must be used
The letter "B" for Belgium if going outside the country
One approved red rear fog lamp

### Rules of the Road

Belgians drive to the right as in the United States. An English version of the *Code de la Route* and the *Illustrated Highway Code* (Via Secura, Brussels) are both available in the bookstores and are excellent source books. The latter, especially, has many pictures and diagrams to clarify and emphasize each rule and examples of every road sign you will encounter.

Always lock your doors when leaving the car—it is against the law to leave your car unlocked. Also, trams and cycling racers have priority. You must stop your car for the latter.

You must have unlimited liability insurance by law, the proof of which is the "green card" issued by your insurance carrier. Comprehensive coverage can be obtained. The cost for both is very high and terms customarily run for several years to avoid even higher premiums. A "diplomatic clause" in the contract will permit cancellation if the insured expatriate has to leave Belgium.

Signs giving directions may be in Dutch, French, or both. It helps to know route names in both languages. Many names are completely different in the two languages.

In case of accident, place the emergency triangle to warn oncoming traffic and exchange the usual data with the other driver. Both parties simply prepare an accident report and both sign it only in cases of property damage. The police are not called in unless there is a disagreement. Report the accident within 24 hours to the police and your insurance company. Where there are personal injuries, the police are brought in immediately to investigate.

Children under 12 years of age are not allowed to ride in the front seat.

### Parking

Street parking is controlled by:

*Blue zones.* These zones are designated by appropriate signs. If you park in them, you must display a *disque bleu* in your window. The disks can be bought in many stores. You mark the time when you arrived on the disk, and it indicates the time when you must move the car.

*Alternate side parking.* The numbers 1–15 and 16–31 indicate that parking is pemitted the first or last half òf the month, respectively. Roman numerals I and II signify odd- or even-day parking.

## Violations

All traffic offenses, except those considered "serious" (see the *Illustrated Highway Code*), can be settled on the spot by purchasing the required amount of fiscal fine stamps at a post office and pasting them on the violation notice, which is mailed or brought to the police station. You cannot use this system if: the offender is under 18; the offense has caused any damage to a third party; or there are more than two offenses charged. Prompt payment is strongly recommended.

Belgium is tough on driving under the influence. The police may stop any motorist for a breath test.

## Automobile Clubs

Royal Automobile Club de Belgique
53 rue d'Arlon
Telephone 230.08.10
Provides travel information and insurance, driving conditions, licenses, and for an extra charge, towing and repairs.

Touring Club de Belgique
44 rue de la Loi
Telephone 512.78.90
Roughly the same services as above.

## Bicycles, Motorbikes, and Motorcycles

Required equipment for bicycles are a license plate for any child over ten, a bell, a rear reflector, a light in front, and a small red light behind.

The minimum age for motorbikes is 16; it is 18 for motorscooters and motorcycles. Licenses and insurance are necessary and crash helmets are required.

# Communications

## *Postal Service*

Considering the lines at post office windows, an expatriate might be justified in thinking that Belgians were the world's champion letter writers. Not so. It's just that the postal system in this country provides so many services besides normal mail delivery: bill paying, banking, the national lottery, family allowance check cashing, issuance of some licenses, payment of traffic fines, and operation of the telephone and telegraph system.

The post office at the Gare du Midi train station, 48 rue Fonsny, is open 24 hours a day plus holidays. All other offices, including the main office, keep normal business hours.

In Brussels mail is delivered twice a day during the week and once on Saturdays. Every region in Belgium has a four-digit postal code number that precedes the name of the town. If the address is a building with more than four letter boxes, it must include the box number. It helps if you use the Dutch spelling for addresses in Flemish areas and French for Walloon locations.

Packages up to one kilo and valued under BF500 can be mailed out of the country from any post office. Above this weight or value, there is a little more red tape. Packages sent to expatriates from abroad that weigh less than 20 kilos and are valued under BF500 will be delivered automatically.

## *Telephones*

Unfortunately, the equipment and lines for telephone sevice have not kept pace with demand, particularly in parts of Brussels. Installation of new service can take several weeks. It is best if you can take over an existing phone as new installations are expensive. If you take over an existing number, the charge will be somewhat less, but not by much. VAT is levied on all telephone charges.

Bills are sent out every two months. Charges are based on units. If your bill exceeds a certain ceiling, your deposit may be increased. Automatic international dialing is available in most areas. One oddity is that conference calls are prohibited. You can only use one phone in your home at a time.

## Telex and Telegrams

There is adequate service for these media. Telegrams can be sent in person at any post office. For night and holiday service, go to Gare du Midi train station or Circonscription Telegraphique de Bruxelles, 19 boulevard de l'Impératrice; telephone 513.44.90. For information call 990.

## Newspapers

There are probably few countries in the world of comparable size and population that publish more newspapers and periodicals than Belgium. In addition to the *International Herald Tribune* from Paris, there are two local English magazines. The *Bulletin,* published weekly, includes an entertainment guide, events of the week, shopping tips, features on personalities, sports, history, current problems, a restaurant column, business news, and very helpful classified ads. Dow Jones began publication from Brussels in 1983 of a European edition of the *Wall Street Journal.*

A very new illustrated monthly, *In Touch,* covers events throughout Belgium and even in some surrounding countries. This English-language publication has an extensive entertainment guide, business diary, articles on shopping, travel, the arts, sports, and a special section for young readers called "Junior In Touch."

## Radio and Television

Both radio and television are state owned and operated in Belgium. There are no commercials. The system is divided into two sections for the two principal languages.

To get more English television reception, try to move into a residence equipped with cable television (available in most areas) or an antenna so that you can pick up channels from Holland, France, Luxembourg, and Germany. With a good aerial, you may be able to get the English BBC channels along coastal areas. A good aerial may also bring in the U.S. armed forces television from Germany. To get French channels, you need the more expensive television set with an interband selector. New installation of cable television is very expensive, but hookups to existing connections are not bad. There is also an annual fee for cable television. Many expatriates rent television sets.

An annual tax on radios and television sets is levied. Failure to pay results in a sizable fine.

# Free Time

A city where one of the most popular events is a 45-mile pigeon race, which is only one of 25,000 races held there each year, must provide some recreation to fulfill even the most esoteric interest. Brussels has everything from a private Brewers Museum to the infamous statue Manneken Pis. It has so much to interest the walker, the viewer, the player, the listener, and the eater that Belgians, quite legitimately, wonder why their capital is not visited by more tourists.

With so much from which to choose, the first priority is knowing how to find out what is going on. Two of the best sources for current entertainment information are the "What's On" pull-out section in the *Bulletin* and the "What, Where and When" guide in *In Touch*. Check the newspapers, *Rendez-vous,* and the American Women's Club of Brussels monthly publication. Other good sources for entertainment information are:

*Brussels BBB Agenda*. A weekly report on events in and around Brussels, including exhibitions, folk festivals, theater, and cinema. It is in French and Dutch with an abbreviated English section, and is available at newsstands each Thursday or by subscription.

*Tourist Information Brussels (TIB)*. (61 rue du Marche-aux-Herbes; telephone 513.89.40). Through its Teletib service, this agency provides information and tickets for many events. For a small annual membership fee, you can order tickets by telephone and pay through your bank.

*Armentor* (61 avenue Louise; telephone 538.40.90). Handles tickets on events in Brussels and Paris; a monthly calendar of events is sent to subscribers.

Films most frequently are shown in their original version (V.O.), so there is a wide choice of English and American films. As in most European cinemas, the picture is preceded by a 15 to 20 minute showing of advertisements, shorts, and previews with a brief intermission before the feature. Usherettes expect a small tip even if they do not seat you.

Ballet, symphonies, jazz concerts, plays, and exhibits crown the cultural calendar of Brussels. The art riches of the country are legendary. After all, Belgium supplied the world with Brueghel, Van Dyke, Memling, and Rubens. With this base on which to build, it is understandable that the collections in museums are truly superlative.

The Théâtre Royal de la Monnaie is the home of the national opera company and the popular and innovative Ballet du XXième Siecle (Ballet of the 20th Century). The satirical puppet theater, Toone, is entertaining even though the language may be incomprehensible. Pop concerts, jazz performances, and rock are heard in larger concert halls and intimate clubs.

There is a very active amateur English-language theater movement in Brussels. Some of the companies are the American Theater Company, Shakespeare Society, and the Gilbert and Sullivan Society. The English-speaking community also has an amateur orchestra and chamber music groups.

Several foreign communities have their own cultural centers:

American Cultural Center
1/C Square du Bastion
Porte de Namur
Telephone 512.22.86

Canadian Information and Cultural Center
5 avenue Galilee
Telephone 219.36.00

American Women's Club Library
1 avenue des Erables
Rhode-Saint-Genese
Telephone 358.66.94

## Sports

American and British colonies have their own active sports' programs. American sports include baseball, basketball, and football (touch, flag, and tackle) leagues, including Little League for children. The international schools have an active interschool competition. Many communes have their own sports complexes. Waterloo has a swimming pool, an omni-sports hall, and many sports clubs from badminton to scrabble.

Sports schedules can be found in the *Bulletin*. Communes publish periodic sports schedules and information.

Golf, court games, and riding require joining clubs. There are only a few golf courses near Brussels, all private. Fees are high, but foreigners sometimes get a special lower rate. There are more tennis and squash clubs. A popular one for both Belgians and expatriates is the Tennis Club Forêt de Soignes. The all-inclusive club (swimming, golf, tennis, and so forth) is not found in Belgium.

The winters are not cold enough to freeze lakes and ponds adequately for skating. Several artificial rinks are open from September to June.

For skiers, the country lacks two key ingredients: mountains and snow. Yet, there are a few runs at nine different resorts less than two hours from Brussels.

Public swimming pools are numerous and inexpensive. The fee covers the use of the pool, showers, and lockers.

Except in certain communes, there are no public tennis courts, only clubs requiring membership. The dues are generally lower than those in the United States. Approximately 350 clubs are listed by the Federation Royale de Lawn Tennis, 164 avenue Louise; telephone 648.74.68. The American Women's Club of Brussels has some private courts.

There are numerous yacht harbors and clubs in Belgium, particularly in Nieuwport. Wind surfing, very popular throughout Europe, is a favorite sport of young Belgians.

## Dining Out

The almost unanimous feeling among expatriates is that it is hard to get a bad meal in Belgium. Food is one of the great pleasures of the Belgians. Brussels has a reputation for fine cuisine and many luxury restaurants. It has one street entirely devoted to restaurants, the rue des Bouchers near the Grand Place, where you can have a "Fleetwood" (gourmet hamburger) at the Cadillac American restaurant or sample *moules* (mussels) served in 50 ways and a glass of Faro beer, a brand that has been brewed for 1,000 years.

## Organizations

Some of the numerous organizations found in Brussels are:

American Club of Brussels
30 avenue Legrand
Telephone 648.51.19

American Chamber of Commerce
50 avenue des Arts
Telephone 512.12.62

American Women's Club of Brussels
1 avenue des Erables
Rhode-Saint-Genese
Telephone 358.66.94

Headquartered in a charming villa in the center of the American colony, this club provides a friend and adviser to newcomers through its hostess program, its publication *Hints for Living in Brussels,* and orientation classes. It is a focal point for social events, courses, tours, and child care. A library, tennis courts, and a tea room are popular amenities.

There are clubs, associations, or informal groups for just about any purpose from political (Democrats Abroad; telephone 395.32.25) to pure fun (Society for Suppression Songsters; telephone 633.31.78). Just inquire and you will find the organization for your interests.

## Churches

Roman Catholic

> Catholic Parish of St. Anthony
> St. Julien's Church
> Chaussee de Wavre and Ave. G.S. Lebon
> Telephone 770.98.85

Anglican/Episcopal

> Holy Trinity Church
> 29 rue Capitaine Crespel
> Telephone 511.71.83

Lutheran

> American Lutheran Church of Brussels
> At the German Evangelical Church
> 7 avenue Salome
> Woluwe Saint Pierre
> Telephone 771.52.40

Protestant Interdenominational

> American Protestant Church
> At the International School of Brussels
> 19 Kottenberg
> Telephone 673.05.81

Presbyterian

> St. Andrews Church of Scotland
> 181 chaussee de Vleurgat
> Telephone 649.02.19

Jewish

> Synagogue de Bruxelles
> 32 rue de la Regence
> Telephone 512.43.34

Baptist

> International Baptist Church
> 17 rue Jacques Hoton
> Telephone 771.92.75

Christian Science

> First Church of Christ Scientist
> 96 chaussee de Vleurgat
> Telephone 647.64.56

## Health Care

Few expatriates have complaints about the Belgian medical system. There are two types of hospitals: public hospitals *(hôpitaux)*, which use their own staff exclusively, and private clinics *(cliniques)*, which provide all the hospital services, but the patient uses his own physician. Most doctors are associated with one or more clinics. When you enter a hospital or clinic for other than emergency care, you are required to pay a sizable deposit on the total bill, based on the nature of your admission and whether you have insurance. You should also have your passport.

Belgium's medical insurance needs are met by the *mutuelle* system. Any employee paid in Belgium or a self-employed individual, including expatriates, should belong. Usually, part of the cost is covered by the employer. There are several different mutual funds from which to select, but they provide about the same benefits. Partial refund of doctors' fees, hospitalization, medicines, and surgery are covered. For additional premiums, smaller risks can be included. (Check to see if your U.S. health insurance program will be honored in Belgium, and see how it dovetails with the local coverage.)

Contraceptive pills are available on prescription. Abortions are illegal except under extreme circumstances. They can be obtained legally in Britain and Holland.

Brussels has a community "Help" service that is staffed with English-speaking personnel to provide 24-hour advice on adjustment problems and marital and family difficulties. It also helps children with learning and behavioral problems. There are in-patient facilities as well. Contact the Community Help Service (102 rue Saint Georges; telephone 647.67.80) Another similar agency is the Human Relations Institute (57 avenue Edmond Masens; telephone 734.12.63), which provides a team of mental health professionals for psychiatric and psychological services.

A unique charitable organization, the Office du Service Familial (208 avenue Winston Churchill; telephone 343.89.34), provides household help in emergencies. The helpers will cook, do light cleaning, shop, and care for children. They accept donations.

## Doing Business in Belgium

Belgium, although one of the smaller European countries, has a lot going for it from a business standpoint. The most important advantage for companies wishing to have representation on the Continent in the EEC is a series of favorable tax treaties with most developed countries, trade ties with a multitude of former colonies, and some peculiar tax laws that give the director of Inland Revenue authority to negotiate your tax load with you. If this sounds somewhat unusual, well, Belgium *is* an unusual country.

If your company is one interested as a representative or nonproducing one (in Belgium), it may qualify for a low tax rate by virtue of a headquarters status. Let's assume that your business is centered offshore in the North Sea and virtually all your employees are located outside Belgium. If your European sales, purchasing, or accounting offices are located anywhere in Belgium, you may be in a position to negotiate a deemed tax on your income regardless of its actual contribution to your company's profit. The rate may be a low 3.4 or 5 percent, depending on the type of business and level of income. This section is rightfully the region of leagues of lawyers and requires careful research. It is mentioned solely owing to its unusual nature and uniqueness to Belgium.

Don't make the mistake of thinking that doing business in Belgium will be all peaches and cream. Belgian labor laws and social benefits are, respectively, among the toughest and most liberal in Europe. Be sure to check your obligations before your staff is hired; afterward it is too late, and termination of an unsatisfactory or redundant employee is a long, tedious, and expensive process. Temination costs can be equivalent to almost one year's employment costs.

With mistakes expensive, a preliminary and extensive preemployment investigation of potential employees is a strongly recommended procedure. You may not mind paying for social benefits for a good loyal worker, but being gouged by a professional job hopper seems to grate on most businessmen's sense of fair play. To discharge such an employee is certain to result in a call from a lawyer and usually ends in a no-win situation. Investigation through any of the professional agencies (U.S. Chamber, Business International) is well worth the time and effort before hiring your first employee. Don't expect local labor to be cheap. Belgian rates are among the highest in Europe. Also, union control is formidable and must be considered.

A good multilingual secretary is a must in Belgium. If your business tends to be of a temporary or semipermanent nature, it may be well advised to investigate concerns that specialize in offering temporary help. This action may also circumvent payment of social benefits, since employment with the service company may continue after your needs have passed. The *International Herald Tribune* runs classified ads daily with offerings for such temporary help.

Unlike his French neighbor, the Belgian businessman will not expect you to speak the three tongues of Belgium, and he will most likely be fluent in English.

Brussels may be the favorite city, but Antwerp is the real business capital of Belgium. Here the old meets the new, and the land meets the sea. Its centralized location and nearness to the major ports of the North Sea, coupled with excellent modern office buildings, qualified personnel, and subprofessional help, and one of the best communications systems in Europe, make doing business in Antwerp very pleasant.

On the negative side loom the exceptional social benefits, which must be a part of economic planning for any business venture in Belgium. While union control is less pervasive than in France, it is nevertheless formidable and must be considered in your forward planning. On the positive side, wage rates, particularly for managers and professionals, are among the highest in the world.

## Legal Matters

### *Visa and Permits*

If your stay in Belgium will be less than three months, the only requirement is a valid passport (or a national identity card for EEC citizens) and an entry visa for citizens of most countries outside North America and Europe. For longer periods, any non-EEC citizen will also need a residence visa *and* a work permit, which *must* be obtained before arrival through the Belgian Consular Service.

*Work Permit.* There are two types. The first is the *permis de travail,* which is applied for by your employer and may take as long as several months to receive. This permit will be valid for at least one year and may be granted for unlimited duration. The *carte profession-nelle* is for the self-employed and is valid for five years.

It is extremely difficult for other family members to obtain work permits after arrival in Belgium. As a result, employment of wives and children is virtually impossible.

*Residence Permit.* The residence permit is granted upon submission of the work permit, a passport, and—for all family members over 12—a medical certificate and police affidavit of good moral conduct.

Upon arrival, registration is required if you plan to stay over seven days. If you stay in a hotel temporarily, the staff will take care of this.

Within eight days of getting into a permanent residence, every foreign national over 12 must register at the city hall (maison communale) of the commune in which you are residing. Brussels consists of 19 communes. Each person will need a passport, residence visa, work permit (for the employed in the family), three photos, and a letter from the employer stating when the employment began. There is a small stamp tax for the identity cards that are issued. When any child reaches age 12, he must obtain an identity card. The cards should be carried with you at all times.

After completing these formalities, you can get a certificate of residence, which is required to clear household effects through Belgian customs.

### *Pets*

There is no quarantine for dogs or cats, but a certificate of good health from a veterinarian within ten days of entry and a rabies vaccination for dogs not less than one month or more than 12 months before arrival are necessary.

Dogs must be registered annually at the maison communale and dog licenses may be obtained there. Some communes levy an additional dog tax.

## _Organization_

Belgium is a civil law country, which means that the primary sources of Begian law are the Constitution of 1831, as amended, and the statutes. Court decisions and legal writing are secondary. The major areas of law are found in a series of codes, such as the Civil Code and the Penal Code. Much of the law is based on the French Napoleonic Code.

Unlike the United States, Belgian courts may not invalidate as unconstitutional any statute that is passed by the Parliament. The legislature is the final arbiter and interpreter of the Constitution. After basic laws have been passed by Parliament, the implementation and details are left to the government to handle through decrees and regulations.

The Belgian judicial structure is divided into 222 judicial cantons, each of which has one justice of the peace. The cantons are grouped into 26 judicial districts. In the principal location for each district there is a district court, a court of first instance, a labor court, and commercial court with the following jurisdictions:

_Justice of the Peace._ Any civil or commercial matter involving less than BF25,000. This court also has exclusive jurisdiction in certain land matters, such as easements, and on alimony.

_Commercial Court._ Handles disputes between businessmen, bankruptcy, and similar commercial matters. Judges in the court are assisted by two lay businessmen acting as associate judges.

_Court of First Instance._ This court has civil, criminal (for minor offenses), and juvenile divisions. Each case may be heard by one or three judges, the latter sitting on special cases, such as civil rights and appeals from the justice of the peace.

_Labor Court._ Each case in this court is heard by a judge with two lay assistants, one an employer and the other an employee. A special department represents the public interest in these matters.

_District Court._ Serves as an arbitrator in jurisdictional disputes of the other courts. In these matters a judge can simply transfer the issue

to this court. It is composed of the presidents of the Courts of First
Instance, Labor, and Commerce.

There is a police court in each of the main urban areas dealing
with misdemeanors and other minor infractions.

Three Courts of Appeals (one in Brussels) with civil, criminal,
and juvenile divisions hear appeals from the lower courts. There is a
separate appeal process for labor matters.

Felonies and other serious crimes are handled by the Courts of
Assizes in each of the nine provinces. A jury of 12 persons is used for
trials involving sentences over five years.

The Supreme Court is more of a regulative body. It only
reviews questions of law. If it reverses a judgment, the case goes back
to the lower court for a retrial. Each panel of this court consists of
five judges, all of whom must agree on any decision.

The Council of State consists of two sections: a legislative
section to advise the government and Parliament on proposed
legislation; and an administrative section that can declare null and
void acts of government officials and regulations on the basis of abuse
of power or violation of essential procedural requirements. The
council cannot nullify acts of Parliament.

As a signatory to the EEC and the Benelux treaties, Belgium
participates in the judicial system of these multinational organizations, but matters involving expatriates personally usually fall outside the scope and interest of these bodies.

An interesting aspect of justice in Brussels is its setting. The 300-
room Palace of Justice dominates Brussels much as St. Peter's
dominates Rome. In fact, the Palace covers an area bigger than the
Roman cathedral.

## Police

Local police forces in major cities handle municipal matters,
traffic, and minor crimes. The Gendarmerie is the national police
force that patrols highways and investigates major crimes. There are
mixed squads for drugs, juveniles, pornography, and other problems
that require special treatment.

Expatriates in Brussels generally feel quite safe, even on the
street at night.

If you are stopped by the police, your car, person, and clothes
can be searched without a warrant. You may be held up to 24 hours
before a formal charge is placed. If charged, you must be brought

immediately before a judge of instruction, who decides whether you should be held. If not released, your case can be investigated for 30 days and indefinitely thereafter so long as the court feels the case is not ready for trial. Bail is rarely granted. You will not be advised of your rights, but you do have the right to remain silent. Usually expatriates convicted of minor crimes will simply be deported.

## Drugs

Narcotics are not as significant a problem for teenagers in Belgium as for their peers in the United States. There seems to be pressure not to use them in the schools.

Nevertheless, the U.S. embassy states that 90 percent of arrest cases involving U.S. citizens are drug related. Possession of *any* amount of a drug is illegal. No distinction is made for hard or soft drugs. It is felt by the Belgian authorities that their country has become a major gateway for the importation of heroin into Europe. The penalty for trafficking in drugs, even marijuana, is a jail term of 20 years. Probation is possible for first-time offenders, but they may have to spend several months in prison before their status is settled by the court.

## Liquor

The retail sale of alcoholic beverages, except wine and beer, is restricted. They are not served in public bars and cafes. Instead, you must go to a private club. But things are not as tight as this implies. Night clubs and cocktail lounges qualify as private clubs since they charge a small membeship fee at the door. Even a brand new member may bring in a few guests.

Beer is king in Belgium. A mild, 2 percent alcohol content beer is even served in schools to older children.

## Marriage and Divorce

The minimum age for marriage is 18 for men, 15 for women. When either party is under 21, the consent of both parents is necessary. The civil ceremony performed at the maison communale is the crucial one in Belgium. Notice is posted ten days in advance. Required documents are birth certificate, a certificate of residence, and, if one of the parties was married previously, proof of divorce or death of previous spouse. No blood test is necessary.

All documents from a foreign country must be authenticated by the Belgian consular office where the documents were issued. They must be translated in French or Dutch by a sworn translator.

A divorce may be obtained in Belgium for a specific cause, by mutual consent, or by separation for at least ten years. Petitions by foreign nationals will be considered only if the residence or domicile of the defendant is in Belgium. No divorce will be granted expatriates if the cause is contrary to the law of the plaintiff's country. In fact, divorces are very difficult to obtain and take a long time (perhaps a year).

## Births and Deaths

Births must be registered within three working days at the maison communale, in addition to the requirements of the expatriates' embassy.

If there is a death in the family, the consular section of your embassy will provide a list of morticians who are familiar with the requirements for disposition of the body for shipment back home.

## Adoptions

Applicants to adopt babies in Belgium are placed on waiting lists for several years by agencies. Expatriates will have to find a child on their own and then go through the court procedure, which takes about a year.

## Banking

### Foreign Exchange

In practice there is virtual freedom of exchange for all purposes for the expatriate. No limit is placed on the amount of foreign currency bought or sold in Belgium. Exchange practices are governed by the Institut Belgo-Luxembourgeois du Change (IBLC), one of the institutions resulting from the Belgian-Luxembourg Economic Union. There are two foreign exchange markets:

#### The Official Exchange Market

This market is used for commercial transactions. The rate is set by the National Bank. All transactions must take place through a bank. For nonresidents, Belgian francs bought or sold in this market are called "convertible francs."

## The Financial Exchange Market

Rates are determined by the free market effect of supply and demand. Generally, this market gives a slightly more favorable rate for the U.S. dollar than the official rate. This market is used for transfers of a financial nature. For nonresidents, francs bought or sold in this market are called "financial francs."

All foreign capital and investment, including earnings, can be transferred freely outside Belgium, but not with Belgian francs. Payments over BF10,000 are made by bank transfer in the currency of the country where sent. For amounts under BF10,000, Eurocheques (see below) can be used. Your bank will determine into what market a particular transaction falls.

For transfers of foreign currency in or out it is necessary to submit a written statement of the nature of the transfer (*notif de paiement*). A deposit or cashing of a U.S. dollar check might be for salary or payment of school tuition.

## Eurocheque System

The Eurocheque System is a system of trans-European payment to which 32 European and Mediterranean countries belong. Individuals are issued checks with a distinctive, standardized design on application at any participating bank. A "Eurocard" or check guarantee card is issued. By utilizing the two, a member can write a check in any participating country in that country's currency and it will be debited against his Belgian franc account. The identity card guarantees payment of any check up to BF5,000 or its equivalent in other currency. Be careful not to have both the card and checks stolen together. The thief would have your checks, your identity card, and a sample of your signature—all that he needs to clean out your account. American banks having the Mastercharge card accept Eurocheques up to U.S. $1,000. Many travelers take a combination of travelers checks and Eurocheques and use the one most advantageous for a particular transaction.

## Banks

The larger Belgian banks have branches throughout the country, and major American banks can be found in Brussels. They both provide full banking services. Generally, they are open from 9 a.m. to noon or 1 p.m. and from 2 or 2:30 to 3:30 or 4 p.m. All that is required to open an account is good identification. There are checking and savings accounts, as well as U.S. dollar savings accounts with unlimited deposits and withdrawals.

Banks offer some other convenient services. They will make monthly automatic payments of your utility bills. Payment of other bills and debts frequently is handled by bank transfer. Checks gradually are being accepted by shops and supermarkets, but often for a minimum amount of BF500. Many banks provide automatic banking and drive-in facilities.

Banks do not return cancelled checks, only a monthly statement of all transactions with a postal charge debited to the account. You can arrange to have the statements held for pickup at the bank to avoid the postage.

## Post Office Banking

The postal system runs a checking and savings account system that rivals banks in popularity, the *Compte de Cheque Postal* (CCP). Each participant in CCP has his own account number. Transfers can be made freely from either a bank or CCP account to another person's bank or CCP account.

## Checks

Checks can be made out to bearer (*au porteur*) and thus be cashed by anyone. If you want more assurance of the recipient, the check can be "crossed" by drawing two lines diagonally across the face. This means that the check can only be deposited in the account of the payee.

Banks can refuse to honor a check if there is insufficient funds, if the check comes from a book not issued by an approved bank, or if the check comes from a book not receipted for by the account holder.

Most banks will not cash checks for immediate credit. The account will be credited only when the check clears.

## Taxation

Belgium is one country that provides a formal, special tax status for expatriates. This program has been revised to make Belgium a more competitive location for international business. The new rules are to be effective for 1983 income, but at the time of writing the final regulations had not been issued. However, the principal features are well known.

To qualify, an expatriate must meet the following requirements, and each employer will have to get a specific advance ruling on these qualifications. The candidate must:

Perform a managerial or scientific research function.

Have been transferred to Belgium or recruited abroad to work "temporarily" in a Belgian subsidiary or branch of a foreign company or in a Belgian company that is part of an international group.

Maintain a nonresident status as determined by the tax authorities. Factors to be considered are the location of the spouse and children, maintenance of a residence abroad, education of children abroad, continued coverage by foreign social security, and other factors attesting to the nonpermanent nature of the assignment and of the expatriate's stay in Belgium.

Qualifying expatriates will be taxed only on income from Belgian sources at the same rate and subject to the same withholding as Belgian residents. Any income earned while traveling outside Belgium for any period is excluded. The rule that travel outside Belgium had to be over 50 percent has been dropped.

The flat 30 percent deduction from Belgian income and special rules for headquarters and research operations have also been eliminated. Instead, certain allowances and reimbursements commonly granted expatriates will be deductible by the employer and not taxed to the employee. These nontaxable payments include:

Housing and cost-of-living allowances
Direct moving costs such as air fare
Educational allowances
Tax equalization payments
Costs for establishing the new Belgian residence

The eight-year maximum for expatriate tax concessions is replaced by a rule that allows the benefits to continue indefinitely so long as nonresident status is preserved.

Any expatriate who does not qualify for these benefits is taxed as a resident Belgian.

The tax rates on the resultant taxable income are progressive over a wide percentage scale, as in the United States. There is a maximum rate of 75 percent plus a 10 percent surcharge on lower income increasing to 20 percent at the top levels. A communal tax rate of 6 percent is charged on the basic tax. The effective tax rate, however, may not exceed 67.5 percent, or 71.55 percent if the municipal tax is added.

Foreign sourced income from real property or professional activities earned and taxed abroad may be exempt from Belgian taxation due to a provision in a tax treaty that exists with the United States. However, these earnings must be taken into account for purposes of calculating the progressive tax due on Belgian sourced income. There is a foreign tax credit of 15 percent on net interest, dividends, and royalties taxed abroad.

Individual taxpayers must file a return in the tax year following the income year within one month from the date the tax return is mailed. If you do not get a form by June 1 you must ask for one. Assessments must be made no later than April 30 of the year following the tax year, but this deadline is often extended. The assessment becomes final unless a valid tax complaint is filed by registered letter with the Regional Tax Director by April 30 of the second tax year following the income year. The tax is collected within two months following the mailing of assessments.

Surcharges can be avoided by making quarterly advance payments equal to one quarter of the tax liability. Salaried employees, including expatriates, have a withholding (*precompte professionnel*).

Belgium has the usual value-added tax on a three tier rate basis— 6 percent for necessities and "services of a social character" (such as farming and cleaners), 16 percent for other goods and services, and 25 percent for luxury items.

# 16

# Assignment Paris

*A*H-H-H, PARIS: Love. Beauty. Lights. Perfection. Writers pour out words of adulation. Singers herald her romance. Artists paint her for posterity.

*Is* Paris all that romantic and beautiful? In recent years, there have been rumblings about the high cost of living and the callousness of Parisians. "If only we could have the city without the people" is a phrase that has drifted back time and again to the States.

There still is the Paris of the starry-eyed romantic who lives on the Left Bank and worries little about the competitive, affluent portions of the city. But, generally, Paris has settled into a sleek, often brittle, competitive lady whose pride must never be challenged. She requires infinite patience, understanding, and, above all, a firm hand to manage.

The people? They are the most elegant, charming, obstinate, unreasonable, self-critical, chauvinistic souls you will ever encounter. And all this can make living in Paris either a delight or a period of absolute frustration.

Let's take a look at the city herself before we tackle the problems of Frenchmen, or more precisely, the Parisians.

A new Paris of skyscrapers and avant-garde design has superimposed itself spottily across the city, much to the dismay of the conservatives who feel that Paris must never change. It has always been like that. When the Eiffel Tower reared its spectacular head back in 1889, Parisians exploded with bitter objections. Words spoken and written then were almost identical with the criticism launched against the radical, supermodern architecture of the Pompidou Center when it was built in 1977 on a decaying piece of property in Beaubourg, an old section of the city not too far from the Hôtel de Ville and Notre Dame.

Old is revered, and deplorable slums—as long as they are of the antique variety that can be transformed into comfortable, contemporary living accommodations—are chic. Painters may still work in Montmartre's old square just behind the Sacre-Coeur, but they no longer live nearby. It is too expensive, for it has become an area of luxurious, renovated homes. The seventeenth-century houses of the Ile St-Louis, which connects by bridge with the Ile de la Cité, where Paris had its birth more than two centuries before Christ, are among the most fashionable in the city.

In addition to cleaning up some slums, Paris has decided to spruce up her better quarters. Hundreds of miles of building fronts have been scrubbed clean over the objections of purists, and metro cars are new and spotless. Paris breathes affluence; and while many of her citizens would debate that image, they, for the most part, are extremely well dressed. The stereotyped Frenchman with the black beret and a bottle of wine under his arm has disappeared.

For the most part, the harmony of Parisian architecture has not been broken by the skyscrapers that now pierce the skyline. Tour Maine-Montparnasse, the 59-story glass tower on the Left Bank, is an exception. As the tallest building in Paris, it stands like a lonely giant, overshadowing the once bohemian quarter of the city that now has settled into a more staid mixture of offices, hotels, and housing units. Other high-rises have been grouped—usually just across the city's borders in the suburbs. La Défense, a complex of contemporary skyscraper offices and apartments just to the west of the city limits, reminds one of EUR, Rome's older suburban bow to modernity.

Change has come to nearly every sector of Paris. The Champs Elysées, still awesome, crowned by the Arc de Triomphe and anchored by the place de la Concorde, has been invaded by fast food restaurants, an automobile showroom, and shopping malls. There still are traces of the elite boulevard of old: the historic Cafe Fouquet, the spectacular Lido night club, and the Grand and Petit Palais.

St-Germain, once an intellectual quarter where great minds met at small cafes to discuss philosophy and art, has become a trendy, "with-it" area of discotheques. And the crème de la crème of Parisian "camp" is a drugstore! The natives have taken the American pharmacy and turned it into something quite different: a complex of boutiques, restaurants, and sometimes a nodding recognition of its true purpose, a tiny pharmacy tucked into an obscure corner.

At times surreptitiously or with firm denial, Paris is becoming, if not Americanized, then very enamored of American products and the American way of life. The stateside spirit of doing a job yourself rather than handing it over to a professional here is called the "D system," and the people are tinkering with motor cars and hammering away on house repairs. With the new trend toward owning a country home, be it a cottage or a grand chateau, there is even more excuse to putter away on home projects.

Jeans (always pressed) are in. Supermarkets and, better yet, the *hypermarché*—stores with over 2,500 square meters of space—are proliferating. Shopping centers have sprung up in the suburbs, shopping malls in the city. Electronic game emporiums cannot be opened fast enough to meet the demand for confrontations between the teenage Parisian and Pac-Man.

Even housing is becoming suspiciously Americanized. Drive through the Paris environs on a Sunday afternoon, and you will see crowds of lookers trooping through modern homes that appear very un-French and very U.S.-suburban-development in style. Apartment complexes like Elysées and Parly Deux have been called *a la Californienne*. Whether the title is justified, they do have swimming pools with shopping centers adjacent, complete with movie theaters and the local version of the drugstore.

There is a desire for "things." In the early 1950s, only 7 percent of the homes had refrigerators, 8 percent had washing machines, and 21 percent had cars. By the mid 1970s, those figures had changed to 90 percent with refrigerators, 72 percent with washers, 64 percent with automobiles, and 17 percent with two cars.

The automobile plays havoc with Paris. The ratio of cars to people is just below the U.S. figure, and how to move them and where to put them have become problems. Paris has more one-way streets than any other city in Europe, and overpasses, tunnels, and expressways run through the inner city, while the boulevard Périphérique encircles it like a lasso.

## The People

The French are different, the Parisian unique. It won't take you long to realize that the average Parisian seems blessed—or cursed, depending on your view—with two personalities. Socially, Parisians are the soul of charm and graciousness; but on the streets, where anonymity prevails, they can be indifferent and at times downright cruel.

One explanation given for the apparent disregard of young lovers—who do not hesitate to display affection far beyond the acceptable limits in the States while standing in a movie queue or waiting on a corner for a light to change—is that as long as you don't know anyone around you, what difference does it make?

The French, and particularly the Parisians, are extremely proud. Their language, culture, city, and fashions, they reason, are supreme. So why shouldn't they be chauvinistic? After all, the word itself originated with a general in Napoleon's army by the name of Chauvin who became so patriotic and devoted to Napoleon that people poked fun at him and began to call patriotism "chauvinism."

Just begin with the premise that any request will probably be met with a negative response. Just as the Japanese often say yes when they really mean no, the French say no when they actually mean, or will finally come around to saying, yes. If all this seems terribly complicated, just keep in mind that the French want to establish the ground rules; once they are certain you will play the game their way, the match can get under way. For example, if you call to ask a question, you probably will be told to call back at another time for an answer. They do not like to apologize, and they tell you how wrong you are with such skill and charm that in the end you wonder if you had the right to question them in the first place.

Just as they have never fully accepted the parking meter, they have yet to acknowledge the full scope of telephone possibilities. They prefer letters of inquiry to questions by phone—better yet, they would like you to come around in person with a note.

Shopkeepers who can appear indifferent on your first visit will give you their undivided attention once you establish yourself as a regular customer. An expatriate related how her butcher ignored all other customers while serving her, no matter how long, undecided, and detailed her request might be. Another American woman presented the owners of a small vegetable shop with homemade cookies at Christmas time. The proprietors were so overcome that they kissed her; on her next visit they had a large box of chocolates, a very expensive item in France, ready as a gift.

The secret seems to be "in knowing you." A smile and a gracious greeting are not enough. Superseding all this is the need to know French.

Dozens of theories have been set forth as to why and how the

French act with such duplicity. France is a formal, not necessarily polite, society. One theory holds that it all goes back to the days of royalty when those at court were bound by protocol to avoid losing favor with the king. The average man, on the other hand, developed a belligerent, rough attitude to assert his independence.

Others say the French, and particularly Parisians, live too much in the past. Their pride in what has been conflicts with what must be today; they become wistful for what was, frustrated by what is, and bitter over what may never be again.

Still others say the toughness developed during the academic years (see Education) carries over into adulthood. Another theory blames the negative attitudes on the strife of urban living coupled with the often damp and dreary weather. Whatever the reason, you can be confident that any hostility is not directed at you personally or because you are a foreigner. They treat each other in the same manner.

There are also a few suggestions by expatriates who have been around Paris for awhile. Don't hesitate to stand firm when you think you are right and argue back (preferably in French). Don't speak to or smile at strangers. It can be considered an invasion of privacy or flirtatious, depending on the sex to whom it is directed. Don't feel guilty if you find that living in Paris is not always delightful. Dress on the formal side. And above all, be prepared for strikes.

The Parisians have an affinity for strikes. You may awake in the morning to find that the electric company is on strike and that bus 52, the one that takes you directly to your office, will not be operating that day.

The Parisian lives for and dedicates his life to the month-long August holiday, when the city virtually becomes a ghost town, inhabited only by tourists and a few die-hard Parisians who decide to stay in town. Leaving Paris takes on such importance during this month that some families have been known to hide out in their apartments rather than be discovered still at home. Many restaurants and shops close down for the entire month of August, and it is not always easy to find needed goods and services at this time. Yet, the city still functions. Those who remain to serve the tourists can enjoy with them the shimmering lighted fountains at night and the sidewalk performers by day.

Rank is extremely important, and decorations help to establish position in the community. The little red ribbon worn in the lapel of a gentleman's jacket designates the Legion of Honor and elevates the wearer to a high position in the eyes of his countrymen. Where you went to school also determines position in life simply through a process of selecting candidates for the best jobs from graduates of certain schools.

The French woman has never expressed the deep passion toward the feminist movement as have many of her counterparts in the States; instead, she has chosen to fight subtly and psychologically. Attractive and chic, she usually is a marvelous conversationalist and often is the real power at home.

One American woman commented on how equal the men and women really are. At the golf club where she is a member, there is no men's dining room, there are no special days for women to play golf, and foursomes are often composed of two men and two women, none of whom is married to each other.

Today bourgeois women are expected to seek jobs after completing their education; but for women of the lower economic classes, staying at home is a sign of prestige. The result has been that about the same number of women are presently employed as worked at the turn of the century.

How do the Parisians view Americans? We are a ball-playing, gum-chewing, Coke-drinking society. Our women, they say, may be pretty and healthy looking while young, but they are not very chic when old. Polyester clothes, wing-tipped shoes, and the no-makeup look tend to annoy them.

Part of the problem for expatriates coming to Paris for the first time is that they have preconceived attitudes of Paris as a city where life will be beautiful. But Paris, like other big cities, has problems. There will be moments, however, that will be pure fun. You may find yourself sitting over a cup of coffee, perhaps in a tiny restaurant in Montmartre, laughing hysterically with the Parisians (but more likely with the tourists) at a shriveled, 80-year-old lady who serenades the audience with off-color songs. Or there will be times when you stroll across the square Furstenberg just as the sun comes out after a rain shower and you will think this must be the most beautiful spot on earth. If you are a woman, you will be charmed when a handsome silver-haired gentleman kisses you three times on the cheek and greets you with the sincere warmth and cordiality that only a Frenchman can display. You will gain a sense of history, a feel for culture, a taste for fresh fruits and vegetables that are among the best in the world along with an appreciation of fine wines and excellent food. But above all you will come away, if not loving the Parisian, at least understanding the Parisian and respecting his city.

## Practical Pointers

*Addressing people.* It is very important to add the term *Monsieur, Madam,* or *Mademoiselle* when you greet, say good-bye, or thank a person. The terms can also be used appropriately at other points in a conversation.

*Shaking hands.* This is the other part of a polite greeting or departure. A woman will offer her hand first.

*Tipping.* Waiters, bartenders, museum guides, theater ushers, restroom attendants, hotel employees, barbers, and women's hairdressers all depend upon tips for a substantial part of their income. Even a gas station attendant will expect something for cleaning the windshield and for other extra services. Deliverymen of all kinds expect a tip. Repairmen, too, will be a little more attentive if they know they will get something extra. The usual tip is from FR1 to FR3, but for deliverymen or repairmen, a drink of wine or beer may be more appreciated. Taxi drivers get 10 to 15 percent.

The concierge requires special attention. The best plan is to start out on the right foot by giving him or her a substantial tip at the beginning. This may mean the difference between receiving and never seeing your mail and packages. They will want a gift at the holidays and another tip when you leave.

In restaurants a service charge *(service compris)* is usually included on the check. No more is required unless you are dining at a very luxurious restaurant where you might want to reward the sommelier or maître d' for special service.

*Flowers.* Sending or taking flowers to your hostess when you are invited to a meal with a French family for the first time will be appreciated. But do not send chrysanthemums because they are used for mourning.

A single red rose can be the sign of special affection for a loved one or special thanks for some act of thoughtfulness.

*Kissing.* Hand kissing is still practiced by the older generation, often accompanied by "Mes hommages, Madam." You don't thank a gentleman but merely say hello or good-bye. Good friends will greet each other with light kisses on the cheeks two or three times.

*Visiting.* Never just drop in to visit a French family. You should call first. Among very close friends invitations are given verbally. On more formal occasions a written invitation is issued. It should be delivered at least ten days in advance and answered within 48 hours. This goes for invitations to business colleagues, casual friends, and neighbors.

*Announcements.* All notices of communions, births, engagements, weddings, and funerals must be acknowledged by a written reply, flowers, or a gift, depending on the occasion.

*Weather.* Temperatures in Paris rarely will drop below freezing and summers are pleasant. There may be an occasional heat wave and it is then, say American expatriates, that they go scurrying for an electric fan. The wettest month is August (average rainfall 2¹/₂ inches), and the driest, March.

*Signs to watch for.* If the word *Livraison* is painted on the pavement, it means the space is reserved for deliveries to a nearby building. *Interdit* on a sign means forbidden, and it may apply to a number of situations, including a warning not to park in the area or not to enter a door.

*Getting around.* One of your first acts upon arriving in Paris should be the purchase of the indispensible book, *Plan de Paris par Arrondissement et Communes de Banlieue,* published by and available at the W. H. Smith bookstore, 248 rue de Rivoli, and at other bookstores and newsstands. It lists every street in Paris and many suburbs, where the street begins and ends, and the Metro stop (see Transportation) to reach it. There are maps of each section and all transportation lines. Public buildings and other points of interest are listed.

Paris is divided into 20 arrondissements. Number 1 is considered the birthplace of the city—the area around the Ile de la Cité. From there, the numbers climb upward in a clockwise pattern of three rings in all. Number 20 is in the last ring on the far east side. Surrounding the arrondissements is the belt highway, boulevard Périphérique. The city proper covers about 40 square miles, but greater Paris with the suburbs is approximately 818 square miles. Parisians are very conscious of the arrondissement in which they live. Addresses will usually include this number; for example, an address in the first arrondissement will have (1ᵉ) following the street name.

Each arrondissement is divided into quarters. These subareas have names rather than numbers and are based on traditional rather than legal boundaries.

Paris employs a five-digit postal zone number that is included in an address before the city. The last two digits of this number indicate the arrondissement number.

*Floor numbers.* The ground floor is the *rez de chaussée* (RC). The next floor is the first floor. The basement is the *sous-sol* (SS).

*Dates.* As in most of Europe, the sequence in writing dates is day first, then the month and year. April 6, 1983 would be 6/4/83.

## To Bring or Not to Bring

In Paris there are very few items that are absolutely not available anywhere at anytime. Sure, expatriates have some things that they get on home leave or recommend bringing from the States: a particular brand, a product whose French equivalent is not exactly the same, or one that is more expensive or of lower quality if bought in France. But these lists are short and more accurately reflect the idiosyncrasies of the expatriate than a general unavailability.

One big decision, as in other 220-volt/50-cycle countries, is whether to bring appliances. The Paris expatriate colony has mixed feelings—there are some definite pros and cons. French appliances are smaller, usually slower, and more costly. Yet they are the right current, they work, and can be repaired more easily. You may find your shopping habits change so you do not need the large freezer. U.S. appliances are big (Do you have room?), costly to ship, and the 110-volt versions require transformers. Even some 220-volt products can be a problem. A couple of expatriates who purchased 220-volt ranges from a discount store in the United States found that the panel lights were on a 110-volt circuit and quickly burned out in Paris. Still, there is nothing as supportive for Americans as having their own tried-and-true appliances.

A few other things mentioned as hard to find are:

Cooking spray for pans for those on low-cholesterol diets.

Your favorite cake mixes. French products are quite different. A few American mixes can be found, but they are expensive.

Maple syrup.

Children's clothing. It is very expensive here.

Sewing supplies. Thread is reportedly unsatisfactory, and invisible zippers are unavailable.

Draperies. If you know the window sizes of your new home, have draperies made in the States before leaving, as costs here are much higher.

Muffin tins.

Disposable diapers. Bring as many as possible, as they are very expensive.

Bedding. Pillows here are square. Also bring bed linens. However, one store in Paris carries American sizes: Chiff Tire (56, rue de Seine [6ᵉ]; telephone 633.14.43).

Clothes. Pack as many as possible, as prices are quite high.

Women's clothes tend to be narrow in the shoulders, the arms are shorter, and the slacks are slimmer.

Shoes. Widths tend to be wider here.

## Housing

"That apartment," said a 14-year-old American boy who had just been shown through quarters that were to become his new home, "is the pits."

"But why don't you like it?" asked the shocked Frenchman who had just conducted the tour. "After all, Madam Claude lived there, and she can trace her ancestry back 400 years!"

Such is the attitude of Paris. Ancestry and housing go hand in hand. What the gentleman very well could have said was, "Her family has occupied the apartment for 400 years."

The Parisians find a place to live and then hold on to it tenaciously, generation after generation.

Locating a suitable apartment in the arrondissement of your choice—or house, if you plan to live in the suburbs—is not easy. Many of the choice apartments are "in the family," so to speak; others are expensive and simply not available. Count on at least several months in a hotel before finding a suitable home.

The town hall or *mairie* is not only the administrative office for each arrondissement but also the neighborhood information center. Their bulletin boards post ads from all types of repairmen. There are many services offered by the mairie: police stations *(commissariat)*, fire stations *(pompiers)*, a library *(bibliotheque municipale)*, medical information, and cultural programs.

There are usually several publications in each arrondissement that describe local activities, emergency telephone numbers, where to find the gas and electric offices, used articles for sale, lists of shops, and so on. Some of these are published by the local merchants and industries in the area.

Each arrondissement is required to have a street market once a week (see Shopping). Information on the day and exact location can be obtained from the mairie.

There is a definite ambience to each arrondissement and its quarters; before deciding on where you want to live, explore the various areas on foot to catch the color and feeling of the neighborhood.

Many newcomers to Paris find accommodations through one of the housing agencies in the city (listed in the Paris telephone book under *agence de location de proprietés* and *location d'appartements.* Here are a few agencies that have been helpful to Americans:

New Resident's Service
26, rue Chalgrin (16ᵉ)
Telephone 500.58.82

Benedict Bureau
10, rue du Mont-Thabor (15ᵉ)
Telephone 073.17.56

George V Immobilier
12, avenue George V (8ᵉ)
Telephone 225.29.97

American Advisory Service
7, avenue de la Grande Armée (16ᵉ)
Telephone 727.43.29

Newspaper advertisements and notices on bulletin boards are two other good sources for housing. Two English-language papers carry housing ads, the *International Herald Tribune* and a free monthly paper, the *Paris Free Voice.* The French papers to check are *Le Figaro* and *France-Soir.* There are several weekly periodicals devoted exclusively to rental and sales of housing: *De Particulier à Particulier, La Semaine Immobilière,* and *Locations Vacances.* These can be found at newsstands and bookshops. Look for *location offres* (to rent), *vide* (unfurnished), and *meublé* (furnished).

The *Wall Street Journal,* which began a European edition in early 1983, has housing ads for major cities.

One of the best guides to Paris for expatriates is UNESCO's *Practically Yours, Paris and France,* 1980 edition (UNESCO Community Service, Paris). It can be purchased for F28 from the UNESCO office, B 1.07, 7, place de Fontenoy. In its excellent section on housing it includes a typical French advertisement and an explanation of the terms:

"15ᵉ, P.à P. Imm. neuf. 4 pces, dbl. liv., 100 m², cuis. équipée, park., tél., soleil, moq., ter., sur jardin, 4.200 F, ch. compr. Tel. 276.31.68, hres. burx."

15ᵉ           15th arrondissement.
P.à P.      The owner, himself, is offering the rental property, therefore you will have no agency fee to pay.
Imm.neuf. New building.

| | |
|---|---|
| 4 pces | Four rooms, plus kitchen, bath and WC. |
| dbl. liv. | Two of the four rooms are living area (either two rooms separated by an arch or a room double the usual size). |
| cuis. équipée | Equipped kitchen; probably has cupboards, stove, perhaps dishwasher, rarely more. If cuis équipée is not specified, you may assume that the kitchen will only contain a sink, rarely cupboards. |
| Tél. | The apartment has a telephone already installed. This is important because if not it could take a long time to obtain one. Even with the telephone already in, you will have to request its registration in your name, if you so desire. |
| soleil | The apartment is sunny—important during Paris's gray, wet winter. |
| moq | Carpeting, most often wall-to-wall in new buildings. |
| ter | Terrace. Not to be confused with a balcon (balcony) which is usually very small, nor a loggia which can be somewhat larger but is covered with an overhang. |
| sur jardin | Overlooking garden. |
| 4.200F | Monthly rent. Gas, electricity and telephone will be extra. |
| ch. compr | This means that the monthly charges for heat and hot water (if their consumption is not individually controlled) are included in the figure above. These charges may also help cover general building maintenance and salary of gardener. |
| hres. burx | Call during usual office hours, i.e. 9.00-12.00, 14.30-18.30. If the ad reads "hres repas" it means to call during meal times, before 9.00, between 12.30 and 14.00 and between 19.30 and 21.00. |

Other terms you might encounter:

*stdg, grand stdg, très grand stdg* A more and more luxurious building in a more and more fashionable area.

*pierre de taille* Cut stone building.

*caractère* Indicates character, unusual or distinctive architecture at best, bizarre or uncomfortable at worst.

*récent* Recently constructed building.

*ancien* Older building.

*tt cft* Has a full-sized equipped bathroom and toilet facilities.

*ref. nf* Newly remodeled or decorated.*

Many buildings containing unfurnished apartments are owned by French insurance companies, which have a rental office for their

---

*Our thanks to UNESCO and *Practically Yours, Paris and France.*

property. Check with these offices for empty units. You can save an agency fee.

The *News,* a weekly publication of the U.S. Missions in Paris, contains many announcements of interest to all the American colony and classified ads for items for sale, housing, and services.

## There's More to Renting than the Monthly Rent

The monthly rent on a Parisian flat is only the beginning. There are sure to be several other changes. The standard lease is heavily in favor of the landlord. If you have used an agency it will charge a fee of about one month's rent. The tenant is responsible for all damage, so there will be a security deposit of one or two months' rent. Utilities may not be separate. There are some taxes on rentals and property that a landlord may try to pass on to the tenant. Parking usually is extra.

The previous tenant, if he has made improvements in the residence, may try to recover their value by charging the new occupant for them. This key money (*reprise*) is not sanctioned legally, but it is not uncommon.

The very complete inventory of the condition of the residence and its contents (*etat des lieux*) is as important in Paris as in other cities.

## Utilities

Landlords do not turn the heat on until the middle of October, and they turn it off by the middle of May no matter what the temperature; by law, they must not allow the heat to go above 68°F. Many residents supplement with portable electric heaters, but check to see if your home is adequately wired for large heating appliances. The costs of heating and water are not normally included in the rental cost of homes or apartments, and you may be charged an additional amount or perhaps receive a refund, depending on the exact amounts used. Ask for an itemized accounting of the charges.

You are expected to pay electric and gas bills.

## Insurance

The tenant, not the landlord, is responsible for any damage to the premises and to the neighbors in case of a water problem, a fire, an explosion, a theft, personal injury, or even items falling from your apartment balcony onto another one. A "tenant's liability insurance" similar to a homeowners policy in the United States is a must.

## Concierge

This individual, long a favorite character of French mystery writers as the most knowledgeable person about nefarious goings-on in apartments, is disappearing except in the most luxurious buildings. Technically, he or she is the building superintendent, and also the deliverer of mail, security guard, and much more. Living without the good graces of your concierge can be burdensome. Newer buildings and many older ones have installed push buttons numbered 1 through 9. The front door is opened by pressing the right code of three numbers.

## Equipment

Paris is one of those cities where you may have to furnish everything including kitchen cupboards, door knobs, a medicine cabinet, lighting fixtures, towel racks, and in very old apartments, even the kitchen sink. One expatriate reported costs of $500 for completing plumbing work in a new apartment so that a washer could be connected.

Refrigerators and stoves are not included in an unfurnished flat.

If the apartment you have rented has a fireplace, remember to have a chimney sweep (*ramonage*) clean it before you ever build a fire. It must be certified that this work has been done. Keep this paper for your insurance in case of a fire.

## Furnished Apartments

Furnished quarters are fairly common, particularly in the Paris area, but they quite often are sparsely furnished. You can supplement with local purchases, but prices are high.

## Residential Areas

There are the usual pros and cons of city versus suburban living. As in the States, you usually get more space for your money the farther out you go; but then you pay in commuting time and costs. Whether it is the suburbs or the city, the west side has been preferred by the expatriates because of the type of housing available, the character of the neighborhoods, its proximity to international schools, and closeness to offices. Here are the favorite residential areas.

### In Paris

Arrondissement 7. Many embassies. Fashionable, bourgeois area. Home to diplomats and, at one time, nobility. Large, old, elegant apartments. Parks and squares. Location of the Eiffel Tower and Ecole Militaire, the American College, the Institut Suffren, UNESCO, the old Gare d'Orsay (a station, now a theater).

Arrondissement 8. Many grand couturiers. Elegant shops and top hotels. Champs Elysées and place de la Concorde. Extremely fashionable. A few newer apartments here. Cours Ste-Marie la Madeleine (school) and Section Monceau (kindergarten and primary school for French- and English-speaking students). Location of American and British embassies. Little space for children to play. Many museums. The Elysée (government).

Arrondissement 16. Stretches westward from the Arc de Triomphe to the beautiful Bois de Boulogne and then south between the Bois and the Seine. Location of the aristocratic avenue Foch, home to many Arab oil magnates. More residential than arrondissement 8. Home of the International School of Paris.

Arrondissements 5 and 6. On the Left Bank. Arrondissement 5 popular with students and artists. Some American business community living here. Much activity on the streets. Luxembourg Gardens. Pantheon. Colorful, less elegant than previous arrondissements. Jardin des Plantes (zoo and flowers). Little theaters called _cafés theatres_. Arrondissement 6 also on the Left Bank. Many bookstores. School of the Beaux Arts (arts, painting).

There are also the pocket areas of revamped, older homes such as Marais, Ile St-Louis, and Montmartre. While these may be charming and picturesque, they tend to be more popular with the French than with the Americans. It can be quite difficult to find a place here, and it could require buying rather than renting. Arrondissement 14 on the far south border is the location of the Cite Universitaire, a popular international housing complex for students.

### The Suburbs

Neuilly-sur-Seine. One of the choicest of all areas both city and suburban. Really an extension of the Paris west side. Metro available.

Just a short distance west and a little north of Arc de Triomphe. Gorgeous apartments overlooking Bois de Boulogne. Homes with small gardens. Huge office complex of La Défense just next door on the other side of the Seine (some American corporations have offices there). Cour Charles de Foucault (this school provides special instructions in French for foreign children). Marymount International School also in this suburb. Very few shops.

Other western suburbs such as St-Cloud (home of the American School of Paris), Garches, le Vesinet, and Croissy-sur-Seine offer charming homes and apartments but necessitate taking a train into Paris and sometimes a bus to reach the suburban train station. St-Germain-en-Laye, even farther out, is a beautiful area and the home of Lycée International d' Hennémont.

## Tips on Housing in Paris

The names of occupants and apartment numbers are not always listed in the building entrance.

Hall lights in an apartment or other buildings can be turned on for three minutes by pushing the *minuterie* button located near the staircase.

House numbers begin from the end nearest the Seine in north-south streets and from the eastern end in the east-west streets.

When looking for an apartment in Paris, try to find one above the fifth floor to catch as much light as possible.

Don't expect to know your neighbors or to be invited home by French friends. The latter is not a case of unfriendliness toward you but simply the closeness of French society. Intimate friends, the ones you invite to your home, are made over a long period of time, sometimes only from childhood days or through close family connections. Then, too, the Frenchman who appears so affluent in public—the car he drives, the restaurants in which he is seen, the clothes he wears, the month-long holiday in August he takes—may live on a very modest scale at home, so modest in fact that he does not want the outside world to view it.

# Education

## The Public School System

To understand the Frenchman is to understand his educational system, for to succeed in it one must be tough, competitive, and oblivious of others and the world around him. Most French families, contrary to the British way of thinking, prefer to send their children to public schools; 80 percent of the educational institutions in the country are free and under the tutelage of the Ministry of Education. Although not the primary reason for public school preference, it does give the Frenchman more money to spend in other pursuits than his British counterpart.

The French approach to education is very structured and unique. The system was designed to be democratic. The rigorous examinations were developed to give everyone a chance to advance and obtain higher educational advantages. But, in actuality, the children of the upper and middle classes seem to end up with the best schooling. An intellectual elitism has been the paradoxical result.

The public school system basically decides what the student's life will be and sets an educational pattern for the youngster from which it is almost impossible to break. Classroom performance determines into what educational field a student will be directed and into what higher level of school he will go. The school itself is indicative of what position in society the student will have. There are no "late bloomers," no misunderstood children who simply need counseling, no chance for a new start in life. The die is cast at a very early age, somewhere between 11 and 15, and to change it is virtually impossible.

In theory an expatriate has a wide selection of educational systems and schools within the system from which to choose. But the choice narrows as he settles down to studying the options. The public school system is open to foreigners; but with the exception of the very early grades, a fluent knowledge of French is necessary. Expatriate parents thinking of placing their children in the public schools to expose them to local culture should give careful consideration as to whether the child can meet not only the academic standards but the psychological challenges as well. Although there have been many reforms since 1968—the year students and others went on strike to protest the system and life in general—the schools still follow relatively rigid national curricula, poles apart from U.S. educational thinking.

Before looking at the other educational systems available in France, let's take a glance at the public school approach. It all begins very democratically with the very important preschool education. Although school is not compulsory until a child is 6, almost 100 percent of the five-year-olds and a high percentage of 3- and 4-year-olds are enrolled in tuition-free preschool classes. Most attend the public schools *(ecole maternelles)*, and it is not just playtime. The primary program assumes that one or more years have been spent in preschool education.

Children enter the five-year primary level at age 5, 6, or 7, depending upon their maturity. The basic program of reading, writing, and mathematics is supplemented by some history, geography, civics, art, music, and physical education. A high rate of failure at this level has plagued France for many years, but reforms are enabling most children to get to the next stage in normal time.

Secondary education for the French child from age 11 to 14 is at the *collèges* for the first level or cycle. They continue their studies of the subjects from the primary level and also begin a foreign language, sciences, economics, and vocational training. During the last two years of this stage there is a period of decision making in which the student, parents, guidance counselors, and school administrators participate in recommending the further educational path to follow, academic or vocational. This decision has great effect on the child's future career. If the consensus is academic, a second language or other science subjects are added. For a vocational career, classes are combined with periods in industry to introduce the student to a wide range of trades from which to select.

After successful completion of the college level, the student receives a diploma: the *diplôme national du brevet des collèges.*

The second cycle of the secondary level, ages 15 through 17, is at the lycées. There, a shorter course is for technical and vocational students. The longer program prepares students for the baccalauréat, the passport to higher education and quite likely the guarantee of a certain status in society. There are a number of baccalaureate series or programs, each with its own academic emphasis. The *bac,* as it is lovingly known by generations of Frenchmen (it was established by imperial decree in 1808), serves a double purpose: it represents successful completion of 12 years of significant accomplishment, and it gives access to a university. The various series can lead to the traditional academic bac; or to one incorporating technological as well as academic study, so that the recipient can consider entering the job market at that point; or to one emphasizing agricultural studies. Subspecialties within these series run the gamut of learning from philosophy to data processing.

The bac examination given at the end of the twelfth grade, usually in mid-June, is the day of reckoning for French students. There are notorious stories about parents bribing for early copies or passing grades. It consists of a written exam in at least five subjects and an oral exam in three or four more. Those who pass the first time, usually fewer than 20 percent, belong to a select group. Others can take the test again in about three weeks, and this session is exclusively oral. If this is failed, then the student must wait a year to take the whole series again.

There are seldom extracurricular activities in either the *collége* or the lycée. School orchestras, drama groups, and sports are rare.

## Universities

The bac is the admission ticket to any university, with the exception of the Grand Ecoles and a few private schools. There are about a dozen of these Grand Ecoles. Graduation from them virtually ensures a position of importance and success in life. A student is required to pass an entrance examination to gain admission. To pass this exam, a two- or three-year postbaccalaureate study is almost mandatory. For this period, the student devotes his full time and energy to studying; admission to this supplementary program is highly selective. These programs are familiarly known as *taupes*.

These elite universities constitute a unique phenomenon of the French system of higher education. The oldest date from the eighteenth or early nineteenth century. Traditionally, they are the training grounds for government leaders, the top civil servants, and the elite of academic, literary, military, and industrial circles. They are under the jurisdiction of several government ministries.

Usually, the regular universities are overcrowded and do not even offer a place for students to get together. No one seems to know for certain exactly how many university students there are in France since it is possible to enroll in more than one school at a time. The figure is believed to be around 700,000.

## Other Educational Opportunities

In addition to the public school system, expatriate children can choose among international schools, such as the American or English schools; bilingual public and private schools where both French and English are used and where the curriculum is international or European; and the strictly French private schools. American children have been accepted in public schools at the lower levels and in some private schools at all levels; when necessary, they have been tutored until they can hold their own in the French language. The following lists are by no means complete, but they include some of the schools that are popular with the expatriate community, particularly with

Americans. For detailed information and a complete listing of private schools in your own neighborhood, consult your arrondissement or suburb town hall or write, preferably in French, to Schola Vox (7, rue Henri-Monnier [9ᵉ]; telephone 878.23.66). The French Cultural Services (972 Fifth Avenue, New York, New York 10021; telephone [212] 570-4400) can be contacted also.

### English-Speaking and Bilingual Schools

American School of Paris
41, rue Pasteur
St-Cloud
Telephone 602.54.43
Located in a nearby suburb, looks very much like a medium-sized urban school in the United States. Coeducational and independent, nonsectarian, fully accredited day school running from grades kindergarten through 12. An American educational program. About 1,000 students of all nationalities. Majority American students. Around 95 percent of graduates enter college. French required in all grades. Hot meals provided and bus service available to most areas in Paris and surrounding suburbs.

International School of Paris
96, bis rue du Ranelagh (16ᵉ)
Telephone 224.43.40
Formerly known as Pershing Hall School. Private, coeducational school from preschool to ninth grade. English is language of instruction but great emphasis on learning French. Class size limited to 15. Enrollment around 200 and usually more than 20 nationalities represented. Uniforms in first through fifth grades. An active extracurricular program. A fleet of taxis provides transportation.

Marymount School
72, boulevard de la Saussaye
9 Neuilly-sur-Seine
Telephone 624.10.51
Founded in 1923 by the Order of the Sacred Heart. Coeducational Catholic school through eighth grade. Other denominations are accepted. American curriculum. Organized with several age groups in one class. No grades. Students bring their own lunch. Can be reached by public bus from Paris.

English School of Paris
Llesna Court
38, quai de l'Ecluse
Croissy-sur-Seine
Telephone 976.29.00
Coeducational school of the British system preparing students for entry into all preparatory schools and colleges in Great Britain. Grades kindergarten through twelfth with some advanced-level courses equivalent to the second year of college in the United States. The U.S. college board exams are given. Uniforms required.

United Nations Nursery School
40, rue Pierre-Guérin (16ᵉ)
Telephone 527.20.24
A private school for children of all nationalities from preschool to age six. Classes half days. Both French and English. No bus transportation.

Lennon School
American Church of Paris
65, quai d'Orsay (7ᵉ)
Telephone 555.63.17
A private, coeducational bilingual school for nursery and kindergarten children. No transportation.

Ecole Active Bilingue
6, avenue Van Dyck (8ᵉ)
Telephone 924.02.04
(The above address is one of several sections and locations for this school. Others are in the 7ᵉ and 16ᵉ arrondissements.)
Coeducational, bilingual primary and secondary school. Preparation for either American college boards or bac exams. Special adaptation classes run parallel to the French classes to help foreign students master French and adjust to the curriculum.

Lycee International
Saint-Germain-en-Laye (Yvelines)
Telephone 963.14.31
A coeducational, primary and secondary day school which, in addition to the official French curriculum leading to the Baccalauréat, offers supplementary American, British, German, Danish, Dutch, Italian, Portuguese, and Swedish national programs.

The school prepares students for college board examinations and the International Baccalauréat. Special intensive French language classes are also available.

The schools listed below have informed the U.S. embassy that they can accept children who do not know French and that special instruction can be given until the child can follow the class instruction in the French language. The embassy suggests that parents make sure that these arrangements and any additional charges are clearly stated beforehand.

Ecole Secondaire Saint-Michel
47, boulevard de Picpus (12$^e$)
Telephone 343.87.65
For boys from ages 5 to 18.

Externat Saint-Joseph
121, avenue du Roule
Neuilly sur Seine
Telephone 624.95.45
For boys ages 6 to 16.

Cours Charles de Foucauld
1, boulevard Richard Wallace
Neuilly sur Seine
Telephone 624.56.16
Coeducational, ages 2$^1$/$_2$ to 18.

Ecole Saint-Sulpice
68, rue d'Assas (6$^e$)
Telephone 548.12.68
For boys ages 6 to 18.

Ecole Nouvelle
30, rue Antonin Reynaud
92300 Levallois
Telephone 737.69.10
Coeducational, ages 3 to 12.

Cours Secondaire Alfred de Musset
33, rue du Champ de Mars (7$^e$)
Telephone 551.00.28
Coeducational, ages 10 to 18.

Ecole Pascal
33, boulevard Lannes (16ᵉ)
Télephone 504.17.75
Boys from ages 8 to 18; girls from ages 8 to 11.

For more information on other schools with this service, contact the Office National d'Information sur les Enseignements et les Professions (ONISEP) (168, boulevard du Montparnasse [14ᵉ]; telephone 325.05.98).

At the college level there is:

American College in Paris
31, avenue Bosquet (7ᵉ)
Telephone 551.21.57 and 705.30.66
U.S. contact: PO Box 133
Demarest, New Jersey 07627
A unique institution in that it is the only independent American college in Europe fully accredited and licensed in the United States to confer B.A. degrees in five liberal arts programs. The campus is in the heart of Paris. Almost 70 percent of the student body of about 500 is American, the rest from over 40 other countries. The faculty numbers about 60. Students are placed in French homes if they do not arrange for their own housing in Paris.

## Shopping

Parisian women dress with a flair. No faded, fringed denims, dirty sneakers, or sloppy shirts for them. They wear jeans, but jeans with class—sometimes so much class that the outfit includes a hat and furs.

"As soon as we saw all the American women tourists wearing pantsuits," one young French woman told us, "we couldn't wear them anymore."

Once again, it was that old spirit of independence. They—both men and women—accept jeans with great enthusiasm but on French terms.

The men are as fashion conscious as the women. One arbiter of men's apparel paid homage to the well-dressed Frenchmen by pointing out that they wear "well-cut drab suits that flatter the body, in contrast with the English gentlemen's suits which are drab and skillfully ignore the body."

It has always been like that in France. As early as the twelfth century, women were being sewn into dresses too tight to slip over their heads. Even Napoleon had an eye for fashion. He never wanted his generals' wives to wear the same outfit twice. In the seventeenth century, the government realized that the couturier fashion industry meant really big business and allowed guilds to be formed that began dictating the styles.

Parisians care about how they look. For the women, there is no quick trip to the grocery in rollers and casual clothing. She has had to fight a subtle, psychological battle to hold her own in a man's world, and dressing well and remaining physically attractive is just one of the ways to do it.

As with the jeans, if the French are to copy something, they make it completely their own. And the art of turning something ordinary into a fashion statement doesn't stop with clothing. The French can take the most mundane kitchen gadget and make it so attractive that you want to have it in full view on your counter. It all adds up to a tempting world of consumer items—but one that can be fiercely expensive.

The big puzzler for the expatriate is not so much where to buy what but how the French do it when everything is so expensive. One answer is that many people buy little but well—one pair of quality shoes, one outfit in the latest style. But there is more to it than that. The French, who for years have thought the more expensive the item, the better the quality, have discovered the discount stores, catalog buying, special sales, and outlet shops. Prices may still be higher than in the United States, although not as bad as the first tour through the local stores would indicate. Sales are held in January, June, and July. Couturier sales are March and July.

Rue du Faubourg St-Honoré remains the city's prestige shopping street, and it is a must on the what-to-see list if not on the where-to-buy recommendations. Prices are high along this street, but merchandise is exquisite. It is here that a buyer must remember the old French saying that translates, "If you like it, you're not to count."

Those arbiters of restaurants, hotels, and night clubs in Paris, Henri Gault and Christian Millau, have arranged for an English-language edition of their very personal and candid guide, *The Best of Paris* (Crown Publishers/Knapp Press, New York, 1982). But entertainment is not the only subject. These two authors have applied their wit and taste to appraising the shops of Paris from antiques to department stores to swimwear. The section "Where to Find" lists sources for just about everything from a hot-air balloon to equipment for a reception.

## Department Stores

A better name, perhaps, would be the "grand boutiques," for clothing sections of these stores are planned with a series of designer's shops rather than one entire area devoted to sportswear, another to dresses, and so on, as is customary in most U.S. department stores. Sales personnel tend to know only the stock available in their small section, and expatriates say it sometimes makes it difficult to find what they want. There are many excellent department stores:

Galeries Lafayette
40 boulevard Haussmann (9ᵉ)
Telephone 282.34.56
Internationally, one of the best known among the department stores. High-quality merchandise. They carry everything from screws to automobile parts; also, items for your home that range from light bulbs to supplies for building an addition. Check kitchenwares for sales.

Bazaar de l'Hôtel de Ville
52, rue de Rivoli (4ᵉ)
Telephone 274.90.90
Check the basement for their *bricolage* (do-it-yourself) *quincaillerie*. Every type of tool is available. They can be rented or purchased. It also has a good housewares department, and clothing is less expensive than at many other stores. An auto repair store can lubricate your car while you shop.

Au Printemps
64, boulevard Haussmann (9ᵉ)
Telephone 285.22.22
Good for men's and women's couturier and ready-to-wear clothing. Its big toy department is a favorite of children.

Some of these stores have branches. Most have restaurants or tea rooms. Hours generally are 9:30 or 10:00 a.m. to 6:30 p.m. six days a week. One night, often Wednesday, some stores will remain open until 9 or 10 p.m.

Fnac, with four stores in Paris, has a membership buying service offering discounts, particularly on photographic, audiovisual, and other electrical appliances. It also provides cultural activities and tickets at reduced prices.

### Discount Stores

Bagg and Carrefour are two huge discount stores located in the suburbs on the route toward Satrouville, east of the Le Pecq circle in Montesson. They carry all kinds of household items, clothing, and food products at discount prices. Hours are Mondays through Saturdays from 9:00 a.m. to 8:00 p.m. Some others are:

Euromarché
1, avenue Général Sarrail (16ᵉ)
Telephone 651.46.11

Monoprix (18 stores)
21, avenue Opéra (1ᵉ)
Telephone 261.78.08

Prisunic (about 10 stores)
60, avenue Champs Elysées (8ᵉ)
Telephone 225.27.46

Uniprix
50, rue Rennes (6ᵉ)
Telephone 548.18.08

The warehouses of some department stores offer household items including furniture, appliances, rugs, and the like (some seconds) at prices that are good by local standards.

Dépôts de la Samaritaine
20, rue Cabanis (14ᵉ)
Telephone 336.49.30

Dépôts de Bazaar de l'Hotel de Ville
97, boulevard Vaillant-Couturier
Ivry-sur-Seine
Telephone 672.45.19

Dépôts Galeries Lafayette
13, quai le Châtelier
Ille St-Denis
Telephone 752.34.72

Dépôt au Printemps
9, quai le Châtelier
Ille St-Denis
Telephone 820.61.01

## Catalog Buying

Clothing, housewares, lawn furniture, and playground equipment are among the items popular in catalog buying. You can buy these catalogs in bookstores. As soon as your order is placed, the money for the catalog will be refunded. The second catalog listed appeals to a slightly younger clientele.

Trois Suisses
64, rue Caumartin (9e)
For mail orders call 584.15.15

La Redoute
1, place Ecole (1e)
Telephone 236.21.43

## Grand Couturiers

All couturiers design two seasonal collections a year. The spring-summer showings open the end of January and run through May. The autumn-winter showings begin the latter part of July and go through mid-December. Most have showings Monday through Fridays at 3:00 p.m. Some have boutique showings at 11:00 a.m.

An invitation card is needed for custom collections, but these are easy to get through the concierge at better hotels, or you may request it directly through the salon except during the two opening weeks of the collection when the press and buyers are in town.

## Permanent Soldes/Degriffe

For all women who have dreamed of owning a grand couturier creation but never wanted to spend the money, here's their chance. These are stores that cut the labels out of the designers' clothes and sell them well below the regular price. While still expensive, they are bargains in comparison with the original. One well known shop is Bab's (34, place du Marché-St-Honoré [1e]; telephone 260.07.87). Check *The Best of Paris* for others.

# English-Language Bookstores

Brentano's
37, avenue de l'Opera (2ᵉ)
Telephone 261.52.50
Carries a large stock of English, American, and French books and paperbacks for adults and children.

Galignani
224, rue de Rivoli (1ᵉ)
Telephone 260.76.07 and 260.73.65
Especially good for new and recent American, English, and French books and magazines.

Nouveau Quartier Latin
78, boulevard Saint-Michel (6ᵉ)
Telephone 326.42.70
Large selection of paperbacks.

Shakespeare and Company
37, rue de la Bûcherie (5ᵉ)
A Left Bank bookstore with an extensive collection of English-language publications and a tradition of providing a haven for struggling professional writers.

W. H. Smith
248, rue de Rivoli (1ᵉ)
Telephone 260.37.97
Books, magazines, and an English tearoom, too.

Children's Book Center
19, place du Marché
LeVesinet
Telephone 966.00.13
Games and toys as well as children's books.

## Miscellaneous

The French customs has periodic sales of goods seized by its agents, particularly clothes, food, and radios. The prices are a bargain. Check with Douane et Transports (24, rue Caumartin [9ᵉ]; telephone 265.77.60) for the nearest location.

Marche St Pierre
2, rue Charles Nodier (18ᵉ)
Telephone 606.92.25
You may receive absolutely rude service, but the bargains in fabrics of every variety (clothing and household) make it worth the trip.

Some areas are known for their specialty in certain items. For example, place Clichy in Arrondissement 8 is famous for carpets, while rue de Paradis in Arrondissement 10 is devoted to tableware. Main shopping streets for antiques are Faubourg St-Honoré (6ᵉ), quai Voltaire (7ᵉ), rue Bonaparte (6ᵉ), rue du Bac (7ᵉ), rue Jacob (6ᵉ), marché aux Puces (18ᵉ), Quartier St-Germain-des-Pres (6ᵉ), and rue des Saints-Peres (6ᵉ and 7ᵉ).

## *Shopping Centers*

Shopping centers, malls, and arcades are changing the buying habits of Parisians, who like the convenience of one-stop shopping.

The most spectacular is the ultramodern, five-level complex, Forum des Halles, rising from the debris of the demolition of the old Les Halles market. Concertgoers at the nearby Pompidou Center may not find the traditional onion soup in the Forum, but they will find restaurants featuring regional cuisines and shops of all kinds connected by glass and steel corridors. Other centers are:

Parly II. Versailles Shopping center. Christian Dior, Charles Jourdan shoes; Boitamôm (children's clothes); Bazaar Hotel d'Ville, Printemps, and Prisunic.

Velizy II. Southeast of Paris. Au Printemps, La Samaritaine, Prisunic, and many other shops. Prices tend to be slightly lower here than at Parly II.

Belle Epine. Between Paris and Orly Airport. Galeries Lafayette plus many shops. Wide variety in price range.

Montparnasse Shopping Center. Between the rue de l'Arrivée and the rue du Depart (15ᵉ). Includes the following boutiques: fashion (women and men), jewelry, perfumes, cosmetics, gifts, shoes, art objects, paintings, Galeries Lafayette, restaurants, hairdressers, and swimming pool.

Palais des Congrés, rue des Boutiques, place de la Porte, Maillot (17ᵉ). Right inside the convention building. Daimaru (Japanese department store), a wide variety of shops, restaurants, hairdressers, and movie theaters. Expositions and the like.

Beaugrenelle (15ᵉ). Near the "Statue of Liberty." Boutiques, four cinemas, restaurants.

## Hints on Shopping

When speaking to sales personnel, begin with *s'il vous plait* and end with *merci*. Always tack on "Madam," "Mademoiselle," or "Monsieur."

When buying major appliances or automobiles, try bargaining on price.

If you need a box for mailing, buy it at the post office. It is cheaper there.

When buying light bulbs, make sure you know what kind of socket is on your lamp. In France there are two kinds of sockets and light bulbs. You have either *bayonette* or *vis*. *L'ampoule a bayonette* has a straight base with two knobs, one on either side. *L'ampoule a vis* has a screw base like an English or American bulb. Check your French-bought lamps and the labels on the boxes before you buy bulbs. A half turn secures the *bayonette* bulb. The largest light bulbs are 150 watts. They are available in most supermarkets and hardware stores and at the Bazaar Hotel d'Ville and Au Printemp.

The smaller shops close for lunch between 12 noon and 2 p.m. Hairdressers close Monday and open Saturday from 9 a.m. to 6 p.m. or 7 p.m. Some have a late opening once a week.

Medical supplies are *not* bought in the *droguerie*. This is the shop for all types of cleaning and painting supplies. You must go to the *pharmacie* for medicines.

Shop the flea markets. It's fun and you may find a bargain. The biggest is Marchè aux Puces Saint-Ouen, porte de Clignancourt (18ᵉ), open Saturday, Sunday, and Monday.

The American Church in Paris conducts orientation seminars. This series includes a pamphlet, *Welcome To The Big Banana,* containing much helpful information on stores and shopping.

The American School in Paris also provides mimeographed material on shopping and other subjects.

## Services

The French, particularly the Parisians, are geniuses when it comes to turning the most troublesome locks into manageable, well-styled coiffures. The Parisian look today is casual—but casual with chic. Don't hesitate to try the little shop in your neighborhood.

If you buy locally made clothing, check the labels to see whether the item is to be washed or dry-cleaned. Certain symbols will give you the answer. A washtub with a number superimposed on it tells you the item is washable and the temperature the water should be. The same washtub with a cross through it indicates that it is not to be washed. A triangle says it's okay to bleach, but a cross through the triangle means "no bleach." A mark similar to the lower case English *a* indicates the clothing should be pressed, while an *x* through the same mark means "no pressing." A circle shows the clothing is to be dry-cleaned, and the letter in the center of it designates the method of cleaning, which the cleaners will understand. The *x* through the circle means do not dry-clean.

If you are concerned about the quality of the dry-cleaning service *(teinturerie)*, check for a blue circle on the cleaner's window, which stands for the International Dry Cleaner's Association. Ask for individual care *(soigné)* for your better apparel. It costs twice as much but is advisable for delicate fabrics and to protect buttons. Expatriates say they send such things as corduroy through the regular services.

When taking clothes or linens to a laundry, check to see if they will be ironed by hand *(finition main)*. One expatriate took four sheets and pillow slips and a few bath towels to such an establishment and was handed a bill for the equivalent of $26. It's the hand ironing that did it. Don't bother to plead with attendants for quick service. It is futile. If they say "Thursday," settle for Thursday. You don't stand a chance of getting it back late Wednesday afternoon.

Laundromats have sprung up around Paris. You are expected to use their soap, at a fee, of course. Better yet, turn the entire wash over to the manager and let her handle it, for a small additional fee.

## Carpenters, Plumbers, Electricians, and Others

First ask your concierge; if this brings no results, check your local town hall for any notices posted there for such services. You also can call the Artisans Service (telephone 720.91.91), which can recommend qualified repairmen.

S.O.S. Depannage (7, rue Linné [5$^e$]; telephone 707.99.99) is a 24-hour service to fix almost any household emergency.

Try the Cleaning Service (telephone 225.98.16) for cleaning jobs.

SVP will move your furniture in Paris and the suburbs (telephone 733.26.00).

## Grocery Shopping and Food Preparation

> The national reputation for frivolity has always astonished me because the French are one of the rare people who take the feeding and clothing of man with utmost seriousness. . . . Out of ten shops on any Paris street, four are devoted to filling stomachs and three to covering nakedness.

Sanche de Gramont's words from his book *The French: Portrait of a People* sum up the French priorities in life. Food and clothing are serious business.

Kings have created recipes for their mistresses, a chef has committed suicide over his restaurant's loss of a Michelin star, and a working-class wife has been known to pack beef bourguinone in her husband's lunchbox. In spite of fast-food chains, the encroachment of supermarkets, and the temptations of frozen foods, the French still dedicate themselves to discriminating shopping and skilled preparation of their meals. When the French do succumb to frozen foods, they usually opt for complicated precooked meals and pass the simple vegetable packages by.

France can feed herself—or almost. The fact that she is underpopulated and provided with good land for growing foodstuffs makes fresh foods of all types plentiful. There are, for example, seven different types of lettuce.

The superb wines also owe something to the French soil as well as the skill of the people in developing and marketing a fine product. But the availability and excellent quality have their side effects. Expatriate men complain of heavy lunches accompanied by wines too good to turn down that make getting back to business afterward tedious and tiresome. Women, too, say they find themselves drinking more because wine is so much a part of life in France. In recent years, however, there has been a trend among the public in general toward drinking fruit juices and mineral water.

You will find that grocery shopping will take longer than at home, not because it cannot be done with one stop at the supermarket but because the temptations offered at the wide selection of shops and markets make one linger. The women say they develop an interest in food that they never had before, and many classes are available to teach the secrets of French cuisine. With the availability of good food and lessons to teach you how to prepare it, you are likely to come home a grand gourmet.

## Types of Shops and Markets for Food Purchases

France reluctantly has succumbed to another invasion of American culture, the supermarket. There are thousands of *supermarches* throughout the country. The super supermarkets, called *hypermarches,* are K–Mart-type stores carrying clothing, hardware, cosmetics, and household items in addition to a complete food market. Prices may run a little cheaper but you will be expected to bag your own groceries. Most supermarkets are located in the suburbs in shopping centers with plenty of parking. Some, however, can be found in the downtown shopping areas near department stores. The popular supermarket chains are: Euromarche, Inno France, Suma, and Saveco. Monoprix and Prisunic are the best known hypermarche chains.

The small grocery chains (*l'épiceries*), such as Viniprix, Codex, Vege, La Parisienne, and Felix Potin, are convenient for Sunday morning and evening shopping.

Good buys on meat can be found at the meat supermarkets such as the Bernard Boucherie chain and Abattoirs de l'Ouest.

Shortly after settling in, explore your neighborhood for a butcher (*boucherie*) and, say expatriates, "Get to know him." Once you have established friendly rapport, service will improve. Some say a tip of one or two francs for special assistance is appreciated, others say this is not necessary. Also locate your neighborhood delicatessen (*charcuterie*) where you can get a fully cooked meal to go as well as ham, cold cuts, salads, and sometimes a catering service for your parties. Food on the move has become surprisingly popular in Paris. Almost every neighborhood has a bakery, delicatessen, cheese shop, and other portable food shops that can provide a delicious and imaginative menu for a picnic in one of Paris's parks or on your balcony. The dairy store (*fromagerie, cremerie*) will carry a selection of over 300 varieties of cheese produced in France as well as butter, milk, and cream.

You will find a large selection of fish available, and there probably will be a good fish market (*poissonnerie*) not too far from your residence. Don't hesitate to ask the attendant to scale, skin, or filet fish or to open shellfish. During the oyster season, orders are filled by poissonneries or by restaurants with outside oyster bars. They provide opened oysters in carry-out leakproof baskets.

The small fruit and vegetable store (*marchand de legumes*) will have a good selection. Fresh produce in France is excellent. But if you do not want the owner to scream at you, simply look at the items without so much as placing a finger on them. You may see the sign *ne touches pas* (do not touch). Ask for ripe fruit, *pour aujourd hui* (for today) or *pour demain* (for tomorrow). You can purchase fruits and vegetables in larger quantities and perhaps a little cheaper at Sycie Agricale Horticale de Saint-Germain, Chambourcey, route Forets de Princesses (off RN 13).

The French head to their neighborhood bakery (*boulangerie*) at least once a day. No meal is complete without bread, and it must be fresh. Breads lack preservatives and will not stay fresh overnight. Yeast is sold in bakeries in 20 gram (2/3 ounce) squares called *levure*.

Markets, both open (*marchés volants*) and closed (*marchés couverts*), are popular with the local people as well as expatriates. Every arrondissement will have stalls set up on the streets several times a week with food direct from the farm. Your local town hall will tell you the location and hours of these markets in your arrondissement. The closed or more permanent markets are a little more expensive than the open ones, but often cheaper than speciality stores. Be sure to purchase the book *Paris pas Cher* (Editions Buy Authier, Paris) for a list of the best market streets in the city.

No Paris food list is complete without the name Fauchon. Its fame has spread worldwide. Behind its doors at 26, place de le Madeleine (8ᵉ) (telephone 073.01.61), can be found foods from everywhere and out-of-season delicacies. Sophisticated, posh, and expensive, top quality is its minimum standard.

There are many different ethnic food stores in the city: Arabic, Oriental, German, and many others. The telephone directory provides a complete listing under *produits etrangers* and *produits exotiques*.

Marks and Spencer Food Department
35, boulevard Haussmann (9ᵉ)
Telephone 742.42.92
Carries English food products such as bacon, cookies, and jams.

Betjeman and Barton English Tea House
23, boulevard Malesherbes (8ᵉ)
Telephone 265.35.94
Another store that stocks English foods.

## *Shopping Tips*

Cook French meats quickly at a very high temperature to keep them tender and moist. They are not aged and have less marbling to release natural fat during cooking. Don't cook over 170 degrees by a meat thermometer or the meat will be dry.

You can buy beef, veal, pork (but not ham), and fowl from the butcher.

Meat may be ordered over the telephone.

Hamburger often is available in the large supermarkets already packaged. Sometimes it is *sur demande,* which means you have to ask for it. Be sure you say *bifteck haché* or you might get something suitable only for animals.

Some helpful terms:

| *French* | *English* |
| --- | --- |
| un kilo | 2.2 lbs. |
| une livre | 1.1 lbs |
| un morceau | a piece |
| une tranche | a slice |
| épais | thick |
| mince | thin |
| la moitié | half a piece |
| boeuf | beef |
| veau | veal |
| porc | pork |
| agneau | lamb |

Baking soda and cream of tartar can be bought at a pharmacie.

## *Liquid Measure*

| *American to French* | | *French to American* | |
| --- | --- | --- | --- |
| 1 cup | .025 liters | 1 centiliter | 0.33815 ounces |
| 1 gill | .118 liters | 1 deciliter | 0.21 pints |
| 1 pint | .4732 liters | 1 liter | 1.0567 quarts |
| 1 quart | .9463 liters | | |
| 1 gallon | 3.785 liters | | |

*Solid Measure*

French solid mesaure is the same as the British.

| American | French | |
|---|---|---|
| 1 teaspoon | 1 *cuillere a cafe* | 5 grams |
| 1 tablespoon | 1 *cuillere a soupe* | 15 grams |
| 1 cup (16 tablespoons) | $^1/_4$ liter less 2 tablespoons | 227 grams |
| 1 cup plus 1 tablespoon | $^1/_4$ liter | 250 grams |
| 2 cups (1 pint) | $^1/_2$ liter less $^1/_2$ deciliter | 454 grams |
| 4 cups (1 quart) | $^9/_{10}$ liter | 907 grams |
| $4^1/_3$ cups (2.2 pounds) | 1 liter | 1 kilogram |
| $^1/_2$ cup less 1 tablespoon sugar | | 100 grams |

These are approximate equivalents for flour weights.

| Cups and Spoons (level measure) | Hard Wheat Flour and All-Purpose Flour (minimum weights) | | Soft Wheat Flour, Pastry Flour, American Cake Flour, and French Flour (minimum weights) | |
|---|---|---|---|---|
| | Ounces | Grams | Ounces | Grams |
| 1 teaspoon | $^1/_{12}$ | 2 | $^1/_{18}$ | $1^2/_3$ |
| 1 tablespoon | $^1/_4$ | 6 | $^1/_6$ | 5 |
| $^1/_3$ cup | 1 plus | 33 | 1 minus | 25 |
| 1 cup | $3^1/_2$ | 100 | $2^3/_4$ | 80 |
| $1^1/_4$ cups | | | $3^1/_2$ | 100 |
| $4^1/_2$ cups | 16 (1 pound) | 454 | | |
| $5^2/_3$ cups | | | 16 (1 pound) | 454 |

In a French recipe 1 *cuillère de farine* usually means 1 heaping French tablespoon or 15 to 20 grams. French flour type 55 is like U.S. all-purpose flour. Type 45 is for pastries, sauces, and crepes. *Farine de ble* is flour made from wheat—both types 45 and 55 are *farine de ble*.

## Wine

Many French buy their wines directly through a broker who takes a personal interest in his customer and selects only the best. But there are a few tips the expatriate might find helpful.

The French advise not to order a table wine at any but the very best restaurants. Table wines in the less expensive cafes and *brasseries* may be a mixture of cheap wines.

The order of drinking wines should resemble a scale that moves from the lightest to the heaviest. Dry wines before sweet wines. Dry white wines before red wines. Red wines before sweet white wines. Young wines before the old. Water rather than wine should accompany vinaigrette, salads, oranges, and chocolate puddings.

## Cooking and Wine Schools in the Paris Area

There are four major cooking schools in the Paris area and one wine school. Further information is available directly from the schools. Reservations should be made well in advance.

### *Major Cooking Schools*

Le Cordon Bleu
24, rue de Champs de Mars (7ᵉ)
Telephone 555.02.77

La Varenne Ecole de Cuisine
34, rue Saint-Dominique (7ᵉ)
Telephone 705.10.16

Ecole de Cuisine Gaston Lenotre
Hameau des Gatines
78370 Plaisir (route de Versailles)
Telephone 460.39.46

Ecole Hoteliere Jean Drouant
20, rue Médéric (17ᵉ)
Telephone 227.63.70

### *Wine School*

Academie du Vin
24, rue Boissy d'Anglais (8ᵉ)
Telephone 265.09.82
The first tuition-supported wine school in the world. Founded in 1973 for the purpose of teaching the fundamentals of sensory evaluation and a general program of wine study.

# Transportation

## Trains and Buses

Getting around Paris is easy. Finding that location can be accomplished by referring to one of the many complete and practical city guides available, such as the *Plan de Paris par Arrondissement,* which can be found at most bookstores and newsstands.

The core of the public system is the Metro, an efficient and inexpensive network of 16 lines. Very explicit maps, signs, and painted lines in stations make finding the right train and transferring simple. There are several ticket plans available, and they can be purchased at Metro station ticket booths or tabac shops displaying the red, white, and blue RATP sign:

Individual tickets or a booklet of ten tickets at a significant savings (these are available in station vending machines as well);

Weekly tickets, the *carte hebdomadaire,* good for six round trips;

The *carte orange,* a monthly pass consisting of an identity card with your picture, which you must supply; and

A go-as-you-please tourist pass valid for a short period of two, four, or seven days.

The tickets are magnetic and are inserted into a canceling machine on entrance, which returns the tickets and permits entry. The canceled ticket, or your longer-term ticket, must be retained to show any inspector. There are fines for traveling without a ticket. Your Metro ticket permits unlimited transfers within the Metro system. Look for the sign *correspondence,* which means "transfer."

Metro trains run from 5:30 a.m. to 1:00 a.m. the following morning.

Metro system tickets are good on the bus lines as well. The bus system consists of 56 routes in Paris and 136 in the suburbs. All the routes are shown on maps available where tickets are sold or in the book mentioned previously. Each stop displays the route numbers of buses that stop there. The routes are divided into stages. A ticket is good for the first two stages traveled. If you travel further, more tickets are collected. Again, you cancel your ticket(s) yourself, except for the carte orange and tourist tickets, which are just shown to the driver. You keep your canceled tickets, as on the Metro, as evidence of a valid fare paid if you are challenged by an inspector.

There is no transfer service on buses. You pay on each change of line.

Service is reduced considerably after 9:00 p.m. and on Sundays and holidays.

The suburban system is the Réseau Express Regional (RER) and the Société Nationale des Chemins de Fer (SNCF). The ticket system is virtually the same as the Metro. Weekly and carte orange tickets can be obtained that are good on both this and the urban system.

The telphone number for the Enquiry Center for the entire system is 346.14.14.

## Taxis

Theoretically, since there are more taxis per person in Paris than in New York or London, they are easier to find. Wrong! Many never get on the street for lack of drivers. This is due to the lucrative private market for taxi licenses. The drivers exploit their monopoly, even to the extent of stopping for meals at the time when they are most needed—12 noon to 2 p.m. and 6 to 8 p.m. Art Buchwald has commented on this: "In New York or London, taxis drive their clients towards their destination. In Paris, you accompany the chauffeur towards his garage or restaurant."

Taxis are available at taxi stands (*tete de station*) and at other usual locations such as airports, stations, and hotels. You can also flag a cab on the street or phone for one, but the meter runs when they are coming to pick you up. One way to get quicker service is to know the telephone number of the nearest cab stand and call it rather than a centrally dispatched cab. A maximum of three persons is allowed in the cab. A driver may take a fourth in the front seat, but the seat is not insured in case of accident.

There are three tariffs—A, B, and C—that can be set on the meter. A is for trips between 6:30 a.m. and 10:00 p.m. within the city limits. B is used for other hours of the day and daytime trips to the suburbs. C applies for night fares to suburbs and trips farther afield, such as to the Paris airports.

The fares, surcharges, and principal rules are posted in cabs and available on a "bulletin" that the driver is required by law to have and show upon request. Of course, it will be in French. There is no feeling among the expatriates that Paris taxi drivers are any less honest than their counterparts in other big cities. A tip of 10 to 20 percent is expected.

## *Your Automobile*

Your automobile can be imported into France duty-free as part of your household effects. As in most world cities, the longer American car in Paris is prestigious but difficult to drive in traffic, hard to park, and expensive to run and maintain. There is really little reason to bring a car rather than buy one in France where all the models of Europe are on display.

If you are 18 or older, you can drive on any of three valid licenses:

Your U.S. license, but only for the first two years.

An International Driver's License issued by one of the U.S. automobile clubs.

A French license obtainable at any time from the prefecture of police (7, boulevard du Palais [4ᵉ]). Your American license will have to be translated, and this can be done there. You will need, in addition, some identification (passport or *carte de sejour*), proof of residence in Paris (a statement from your landlord or concierge,) and two photos. You will not be required to take a driver's test if your old license is still valid.

Don't think a valid license is all that you need to drive. You must carry the following on your person or in the car:

Registration certificate (*carte grise*) obtainable from the police prefecture in your area.

Insurance papers, the "green card," which permits travel outside of France as well as inside.

A tax stamp (*vignette*) placed on the lower right-hand corner of the windshield. The stamps are issued in November, and the cost varies with the age and the horsepower of the car. You need to present your carte grise to buy one.

A distress signal, usually a triangular reflector.

An accident report form (*constat amiable d'accident*).

A parking disk for the blue zone parking areas.

A black and white nationality plate.

Despite an obvious need, the Parisians have been loath to accept any order in or organization of their parking habits, and today parking is terrible. The "blue zone" system was started in the 1950s in the central areas. The driver puts a card in his front window indicating the time he is due to depart, no more than 120 minutes after parking. This system was chosen over meters, which Parisians thought would destroy the aesthetics of their boulevards. Paris was one of the last major cities to install them. Now there are thousands. Areas marked *payant* have machines nearby instead of individual meters. Tickets are obtained from them and displayed on the car. These, and many new underground parking facilities, have improved the parking situation. Paris's first mayor, Jacques Chirac, stopped the practice of parking on sidewalks. He instituted 16 miles of concrete and metal posts to bar cars from blocking pedestrian walkways. If you transgress, you will be ticketed by the Paris meter maids or have your car hauled away or fixed so that it can't be moved until the police release it. If you get a ticket, you can take care of it immediately by purchasing a special stamp in the amount of the fine from any tabac shop and mailing the ticket with the stamp affixed to the police.

Liability insurance in the amount of at least U.S. $100,000 is compulsory. A short-term policy (21 days) can be obtained at the French border point of entry. The procedure for an accident is much like that in the United States, except that both parties fill out the accident report form required to be carried in the car. Report the accident to your insurance company within 24 hours. From there on it is in the hands of the French insurance companies, which are just as slow to part with money as their counterparts in other countries.

Driving regulations are available in English at bookstores. One of the basic rules is that the car on your right has the right of way. In a city with so many traffic circles, this is crucial to know because the French expect everyone to their left to yield. Seat belts must be worn. If you have had any trouble with your children about sitting in the front seat, you will love the rule that prohibits children under 12 from riding in the front. Blowing your horn is done only for a real emergency. At night, flicking the lights serves the same purpose.

## Communications

### *Radio and Television*

For many years, radio and television in France were under the complete control of a monolithic state organization, and they were considered tools or resources of the party in power. Rather than introducing independent commercial television, the government allowed advertisements on its own channels at certain periods. A scandal, *la publicite clandestine,* broke open in 1971-72 to reveal that television producers had been taking bribes from firms to plug their products. This sparked a complete reorganization in 1975; seven entirely separate program, production, technical, and administrative companies were set up, but they are still under the ultimate control of the government. The results have been news that is more objective and livelier and a more diverse and individualistic character in the separate networks.

There are three television channels, all in color. They transmit with the French-developed SECAM color process, which is not compatible with the PAI system used in many other Western European countries. Portions of France can pick up a border station, those transmitting from just outside French boundaries. Tele-Luxembourg has a French audience in Lorraine several times larger than its own national audience. These stations provide much more popular programming. But the French government has managed to acquire controlling interest in most of these companies.

Radio programs are broadcast on five national networks, one of which operates 24 hours a day. Just as with television, radio has its border transmitters, which reach most of the French population.

There are few programs in English on either radio or television.

If you buy a television set, you will have to pay an annual tax that is fairly steep (about U.S. $75 for color television). Only a very few homes have cable.

## Telephone

The beauty of Paris owes a good deal to the buried lines of the telephone system. Until recently, one of Paris's frustrations was the long wait for new telephone installations and service. The saying was that half the country was waiting for a telephone and the other half for a dial tone. But take heart. The French post office (or PTT), which runs the telephone system, has started an ambitious program to meet the demand for phones and to launch a new electronic age for telecommunications. Electronic directories, a small video screen with a keyboard, have been introduced on a trial basis. The screens not only provide all types of phone information, but also have the potential for data and many other information outputs.

Another innovation are pay phones that accept a magnetic card sold at newsstands and tabac shops. The cost of the call is deducted electronically from the face amount of the card.

New, modern phone booths have been installed throughout Paris. Cafes and bars no longer are the only place to make a call.

Although telephone numbers in Paris and immediate suburbs are of seven digits, the exchanges used to be named, and these names are still used unofficially. The first three letters of the name (BAB for Babylone) correspond on the phone dial to the first three digits of the number.

Calls to any Paris number can be made from any public telephone for half a franc. Most cafes will have a telephone operated by a token (*jeton*) obtainable from the cashier. For both types, after your party answers, you must push a button at the lower right-hand side to complete the connection.

Long-distance or international calls must be made at a post office or at a few cafes that have *Telephone Inter* service. You pay in cash after completion of the call. Direct dialing long-distance service is available for private phones.

There are two directories: *alphabetique* (alphabetical list) and *professions* (similar to the yellow pages).

People who rent will not necessarily be listed in the directory because the number is still in the name of the owner. You can request the PTT to list you at no extra charge.

Payment of the telephone bill should be made promptly within two weeks from the date it was sent; otherwise, your service may be cut off and restoration is difficult. Unless you place a call through an operator at an extra charge, long-distance calls are not itemized. Another improvement by the PTT is an experiment in providing itemized bills for a small additional fee.

One help in completing calls is learning the French words for each letter, so that you will be able to spell out a name—for example, *anatole* for *A*.

The PTT puts out a little booklet with the alphabet words and lots of other useful information—*Pour Telephoner de Paris,* available at any post office.

Wireless facilities (telex, cable, and so on) are better but can still be improved.

## Postal Services

Normal post office hours are from 8:00 a.m. to 5 p.m., except Saturday when they are open only until noon. The main post office (52, rue du Louvre [1ᵉ]) is open every day around the clock.

Letter mail has two principal rates: tariff normal and a reduced rate, about 20 percent less, which has lesser priority. Within Paris there is a unique system for sending messages in special forms by pneumatic tubes. Usually delivery is within four hours, except on weekends. These letters can be dropped in special boxes in any post office. The rate is close to $2.

There are also special delivery services for priority mail outside Paris: registered letters (*lettre recommandee*) and letters with a return receipt (*avis de reception*).

Packages over two kilos to be sent by either airmail or surface must be mailed at the central post office for each arrondissement. Post offices will not accept packages sealed with anything but twine—no scotch tape.

## *Newspapers*

Paris is the home of the *International Herald Tribune,* the only English-language daily published in this city. The *Paris Free Voice* is an English-language monthly primarily featuring articles and announcements on cultural events, but with a helpful classified ad section. London papers and the new European edition of the *Wall Street Journal* are available daily.

## Free Time

In England, everything is allowed except what is forbidden.
In Germany, everything is forbidden except what is allowed.
In Russia, everything is forbidden, even what is allowed.
In France, everything is allowed, even what is forbidden.
From *Paris* by Rudolph Chelwinski

Entertainment can be absolutely free (or nearly so) if you are willing to explore by foot the tiny nooks and alleyways that give the city her charm, or if you sit for hours at a sidewalk cafe and simply watch the world go by. Paris oozes history accentuated with the avant-garde, flaunts sophistication with touches of naïveté, and parties with overtones of melancholy.

Catch the shows that play in the giant plaza in front of the Pompidou Center. Mimes, jugglers, magicians, and just plain kooks have their moments of glory entertaining for free or for just a few coins anyone might like to throw into the performers' hats.

London and New York may have raced ahead in the formal art world with more galleries and shows, but Paris is still the place to see artists with their easels set up on the sidewalks, painting the most popular subject, the city itself, or ready to give a tourist a quick portrait sketched while he waits. It takes a permit to set up shop in

Montmartre or the other popular squares that tourists frequent, something many artists do not have. You may see a mass exodus when someone gives a signal that the *flics* are on the way to check credentials.

All the world's roads, culturally speaking, may no longer lead to Paris, yet the city is still able to hold her own. Plays, concerts, movies, and libraries are there for the expatriate to enjoy. But above all else, films and the art of cinematography have a premier position in the French cultural world.

The French are film addicts. They love just about anything put on celluloid, from the first pictures to the latest avant-garde productions. Foreign films are just as popular, and you can often catch one in English. Just check the billing to see if a "VO" is shown, and you will know that the sound track is in the original version.

Paris has a wealth of theater. The boulevard theaters, light, often bedroom farces, have been around for a long time. The state and the city of Paris subsidize theater, some of which exists in the suburbs. In recent years, the cafe theater, the *revue,* and one-performer shows have become popular.

New life was pumped into the famous Opera in the early 1970s when the building was renovated completely at a cost of 15 million francs and Rolf Liebermann, director of the Hamburg Opera, was persuaded to take over the Paris house. Today, Liebermann has left, but its musical quality is said to rival the Met or La Scala.

On the lighter side, discotheques, jazz clubs, and bars offer a world of variety and entertainment.

Several weekly magazines, unfortunately all in French, list cultural and entertainment events. One available at newsstands is *Pariscope*.

Many Parisians find their ultimate entertainment in dining at one of the city's superb restaurants or at a quaint inn run by its owner/ chef in the suburbs. You will have a chance to test the recommendations of Michelin and Gault/Millau.

Le hamburger, the ubiquitous symbol of America's fast-food revolution, is invading the City of Light. American tourists find many of the popular chains from home at the best addresses in Paris and filled with the locals. One favorite spot for young expatriates, Mother Earth's, 66, rue des Lombards, even has free buckets of popcorn.

An intruder from across the channel, the tea room, is replacing the sidewalk cafe as the place to go for quiet conversation and to dally over a pot of English Breakfast or Darjeeling and crumpets.

When you tire of all the city has to offer, you can head into the country, not just for sight-seeing but to learn a craft or to visit a family. You can also rent bicycles at many railroad stations and pedal around the countryside. The list can go on indefinitely.

## Museums

Paris's newest art museum, the Centre National d'Art et de Culture Georges Pompidou (better known as the Beaubourg), is also the city's most controversial museum. Designed in an architectural style that might be called the "power plant" school, its utilitarian modernity rivals any of the works of art it houses for color, style and far-out originality. It has become the most visited site in Paris and justly so. On display is the world's greatest collection of modern art and sculpture, a reference library, a cinematheque showing classic films from all over the world daily, an industrial design center, a cafeteria, and usually several special exhibits.

Even the most eclectic museum lover can be satisfied among the rest of Paris's 100 or so museums. Traditionalists will haunt the Louvre. The more adventuresome may try the Musee de la Machine a Ecrire (the museum of typewriters) or the Las Vegas Museum, featuring amusement machines from carnivals and casinos.

Most state-owned museums are closed Tuesdays and open Sundays. *The Best of Paris* has an excellent section on museums.

## Lectures

Perfect your French and take advantage of the dozens of public lectures offered at the College de France on just about any subject you can name. These are free, but no credit is offered. Contact the College de France (11, place Marcelin-Berthelot [5ᵉ]; telephone 329.12.11).

The Women's Institute for Continuing Education is another possibility. It holds monthly meetings where expatriate women share experiences and advice. One seminar covered ways for foreigners to get into business in France. For more information, contact the American College (31, avenue Bosquet [7ᵉ]; telephone 555.91.73).

# Libraries

*Mairie* ("town hall")
Each one in Paris has a library for the use of residents of that arrondissement. Some have a few English books.

The American Library in Paris
10, rue du Général Camou (7ᵉ)
Telephone 551.46.82
One of the oldest, private American cultural institutions in Paris. There are branches in Grenoble, Montpellier, Nancy, Nantes, and Toulouse. It is an endowed membership library with over 150,000 volumes and 700 periodicals.

Library of the British Council
911, rue de Constantine (7ᵉ)
Telephone 555.54.99

Many bookstores maintain rental libraries. Ask for the *abonnement de lecture*.

# Theaters

Very little English-language theater is found in Paris. Those productions that are presented are amateur ones within the English-speaking expatriate community. One professional group, the Living Theater, presents a mixture of English and French productions at the Théâtre de l'épeé en bois, Cartoucherie (12ᵉ); telephone 808.39.74.

The renowned French theaters are worth a visit even if your French is not the best. Go see the Comédie Francaise—performing the great dramas of the seventeenth century and modern plays from the world's top playwrights—and the Théâtre de la Ville. Cafe-theaters present lighter fare and are very popular.

Tickets can be obtained through agencies such as Une Semaine de Paris, 2, avenue Matignon (8ᵉ), and American Express, Comptoir des Théâtres, 2, place de la Madeleine (8ᵉ); telephone 260.20.41.

# Operas and Concerts

Music, while not quite achieving the recognition of French art or French cuisine, is an important part of the Parisian's life. Paris truly is a city of sound and lights.

When Liebermann came to revitalize the Paris Opera, a relatively lesser known conductor, Georg Solti, took over the podium of the Orchestre de Paris. He applied his brilliance to that orchestra just as in his next move he raised the quality of the Chicago Symphony to the peak. Now conducting the Orchestre de Paris or the other major orchestras of Paris is a considerable musical honor.

Other classical concerts and recitals of world-famous artists fill the Théâtre des Champs Elysées, other concert halls, and the naves of many of Paris's beautiful old churches.

The top jazz, rock, and pop performers appear regularly in Paris.

## Night Clubs

If a tour group were conducting a truly representative sample of Paris night life it could take several evenings. The Lido, Crazy Horse, Folies Bergére, Moulin Rouge, and Régines are just the tip of the iceberg. *The Best of Paris* lists many other spots: ballrooms, cabarets, discos, jazz, and private clubs.

## Restaurants

A well-known restaurant critic once severely downgraded a highly respected dining room when the waiter failed to ask him what kind of oil he wanted in his oil-and-vinegar salad dressing. The French not only accept such reactions as perfectly normal, they probably spend more time than any other people in the world discussing food.

You, too, will probably fall into the local habit of analyzing, discussing, and hunting out new restaurants. Remember, eating is not something you do simply to stay alive. In France food is what life is all about.

Almost all restaurants offer two types of meal choices: a la carte and *le menu*. The former has the same connotation as a stateside menu, while the latter is a meal at a fixed price that usually includes an appetizer, a main dish, some cheese, and/or a dessert. Coffee is never included. In the countryside, you may be offered a tourist menu, which means that wine and the tip are included in the fixed price.

It is advisable to reserve if you are going to a restaurant, especially during the weekend. Some restaurants are closed on Sunday or Monday.

## *Sports*

While every type of sporting activity is available in France, the people tend more toward the role of observer rather than participant. They love to bet on the horses, and come Sunday, you will find the extended family convened to pool talents and resources in picking the winning combination.

For the expatriate, there are innumerable choices either as observer or participant in the sporting field. Check the telephone directory for sporting associations or leagues; for information on facilities, be sure to inquire at your local town hall.

### *Cycling*

Cycling is a popular sport in France. Bikes may be rented from the French railways (SNCF) and are available at many railway stations. Additional information may be obtained from the offices of the French railways and from the Touring Club in France.

The Federation Francaise de Cyclotourisme (French Federation for Cycling Tours) (8, rue Jean-Marie Jégo [13ᵉ]; telephone 580.30.21) organizes cycling excursions to all regions of France. For more information, you also can contact Bicy-Club de France (8, place Porte de Champerret [17ᵉ]; telephone 766.55.92).

### *Boating*

There are 3,000 miles of canals linking 25,000 miles of rivers in France, and what better way to see the country than on a houseboat?

### *Swimming*

For swimming pools, look on the Michelin maps for *piscine*. Don't be shocked if topless swimming is allowed.

### *Leg Exercise*

France is crisscrossed by 10,000 kilometers of footpaths. Just follow the red and white markers, and you will be taken into picturesque and offbeat areas of France. *Topo-Guides* is a publication that will give you all the details about the itineraries, places of interest along the way, and where you can find food and lodging. It is an excellent way to get acquainted with the real French countryside.

## Golf

There are several clubs around Paris that allow nonmember expatriates to play, but fees are very expensive.

# Young People's Activities

If your children start to complain, "I don't have anything to do," you might point out what is lined up for local youngsters. They may change their attitudes. Many Parisian families of the upper social strata route their teenagers into dancing clubs—known as *rallyes*—where for five years they are kept busy at formal parties under the watchful eyes of moms and dads. But for the expatriate youngsters, such groups (gratefully) are beyond reach. Instead, Paris will offer museums, parks, sports, and hundreds of sights to intrigue them. While streets may be too clogged with traffic to make it safe to pedal a bike, families can put their bikes on a train and head to the country. Try Gare d' Orsay Station for this because they will allow you to put your bike right on the train yourself.

### Museums of Interest to Young People

There are many museums of special interest to children. If they enjoy uniforms and arms, they might like to visit the Musee de l'Armee (Place des Invalides [7ᵉ]; telephone 555.92.30).

The science museum is fascinating, with experiments conducted by the staff every afternoon: Palais de la Découverte (avenue Franklin D Roosevelt [8ᵉ]; telephone 359.16.65).

Don't miss the history of Paris through the centuries at the Musee Carnavelet (23, rue de Sevigne [3ᵉ]; telephone 272.21.13).

### Zoos

The largest zoo in Paris, Zoo de Vincennes, at the southeast edge of the city, is not very attractive. The younger set might enjoy Jardin d'Acclimatation in the Bois de Boulogne. There are miniature trains, a zoo, rides, and a bowling alley. Go to the little farm. You'll have chocolate and cake among the geese and the lambs. You can rent this place for a birthday party (telephone 745.47.65). It's expensive, but you'll never forget it!

### Theaters, Concerts, and More

For Jeunesses Musicales de France, you may buy a card for a year. With this card, young people can attend a concert and a program once a month. They do not give lessons. For lessons, contact the Conservatoire International de Musique (8, rue Alfred de Vigny [8ᵉ]; telephone 622.56.04).

In nearly every Paris arrondissement and the surrounding suburbs is at least one youth activities center. It is a great way to meet French children. All types of activities take place here, from theater to dancing. Sports are also included in the program. For information, inquire at your local town hall.

Another attraction is the circus: Cirque d'hiver (110, rue Amelot [11ᵉ]; telephone 700.12.25). It is not the American three-ring variety but an intimate, fascinating show the kids will enjoy.

There are innumerable private classes around Paris where young people can study dancing, theater, music, arts, and crafts. Again, check at the local town hall for classes near you.

### Vacations

Young people can find all types of vacation possibilities that will meet their age and interests.

Rest vacations. A youngster camps and stays in the mountains, on the seashore, or in the country. Some offer organized activities. Sports, hikes, and so forth are part of the program.

Action vacations. Schools in this category teach handicrafts, sailing, ecology, and community work, organizing young people's volunteer work projects, and combining useful tasks with cultural activities.

Study vacations. During the summer all French universities organize French-language and literature courses for young foreigners. Most offer diplomas at the end of the study.

### Films

Children's shows are listed as _films pour les enfants,_ but to make doubly sure that you want your child to see it, check around. It may not meet with your approval.

The American Library, the Canadian Cultural Center, the Musée des Arts Decoratifs (107-109, rue de Rivoli [1ᵉ]; telephone 260.32.14), and the Musée Guimet (6, place d'Lena [16ᵉ]; telephone 723.61.65) show films for children. Check with each for showings.

### Tips for Young People in Paris

When you order a birthday cake, be sure to order it _sans liqueur._ Otherwise, it may come doused in alcohol.

Contrary to all you have heard about young children drinking wine in France, don't try giving it to your children. The French *do* frown upon this.

Churches and international schools also have many activities for children. For information on children's activities in Paris, contact the Centre d'Information et Documentation Jeunesse (101, quai Branly [across from Hilton Hotel] [15ᵉ]; telephone 566.40.20). They'll send you a lot of addresses in France for summer or winter vacations.

### Baby-Sitters

Once you are settled, you will probably learn of American and French teenagers willing to baby-sit. But until that time, you might like to obtain a sitter from one of the institutions listed below. Be sure to find out all the costs involved—meals, transportation, and so forth. Expect to pay at least the equivalent of $2 an hour, probably more.

Institut Catholique
21, rue d'Assas (6ᵉ)
Telephone 222.41.80

Centre Régional des Ouvres Universitaires Scolaires (CROUS)
39, avenue Georges Bernanos (5ᵉ)
Telephone 329.12.43

## Organizations

It astounds many expatriates to learn that the two most important centers for Americans are the American Legion Building at 49, rue Pierre-Charron (8ᵉ) and the American Church in Paris at 65, quai d'Orsay (7ᵉ); telephone 551.38.90.

The church, established in 1857, is the oldest private American institution abroad and the first American church founded overseas. The chancel contains two Tiffany windows officially classified as historic monuments by the French government. There are many meeting rooms, a gym, library, and other facilities for its four-phase program. Preeminent is the religious program in the protestant tradition. The music program sponsors classical music series and contemporary concerts. The young adult ministry plans Bible study groups, an annual crafts festival, and a resident theater group. As a community center, it serves as a home for a nursery school, counseling service, an Alcoholics Anonymous chapter, and a program for aid to refugees. The very inexpensive dinners in the dining room after the Sunday service are a great place to meet and make friends.

The American Legion headquarters houses a number of other expatriate organizations:

The American Legion
This organization is not limited to veterans; other Americans can join for a reasonable fee and use its restaurant (it has a Sunday brunch) and take part in bridge, bingo, and other social activities.

The American Women's Group in Paris
Telephone 359.17.61
The offices for this group of over 500 women, primarily American but also from many other countries, is in the building. It has a busy and diverse program of teas, meetings, seminars, tours, and other activities to promote U.S.-French understanding.

The American Club of Paris
Telephone 359.24.33
The club claims that its roots go back to the weekly dinners hosted by Ambassador Benjamin Franklin for his fellow countrymen in Paris in 1777. This group, like the Women's Group, has no club rooms or facilities other than the office in the Legion building. Its meetings and other functions are conducted primarily at luncheons.

The Association of Americans Resident Overseas
This is a nonprofit organization to promote actively the needs and rights of Americans overseas.

Some other organizations of which to be aware are:

SOS Help
Telephone 723.80.80
An English-speaking crisis line in Paris.

Association France-Amérique
9, avenue Franklin D. Roosevelt (8ᵉ)
Telephone 359.56.46
Promotes cultural relations between the two countries.

## Churches

There are a number of churches that those in the expatriate community attend. Some that are very popular, besides the American Church in Paris already mentioned, are:

American Cathedral in Paris (Episcopal)
23, avenue George V (8ᵉ)
Telephone 359.17.90
This church is a religious and social focal point for many Americans. It has a busy and worthwhile program similar to its counterpart, the American Church.

Saint Joseph's Church (Roman Catholic)
50, avenue Hoche (8ᵉ)
Telephone 227.20.61

Liberal Synagogue
24, rue Copernic (16ᵉ)
Telephone 727.25.76

St John's Lutheran Church
147, rue de Grenelle (7ᵉ)
Telephone 705.85.66

## Health Care

Standards of medical care are quite good in France. In many cities there are public hospitals and private clinics that provide adequate medical care and emergency assistance, although many expatriates go to the American Hospital of Paris.

### *French Public Hospitals*

French Public Hospitals *(Hôpitaux de l'Assistance Publique)* provide adequate emergency medical care, but the accommodations might sometimes be considered below the American standards. The emergency wards of the public hospitals are fully staffed around the clock, and the *Police Secours* (French Safety Police and Ambulance Service) will take a patient to the closest French public hospital in the event of an emergency, unless the patient requests that he be taken to a specific private hospital or clinic.

## French Private Hospitals—French Clinics

French clinics are usually small private hospitals, many of which specialize in one or two types of surgery. They are located throughout Paris, and the equipment and standards can be compared favorably with small private hospitals in the States. A person does not usually enter a private French clinic unless the person's doctor is associated with the clinic.

## American Hospital of Paris

This hospital has a staff of English-speaking doctors and nurses and a high standard of medicine with modern methods of diagnosis and treatment. In addition to the medical, surgical, and obstetrical departments, the hospital maintains a dental clinic and an out-patient department.

American Hospital of Paris
63, boulevard Victor Hugo
Neuilly-sur-Seine
Telephone 747.53.00

There is also a British hospital:

British Hospital
48, rue de Villiers
Levallois Perret
Telephone 757.24.10 or 757.22.58

## Medical Assistance, Pharmacies, Dentists

In the event of urgent medical problems requiring immediate attention, dial: 17—SAMU, which stands for *Service d'Aide Médicale d'Urgence,* the national emergency organization in France. It has a 24-hour service and processes the information and means necessary to give medical assistance.

In addition, you also can call SOS Médecine (telephone 337.77.77). This is a private company where doctors are available on a 24-hour schedule for house calls. Bills for services are to be paid immediately by patients.

Pharmacies are indicated by a green cross sign, and a few are open at night, on Sundays, and during holidays. All pharmacies rotate on this duty, and those that are closed display the name of the pharmacies open in the district. The local police station will also have this information.

Anyone who is taking an American prescription drug should verify before leaving the United States whether a satisfactory equivalent is available in France. However, when already in Paris, contact either of the organizations listed below to verify whether a satisfactory equivalent is available:

> Pharmacie Centrale des Hôpitaux
> Service de Documentation
> 47, quai des Tournelle (5ᵉ)
> Telephone 633.01.40

> Syndicat National de l'Industrie Pharmaceutique
> 88, rue Faisanderie (16ᵉ)
> Telephone 504.62.90

Pharmacies, also, are available for emergency first-aid treatment.

Prescriptions for eyeglasses are readily filled, although prices are high.

Dental care is above average in France. There are many American-trained dentists who have the latest equipment.

There are no special precautionary measures to take with respect to health conditions in France, but it is advisable to be immunized against typhoid, small pox, and tetanus. The water in Paris is safe to drink; however, the handling of meats and vegetables in the open market is not as strictly regulated as in the United States.

## Doing Business in Paris

### *Dichotomy: A National Image?*

American businessmen in France fall clearly into one of two categories—they either love it (Francophiles) or hate it (get me out now). The degree of love or hate depends on the knowledge or ignorance that the businessman has of the business climate, the country, its people, its history, its culture, its national objectives, and its politics.

Unfortunately, the average Frenchman does little, if anything, to salve the feelings of the less-than-knowledgeable executive. A

Frenchman, unlike many nationalities, does not appreciate an American's effort to speak his language. High school or college French will not suffice in the business world, and the Frenchman will soon let it be known that if you are not completely fluent in his language, stick to English or get an interpreter. The Francophile will appreciate that the reasoned approach requires such an attitude because of the many idioms and subtleties of the language, particularly voice inflection or pronunciation that can seldom be learned in the classroom. The non-Francophile will not know of, or appreciate, such action on the part of the Frenchman, so he will be driven even further into the corner of those who would rather be some other place.

As in most European countries, the visitor is expected to make the first move toward establishing a relationship; but it must be done according to the protocol of that country. Invitations are seldom, if ever, issued informally. Written and formal invites will receive a written and formal acceptance or regret. A simple telephone or verbal invite will be ignored, overlooked, or rejected. An over-the-fence suggestion will just not get the job done. In business this formality is even more important. A written request will get an appointment or a reply, whereas a drop-in will be kept waiting or told that an appointment is required owing to the business commitments of monsieur. Why waste your time? Make a formal request. A formal request, like an invitation, requires an answer; and the result is that your request will usually be granted.

## *Know Your Rights*

French law is based on the Napoleonic code. The unwary or ignorant businessman can easily run afoul of it, particularly in decisions governing relations with employees.

Like many European countries, the penalties for false discharge of an employee may be severe. The unknowing businessman may find himself making a settlement for many times the actual wage paid to an employee. Even if the discharge is not for false reasons, the cost can be high. Social benefits are expensive and extensive. Depending on needs, the newly arrived businessman may wish to maintain his staff at minimum and contract for as many services as are readily available. A detailed study of your duties and rights as an employer should be made by competent French lawyers and seriously studied by the potential expatriate businessman.

## *Labor*

As a rule of thumb, expect social benefits to be 50 percent greater than U.S. benefits. While on the subject of rights, duties, and employees, the strength and depth of French labor unions should be mentioned. The largest and most powerful union is communist led and communist controlled. As could be expected, social demands are great and ever-increasing.

Labor laws are stringent and, in a socialistic environment, favorable to labor. The size of your labor force may make your business subject to industrywide bargaining or special requirements concerning benefits. As in Germany and England, participation in the management of the business is a goal of French labor. Here again, the need for competent French legal counsel is obvious and should not be taken lightly.

In France, as in most other European countries, overregulation is the name of the game; so don't expect to find less than you are used to in the United States. The red tape is not insurmountable, but it is formidable. It should not become a concept killer for your venture, but it certainly should be considered in the economics and time consumption for doing business in France.

French life is full of inconsistencies, probably reflecting conflicting impulses within the average Frenchman. On the whole, the average Frenchman is conservative in dress and life-style and truly individualistic. This is especially so in rural areas, but one sees this even in the larger cities; yet the national vote will be liberal or left wing by better than a 50 percent majority. How do you reconcile this vote with conservatism? Continuing this dichotomy further, since the mid 1930s, the French government has moved increasingly into nationalism of industry, railroads, utilities, air travel, communications (telephone, telex, postal, radio, and television), banking, and heavy industry such as automobiles. Nationalized industry and socialism do not fit a highly individualistic personal portrait.

Frenchmen pride themselves on their honor, but the French government reports that there is widespread tax evasion at all levels of the society—again, a somewhat inconsistent performance that is as baffling to the French as to outsiders.

The average Frenchman considers himself to be highly individualistic, but at the same time, like his cross-the-channel parallel, he expects his government and his labor union to provide all his needs from cradle to the grave—including vacations of one month to five weeks, at least 11 official holidays each year, and retirement at age 60.

All of the above, of course, with no increase in productivity. Individualistic, perhaps, he likes to think; but in reality, he is increasingly dependent on his government and demanding that it do more for him.

With so many factors, can the American businessman in Paris find a way to conduct his business and still stay sane? The answer, of course, is a resounding yes—if you . . .

## Understand the People

Understanding the people may be difficult, but it is not impossible. If one word characterizes the people, *pride* may be that word. The American businessman will do well to respect the pride of the French. Their history gives them the right to be proud of their heritage.

## Know the Business Climate

The French romance with socialism has taken its toll of major businesses, and the result is that France sincerely needs the input and output from major multinational firms. With nationalization of major industry, the remaining small, family-owned, often undercapitalized business does not have the muscle to compete in today's world of high technology and intensive capital investment. France is eager to welcome the influx of foreign capital in the purchase of small French firms and the transfer of management know-how, capital, and technology into the French economy.

From a national-need standpoint, the climate for business is favorable. With this knowledge, you can proceed to do business in France if you . . .

## Know the Rules

Before embarking on a business venture in France, you should be sure that you can obtain a work permit. While detailed rules are available from any consultant, from the U.S. Department of Commerce, or through various private organizations such as Business International or the U.S. Chamber of Commerce, general rules will allow key U.S. personnel to enter if they are top management or supervisory. Local personnel must be employed in jobs not filling this general rule.

### Know the Customs and Manners of Business

If the English businessman worships the business lunch, his French counterpart disdains them as an invasion of privacy and an affront to his gastronomic fastidiousness. To discuss business at lunch with a Frenchman is to lose him as a client, benefactor, friend, or associate. To blunder further, if such is possible, simply invite him and his wife to dinner and discuss business. This action is guaranteed to chill, if not freeze, all future relations with him.

Equally disdained is the "small talk" frequently associated with the sales pitch of American business. To really turn a French businessman off, start with small talk aimed at his personal life. The highly private life of the Frenchman is just that, and your discussion of his family, marital status, or place of residence will brand you as an insensitive meddler. Keep your discussion to your own problems, product, or proposition, or sports, and only discuss personal items if they are first brought up by the French businessman. He will respect your management skills and technology, but meddling in his private life will get you two things: contempt and the boot. Don't seek to shift the talk to politics, for next to his private life, a Frenchman's politics are to be discussed only if he brings up the subject. Keep your sales pitch low-key.

The average Frenchman appreciates intelligence, education, and position. He also resents any affront to his own ability, education, or intelligence; so avoid any tactic that in any way could be construed as being pitched toward lower intelligence or skill. Childlike prattle and sales procedures aimed at ten-year-old intelligence will kill any chances of success. If in any doubt, treat your French colleague as if he knows more than you think he really does. Give him the chance to ask for more or for clarifying details. Pressure sales may have a place somewhere in international business relations, but that somewhere is definitely not in France with French businessmen.

Your French counterpart will respect you and make your stay in France enjoyable if you . . .

### Remember Small Courtesies

One such courtesy is retaining a formal relationship until you are invited to call him by his first name. Avoid familiarity until you are sure of your standing, and then be careful when and where you use the newly acquired right to call him by his Christian name. Familiarity in the presence of others who do not have a similar relationship places him in the unenviable position of either offending you or the other person or having to extend a similar right to the third person. In any case, he will not appreciate your actions. As a rule of thumb, if in doubt, keep it formal.

## Legal Matters

### *Visas and Permits*

To work in France, non-European Economic Community (EEC) nationals must have a work permit *(carte de travail)*. Obtaining this permit requires submission by the prospective employer of the foreign national's contract of employment (which must be in French to be enforceable) to the labor authorities. If approved, the contract is sent to the consultant nearest the residence of that foreign national. A medical examination is required. The three types of permits granted are:

Temporary work permit *(carte A)*. Limited to one year for a specific occupation in a specific locality.

Ordinary permit *(carte B)*. For three years but with the same occupational and geographical limits.

Permit for all salaried occupations and professions. Granted for ten years, renewable, and not limited in occupation or location.

If you plan to be in France longer than three months, you must have a residence permit *(carte de sejour),* which is issued once your work permit is approved. Residence permits can be obtained from the local police prefecture after your arrival. They are issued in three categories roughly comparable to the three types of work permits. The third category, the privileged permit, is issued subject to a medical examination and an administrative investigation.

Certain top-level executives, such as the managing director of a branch or subsidiary of a foreign enterprise, commercial agents, and owners of individual enterprises, obtain a commercial card *(carte de commercant)* instead of work permits. These can be issued abroad through a French consulate. American applicants are required to show proof that they have never been bankrupt in the United States or France.

Procedures for these permits can take several months.

## Prison Treaty

France is one of a handful of countries with which the United States has concluded a treaty allowing citizens to serve prison terms in their own country for crimes committed elsewhere.

## Taxes

It has been said that a French child is taught that love of country is sacred, but that juggling one's taxes has its charms. The expatriate will not have had the benefit of this educational experience. Despite whatever ingenuity the French taxpayer practices, foreigners had best stick to the law without improvisation. Before an expatriate can leave, he will have to obtain a *quitas fiscal* (tax clearance), attesting to his full compliance.

Any person, including a foreign national, who has his domicile in France is subject to tax on worldwide income from whatever source unless relieved by a tax treaty. An individual is considered domiciled in France for tax purposes if he maintains his permanent or habitual residence there, transfers his "center of interest" to France, or is either salaried or independently employed in France.

Individuals domiciled outside and maintaining a residence only in France are taxed only on their French source income. The tax authorities can change an imputed income, however, based on external indications of wealth and three times the rental value of any dwelling in the country. The Franco-American tax treaty eliminates this dwelling income for U.S. nationals domiciled in France. American citizens having no French residence are not subject to any French tax on services rendered if they spend less than 183 days a year in France, if their salary is paid by a nonresident employer, or if the employee's salary is not deducted from the income of a French branch or subsidiary of the employer.

Individuals are taxed on the sources of income that are roughly comparable with those taxed in the United States. One unique feature is that the head of each household has to pay on the entire income of his family. Allowances such as overseas hardship, cost of living, education, and tax differentials are all held to be income. There is only one exception. The French love their language, so French-language lesson allowances are not considered income to the recipient.

There is a standard deduction from salaried income that varies somewhat, but usually results in your being taxed on about 72 percent of such income. Alternatively, you can elect to itemize business-related expenses.

The resultant tax is computed per "share." The taxpayer multiplies the per share rate by the number of shares allotted to him. The number of shares increases with the size of the family.

The tax return is filed by February 28 for the preceding year. The local tax inspector reviews the return and forwards it to the tax collector. He sends out notices of taxes due between July 15 and December 15. The previous year's taxes, already determined, are payable in three installments. Foreign nationals in their first year in France will normally pay their first taxes in September following the year they arrived. The rates reach a maximum of 60 percent, but there are surcharges for higher incomes. No provision for withholding is made for persons domiciled in France.

## Customs

Several documents are required to process duty-free shipments of personal effects and household goods. These forms can be obtained from a consulate, and a couple require stamping by the consulate. You will have to make a sworn statement on the inventory that all effects have been used for at least six months—one year for an automobile. The inventory must be in French.

## Pets

No animals are admitted into France under three months of age. Dogs and cats more than one year old need only a rabies vaccination certificate. Between three months and one year of age, dogs and cats require the rabies vaccination certificate; a certificate of origin and health stating that the animal comes from a place with no rabies outbreak for the last three years and dated no later than five days before the journey begins; a distemper vaccination certificate for dogs; another vaccination certificate for dogs against virus-hepatitis illness; and a vaccination certificate against typhus for cats.

For more specific information, contact the Ministere de l'Agriculture, Direction de la Qualite, Bureau de la Reglementation Sanitaire aux Frontieres, 44-46, boulevard de Grenelle, Paris; telephone 575.62.25.

## Exchange Control

France has an elaborate system of exchange control. Even gifts to relatives abroad sent by French residents must have prior authorization. A foreign individual is considered a resident for this purpose after two consecutive years of residing in France. Be sure you clarify your rights and obligations under these regulations with your attorney, banker, or accountant.

## Banking

The French banking system is not too dissimilar from that in the United States. Many American banks maintain branches in Paris. An overdraft on your account without proper prior authorization is considered very serious, so watch your account balance. Stop-payment orders are allowed only in cases where a check is lost, stolen, or the payee is bankrupt. Checks delivered by a bank are normally "barred" (imprinted with parallel lines), and are endorsable only to a bank or other financial institution. Nonbarred checks are available but have to be requested; these require a stamp duty of about 1F per check. Cancelled checks are not returned with the account statement.

# 17

# Assignments Rome and Milan

*I*T'S A FUNNY THING ABOUT ROME. Although crammed with antiquities, she has the knack of making everyone feel young again. It is just one of the reasons expatriates say they like living in the Italian capital city.

Another is the flavor of her historic sections. Your first impression may be one of crumbling, cluttered buildings. But, gradually, as your eyes adjust, the real beauty of 28 centuries of development reveals itself—in a Roman column, an ornate fountain in a nondescript square, or a garden of colorful flowers and lush vines almost concealed by a magnificently carved wood and stone entryway. The light—that strange, penetrating, vibrant sunlight that seeps into the streets and reflects across the roofs—will lift your spirits and perhaps touch your soul as it has done to artists and writers throughout history.

Yet antiquity carries a price tag that some find too high.

Irving R. Levine, a television network correspondent formerly based in Rome, summed up the problems of Rome's civic old age by saying in his book *Main Street Italy,* "Time here is measured by a calendar of greater dimensions." He went on to explain how a scholar who was doing research in the Vatican library asked for a certain book from the stacks. The slip for the requested book came back with a note explaining that this particular book had been missing since 1530.

One expatriate, after describing the interminable red tape involved in doing anything official, summed it up by saying, "That's Rome," as if this explained all deficiencies. A resident of longer standing advised, "Take the time to live in Rome."

Whether it is due to a new-found sexual freedom, making vicarious thrill no longer necessary, or to a growing sophistication on the part of Italian men, the *papagalli*—those sidewalk Romeos who taunted women with suggestive remarks and pinches—are becoming a thing of the past. The contemporary Italian gentleman uses the diplomacy of a papal envoy along with the chicanery of a Borgia count. But who is to fault him? After all, when he tells an elderly woman she becomes more beautiful with each passing year and generously sheds his flattery over foreigners and natives alike, you decide he really deserves an Oscar.

The weather is rated as delightful by expatriates. "We even have lunch on our terrace in February," said one couple. Many told how their flowers bloom all year.

This is not to say that Rome does not have its unpleasant days. It definitely does. In fact there are many winter days that are cold and cloudy and penetratingly damp. But freezing temperatures are rare, and on the few days they do hit the city, people slip paper bags or some type of protection over their potted plants, and the plants usually pull through unscathed. The annual rainfall averages 33 inches, and the wettest season is autumn. Summers are hot. You will find yourself dodging patches of sunlight along the sidewalks to stay a little cooler. The thick walls of the older buildings, which usually are without air-conditioning, keep the rooms amazingly cool. Sun-dresses are very popular with women during the hot weather and sandals are a good solution if any walking is to be done. Normally, shorts are out. But if the current fashion trend favors this briefer wear, the Romans will follow fashion.

There are many Romes. There is the city of fashionable couturiers, cafes, and lovely shops hovering around the Spanish Steps. Sharing this facet of Roman life is the Via Veneto, a ten-minute walk east from the Spanish Steps. This street was once the scene of La Dolce Vita (not just the movie version, although part of it was filmed here), the hangout of the swinging, with-it generation who patroled the length and breadth of her, seeking excitement. Today the scene has changed, and the Via Veneto, which also plays host to the American embassy, is more popular as a tourist spot and a meeting place for Roman matrons who rendezvous with their friends at Doney's or Café de Paris for an ice cream or coffee.

There is the Rome of magnificent palaces, 50 within one square mile, many that go almost undetected because of their modest exterior; and there is the Rome of Trastevere, once a favorite haunt of thieves, later a slum, but recently rediscovered and now a favorite residential area and location of many good restaurants.

There is the Rome of history, not just ancient history with the remains of the Colosseum and the Forum, but the Medieval city as well, with its churches that became the models for ecclesiastical buildings for centuries to come. There is the city of the Renaissance period, when street plans and squares emerged that were to establish the beauty of Rome; and then there is the Baroque city of the seventeenth century, typified by Bernini's colonnade that outlines the elliptical piazza of St. Peter's and his many fountains that have contributed to the romance and splendor of Rome. Nevertheless, it is twentieth-century Rome that is the most surprising. Mussolini's city of tomorrow, the Esposizione Universale di Rome (EUR), as it is officially called, was Mussolini's dream of a new Rome. Today, its marble buildings are starkly modern; its sports arena, exhibition halls, theaters, and contemporary living quarters are in such sharp contrast to Rome proper that at first viewing you find it an unbelievable anachronism.

The Eternal City is undergoing an attack of schizophrenia, trying desperately to preserve its heritage while keeping pace with progress. The traditional Roman three-hour lunch break, so delightful in the summer after a large meal, is being challenged by an outside world in which business doesn't stop. Homemade pasta competes with new pasta machines. Subway construction is delayed because the tunneling unearths ancient artifacts. Even the Vatican radio has a very popular disk-jockey program, "Studio A."

Heart and soul of the Catholic world with the independent city-state of the Vatican inside its borders, Rome also claims the oldest Jewish community in Europe. The Jews first came to Rome as slaves, over a half century before Christ; another group was brought from Jerusalem about 100 years later to work on the construction of the Colosseum.

It is easy to meet the Romans. Friendly, gregarious, they are anxious to present their _bella figura_ to you. This means more than just "beautiful figure"; it is the style or public impression the Roman presents, and even includes a bit of the oriental concept of "face." Establishing true friendship is more difficult and will take determination on your part.

Rome is most captivating on a warm summer's evening. Children lick ice cream cones of date or watermelon ice as their parents browse in the shops; young travelers from many lands stop to rest beside the fountains; and sophisticated Romans relax at an outdoor cafe in a quaint piazza filled with flowers. All historic Rome is a sound and lights show that entertains for hours. One night like this can overcome days of heat and frustration.

## The Language

Italian is the national language of Italy only, although it is spoken in parts of Switzerland and in the many Italian enclaves around the world. Even the official languages of the United Nations Food and Agricultural Organization in Rome do not include Italian. Nevertheless, learning Italian is the key to really understanding, and being truly accepted in, Italy. It is a musical language that lends itself to both beauty and vagueness of expression. A foundation in another Romance language will help.

Another language you will have to learn for yourself from observation and practice is the language of the Italian hands and face. If you can develop this without being self-conscious, the gestures of a raised eyebrow or an uplifted palm can add seasoning to a bland conversation.

## Housing

Finding housing has become very difficult in the past few years. The principal cause is the issuance by the goverment of a Fair Rent Act in 1978 to protect the tenant from unfair rents and to provide some security of tenure. The result has been that landlords find it advantageous to sell their apartments or even withdraw them from the market to stand vacant rather than commit to a lease with rent they consider inequitable. Thus, the number of available units for expatriates is decreasing. Landlords only wish to rent to someone for a short term, and then usually furnished, which can mean only one or two pieces of furniture. Expatriates needing a place for one to three years will be more attractive to owners.

There are no enclaves to which expatriates gravitate; nor is there any particular geographical area that is favored. Selection may depend upon the location of the office, the children's school, shopping, and transportation. The choices run the gamut from a residence in the historic central area with lots of atmostphere, charm, and headaches to a modern, more practical apartment in EUR (see below).

Finding the right spot can take time, perhaps several months, if you have your heart set on a spacious apartment in one area. In the meantime, there are several good residence hotels with kitchens, and one has a pool. Most important, these residences come equipped with a telephone. A couple are:

Residence Cavalieri
Via Cadlolo (near the Hilton Hotel)
Telephone 344.241

Residenza Duse
Via Duse 5 (near Parioli)
Telephone 805.841

## *How Do You Find Housing?*

Everyone agrees that the best way by far is dogged, unrelenting foot power and word-of-mouth. Ask all your new friends and business associates about vacancies or those that may be coming up soon. Explore areas and pick out several you like. Then prowl the streets watching for *affittasi* (for rent) or *vendesi* (for sale) signs. If you see a building that appeals to you, ask the portiere about vacancies.

If you haven't the time or patience for your own search, check the ads in the two English-language papers and *Il Messaggero*. Thursday and Sunday are the big classified ad days.

An English-speaking agent may help, but owners are reluctant to incur any of the fee. Some agents may even try to charge you just to look at an apartment. Of course, there is nothing approaching multiple listings. Get current personal recommendations before going this route. The American Women's Association of Rome (Hotel Quirinale, Via Nazionale 7; telephone 475.52.68) and the Food and Agricultural Organization of the United Nations headquarters at Viale delle Terme di Caracalla try to keep current on agents. One mentioned by several expatriates is Internazionale Immobiliare (Ms. Gerhig; Via Veneto 96; telephone 475.9561).

If you can avoid it, do not move to Rome—or any other part of Italy—in August. This is the traditional month for the Italian holiday, *Ferragosto*. Just as in France, the Italians live, plan, and dedicate their lives to their summer holiday. Cities are almost in limbo. The department stores, some gas stations, some restaurants, and the essentials to keep the cities alive still function. The small shops close for the month; apartments and houses are shuttered; and the transportation arteries from the cities almost have an aneurism. Landlords disappear.

## *Where to Go*

Il Centro. Narrow streets, old buildings with scruffy exteriors concealing palaces and villas with Renaissance interiors. All buildings, ancient and twentieth century, blend into a facade of rundown splendor—commercial establishments on the ground floors, street noise, antiquated services, high rents, convenience, parking problems. Upstairs are elegant, old apartments with beamed ceilings and parquet floors.

EUR (Esposizione Universale di Roma). Built by Mussolini for an exhibition to commemorate 20 years of Fascist rule, was to be the "Third Rome." Planned community of gleaming white marble buildings, housing government ministries, company headquarters, museums, and conference centers. Modern apartments and villas surrounded by yards, sidewalks, and spacious avenues. Plenty of parks, fountains, and playgrounds. Good transportation to the center via the Metro. Near beaches and Fiumicino Airport. Apartments similar to those in the United States with modern kitchens. Five miles south of central Rome. Not as many stores as other areas.

Trastevere. Just across the river from Il Centro. Narrow streets. Greenwich Village of Rome. Lots of restaurants. Small flats. "Discovered" and becoming fashionable and expensive.

Parioli. Embassy area in the city. Trees. Luxury apartments, some with terraces and fireplaces. English-speaking cinema. More international.

Ponte Mario. Area within Rome near the Hilton Hotel. Good panorama of the city.

Aventino. An area of private homes and newer apartments on one of Rome's seven hills.

Popular suburban areas are:

Casel Palocco. Another planned community farther south from the EUR. Parks, churches, large shopping center and Rome's only drive-in movie. One- and two-family villas. Low-rise apartments with gardens, terraces, and fireplaces. Big kitchens. Swimming pool. A little out of the way.

Olgiata. A most elegant, protected area 12 miles out. Expensive.

Two-family houses, but each may have 20 roooms. Own golf club, shopping center, and beauty salon.

Avila. A compound along the Via Cassia for modern apartment living. Both Olgiata and Avila are located along the Via Cassia, a lovely main road north of Rome that has only two lanes. Rush hour traffic is horrible. On the other hand, Via Cassia is the location for several of the international schools, particularly the Overseas School of Rome. Residents living in the southern areas of EUR and Casel Polocco have to keep the length of the school commute in mind.

## Housing Tips

In an apartment building, if you are on a lower floor, you may have more noise. Let's face it, Italians can be quite vocal. On a higher floor, water pressure may be low.

_Unfurnished_ means completely bare in Italy. Unless you buy them from the previous tenant, you will have to provide light fixtures, appliances, closets, cabinets, and perhaps even hot water heaters and a toilet seat. A few newer luxury apartment buildings may have central heating and hot water.

Even with central heating, you may freeze before the official time for providing heat begins or after it ends.

Since driving and parking are such problems, check to see what bus lines are near your intended residence and how often and how late they run.

If you intend to do any remodeling or restoring of units in Rome, check with an organization called Belle Arti, which controls such things in order to preserve Rome's heritage. If you only have to clean your new home, cleaning services are listed in the yellow pages under _imprese di pulizia_. Painters are _imbiancatura_.

Elevators are considered a mode of transportation for going up, not down—and that's when they are working. Some require a 10 lire coin, so keep them handy, if you can find them.

When renting a furnished apartment, a meticulous inventory by the landlord is checked off with the new tenant. Make sure every defect is noted. A picture of a big item showing the current condition is a help.

It has been difficult to install modern plumbing in Il Centro and Trastevere. In many cases, the bathroom has been added to the side of the building.

Street numbers are confusing. The numbers are not necessarily consecutive or with odd on one side and even on the other. Numbering begins on one side, runs to the end of the street, and continues back up the street on the other side. Street names are written on the walls of buildings, but not at all corners.

Electricity in Rome is dual to say the least—two currents, two types, and two companies. Rome is in the process of converting from 125 to 220 volts. The cycles for each voltage is about 50, but this tends to fluctuate. In older buildings, you will find both currents; in the newer, 220 only.

There is an ordinary rate for lighting, and an industrial rate for running appliances. The former is much more expensive and is used with smaller plugs. The additional cost is to encourage conservation by keeping ordinary illumination to a minimum. The industrial circuit uses heavier plugs.

The ENEL is the government-owned national electricity utility. It is acquiring the older private companies. The Rome city-owned utility, ACEA, still exists.

You will probably have to increase the kilowatts to your apartment by having additional current brought in. Be sure to get a meter if one is not installed already.

Some units have fuse boxes, but the newer ones have circuit breakers.

Bills are issued every three months after you read your own meter and report the reading. Prompt payment is absolutely necessary. You can arrange for your bank to do this.

Because of the expense of electricity, even U.S. appliances that have been fixed for the local current or through transformers are costly. Italian appliances are smaller and well designed. You will have to weigh the cost and convenience of your appliances from home versus putting up with a washer that can do only two bluejeans at a time. Keep in mind that it is very difficult to repair an imported product.

Gas is used for stoves and heating water, and it is not too expensive. The nozzles and jets of the U.S. stove may have to be adapted. The typical Italian stove is quite small.

Central heat is oil in most cases.

Water is free, or there may be a small charge in the lease if there is central hot water.

A good way to purchase 220-volt U.S. appliances is to buy used ones from departing expatriates. You can usually find appliances at the international moving companies. Families leaving Rome have to clear their apartment but do not want to ship the wrong voltage appliances home. They leave them with the movers, who build up an inventory of used pieces they are glad to sell.

The hours for central heating in winter are voted on by the building occupants. Typical times are from 8 a.m. to 10 a.m. and then from 5 p.m. till 9 p.m.

Check for termites. They have been a problem since the war. The Vatican was one of the first places hit by these pests.

Inspect plumbing. It is hard to get leaks fixed after you move in.

## Legal Considerations

The typical expatriate lease is from one to three years. Usually, a diplomatic clause can be negotiated, permitting leaving before the term expires owing to a transfer. It is quite common to have an official lease at a reasonable rate for the landlord's tax declaration and then a side agreement for an undisclosed supplementary rental. This means you should be very careful to get good legal advice when negotiating a lease.

The lease contract will also establish what other costs are the responsibility of the tenant. Customarily, heat and utilities are paid by the lessee. In apartment buildings the prorated amount for heating is based on the square meters of the unit and the number of heating elements in the radiators, unless there are separate meters.

You may have to pay for your share of the doorman, other staff, elevators, and other charges that typically are included in the maintenance fee for a U.S. condominium.

You will have a substantial down payment of three months' rent to make on any unit. This serves the usual purpose of protecting the landlord against damage. But another reason for this hefty initial payment is that the landlord doesn't want to get stuck for large telephone bills. International telephone charges may take several months to show up on a bill. By that time, the previous tenant is gone. So the landlord holds the deposit until he is sure all the tenant's bills are settled. In some cases, a guarantee of payment by your company can avoid or reduce the deposit.

Home robbery is a growing problem. Some expatriates have been hit three or more times. Alarms, big dogs, bars on windows— all are only partially effective as deterrents. Expatriates recommend not renting quarters on ground or top floors. The lower location provides easy access, and thieves often swing down from rooftops into the top floors. There is a semiprivate patrol of "night police," who are reimbursed by the neighborhood residents, that is helpful in some areas. Fortunately, there has not been much physical violence or vandalism so far.

## Domestic Help

Most expatriates find that live-in help is too expensive now, and that part-time help will suffice. Part-time maids receive a monthly salary for several hours work each day, which is still less than the U.S. equivalent wages; but then you have to add the social benefits for your Italian employee—about 40 percent of the salary—the thirteenth month payment, and vacation payment. Word-of-mouth is the best way to find help. Personal recommendations are important. Agencies are considered less reliable.

When you realize the legal requirements and red tape involved, you may have second thoughts about having hired help. Make sure your employee has a work certificate, parents' written permission if under 18, papers for welfare requirements, medical insurance papers, and an identification card. After hiring a part-time maid you must report this to the Instituto Nazionale per la Previdenza Sociale (INPS) at Via dele Ambra Aradam 5.

To comply with welfare requirements, you must buy weekly stamps at the INPS office or a tobacco shop and paste them in the INPS booklet of your employee.

If you hire a foreign au pair to live in, she must be registered with the police.

Part-time help hired on a monthly basis get the same benefits as full-time help—two afternoons off a week (usually Sunday and Thursday), the thirteenth month salary bonus, two weeks paid vacation, a long leave for pregnancy, 15 days notice of termination on both sides, and a complicated termination payment.

There are girls who will work a prescribed number of days on an hourly basis. They have similar but less complicated laws regarding their employment.

Handling help in the proper legal manner calls for a great deal of diligence and patience.

## Education

Picking the right international school in Rome has been made relatively easy since the formation of the Rome International Schools Association (RISA) in 1974. This group now includes almost all the schools in Rome that teach in English. Besides the common language of instruction, these schools have independence from the state school system, a curriculum typical of a country outside Italy, and students and faculty from a number of nations. A directory, issued each year, gives a one-page summary of each school and its courses and facilities and can be obtained from any of the schools. The principal ones are:

The American Overseas School of Rome (OSR)
Via Cassia 811
Telephone 366.4841
Founded in 1947, this is the oldest of the nondenominational, coeducational, day schools located in one of the favorite residential areas of expatriates. The school provides a basic American curriculum beginning at the nursery level and going through high school. Enrollment is about 600 students—perhaps close to half from the United States and the other half about equally divided between Italian children and those of other nationalities. Students are prepared for entrance into British or American universities. Facilities include two libraries, a gym, auditorium, tennis courts, soccer field, and a Roman theater on a six-acre campus. It has advanced placement courses in many subjects.

Saint Stephen's School
Via Aventina 3
Telephone 575.8494
A coed school for grades 9-12 founded by a former headmaster of Kent School in Connecticut and patterned after an eastern boarding school in approach. Enrollment of about 130, of which less than half board. Situated in the heart of Rome on a two-acre site with good academic and sports facilities. The faculty numbers 16. Strong college preparatory curriculum.

St. George's English School
Via Cassia, Km. 16
Telephone 699.0141
Another of the international schools located along the Via Cassia near the expatriate community. It is a nondenominational English day school for both boys and girls from kindergarten through grade 12. Enrollment is approximately 800; about 65 percent are British, but well over 50 other nationalities are represented. The program is the British curriculum leading to further university education.

Marymount International School
Via di Villa Lauchli 180
Telephone 327.3349
Catholic day and boarding school run by the Sisters of the Sacred Heart of Mary primarily for girls from nursery through

grade 12 but they accept boys up through the third grade. It follows a college preparatory curriculum. Most of the 320 or so students are American, but 20 other nationalities are represented. Boarding facilities are available for about 100 girls from grades 9 through 12.

Notre Dame International School
Via Aurelia 796
Telephone 625.051
Catholic resident and day school under the auspices of the Brothers of the Holy Cross of Notre Dame, Indiana. It provides the standard college preparatory course from grade 4 through high school. About 350 boys are enrolled. Girls are accepted in grades 4 through 8 only. Boarding facilities for 125 boys.

St. Francis International School
Via Cassia 645
Telephone 36.60.657
Catholic coed day school operated by the Sisters of the Order of St. Francis for 140 students. A standard American curriculum is used.

The above schools have several things in common: they are fully accredited in the United States or England, have excellent facilities, good student–faculty ratios, present a strong academic program to prepare for college exams and acceptance, and have varied extracurricular sports and activities programs. They are also expensive. Some have a capital assessment that is not refundable. They have very limited ability to take handicapped children. The number of expatriates in Rome is decreasing so the schools are accepting more Italians and other nationalities.

The Italian nursery schools (*asilo*) are very popular among expatriate mothers. They provide a preschool program for 3- and 4-year-olds and introduce American youngsters to their Italian counterparts. They can be found in almost every neighborhood and are inexpensive.

Other schools in the association provide nursery care, such as the Ardeatina Nursery and Infant Group (Via della Formelluccia 40; telephone 54.07.586), which is located near the countryside in a small modern villa with a beautiful garden. It has an international staff and takes children of all nationalities.

Some other schools provide a more specialized academic program. The New School of Rome (Via della Camilluccia 669; telephone 328.4269), for example, employs the Open Plan System and emphasizes individual progress for its students from ages 5 to 19.

There is a wealth of academic possibilities from which to choose for college-level courses and beyond. The U.S. embassy has compiled a list of over 50 American institutions operating in various Italian cities, and not including many other American schools that sponsor summer programs. Such well-known U.S. colleges and universities as Bryn Mawr, the University of Dallas, Loyola, Notre Dame, and the University of Washington have special courses, programs, or institutes in Rome for their students.

There are international grade and high schools and advanced educational programs in many other principal cities in Italy. (See the section on Milan for schools in that city.) A list of schools for English-speaking students is available from the Instituto Italiano di Cultura (686 Park Avenue, New York, New York 10021; telephone [212] 879-4242). The Institute also publishes a catalog, indexed by subject, of summer and year-round courses in Italy.

With such a choice of high-quality international schools, it is unlikely that the Italian school system will be considered by expatriates. Yet families of Italian extraction or others may give some thought to what this system is like. The hallmark of the Italian system is uniformity. All schools, whether public or private (most of which are Catholic), are under the direct jurisdiction and control of the Ministry of Education. The same curriculum and organization are found in all schools. Transfers are easy, and degrees from all schools have just about the same value. Teachers are civil servants of the national government. Teaching has become very politicized and strikes are not uncommon. There are no special programs to aid any student not fluent in Italian. The various levels are:

Kindergarten (*scuola materna*). Optional for 3-5-year-olds.

Elementary school (*scuola elementare*). Grades 1 through 5. The core is reading, writing, and arithmetic with science, geography, history, music, art, and physical education as adjuncts. Religion is optional.

Middle school (*scuola media*). Grades 6 through 8. Now a foreign language is added. Completion of this level marks the end of compulsory education.

If the student decides to continue his education, he goes on to the upper secondary school, *scuola secondaria di secondo grado*, or *liceo*, for three to five years, from ages 14 through 18. He must make a decision on his future occupation because there are technical, teacher training, vocational, and art schools in addition to the more classical program. The choices available in the classical licei emphasize Latin, Greek, another modern foreign language, philosophy, history, mathematics, or science. All the upper secondary schools provide access to universities upon graduation.

Italian children study very hard. Exams predominate at all levels. There is no social life or extracurricular activities connected with the schools. Failure is an ever-present possibility even in the lower grades.

## English-Language Schools in Other Cities

### Florence

The American School of Florence
La Torre di Bellosguardo
Via Roti Michelozzi 2
50124 Florence
Telephone 228.145
Coed with an American curriculum from nursery through high school. About 150 students.

### Genoa

The American International School of Genoa, Inc.
Via Angelo Carrara 14
16147 Genoa
Telephone 386.528
Coed for kindergarten through grade 8. Good pupil-teacher ratio. Italian compulsory. About 60 students.

### Naples

John F. Kennedy American School of Naples
Mostra d'Oltremare
80125 Naples
Telephone 615.993
Private nondenominational coed school from first grade through high school. Approved by both the New York State Board of Regents Program and the British General Certificate of Education.

*Trieste*

The International School of Trieste
Via Beirut 31
34014 Trieste
Telephone 224.270
Coed from nursery to grade 8. American curriculum. About 110 students.

# Shopping

Nearly everything is available now in Rome except McDonald's and other fast-food chains.

Almost all shopping for clothes and household articles still is done in small shops where you get personal attention. There is really only one department store comparable to those in the United States, la Rinascente in Piazza Fiume, where you can find furniture, hardware, kitchen gadgets, stationery, camping equipment, and appliances. A branch for clothing only is at Piazza Colonna. Both are quite small by American standards.

Two chains with several branches each, UPIM and Standa, carry slightly lower quality merchandise. They also have supermarkets attached.

Some other leading stores and markets are:

Coin
Piazzale Appio
A higher quality clothing store.

Morassutti (three branches)
For hardware, kitchen and bathroom supplies.

Porta Portese
Rome's biggest and best-known outdoor flea market held every Sunday morning. Mostly junk and secondhand items, but maybe an antique will be found that makes the search worthwhile.

Other shopping is by streets or districts from the Via Condotti, where top quality and current fashion are shown in ultramodern or classically understated boutiques, to the new "African district."

One must for newcomers to Rome is the recently published *Destination Rome* by Virginia Valentini, which covers shopping in more detail as well as other aspects of living in this city. It is available from the American Women's Association of Rome or in English bookstores.

## Shopping Tips

Italy is an international fashion center. Many of the top couturiers are headquartered in Rome and Milan. Others from Paris and London have shops in Rome. And who hasn't heard about the smart, chic Italian look for men?

Undoubtedly, one of the premier shops for women's clothing is located just at the top of the Spanish Steps, Anna Manieri (Piazza Trinita de Monti 18; telephone 679.3103). The charming proprietress is a transplanted American who creates exquisite designs that appeal to—and also fit—expatriates. She is always willing to pass on the wisdom gained from many years in Rome to newcomers.

Many expatriates report that children's clothing is rather frilly and impractical. They recommend that you bring along a complete supply of children's clothes and supplement it on trips home. The one exception is shoes, which are a good buy. Gradually, more wash-and-wear clothing is becoming available.

*Rome for Children,* by Nicoletta Alegi and Deirdre Ryan, still is an excellent guide to shopping and entertainment for children. It is available in English bookstores.

Rome can be the place where you find that ultramodern furniture or an exquisite antique to prize forever. Both will be expensive. If you are really knowledgeable, you might unearth a bargain at the flea market at Porta Portese or in the countryside.

For china, crystal, and kitchenware, visit Leone Limentani (Via Portico L'Ottavia 47/48; telephone 654.0680). This store is an example of the smaller shop where bargains may be found. Located in the old Jewish quarter of the city, it is usually crowded with local patrons. The shop carries bargains in dishes (often seconds), crystal (including Waterford), and beautiful copper pots and other kitchenware.

A word about store hours. All stores except hardware shops and food stores are closed Monday mornings. Food stores are closed Thursday afternoons, hardwares on Saturday afternoons. If there is a holiday during the week, the stores will stay open on the usual closing days. In winter, stores are closed between 1 and 3:45 p.m. and between 1 and 4 p.m. in the summer. Food stores often remain closed until 6 p.m. in the summer. These are the customary practices, though there may be slight variations. Knowing the hours of your favorite shops is vital if you want to save gas and shoe leather.

Sales _(saldi)_ and discounts _(sconto)_ are often the most permanent signs in the shops—some genuine, some not-so-genuine. Bargaining is still part of most transactions. One expatriate said her Italian friends could always get something cheaper. Shopping one-upmanship is a serious game in Italy.

Expatriates report women's underwear is cheaper and more practical in the States.

If you have a foot width narrower than B, you will be hard to fit in Italy, so you might want to pass up the Italian Ferragamo for a more practical pair from home.

There are a handful of bookstores in Rome either specializing in or maintaining a large selection of English-language books. One well-known shop is the Economy Book Center (Piazza di Spagna 29; telephone 679.0103), located very near the Spanish Steps.

## The Italian Cuisine

There are two important things to know about Italian cuisine: first, for centuries, this cuisine was the dominant one in Europe from which the French and others developed, and second, Italian cooking is very regionalized and therefore quite diverse and ingenious.

The excellent volume of the Time-Life Food series, _Cooking of Italy,_ by Waverly Root, credits the marriage of Catherine de Medici to King Henry II in the sixteenth century with bringing to France the secrets of the relatively advanced cooking of Italy. Not only was the cooking and preparation elaborate, the presentation of Italian foods in the sixteenth and seventeenth centuries was beyond anything that is or could be done today.

Many dishes not now considered Italian in origin did in fact originate there—turtle soup, french fried potatoes, and fruit pies. Italy certainly developed and made popular melons (the cultivation of which was begun in the town of Cantalupo), coffee, and ice cream.

Regionalism in Italian cuisine results in two main groupings: one is based on the principal cooking fat used, butter in the north and olive oil in the south; the other on the principal type of pasta, ribbon shaped in the north and tubular in the south. Yet this is really too simplistic. Italy has several quite distinct districts where a highly individualized subcuisine has been developed. Studying the regional differences can be an enjoyable avocation.

# Grocery Shopping

In a country where the housewife has the reputation of being a great cook, and there are no fast-food chains imported from America, you just know that purchasing and preparing food are important everyday occupations of the Roman homemaker.

Many Italian housewives follow the traditional pattern of buying their food each day. It takes time but ensures freshness. Americans in Rome usually stick to the supermarkets, but complement those purchases with the delicious fruits and vegetables sold by vendors in the open markets or small shops. The biggest open market is at Piazza Vittorio.

Practically everything is available in the Italian supermarkets, either imported or in the Italian equivalent. You will find a large liquor section in every supermarket. Meats are prepackaged. Some stores where many Americans shop will have a few cuts similar to those in the United States. The leading chains are Standa, GS, UPIM, and others listed in the yellow pages under *supermercati*.

Italians are very careful about preservatives. Crisco and Bisquick, for example, cannot be sold.

The little shop is still the mainstay for food shopping. They are highly specialized, each gets a license to handle only certain items. This means, of course, that you have to go to several shops to get everything you need. Most expatriates report that they enjoy the personal touch the small shopkeeper provides. He will deliver if you live close by.

If you have trouble finding salt, go to a tobacco shop marked with a big *T* outside. Salt is a state monopoly—as are tobacco and matches—and is sold in the *tabaccheria* (although you can find these products in some of the larger supermarkets, too). The licenses for these shops are limited, and veterans and the handicapped are given preference. There are two types of salt: table salt and coarse used for salting water for cooking pasta.

Other state monopoly items sold in these shops are postage stamps, bus and metro tickets, playing cards, and some legal stamps for official documents.

Some of the important small specialty shops are described below.

## Pasta

Pasta is, undoubtedly, the national dish. In one national cooking contest, 19 of the 20 prize winners were pasta dishes. Most Italian cooks contend that the best is homemade. You can buy prepared pasta at supermarkets or at the *panetteria*.

## Breads, Cakes, and Rolls

The *panetteria* also supplies freshly baked bread and rolls each day. Just as in France, there are no preservatives, so the bread products become stale quickly.

There are hundreds of different varieties of bread products. Sliced bread, *pane americano,* similar to that in the United States, can be found in the supermarkets.

## Meat and Fish

Beef is not very good, except for that from Tuscany, which usually goes to restaurants and hotels. As a result of membership in the EEC, imported frozen beef is increasing. Veal, on the other hand, is very good. Both beef and veal, together with game and fowl, are found at the *macelleria*. The Italian butchers prepare their cuts differently, and they often debone the meat.

Fish are found at the *pescheria*.

## Delicatessen Products

Deli items, including pork, are sold at the *salumeria*. Here also you can find the delicious Italian cheeses: parmigiano and its cousin made from sheep's milk, pecorino; the soft, chewy mozzarella, made from water buffalo milk; ricotta, similar to cottage cheese; soft cheeses of the Po Valley such as stracchino; slightly firmer cheese like the famous Bel Paese; fontina, nearest to American cheddar; provolone, in all its sizes and shapes; and gorgonzola, a blue-veined cheese. There are hundreds of subtypes and varieties to sample, so cheese lovers will be ecstatic.

## General Grocery

This is the *alimentari* or *drogheria* where you get canned and bottled products. They are similar to the neighborhood convenience stores in the United States.

## Fruits and Vegetables

Delicious fresh produce, in season, is found at the *ortolano* or *fruttivendolo*. Expatriates are warned not to pinch or probe the fresh fruit or vegetables. You may also buy eggs at these shops.

## Dairy Products

Milk, eggs, and butter are bought at the *latteria*. The refrigerated milk is good, but the containers could stand improvement. The unrefrigerated milk sold in cartons is all right for cooking.

## Ice Cream

Italy is justly famous for its ice cream, which is found at the *gelateria*.

There certainly are more than 31 flavors of ice cream. One outstanding example of Rome's many excellent gelaterias is Gelateria dele Palma near the Pantheon. Here they help you select your fruit ice by placing a slice or a berry on top of the container in the case to identify the flavor.

## Other Shopping Hints

When you have your mouth set for a particular food from home or a delicacy that you cannot find anywhere else, go to the elite of food shopping areas, the Via della Croce. Here you can get peanut butter, cranberry sauce, pumpkin pie filling, and many other gourmet items from around the world.

A good introduction to Italian cooking is the cookbook prepared by the Parent-Teachers Association of the Overseas International School, *Overseas Selected Recipes*. In addition to some not-so-basic (rabbit in piquant sauce) recipes, this book has a wealth of helpful information on marketing (with a list of English-Italian names for most foods), oven temperature equivalents, and many helpful hints to avoid cooking catastrophes at the start.

## Transportation

Transportation in Rome revolves around the Italian driver of his car, bus, or motorbike. No wonder there are so many Italian racing greats. The streets of old Rome make a challenging Grand Prix course, particularly during the four—yes four—rush hours in the morning, evening, and at the lunch break.

The principal public transportation system is the bus system supplemented by an old and one new subway. The fare is ridiculously cheap regardless of distance, but there are no free transfers from line to line. Even cheaper monthly passes are available. Warning! Cash is not acceptable for paying fare. You must buy a ticket or book of tickets at the tabaccheria.

You can enter either at the front or rear doors of the bus. The front is for those passengers with passes, the rear for individual ticket holders who cancel the ticket by inserting it into a machine near the rear door. English signs warn against violators. Occasional spot checks are made for properly cancelled tickets by the authorities. You exit through the middle door.

Route maps are available from the bus company stand in front of the railway station *(Termini),* at newsstands, and in the yellow pages. The routes are easy to follow since each stop has a sign with numbers and the main stops for the route. Be aware that buses stop in the evening between 9 p.m. and 11 p.m.; the exact time is shown at each stop.

Late in 1979 Rome finally completed its second subway line (line A) traversing the center of Rome and with stops at many of the most important centers such as the Termini, Spanish Steps, and near the Vatican. The older line B connects with this new line at the Termini with free transfer privileges. It runs from the Termini to EUR. A branch goes to Ostia Antica and the beach. Both lines are called the "Metropolitan" or "Metro" and stations are marked with a large "M."

Ticket machines at each station on the A line disperse tickets for the same low fare as the buses. Coins are deposited in the same amount on the B line. No change facilities are provided for larger denominations so you must have the appropriate coins before entering. The Metro cars are clean but not air-conditioned.

Metered taxis are bright yellow or dark green and black. Because of traffic conditions, cabs seldom cruise for fares. The best place to get one is a taxi stand, and all stands in a neighborhood are listed in the yellow pages with the telephone number at the stand. When the cab is engaged, the meter starts ticking when the driver leaves the stand, and a small service charge is added. There are also surcharges for Sundays and holidays and fares at night (10 p.m. to 7 a.m.), for more than two passengers, for luggage, and for trips out of the city (the airport fare is double the meter). A telephone call to 4999 or 3570 will bring you a radio cab.

Unmetered cabs do operate. Generally, they are safe and not overly expensive, provided you know what a fair price is to your destination and negotiate it beforehand.

## Your Car

The extremely high cost of gas, very tight parking facilities, the high license fees for American cars, and the quality of Italian cars are all good reasons to leave your U.S. automobile behind.

Driving is challenging. The historical significance of Rome prevents any widening or new construction of roads in those areas where monuments to the past might be disturbed. Of necessity, some streets in the central district are solely for taxis and buses. Many others are one-way. A fairly wide street may have a beautiful fountain in the middle blocking the traffic flow like a cork in a bottle.

Parking is next to impossible. "Lots" are wide places in the street where, for a small tip, an attendant will try to squeeze your car into a spot that may leave it looking like a solitary pier jutting out into an ocean of traffic. Never fear, the attendant does prevent one of the other prevalent risks of car ownership: theft.

In limited parking areas *(parcheggio limitato)* you must display the parking disk *(disco orario)* to show when you arrived and when you will leave.

Double parking, although not legal, has been developed into a fine art in Rome. Sometimes cars illegally parked are towed away. Part of your Italian cultural learning process will be finding where it is safe to park in violation of the traffic law but in accordance with the Roman law of necessity.

There are now two large underground parking lots, one behind the Via Veneto and the other under the Villa Borghese connected by tunnel with line A of the Metro. Expatriates advise that the Roman police are becoming a little more generous in giving tickets for wild parking.

## Licenses

Expatriates can drive on a valid U.S. license for three months *if* they get a translation from the Italian Automobile Club (ACI) (Via Marsala 8; telephone 49.98), which will be given free of charge. Thereafter, you must have an Italian license. Your U.S. license can be converted to an Italian one by obtaining a sworn translation at the U.S. embassy and then taking the translation to the office of the

Automobile Club. The minimum driving age for cars is 18, which causes a lot of American teenagers distress and their parents relief—until they learn that the legal age for motorbikes is 14.

The ACI provides many of the same services as the AAA: towing service, tourist assistance, discounts in affiliated hotels and restaurants, and road conditions. The Rome Phone Assistance Center (telephone 421) gives road and weather information in English. The emergency number is 116.

The car license is permanent. The equivalent of the annual fee at home is the road tax *(bollo)*, which is paid periodically; the fee varies depending on the size of the car. You can pay the tax and get the necessary sticker at the post office or the ACI. The sticker goes on the windshield.

If you have a car radio, there is an annual tax payable at the post office. The receipt is stamped on your car registration book *(Libretto di Circolazione)*.

Insurance with an Italian company, or an Italian subsidiary of a foreign firm, is mandatory and expensive. A small insurance certificate must be placed on the windshield next to the bollo. To leave the country, the universal "green card" is required.

### *Driving—If You Can Call It That*

Driving on the right is the rule in Italy, as in most of continental Europe. The speed limit within urban areas is 50 kilometers (31 miles per hour). On weekdays you will be lucky even to approach that speed. When stopped for an emergency, you must have the red triangle warning device that is put on the road 50 yards behind your stationary car. Failure to observe this precaution brings a fine.

Check the hours for gasoline stations. Sundays, holidays, and lunch time are notorious for closed pumps. There are a few self-service stations in the center of Rome that operate automatically for a 1,000 or 5,000 lire note.

Along the Autostrada, which runs the length of Italy from Milan to Reggio Calabria, there are telephone boxes about every mile from which one can summon medical or mechanical assistance. Directions are in English as well as three other languages.

A pamphlet—"Driving in Italy"—showing all the road signs and shapes, is distributed by the government and can be obtained through the ACI.

Accidents are almost a form of recreation to the Roman. The slightest touch of two cars will result in a dramatic, emotional confrontation between drivers that calls upon their greatest oratorical skills and allows spectators the pleasure of feeling as if they were judges at a debating contest. Unless you are a driver held up in a jam resulting from all this, you can enjoy this theatrical performance with the other Romans.

# Communications

## *Post Office*

One observer of the Italian post office system has said that it is in "terminal chaos." Important documents are sent by private courier services. The post office is burdened by labor disputes, lack of manpower, and failure to modernize. Postal delays affect everyone.

As in most European countries, the post office performs several functions besides mail delivery. But to avail yourself of these services, you have to be up and about early in the day. The branch post offices are only open from 8 a.m. to 2:30 p.m. for most functions, and often there are long lines. The main office at Piazza San Silvestro is open all day. If you just need stamps, these can be purchased from any tabaccheria. The Vatican issues its own stamps but has the same rates as the government system. Electricity, gas, telephone bills, and traffic violations can be paid and overseas cables and telegrams can be sent from any post office.

Packages must be tied with string and not sealed with tape. If the package weighs more than one kilo, the string ends must be sealed with wax or lead obtained from a stationery store.

Mail is delivered daily, except Sundays and holidays.

Receiving a package involves both customs and the post office. You may be charged a fee on delivery or asked to pick it up. If your friends and family send packages marked "unsolicited gift" *(regalo),* duties may be less.

## *Telephones*

You will have to wait and wait and wait for phone installation unless there is already one in place in your residence. If you are fortunate enough to inherit a phone, you will still need written permission from the former holder to transfer it to your name.

The directory yellow pages are one of the most practical guides available for any number of things. Get them even if you can't get the phone. Along with the directories you get a booklet of invaluable information, "Tutto Citta."

There is direct dialing for calls within Italy and to some other European countries. Most international calls are placed through the operator, who will give you the duration and charges after the call is completed.

There are several different types of public phones. Originally, there were few public booths and phones were found in bars and restaurants. These took a special slug, a *gettone,* which was purchased in the bars. Once the other party answered you had to push a button near the slot to complete the connection. There are a few of these older phones still around. The newer phones accept 100 or 200 lire coins.

If the word *teleselezione* is printed on a phone, you can make direct international calls by inserting more gettone or coins.

Bills are mailed every three months. When you move into your residence, check the first few bills to make sure you are not paying for calls of the previous occupant. Direct dial calls are billed by the length of time and units used. Long distance, telegrams, and cables are totaled. If you want a breakdown, go to the telephone company office and ask to see the *cartellini.*

## Newspapers, Radio, and Television

The Rome English-language papers are the *Daily American* and the *International Daily News,* both containing a good selection of Italian, U.S., and international news. London papers can be found at some of the larger and more central newsstands.

There are many television channels and many imported U.S. shows, but all are in Italian. Now, on a typical evening, an Italian viewer can tune into a show illustrating sexual positions, English or French lessons, a spaghetti Western, several commentators discussing a recent kidnapping, or films brought in by relay from France.

Much of the programming is game shows and films. Underlying some is a blatant pornographic theme. One station in Rome showed *Deep Throat* (outlawed in cinemas), and the city came to a standstill. There is some effort to stop or reduce the preoccupation with sex. Several stations have been warned.

## Free Time

The amateur historian or archeologist will never become satiated in Rome. Rome has more than 50 museums, innumerable monuments, excavations, catacombs, galleries, basilicas, and many other cultural and historical treasures.

Interested in a more contemporary cultural experience? Rome offers music, opera, the cinema, and theater. There is an emerging night life devoted to disco.

Those interested in less structured entertainment can follow the example of many Romans—there is nothing to top a leisurely meal in a good restaurant and mingling among other Romans in the piazzas and alleyways of Il Centro and Trastevere.

Your key to where to go and what to see will be the magazine *This Week in Rome,* an English/Italian weekly covering art exhibitions, libraries, museums, current entertainment, sports events, shopping, and tourist information. The two English newspapers also provide current listings.

If you are looking for something more festive, there are many celebrations in the villages surrounding Rome, particularly on each town's Saint's Day. One of the most famous is the Palio delle Contrade in Siena, with its world-famous pageant and horse race in the city square on July 16.

American businesses, chambers of commerce, and the embassy have been partially successful in finding some jobs for teenagers in the summer. Some Italian families arrange to have an American child stay with them for a few weeks to tutor their children in English and other subjects.

## Theaters and Films

There is a very active theater in Rome, but many expatriates miss this because the productions are almost always in Italian. Even with only a rudimentary knowledge of the language, it can still be interesting to see a local performance of a U.S.-origin musical or drama.

The Teatro Tenda (Piazza A. Mancini; telephone 39.39.69) features performances in several languages, occasionally English. The Teatro Goldoni (Vicolo dei Soldati, just north of the Piazza Navona; telephone 656.11.56) also offers English productions.

Only one movie theater shows English-language films on a regular basis. This is Pasquino, Vicolo del Piede 19 (in Trastevere); telephone 580.36.22. On weekdays you will see a substantial portion of the older students from the international schools here.

Santa Susanna Church (Via Venti Settembre; telephone 475.15.10) shows English-language films for the whole family. Monthly bulletins can be obtained from the church.

## Opera, Concerts, and Ballet

The Rome Opera (Piazza Beniamino Gigli; telephone 461.756) still takes second place to La Scala in Milan in quality of performance and magnificence of its opera house. Nevertheless, Italian opera is a cultural treasure that few other countries can hope to duplicate. The summer seasons of opera and performances of visiting companies at the Baths of Caracalla are spectacular. The giant stage, set in the ruins of the old Roman baths, provides an exciting backdrop for bravura performances of *Aïda* complete with elephants. Tickets are obtainable only two days ahead from the box office at the opera house.

There are many concert series, recitals, and other musical events. The most famous hall is the Accademia di Santa Cecilia (Via dei Greci 18; telephone 67.93.677), which has its own orchestra.

Ballet is presented almost entirely by a few visiting companies at the opera house or Caracalla.

### *Restaurants*

Rome has more than 5,000 restaurants. There is an old Italian saying that describes the Italian approach to food: "Your food is your health's best protector."

There is not just one type of restaurant. You have a choice of ristorante, trattoria, pizzeria, café, gelateria, or bar. The sophistication of the cuisine and decor is roughly in that order, with the ristorante at the top. Trattorias are more unpretentious with a simpler, although not necessarily lower quality, menu more closely associated with the working class. Bars sell espresso, tea, soft drinks, and ice cream besides the usual alcoholic beverages. Many will add milk, yoghurt, sandwiches, small pizzas, and cakes. Pizzerias sell exactly that—but often not at lunch time. Most of these places open at 7 or 7:30 p.m.

A gelateria specializes in ice cream and sherbet concoctions, but will have some sandwiches and perhaps pizza also. The cafe offers leisurely enjoyment—either inside or at an outside table—of the passing scene over a cup of espresso or a light snack. You are welcome to stay as long as you wish. Bars, cafes, and gelaterias often require that you select and pay for your food at the cashier in the front before you receive it. The cashier gives you a receipt that you present to the waiter.

As in most world capitals, you can find restaurants featuring French, Chinese, and other national dishes. That great American export, the fast-food chain, has not penetrated Rome.

When Italians dine at night, they begin at 9 or 10 p.m. It is not unheard of for a group to sit down for dinner at midnight.

The usual bill will include a cover charge *(pane e coperto)*, and a service charge of 15 percent. An additional tip to round off the total is customary. Almost all dishes are a la carte, although some places offer a fixed-price dinner for tourists. House wine is decent in most places. Bread is typically served without butter.

For a snack, try a *tavola calda* where dishes are chosen cafeteria style.

Children will have to try Snow White's Poisoned Apples, an ice cream concoction at Biancaneve on Piazza P. Paoli.

Night life in Rome depends more upon the clientele than upon the performers for a show. Most spots are fairly intimate with a singer or small musical group and, more and more, a disco.

## Organizations

Americans in Rome have no formal club facilities for dining or recreation. The principal social clubs are the American Club of Rome and its companion organization for women, the American Women's Association of Rome (AWAR).

They maintain a small business office in rooms on the first floor of the Hotel Quirinale, Via Nazionale 7. Telephone for the American Club is 474.32.31 and for AWAR is 475.52.68. Both clubs, especially AWAR, sponsor many programs on culture, the arts, wine tasting, and various aspects of living in Rome. The women prepare the excellent book, *Destination Rome.*

The Church of Santa Susanna is the parish church for Americans in Rome. The Santa Susanna Guild, open to any English-speaking woman, assists in the spiritual and charitable functions of the church. It is very active in helping newcomers, and it publishes a booklet, *As Romans Do,* with some very practical information. The Guild also maintains the only free public lending library in Rome, with over 5,000 books from current fiction to philosophy. The Guild's address is Via Venti Settembre 14; telephone 475.15.10.

## *Sports*

Politics may be the main topic when a group of Italians meet, but soccer is a close second. And if soccer is the principal sports passion, betting on soccer, and horses, and lots of other things, is perhaps the "sport" with the most active participants.

Rome is blessed with some very modern sports facilities, built either for the XVII Olympic Games in 1960 or by Mussolini as monuments to his love of Italian sports. In addition to being versatile sports arenas, many are also architectural landmarks by some of Italy's renowned builders such as Nervi. One example is the Foro Italico, consisting of a 100,000 seat Olympic Stadium used for soccer matches. There are also the Marble Stadium, entirely constructed of that stone, the Swimming Stadium with several racing and diving pools, and a covered Swimming Stadium.

Rome has not one but two soccer teams, Roma and Lazio. There is a game every Sunday during the season. Tickets are expensive and difficult to get. If you are uncomfortable in very large crowds, stay away from the matches—they can get rowdy. The American Overseas School has a good soccer program and summer camp.

Cycling is one of the favorite amateur as well as professional sports. The highlight is the annual Giro d'Italia.

Some sports seem linked with the number two in Rome. There are two public pools, two bowling alleys, and two golf courses. Both the golf clubs are private, one in the Olgiata residential complex on Via Cassia 1951.

The Italian coastline with its many natural harbors is ideal for sailing and power boating, but berths are in short supply. If you bring your own boat to Italy, it must have a *carnet*. Insurance is compulsory.

Other sports increasing in favor with Romans are tennis (there are many private clubs and some public courts), riding, basketball, and skiing. For the latter, the resorts in northern Italy are far superior to the limited facilities within two hours of Rome.

The nearest beach to Rome is the Lido di Ostia, often called the Roman Riviera. There are cinemas, restaurants, and bikinis. The Metro will take you to Ostia Antica near the shore from the Termini railway station. Summer weekends are mob scenes at the beach and on the roads between it and Rome.

There are over 500 official camp sites, the details of which can be obtained from the Italian Camping and Caravanning Federation (Via Vittorio Emanuele II, Florence; telephone [055] 88.23.91).

# Churches

The major English-speaking churches are:

Anglican
> All Saints Church
> Via del Babuino 155
> Telephone 679.43.57

Baptist
> First Baptist Church
> Piazza San Lorenzo in Luciana 35
> Telephone 679.53.90

Episcopal
> St. Paul's American School
> Via Nazionale corner Via Napoli
> Telephone 463.339, 470.328

Jewish
> Jewish Synagogue
> Lungotevere dei Cenci
> Telephone 656.46.48

Presbyterian
> St. Andrew's of Scotland
> Via XX Settembre 7
> Telephone 475.1627

Salvation Army
> Via degli Apuli
> Telephone 495.62.85

Catholic churches with English masses are:

Santa Susanna (Paulist Fathers)
The American Catholic Church of Rome
Via XX Settembre 14
Telephone 475.15.10

San Clemente (Irish Dominicans)
Via Labicana 95
Telephone 75.57.32

San Silvestro
Piazza San Silvestro
Telephone 679.7775

Saint Patrick's
Via Boncompagni 33
Telephone 465.716

## Health Care

While a few expatriates give the Italian medical facilities credit for adequate emergency care, most recommend treatment elsewhere for long or serious illnesses. Dental treatment is reported to be quite behind the state of the art in the United States. The American embassy, as it does in other countries, provides a list of doctors and dentists but without any recommendations.

For emergencies you can call the Italian Red Cross at 51.00 or the general emergency number, 113. You will be taken to one of the bigger hospitals with emergency services *(pronto soccorso).*

There are several 24-hour pharmacies in Rome. One is Carlo Erba, Via del Corso 145; telephone 67.90.866.

### *Medical Tips*

Just because a doctor has the title *Professore,* it does not signify necessarily that he is a professor of medicine.

If you are rushing to the hospital in your car, something white held outside the window while sounding the horn signals an emergency and will help clear traffic.

The Red Cross *(Croce Rossa)* is not a volunteer charitable organization. Also, there are the Green Cross, White Cross, and so on.

If you have a family member in the hospital, nursing care is very perfunctory. It is up to the family to provide all the amenities.

Doctors, usually, do not give a prescribed injection. Instead, you go to the druggist to buy the medicine and the syringe. Then you find someone to give the shot.

Most doctors and hospitals keep incomplete records, so keep copies of your lab work, shots, and other medical history.

One of Rome's hospitals, Santo Spirito, is the first to be founded there and may be more famous for its priceless frescoes than for its medical care.

# Milan

Milan is Italy's second largest city and boasts the country's highest per capita income. It has been called the city where the new Italy meets the old.

It is a steel-and-glass capital of industry, commerce, and finance with modern and even daring high-rise offices. No surprise, then, that the city's most popular fair is the International Milan Fair for commercial and industrial exhibitors. This is the main fair, but there are many smaller fairs, expositions, and shows held throughout the year for all sorts of products and services.

Yet Milan is also the home of da Vinci's *Last Supper* as well as many other art treasures that survived the bombing of World War II. Throughout history, the city has been captured, occupied, destroyed, and rebuilt many times. Among its rulers have been Attila the Hun, Charlemagne, the Sforzas, and Napoleon. Surviving the benevolent ministrations of such charming occupiers has given the city a strength and resiliency that has stood it in good stead. Its people have a reputation for being more hurried and laconic than their southern neighbors.

The center of Milan was established at the Piazza del Duomo as early as the twelfth century. The pattern of growth has radiated from this focal point ever since. The province of Milan now covers an area of 1,065 square miles and is both a rich industrial region and an agricultural region.

Tourists tend to overlook the attractions of Milan in favor of those of Rome or Venice. Loyal Milanese expatriates swear that in any other country the castles, art, and museums of their adopted home would be premier sights. They also point out that Milan is near the beautiful Italian lake district, close to excellent skiing in the Alps, and has the attractions of its neighbors France and Switzerland for vacations and shopping.

Because of the friendliness of the people of Milan and the limited number of organizations for Americans or expatriates as a group, the foreign colony is less close and segregated than in many other European cities. In other words, the expatriate becomes more a part of Milan rather than an interloper.

Milanese expatriates do not seem envious of their southern cousins in Rome. One summed it up by saying, "This is a city where you can get things done."

Expatriate living in Milan is much the same as in Rome—

housing is scarce, telephones are difficult to get, medical facilities are limited, shopping facilities are comparable, etc. This section highlights the unique and different things that the expatriate in Milan will encounter.

## Weather

Good weather cannot be listed among Milan's attractions. It is cold, wet, and foggy during the winter. Often the fog is so thick that you cannot see across the street. The Milan national airport, Linate, is closed more than any other airport. Even Malpensa, the international entry, is fogged in frequently. The summer is not quite as hot as Rome's, but it can still be stifling.

## Housing

It is difficult for resident expatriates to pinpoint any particular area where Americans or nationals of other countries congregate. They live all over Milan from the center to the suburbs, primarily in apartments but a few in lovely villas. Two places, however, are popular:

San Siro. A large area of both villas and apartments, with rather nebulous boundaries located near the Milan International Fair grounds. The apartment complexes here may have pools and tennis courts.

Villagio Maggiolina. A protected area (fence and gatehouse) with approximately 30 two-story units containing apartments very close to American style in layout.

Americans are spreading outside of Milan to Monza in the north, Gorganzola in the east, and even as far as Lake Como.

The best source for housing information is word-of-mouth. Church and school bulletin boards are other locations to check. Also watch the ads in the *Corriere della Sera* and *Il Giorno* newspapers.

## Domestic Help

Expatriates find the prospect of obtaining help not much better in Milan than in Rome. The competition in Milan is the better paying industry jobs for young women. Live-in help is extremely rare.

## Education

There are three English-speaking schools:

The American Community School of Milan
Villaggio Mirasole di Opera-Noverasco
(just inside the Milan ring road)
Telephone 524.1546
This nonprofit, parent-owned, independent, nondenominational, coed school celebrated its twentieth anniversary in 1983. It has an American oriented curriculum from nursery through high school. About 45 percent of the students are American and an equal percentage are Italian. The rest of the approximately 500 students are from several countries. Excellent facilities and comprehensive sports and extracurricular activities make this a recreational as well as educational center for its students.

Sir James Henderson School of Milan
Vialle Lombardia 66
Telephone 285.0257
This is a British community school with an accent on preparation for the O and A levels. It accepts children from nursery age through 14.

International School of Milan
Via Osoppo 4
Telephone 639.408
This is a private, bilingual school preparing students for both English and American exams. Classes run from prekindergarten through high school. It has almost 700 students, mostly Italian.

Many American mothers take advantage of the Italian nursery program and send their children to the *asilo* in their neighborhood.

## Shopping

The pattern of shopping and availability of items is very much the same as in Rome, although there are some local variations. Milan is the center of haute couture. Ken Scott, Sergio Armani, Missoni, Roberta di Camerino, Mila Schon, and several other internationally famous names have their salons and boutiques in this city, primarily along or near Via Montenapoleone, Milan's premier shopping street. This is the area where you can get Ferragamo shoes, Gucci handbags, and exquisite jewelry.

Standa, Coin, and a subsidiary of Rinascente, Upim, are the three lower-price department stores. La Rinascente is headquartered in Milan. Its main store on the northern arcade of the Piazza Duomo is comparable to a quality U.S. store.

J. C. Penney is in Milan at Via San Pietro dell Orto.

One of the leading grocery chains carrying American products is Esselunga. Their stores are marked by a big _S._

## Transportation

Milan's Metropolitan subway system has two crossing lines: the green (line 2) and the red (line 1). Tickets are purchased before you go through the turnstile for slightly more than the Rome fare. The big advantage in Milan is that you can get change or tickets at the magazine stands at the bigger stations. The Milan Metro symbol is "MM."

Above ground, there are both trams and buses. Tickets are obtainable from the tobacco shops, as are daily and monthly passes. You have 70 minutes from the time you validate your ticket in the machine at the rear entrance to use free transfers anywhere within the system.

A word of warning about the Milan train station and perhaps for all stations in Italy. It is not hard to miss your train even if you are there on time and search diligently for the right track. One expatriate's train left without him because the station attendants were on strike and were not putting all the departure announcements on the big board. When asked for an explanation, they said the strike included not giving out any information in a foreign language.

Parking in Milan is easier than in Rome. You can find parking places in the city where an attendant will watch the car for two hours for a pittance. The city fathers, however, have established a green zone _(zone verde)_ in the old town center where parking is allowed only at limited times.

The Automobile Club of Milan is located at Corso Venezia 43; telephone 77.45. The highway emergency number is 116.

As in Rome, gas stations have odd hours. Only about 2 percent stay open on Sundays and holidays.

## Free Time

The cultural resources available to the Milan resident are not as extensive as those in Rome, but they are of the highest quality. To opera fans, La Scala is the epitome against which other performances are measured. The Milan museums have one of the world's greatest collections of art. Architectural achievements include the ultramodern Pirelli building and the classic arcade Galleria Vittorio Emanuele II, built in the form of a cross with an octagonal glass-and-iron dome in the center.

Milan offers enough music to satisfy even an Italian, and it needs no translation for the expatriate:

Teatro alla Scala
Piazza alla Scala
Telephone 88.79
This renowned house has a ballet season beginning early in September and then the opera opening December 7. Tickets are extremely scarce and expensive. Some of the boxes have been owned by companies or families for generations.

Concerti Sinfonici del Conservatorio
Information: Via Montenapoleone 23
Telephone 706.850
Presents a series of orchestral concerts, recitals, and a young people's series on Saturdays.

Musical events, concerts, and other current events in Milan are listed in the newspapers and in the monthly publication of the tourist association, Ente Provinciale per il Turismo (EPT), entitled *Milano Mese*. The Publication lists sports and gallery openings as well. The EPT information offices are located at the Piazza Duomo (telephone 808.813) and at the Central Station (telephone 206.030).

The EPT also publishes *Tutta Milano,* an excellent guide in English. It lists many parks and gardens, galleries, museums, palaces, churches, and other attractions. The best-known is the *Duomo,* actually the cathedral itself, but generally used to refer to the huge square on which it faces together with the Galleria Vittorio Emanuele II. The Duomo is the world's third largest cathedral (after St. Peter's and the Seville Cathedral) and is richly ornamented both inside and out.

Theater in Milan is exclusively Italian.

Of over 200 cinemas, only one, Teatro Angelicum (Piazza S. Angelo 2), shows English-language films.

Milan offers ample facilities for those who want simply to enjoy a good restaurant or an evening of entertainment in a night club.

Social life in Milan revolves around its schools, churches, and the two social clubs listed below. In-town functions tend to be on Tuesdays through Thursdays, as the weekends are spent outside Milan traveling, skiing, hiking, or doing some other recreation.

Teenagers go in groups to discos, to the one movie showing English-language films, or to school functions. Drugs have not become a significant problem as yet.

## _Sports_

In Italy there is soccer—and then the other sports. Soccer is not neglected in Milan. The Stadio di San Siro seats 100,000 avid spectators who watch the two Milanese teams, Milan and Inter.

Horse racing can be found at the Ippodromo del Trotto a del Galoppo at San Siro and the Ippodromo di Mirabello at Parco di Monza.

_Tutta Milano_ lists the locations of sports federations and facilities for almost every activity. Adequate provisions can be found for most sports, but there are some exceptions or points you should know about:

Golf. The first public golf course in Italy was opened recently, Mirasole, next to the American Community School. It also has tennis and swimming facilities. There are several other private clubs but the high initiation fees, which are not refundable, discourage expatriates.

Swimming. The Italian lake country is a favorite swimming spot for expatriates. So are the beaches, but these are mildly polluted from time to time.

Tennis. With the boom in this sport, there are never enough public courts. Private clubs are the answer if you can afford them and are admitted.

Skiing. This is a favorite recreation for expatriates in the winter. There are a few slopes near the city for weekend trips, such as Foppolo Mera. The better facilities of Switzerland, France, and Austria, as well as in the Italian Alps, are close enough for weekend trips.

Many expatriates take advantage of the lakes and mountains near Milan to rent apartments in resort areas for skiing in the winter or for swimming and other recreations in the summer. This is the way to see some sun from November to April. More and more developments are going up, so these retreats are relatively inexpensive.

## *Organizations*

Benvenuto Club. This club has no official address but meets Tuesday mornings from 10 to 12 at the Jolly President Hotel, Largo Augusto. It is a very active English-speaking women's organization of over 700 members from 41 countries, the majority being English and American. The club sponsors luncheons, coffees, excursions, 21 specialty activity groups, an arts and crafts fair, and many other worthwhile activities. One of its important community services is the publication of a booklet on living in Milan, *Benvenuto to Milan*. A new edition is expected soon. Another publication is a monthly newsletter, *Town Crier,* which provides information on current activities and invaluable advertisements.

British-American Club (Corso Venezia 18; telephone 780.095). Although not as many Americans belong to this club, it still is an excellent medium to meet new friends and exchange information.

## *Churches*

There are several English-speaking Catholic and non-Catholic churches in Milan. *Tutta Milano* lists all the churches and provides much other useful information.

## Doing Business in Italy

Italy is a paradox. Few businessmen—or for that matter, individuals involved in international affairs—are unaware of the myriad problems that have befallen this remnant of the Roman Empire. For years the lira has been a soft and very weak currency in international banking circles. Inflation and the printing press money policies of various governments have, at times in the past, been so blatant that international money markets would not even speculate in futures for the Italian currency. Coalition governments have become the "name of the game," with governments being formed and falling with such frequency that for a while the "in" thing was to predict next week's government with the same rationale as picking the winner in a high school football game.

Terrorism has become a way of life for politicians, military personnel, and high-ranking businessmen who have become targets for kidnapping, murder, and, more recently, the infamous "kneecapping," or shooting the legs from under prominent persons.

With galloping inflation, virtually no stability in government, and terrorism as a way of life, one has to question why anyone in his right mind would want to work as an expatriate in Italy. The fact is that Italy is a favorite for expatriate workers—and this is the paradox. An overwhelming majority of the expatriate businessmen interviewed would welcome continuation of work in Italy or would return to Italy without reservation. Perhaps the magic in "Arrivederci Roma" still lives, or maybe the recall of scenes from *Three Coins in a Fountain* is just too poignant, making the few paltry inconveniences just mentioned a small price to pay for the good life on the Italian Riviera or on the sun-baked shores of the Mediterranean.

The weather, too, is a study in contrasts, making north and south more like two separate countries. There is sunny southern Italy with its perpetual summerlike weather, and northern Italy with its four seasons—actually more like two seasons. Spring and fall in northern Italy are very beautiful, especially if you happen to be around on the two or three days that they are present each year. If you miss those two or three days of fall and spring, the summer-winter concept is probably your recollection of a typical year.

If Rome is the air, tourist, and cultural center of Italy, Milan has to be the business center. Milanese winters typically have cloudy skies, and air travel into and out of this business hub during this part of the year is uncertain. The chances for landing at an alternate airport are about as good as getting into Milan. Recent improvements in air traffic control and instrument-landing systems have helped, but there are still many days when weather is below landing minimums for aircraft.

Actually, there are many reasons why Italy is a favorite of multinational managers. It is a bridge between Western Europe and the North African countries bordering the Mediterranean. A lovely (southern Italy) climate and a key crossroad air center make Rome a travel center to and from the Middle East. With the civil strife in Lebanon, many multinationals felt that a new address in Greece or Italy was the best way to continue to serve the Middle East and still not be completely removed from the area.

In addition to being a major exporter of hard goods such as automobiles, trucks, and machinery, Italian engineers and technicians have kept the power stations and major transportation systems in operation in many developing and underdeveloped countries. This influence has led to favorable trade relationships with most nations of the world. As a result, Italian trade treaties often make it beneficial to multinationals to have an Italian branch office.

When asked about his preference for overseas living, an 11-year expatriate stated that Italy would be his top choice for a return assignment. For a person who has lived in several countries ranging from India to the United Kingdom, this has to say something about the business climate in Italy. Simply put, expatriates enjoy the Italian people, the Italian food, the Italian climate, the Italian wine, the Italian businessmen, and just plain living in this land of contrasts. (It is just possible that the nearness of his Italian office to the excellent skiing areas of the Italian and Swiss alps could have influenced the thinking of this avid skier and expatriate businessman; but this, too, is part of the lure for expatriates in Italy.)

Regarding the terrorism and previously mentioned inconveniences, this businessman merely says, "The press distorts things in Italy too; as long as these excesses are still news and not the everyday norm, I'll still pick Italy as my favorite overseas post. Others may disagree, but really, Italy has a lot of things going for it from a business standpoint."

## Legal Matters

### *Visas and Permits*

Getting the necessary documents to reside and work in Italy takes some diligent planning and attention to detail.

Working in Italy requires an employment permit *(permesso di lavoro)*. Your prospective employer (or yourself if you are self-employed) first requests a "certificate of unavailability" from the local Provincial Labor Office *(Officio Provinciale del Lavoro e della Massima Occupazione)* attesting to the lack of qualified Italian workers for the position. If granted, the certificate is taken to the nearest police station *(questura),* and a request for authorization to enter Italy is made. This request will be granted provided that there is no adverse information about the prospective employee in the police records. This document is forwarded to the employee to use in obtaining a visa. If you think this sounds time-consuming, you are right. Generally, however, senior positions in American subsidiaries can be filled by expatriates without too much trouble over work permits.

If you are planning to stay in Italy more than three months, you enter as a resident rather than as a tourist, and you must have the appropriate visa. The formalities of a residence visa take time as well. Check with the Italian consulate for details.

Within three days after arrival in Italy, all foreigners must register with the police and get a permit to stay as a resident or tourist. Your hotel will probably take care of this and you will turn over your passport for this purpose.

During the next 20 days, you must register with the Vital Statistics Bureau (Anagrafe) in the city where you will reside. This is the step that permits you to bring your personal effects in duty-free. When you leave to return home, you should cancel your registration with Anagrafe. This step, in turn, permits exportation of your belongings and avoids assessment of taxes after departure.

Now you are duly entered and registered.

## Legal Rights

Italy is a civil law country with a career judiciary. The principal law of the land is the Constitutional Law of February 9, 1948. Freedoms of speech, press, movement, and association are safeguarded. Personal liberty and domicile are inviolate except for officially authorized arrests or searches. There is a presumption of innocence. In general, aliens enjoy these same civil rights.

## Court System

The highest legal tribunal is the Constitutional Court, composed of 15 judges, which is the only court empowered to determine questions of the constitutional legality of laws and acts. There are some administrative courts that handle specific controversies between individuals and the government, such as tax matters or the abuse of power.

The procedure in an Italian court, while designed to accomplish much the same ends as the system in the United States, is quite different from what Americans have seen in hundreds of television courtroom scenes. For example, the parties and any other persons having an interest in a dispute cannot testify. Be sure to get legal counsel if you become involved in any controversy.

## Marriage and Divorce

Anyone marrying in Italy has to be in love to get through the red tape involved. There are many certificates, sworn statements, and legalized declarations required by the U.S. embassy and Italian government authorities. Civil ceremonies require posting of a notice at the city hall for two weeks, but this can be waived in some cases.

The civil ceremony is performed at the city hall with two witnesses and an interpreter if one is needed. Most non-Catholic clergymen require a prior civil ceremony. A religious marriage by a Roman Catholic priest will suffice by itself if duly registered with the Anagrafe.

The U.S. embassy provides a booklet on all these requirements.

Divorce is permissible in Italy now, but the requirements and prerequisites are stiff, as one would expect. If possible, the procedures are even more time-consuming and frustrating than those for a marriage. If a divorce is being considered, forget Italy and go back to the United States, provided you have maintained residence there.

## Births

Two registrations are recommended for any baby born in Italy: the birth should be registered within 10 days with the Anagrafe and it should be registered at the U.S. embassy to provide for U.S. citizenship and birth records. The child takes the nationality of the parents, but there are some important exceptions. A child born to aliens resident in Italy for 10 years at the time of birth, or who has an Italian father, mother, or grandfather on his father's side, has some options to elect Italian citizenship, such as entering the Italian military service. Most of these options constitute a denunciation of U.S. citizenship. Again, if you have any doubt on the citizenship of your newborn, check with your attorney.

## Death

The transfer of the body of the deceased for burial is a relatively simple matter in Italy. Some administrative authorizations are required but easily obtained. They should be cleared through the embassy when the death is reported.

There is one non-Catholic cemetery in Rome—the one where Keats is buried. Any non-Catholic foreigner may be buried there if he had been living in Rome for a six-month period prior to death.

## Women's Rights

The principle of nondiscrimination is set forth in the constitution. Some legislative progress has been made to implement this position. For instance, in 1968 and 1969 some decisions of the Constitutional Court declared invalid the provisions of the penal code concerning adultery on the grounds that there was inequity between the sexes. Consequently, adultery is no longer a criminal offense. In 1977 a law was passed dealing specifically with the prohibition of discrimination based on sex in employment and labor relations. Women can own property now, too.

Although Italian women may be making headway, the position of expatriate women is frustrating. An American woman who marries an Italian becomes an Italian citizen automatically, although she does not necessarily lose her U.S. citizenship. As an Italian, she is allowed to work. All other American women and children cannot get work permits, except in the most extraordinary circumstances. Taking a job requiring English-language ability no longer is the answer since Italy is in the EEC with England and the latter's citizens get preference. Even the international schools have become subject to Italian labor laws, which complicates their activities greatly.

## Exchange Control

Nonresidents are subject to complicated laws with regard to funds derived from activity carried out in Italy. There should not be a problem for ordinary transactions in connection with daily living. If you plan any business investments in Italy or other exceptional transactions requiring transfer or exchange of funds, you should check with your banker or lawyer.

## Drinking

There is no legal drinking age in Italy under which children are prohibited from consuming beer, wine, or liquor. Most expatriates know their children will be exposed to the availability of liquor, particularly beer and wine. They feel that the great majority of U.S. children handle this well. They report peer pressure discourages excess drinking. Perhaps a society where it is not such a "forbidden fruit" helps discourage abuse.

## Taxes

The Italian tax system is no longer the chaotic, oft-ignored, archaic program it once was before massive reform in 1974. A new, simplified, predictable system of direct and indirect taxes and an efficient method of record keeping and enforcement is in effect.

Individuals are subject to two taxes: personal income tax (IRPEF) and local income tax (ILOR). Only the former is collected for salaried and other employment income. Both are administered nationally, but the ILOR is allocated to provinces and municipalities.

You are a resident for Italian tax purposes if you are registered with Anagrafe, or if you reside in Italy more than six months in a year, or if you have your principal office or interest there. This covers virtually all expatriates. As a result, your income from any source is taxable. Nonresidents are taxed only on their income from Italian sources.

No special concessions are granted expatriates in calculating income. Your gross income includes that from almost any source, except for capital gains that are not made because of speculation or that are not connected with a business. For example, if you purchase an antique or a painting and resell it in less than two years, the gains are taxable because the transaction is presumed speculative.

Expenses incurred for production of each type of income—local taxes, social security contributions, some insurance premiums, medical and funeral expenses, alimony, and school fees—are deductible in arriving at net income. For a salaried employee, there are no special allowances for business-related expenses. Certain "independent" persons, such as a company director or an author, get an allowance of 10 percent to cover all expenses. Charitable contributions are not deductible. Personal allowances in the form of rebates deductible from the tax are provided for the taxpayer, dependent spouse, and children. Credits are available, to some extent, for taxes paid abroad where foreign income is produced.

A few special income categories are taxed separately. Two that might be applicable are indemnities for employment termination and the par value of shares received as stock dividends. Note that an expatriate may have a few shares of an Italian corporation in his name to provide the requisite shareholders. He should make sure that the documentation indicating that he is only a nominee shareholder is clear so that he will not be subject to this stock dividend tax if such a dividend is declared.

The United States and Italy have concluded a tax treaty that provides that compensation for personal services, professional fees, and certain other income is—subject to some qualifications—taxable in the country where such service or income was rendered or earned.

There is a withholding system for wages, professional fees, interest, and dividends.

Each employer gives his employees a tax withholding form

shortly after the end of the calendar year, just as in the United States. The employee or any self-employed individual is required to file a return by May 31 for the preceding year. If there is no income except salary and no special allowances, the employee can simply sign the form from the employer and send it in. The big difference in Italy is that the return must show that the proper taxes have been withheld or paid prior to filing. In effect, Italians assess themselves. Individuals subject to the IRPEF must pay 75 percent of their tax by November of each year on any income that has not been subject to withholding. The difference between this payment and the taxes shown as due at the end of the year is the amount paid when the return is filed. An overpayment in November is refunded with some interest.

This system works! As a result, a tax clearance when an expatriate leaves is normally not required.

The major indirect tax is the Italian version of the value-added tax (IVA). The ordinary rate is 14 percent. Reduced rates are provided for food and essential items—35 percent for luxury items and certain motor vehicles.

Another tax that you will experience is the registration, or stamp, tax. This is collected on any legal document: contracts, deeds, receipts, promissory notes, and any other document with legal effect connected with a transaction on which no IVA has been paid. Tobacco shops sell special stamped paper, _Carta bollata,_ on which to prepare many of these documents. The rates vary depending upon the amount involved and the type of transaction.

One point to watch: If a company has U.S. personnel who travel frequently to Italy, be sure that they do not accumulate six-months time in the country or they will be subject to taxation.

## _Other Legal Tips_

Dogs not on a leash must be muzzled.

Each restaurant is required to give you—and you are required to accept—an official receipt.

If you are closing a bank account, be prepared for delay and red tape.

American cars must be "nationalized," meaning made to conform to Italian specifications. This may only involve changing the lighting.

The parking ticket on your car will be followed up within a few days by a notice and form to make payment at the post office.

You are presumed guilty if you have a traffic accident unless you can show you did everything possible to avoid it. With two vehicles, the presumption is shared equally. Compulsory third-party liability insurance is expensive as a result. If involved in an accident, do not succumb to the Italian practice of a heated debate at the scene. Let your insurance company handle it without being burdened by any admissions from you.

# 18

# Assignment Hong Kong

*B*ACKPACKING IN HONG KONG? "Ridiculous," you say. "That's the spot for calculators, jade, big business deals, and perhaps a trip over the border to China." But roughing it in the countryside is not exactly the bill of fare for this jam-packed colony where there is scarcely room to make your way along the sidewalk.

But you *can* backpack in Hong Kong, and the very fact that you can gives you insight into how varied and surprising your life will be in this British Crown Colony at the southeastern tip of China. If there is any truth to the old adage that variety is the spice of life, then living in Hong Kong is like sampling a delicious hot curry created by a master chef and assembled with such skill as to fascinate and tempt you but never to overpower you.

Nearly everyone comes to Hong Kong prepared for a small, crowded, insular community. But the colony really spreads over a tiny piece of the mainland and 235 South China Sea islands, many of which are sparsely populated, rugged, and ideal for getting away from it all.

A word about names for Hong Kong is needed at this point. It is still a British Crown Colony, but the old term "colony" is out of style. "Territory" is now used, despite its primitive connotations. This should not be confused with the "New Territories," which refers to just a portion of the mainland. In all, Hong Kong consists of

Hong Kong Island (or "the Island"—29 square miles in area), Kowloon just across the border on the mainland, the New Territories behind Kowloon stretching to the China border, and the other South China Sea islands (mainland and islands covering a total of 365 square miles).

Everything in Hong Kong seems to be done in the midst of a crowd. Newcomers have to adjust quickly to the mobs of people whenever they move about. Conditions are crowded because 80 percent of the Territory's 5.2 million people live along the coastal fringes of the Island and mainland. Though entry from China is severely restricted by both sides, Hong Kong still gets an average of 150 illegals per day. In recent years, fleeing refugees from Vietnam have added another big group.

One of the best guides on Hong Kong, the *Insight Guide,* describes how the Chinese cope:

> Perhaps the key to understanding the people of Hong Kong is to understand the mechanism which allows the society to function normally under such closet-like circumstances; they are people living on "borrowed land" and "borrowed time" in a city constantly in the excited state of a packed stadium during a championship match. A built-in mechanism within each individual—like an automatic valve that shuts when pressure approaches the unbearable—keeps such tension from surfacing.

Westerners need to find their own release mechanisms to survive. For some, the thrills and challenges of working in such an exotic business climate are enough. Others immerse themselves in activities within the international community. For a few, only the anticipation of home leave carries them through.

Indicative of how your life will merge with other foreigners in Hong Kong is the annual father-son baseball extravaganza with the resident Japanese. The youngsters slug it out first on the diamond, followed by the dads' game. While the American boys may take the game rather seriously, once it is over they head for the nearest McDonald's for a hamburger and Coke. The Japanese kids, however, fall into line for stiff calisthenics and training for the next game. A few days before the international match, the American fathers scout the playing field to determine if the Japanese fathers are into their usual intense pregame practice sessions. Not only are they on the diamond—the Japanese fathers enter the practice games with all the fervor and dedication assigned to a multimillion-dollar business deal.

Hong Kong is truly an international city in spite of the fact that

98 percent of her population is Chinese. As a British colony, she carries the overtones of a Western culture, but her roots are deeply embedded in oriental soil. English, however, is spoken in many shops and restaurants, and many commercial transactions are conducted in this language.

Many local Chinese speak Cantonese, and most of the "foreign" languages you hear will be this harsh tongue of the people who come from the Kwantung province of China, which borders the Territory to the north.

Certain attitudes among the Chinese are traditional. They are loyal to family and friends, they tend to be emotional, they love noisy parties, they work hard, and they are rarely drunk but they love to gamble. They live by a strict code of responsibility to mates, parents, children, and close friends, but their lack of concern for those outside their immediate circle develops into the rude, aggressive behavior of pushing, slamming doors, and uninhibited driving in public.

For years, expatriates were referred to by the Chinese as _gwailos,_ literally, "foreign devils." Perhaps a sign of toleration or partial acceptance of the international community is the use now of the term _sayan,_ which just means "western foreigner." The biggest _sayan_ group is still the British, followed by Indians, Americans, and Australians. But there are nationalities from everywhere.

Many expatriates are sent by multinational companies; others come to make quick fortunes. Still others settle in Hong Kong for the excitement and flavor of international life. Nearly everyone appears to be living in Hong Kong temporarily.

The Territory is the transportation hub of the Orient. Over 900 scheduled flights go in and out of the airport each week as well as hundreds of nonscheduled services, making it one of the busiest terminals in the Far East.

What really makes Hong Kong thrive is its harbor. Both from a scenic and economic standpoint, it is the focal point of life in the Territory. If you also include the airport, gateway for tourists and residents, you have the heart and soul of Hong Kong.

The harbor of over 23 square miles rivals any other harbor in size and beauty. There are few sights that can compare with the harbor at sunset as seen from the balconies of apartments above Victoria— unless it is the lights of the many ships at anchor, which are like sequins on the rich, velvet blackness of the water at night.

Each month more than 750 ocean-going vessels and 3,000 river steamers and smaller craft use this port. It boasts the third largest and one of the most modern container terminals in the world. With its reputation for the fastest turnaround in Asia, for charges that are among the lowest in the world, for minimum regulation by the Marine Department, and now its access to its gigantic northern neighbor once more opening, the port is Hong Kong's greatest insurance of continued good health.

It doesn't take long to find your way geographically around this Territory. Victoria on Hong Kong Island is the capital, but no one ever uses her proper name. Instead, residents simply refer to the area of government buildings, financial institutions, hotels, and shops as "Central." The Star Ferry, which connects Hong Kong Island with Kowloon on the mainland, docks at the foot of the Central District.

Rising above Central and its bordering communities is the rugged hillside, with row upon row of high-rise apartment buildings; towering over it all is "The Peak," an exclusive residential area.

On the far side of Hong Kong Island is Repulse Bay, a very popular residential district and the location of the once proud and elegant Repulse Bay Hotel, now the victim of the demolition ball in the interest of progress.

Aberdeen, famed for its thousands of boat people and a gigantic floating restaurant, is also on this side of the Island along with Ocean Park (see Free Time).

From the Island to Kowloon is only a ten-minute ride on the Star Ferry, and even quicker by tunnel or subway. While Central on the Hong Kong side is the chief financial and governmental center, Kowloon is known for its commerce and manufacturing. To tourists and residents alike, they offer hundreds of shops; arcades such as the Ocean Terminal; a three-tiered esplanade, lined with prestigious boutiques; hotels, bars, and restaurants. Stretching from Kowloon to the Chinese border are the New Territories, where modern high-rise apartment blocks are beginning to intrude into once quiet farmland and old Chinese villages.

The infamous shanties that once blotted the hillside on Hong Kong Island are not nearly as prevalent as a decade ago when the government undertook a rigorous program of public housing construction. Much of the population today lives in towering concrete blocks of government-owned apartments. The largest housing estates are cities within themselves, accommodating 150,000 people and containing shops, schools, and medical facilities.

Not too many years ago, Hong Kong had a reputation for country club living. A beautiful coastline, luxurious apartments, many clubs, months of warm weather, and miles of shoreline for swimming and boating were at the disposal of expatriates. Such a life-style may still exist for a few, but more often it is not readily available to the newly arrived resident.

One of the major frustrations for new expatriates is the monumental traffic jams, coupled with the lack of parking space and crowded sidewalks—where pushing is quite common and placidly accepted. Air pollution is irritating at many times. Some foreign residents commented that families who have any member with a continuing serious medical problem or a learning difficulty should think about not accepting an assignment to the Territory. Psychological problems, however, were reportedly being handled moderately well.

"We have all the luxuries here in Hong Kong," said one American woman. "It is the necessities that are hard to come by."

While these add up to some serious problems to consider, most are not insurmountable. Once you find an apartment, you will probably have a spectacular view of either the South China Sea or the harbor. It is not so difficult to find domestic help, and expatriate women find that they are freer to enjoy life. Even party giving becomes easy and good caterers are plentiful.

How do women spend their time? There is an active social life. Organizations such as the American Women's Association, which does a fantastic job, not only help newcomers get acquainted but also contribute magnanimously to community life.

There are no legal restrictions on employment for wives of husbands who have work permits. In practice, though, jobs are difficult to get either because Cantonese is required or because there is a local preference policy. Even when a job is found, the pay may be too low to make it worthwhile. (The League of Women Voters, a very active organization in the Territory, has just published an informative booklet describing the requirements and opportunities in all fields. It is entitled _Educational and Employment Opportunities in Hong Kong for Expatriate Women,_ and it can be found in the South China Morning Post bookstores.)

Living in the Territory provides an opportunity for the expatriate to study firsthand the historical background that has been the context for recent popular novels and films. The sullied ancestry of Hong Kong may have been the inspiration for the many Kung Fu movies produced here. Pirates and opium were two of the most important factors in the development of this law-abiding model of propriety.

Before the British occupation, Hong Kong was a small fishing village; it was also notorious for its pirates. When Britain began trading with China, the harbor was a logical place to stop to replenish supplies. The ships were often full of opium, tea, and silks on the return run to the West. This trade was important to Britain. Each side tolerated what they considered to be the "boorishness" of the other to maintain trade.

The Chinese placed severe restrictions on the British "barbarians." They could only trade through one port, Canton, and only at certain times. Families were not allowed and were left in Macao. It was illegal for a trader to learn Chinese.

In 1799 Emperor Tao Kuang declared opium illegal in China, but this did not stop the lucrative trade. It just went underground. In 1839 the British colony in Canton was barricaded until the supplies of opium, "foreign mud," were handed over. This affront to British sovereignty brought on the first Opium War (1840–42). When the parties negotiated a cease-fire, Britain acquired Hong Kong Island in perpetuity. Not everyone felt this was an important acquisition.

Hong Kong's status was confirmed by the Treaty of Nanking (1842), and five other ports were opened by China for trade. The strategic and economic importance of the Island was soon evident.

In 1860 the Convention of Peking granted part of Kowloon to the British in perpetuity. This grant came after one of Britain's diplomats was shot on his way to Peking, and China had to make amends. The New Territories were granted in a 99-year lease that expires in 1997. This lease also included 233 islands (which help make boating one of Hong Kong's most popular recreations). It is anybody's guess as to what China will do in 1997. Experts have felt strongly that China would not change the status quo. Recently, however, there have been disquieting indications that the issue is still unresolved in Peking.

Hong Kong is one of the last jewels remaining in Britain's colonial crown. As a Crown Colony, the Queen's appointed representative, the governor, is the head of government and presides over the two principal policy-making bodies, the Executive Council and the Legislative Council.

The government seems to work. Hong Kong is financially self-supporting. Although its near total dependence on imports creates a deficit trade balance, this is overcome by considerable earnings from tourism and a sizable annual inflow of capital.

One of the great advantages of living in Hong Kong is that you will have a chance to experience two cultures at once, the British and the Chinese, plus mingle in a truly cosmopolitan international community. To quote a retired Latin and Greek teacher from Philadelphia, who became so enamored of the colony during a round-the-world trip that she never left: "Where else can you find all this?"

# Housing

Housing is one of the critical problems a newcomer faces, primarily because of the extremely high rents. Plan on several thousand U.S. dollars per month for a modern, multibedroom apartment on Hong Kong Island.

Virtually all expatriates in the Territory lease apartments in high-rise buildings on the Island. There are very few one-family dwellings available. Some townhouses have been built with miniscule yards and a living area no larger than the average apartment; land is too expensive to construct anything but high-rise buildings these days.

Traffic, schools, and the location of your work influence strongly where you will want to live. Since most Americans work and send their children to school on the Island, they live there as well in order to minimize travel distances during the horrendous rush hours.

## *How To Find Your New Home*

Many companies lease apartments for their people. Usually these are very nice units, adequately equipped and in a preferred area. If your company has such a place, you are fortunate. Otherwise, be prepared for a one- to three-month period of looking around for something acceptable. While you are looking you can stay in a hotel or a "leave flat." The Hong Kong hotels are deluxe and can provide suites or connecting rooms for families. Many have refrigerators in the rooms; some even have swimming pools. Cooking in the room is, technically, forbidden and certainly frowned upon in practice. Unless there is a heavy demand for rooms, you can get a long-term reduced rate. Apartment rents are so high now that companies may not care if you stay a little longer in the hotel.

The other alternative, the leave flat, allows you to rent another expatriate's apartment while he is on leave or otherwise not occupying it. These are more readily available in the summer when many expatriates take their home leave. The usual rental term is from one to three months. You pay the rent and the salary of the maid. If you are lucky, you may get the use of a car or boat. These leave flats are advertised in the English newspapers, club bulletin boards, and by word-of-mouth.

One American who stayed in a leave flat explained that while these temporary apartments do provide more space and cooking facilities, they also put you on your own immediately; it becomes slightly more difficult to make friends. If you are forced to stay in a hotel, you meet others in the same predicament and a camaraderie develops among your group of newcomers. Yet, others say that having an opportunity to test out the neighborhood in which your leave flat is located is a big plus.

Your company may have someone to assist you in your apartment search. If not, use the same sources for finding a permanent location as for a leave flat, but also try the many real estate agents. Three of the largest and best known are:

Hong Kong Land Co., Ltd.
Alexander House, 5/F
16-20 Chater Road
Hong Kong
Telephone 5-265471

Jones Lang Wootton
Sutherland House, 9/F
3 Chater Road
Hong Kong
Telelephone 5-217171

Riggs Realty
Dominion Centre, 4/F
37-59A Queens Road, East
Hong Kong
Telephone 5-284528

## *Where to Settle*

There are three areas on the Island where Americans have resided for several years and that still attract the greater portion of the international expatriate community. Table 6 describes the essentials of each.

Although there is much development of new housing in Kowloon and the New Territories, very few expatriates opt for this area. Recently, Harbour City, a new complex of luxury apartments (about

# Table 6

## Areas Where Americans Settle in Hong Kong

| Area | Location | Advantages | Disadvantages |
|---|---|---|---|
| Mid-Levels (including Conduit, MacDonnell, Kennedy, Magazine Gap, and Robinson Roads) | Halfway up Victoria Peak from the Central district; about ten minutes by taxi, bus, or car from Central | Closest to offices, shops, American Club, restaurants, Star Ferry, et cetera in Central district; in some areas within walking distance of Central; beautiful view of harbor; some new buildings but generally older units (can be a disadvantage, depending upon your taste); easiest access to Kowloon from the Island; near Island School; more international than purely American | Less convenient to the Hong Kong International School, although there is bus service; is on steep terrain and difficult to walk; traffic congestion; little play area for children; bad public transportation to beaches and the other side of the Island |
| The Peak | At the top of Victoria Peak and connected with Central by the Peak tram | Cooler in summer; use of Peak tram; traditionally the most exclusive; good views of both harbor and South China Sea; near German-Swiss International and Peak Junior schools; apartments older and more gracious, some with fireplaces | Further from Central; very humid and foggy at certain times of the year; relatively few shopping facilities nearby; greater exposure to typhoons |
| Repulse Bay (including Shouson Hill, Stanley, and Deepwater Bay) | On the south side of the Island about 25 minutes from Central in nonpeak rush-hour traffic | Newer units generally; more open, suburban feeling; near beaches; close to the Hong Kong International School; good American shopping; near several golf and other clubs | More Americanized and less international; furthest from Central; some newer units skimping on balconies and other amenities; beaches very crowded on summer weekends; lots of littering |
| Kowloon (including Waterloo Hill and Yau Yat Cheun) | On the mainland side | Cheaper rents; some one-family and garden units; convenient if office on this side; more open and flat; more a Chinese than an international community | Long commute to the Island; less prestigious; fewer foreign residents; less Americanized shopping; noise in some areas from Kai Tak Airport; generally smaller units; not as scenic |

3,000 square feet), opened in Kowloon along the waterfront and was rented quickly. Further phases are planned.

There are other new luxury complexes in the planning stages for Hong Kong, and even some on Lantau Island, which is the largest of the outer islands. Future plans call for Lantau to be linked with Kowloon by bridge and tunnel. A ban on further construction at the Mid-Levels has been lifted and new projects are under way. Some Europeans live on Lamma Island and commute daily by boat.

## *What You Get*

You get the bare rooms and not much more. By law the builder or owner need only supply very limited plumbing, kitchen facilities, and wiring. The new tenant has to furnish cabinets, appliances, additional electrical equipment, and fixtures.

Generally, apartments run from 1,500 to 4,000 square feet. A typical unit will consist of two or three bedrooms, two bathrooms, a big living room/dining room (although there are many with separate dining rooms), a kitchen, a maid's room and bath, and a balcony. One parking space is alloted free of charge in most buildings. Additional spaces are sometimes difficult to obtain.

Rarely is there any central heating. Although Hong Kong lies just inside the Tropic of Cancer, winter months can be cold and damp, as a chilling wind sweeps down from China. Summer months are extremely hot and humid. The problem is solved by the reverse-cycle air-conditioners (heat and cool units). Another solution is room heaters that can be moved about. You will need to buy water heaters—or "geysers," as they are known in England—for the kitchen, bath, and laundry, unless they have already been installed by the previous tenant.

Many apartments, particularly in the Peak area, have "hot rooms," usually large closets in which items such as leather goods, some foods, and clothing can be stored to combat the high humidity. Most closets have electrical outlets for heaters or bulbs to combat mildew.

If you need a repairman, he will gladly come—to check it out. Then someone else will have to come to do the work. If this is the limit of your repair experience, consider yourself lucky. It sometimes means severe frustration with the ever-obliging but mechanically inept service staff.

Electric current in Hong Kong is 220 volt/50 cycle. Since it is difficult to obtain adequate wiring for electric ranges, most people use gas ranges. Many apartments have a higher-power 15 amp wall plug for air-conditioners and similar appliances. Three-pronged plugs are standard.

Walls are literally as hard as nails. It is difficult to drive a nail or hanger into the hard concrete mixtures that are used in wall construction. Locally, you can buy the necessary high-carbon steel hangers that will do the trick.

Most of the older high-rise buildings have limited parking facilities, very little surrounding grounds, and only occasionally a pool. The new complexes being built and in the planning stages are multibuilding designs with pools, tennis courts, clubs, and other recreation areas.

## What it Costs

Rents are exorbitant! Over the past four years rents have soared due to the boom in the establishment of banks and other financial institutions and the increase in trade with China.

Besides the rent, you will be required to pay the "rates" or property taxes (11½ percent of the annual rental value established by the government—which is now below the actual open market rental value), management or maintenance fees (which can be several hundred to a couple thousand U.S. dollars a month), one-half of the government stamp duty at ½ percent of the annual rent, and your share of any legal costs. No key money is required. There may be a fee attached to any agent you use. All utilities will be paid by the tenant, and electricity is expensive. Running air-conditioners in the summer generates sizable electric bills. Some companies pay or contribute to the payment of these bills.

## Legal Considerations

The standard lease form is very favorable to the landlord, and very little is negotiable. The American Chamber of Commerce can provide some help in what tenants can do to protect themselves, or you can consult your attorney for advice. The basic rule is to take nothing for granted and negotiate on any point that you have doubts about or that is not covered.

If the fixtures and other improvements a tenant makes are removable, they are considered his and not the landlord's. The lease will not cover this, but a tenant should try to get agreement on this point from the landlord before making any installations. The tenant can elect to sell these fixtures to his successor.

A rather complicated series of laws concerning rent control and tenant security have been passed since 1973. Their application depends upon the age and the government-estimated rental value of the building. Even lawyers and real estate agents have difficulty understanding all the ramifications of these laws. The Hong Kong Commission of Rating and Valuation can answer any questions. The number for inquiries is 5-7957666.

One interesting result has been that landlords continue to prefer a lease with a corporation as the tenant in order to better secure rent payment and performance. However, now they also want a provision stating that the unit is "for the individual use of" the corporation's employee in order to obtain some benefits for landlords on personal leases.

## *Other Housing Pointers*

Electric wires are often not enclosed in conduits and are simply strung along the surface of a wall or ceiling.

The top floor of a high rise can be hot.

Older apartments have little closet or storage space unless installed by a previous tenant.

Lobbies will be quite bare.

## Domestic Help

The days of employing Chinese domestic help have just about ended. Young Chinese girls can find better pay and more independence in other jobs. Their replacements are young women from the Philippines and a few from Thailand. They are often fairly well educated and able to speak English. Their disadvantage, of course, is their lack of knowledge of the Chinese language and customs. You must pay their transportation to Hong Kong and guarantee their return home. Besides the air fare, you must also pay for their visas and extensions.

A live-in maid works six days a week, and a part-time girl works on a schedule agreed on in advance. For either, the wages are reasonable by Western standards. They are entitled to about a week's vacation at Chinese New Year and a bonus of one month's salary. Live-in maids are provided a room, some clothes, and occasionally medical expenses. A small television set may help to keep an exceptionally good maid. It is wise to obtain insurance coverage for your maid and to have a periodic health check.

Customarily a maid can be terminated on a month's notice, or sooner by paying a month's wages in lieu of notice.

## Children in Hong Kong

Children can have a difficult time adjusting to the comparative lack of freedom forced upon them by the life-style in the Territory. Small children in high-rise apartments face a life not unlike that in a large U.S. city. Someone must watch all their activities. Employing a trustworthy maid helps. Older children and teenagers also have fewer free-time opportunities, and jobs are hard to find. Parents say the answer is to get them involved in lessons, clubs, school activities, and sports. The terrain precludes bicycling and roller skating, things taken for granted in the United States. There are leagues for baseball, but none for soccer.

## Education

There is no free education for English-speaking children in Hong Kong. Students either attend government-subsidized schools with a relatively low tuition, or private schools with tuitions comparable to private institutions in the United States. All are coeducational. Many require uniforms.

Most American children attend the Hong Kong International School (6 South Bay Close, Repulse Bay, Hong Kong; telephone 5-92305). This school is sponsored by the Lutheran Church, Missouri Synod, and is fully accredited. Its curriculum is American, with special emphasis on foreign languages. More than 90 percent of the graduates go on to higher education in the United States. About 1,400 students attend kindergarten through twelfth grade. The majority are American, but there are children from many other countries. The staff numbers over 100.

The school plant and facilities are modern and attractive. There are active sports, music, and drama programs. As other activities for children in Hong Kong are limited, the school has an active and diverse extracurricular program. Uniforms are required in the primary grades. Bus transportation is available for an extra charge. Generally, the Hong Kong International School gets good marks from the American parents.

Other private schools are:

German Swiss International School
11 Guildford Road, the Peak
Hong Kong
Telephone 5-96216
This school has a stream for English-speaking children, providing instruction in both languages but preparing them for the English exams. It covers primary and secondary years.

L'Ecole Française Internationale
Borrett Road off Bowen Road, Mid-Levels
Hong Kong
Telephone 5-242907 / 5-237807
The L'Ecole is entirely a French school. Ground has been broken for a new campus at Jardine's Lookout on the Island, which will allow for expansion to about 700 students.

Two other national schools are:

Hong Kong Japanese School
157 Blue Pool Road
Hong Kong
Telephone 5-746479

Kellett School
2 Wah Lok Path
Wah Fu, Aberdeen
Hong Kong
Telephone 5-518234
The Kellett School is a new primary school in the largest housing estate on the Island. It follows the British system.

The English Schools Foundation built and administers, with considerable financial support from the government, several primary and secondary schools. These prepare students for the exams prerequisite to admission to British universities. Each school covers a specified area and accepts students only from that area. There are five primary schools on the Island: Kennedy (Mid-Levels), Glenealy (Mid-Levels), Quarry Bay (North Point), Peak (The Peak), and Causeway Bay (Causeway Bay). The secondary schools are the King George V School in Kowloon and the Island and South Island Schools on Hong Kong.

The Island School (20 Borret Road; telephone 5-247136) is considered quite good. There are about 1,200 students in this excellently equipped institution. Graduates go on to universities in both the United States and England.

Places in all the English-speaking schools are much in demand, so you should notify either the individual private school or the Foundation schools through the Foundation office (G.P.O. Box 11284) as soon as possible about your move to the Territory and your educational needs.

For preschoolers there are many private nursery schools. These will supplement the care of children provided by your maid. Bulletin boards at clubs and schools as well as the newspapers are good places to learn about these services.

If you have dreams of placing your child into the Chinese educational system to soak up the culture and learn the language, forget it. Like the Japanese educational program, this one is highly competitive; entrance exams run throughout the programs, making it terribly difficult to get into top schools and just about impossible for an expatriate to be accepted unless he is fluent in the local language. The frustrations, the competitiveness, and the strictness of the system would make the emotional strain on a Western child too severe.

Very little is available in the Hong Kong educational system for handicapped or gifted children. The government offers some speech assessment and therapy. There are two classes in the primary schools, but only for the less severely handicapped. Bear in mind also that the hilly terrain of the Island is a great problem for the physically handicapped. At times, parents have organized and funded private care and training for their children. Parents of gifted students often supplement the schools through correspondence courses. The Hong Kong International School does have advanced placement classes.

While there is no prohibition against non-Chinese enrollment in the two universities, the University of Hong Kong and the Chinese University, most expatriates send their children abroad for higher education, as do many of the more wealthy Chinese families.

Hong Kong University, the Hong Kong International School, and the Island School offer adult courses and evening courses in a variety of subjects from archeology to personnel administration.

## Weather

While Hong Kong has a subtropical climate, you will need some winter-weight clothes and possibly a coat for the first three months of the year. The Chinese women love to wear their furs at that time. The summers are hot and humid, creating a mold and mildew problem. Dehumidifiers or small heaters can protect clothing, camera equipment, and other susceptible articles. Typhoons menace Hong Kong. You should familiarize yourself with the ten-point warning system and know what to do when one of these Asian hurricanes hits.

## Shopping

In few other countries does shopping—where to go and what to buy—occupy such a prominent place in the life of the inhabitants, of the expatriates, and particularly of the tourists. Hong Kong is still considered the giant, duty-free, bargain-basement emporium of the world. Why else does shopping occupy such a major part of tourist literature? Where else can you find shopping malls and boutiques even in the most dignified office buildings? But before you open your wallet, some observations are in order. Inflation and rising wages have caused significant price increases. The camera you have long coveted may be cheaper in New York or perhaps Singapore. Nevertheless, luxury buying is on the upswing. Hong Kong has more Rolls Royces per mile than anywhere else, is the world's biggest consumer of fine brandy, and is the second largest import market for Swiss custom gold watches. All the leading haute couture designers of the world are represented in the Territory. Expatriates report that all the big items are available; it is only the little things, like chocolate chips, that are often hard to find.

Inevitably, you will be involved in shopping for "bargains," either for yourself, visitors, or friends back home. You may even find a good buy in a Korean chest, silk material from China, ivory, jade, gold, or a complete hi-fi outfit. There are many guides available, such as *The Hong Kong Shopper* by Michele Kay, the author of a weekly column on shopping in the *South China Morning Post*. It is a little out of date, but still a very complete listing of every category from antiques to toys and with some good general advice. You can find it in most bookstores. The Hong Kong Tourist Association issues *The Official Guide to the Best of Hong Kong Shopping,* available free of charge at its bookstore in the General Post Office Building on the Island and at Kai Tak Airport. Part of the charm of Hong Kong is "discovering" the shop that no one else knows.

Bargaining is customary but not universal. Fixed prices are quoted in several mainland Chinese stores, the department stores, and established branches of foreign stores. In the local shops and stalls, try your luck.

Be sure to get recommendations. Provide complete measurements for anything made to order. Experienced expatriates say a 75 percent rate of satisfaction is about par.

Some of the most interesting shopping takes place in the alleys connecting main thoroughfares in the Central district. Most have become well known for the merchandise in which they specialize. So you have a cloth alley, a flower alley, a hardware alley, and so on.

In 1974 the government formed the Consumer Council to protect and promote the interests of consumers of goods and services. It has sufficient funds and staff to make it an effective source of information on dealers for particular brands, product safety, product testing and evaluation, and service. It plays an active role in consumer complaints. The head office is at 6 Heard Street, Hong Kong; telephone 5-748297. The advice and complaint number is 5-747388.

## *Getting Settled*

### *Appliances*

The Consumer Council is an excellent source of information on which types of electric appliances to buy, as well as where to buy them. Also check with the Hong Kong Electric Co., Ltd. (Home Management Centre, 44 Kennedy Road, Hong Kong; telephone 5-7906535) or the Hong Kong and China Gas Company (Leighton Centre, Leighton Road, Hong Kong; telephone 5-760493). The ability to install and repair these appliances should be considered in your selection.

Used appliances can be purchased from departing families, and they are found advertised on bulletin boards, in the American Club newsletter, or the *South China Morning Post*. One shop that handles them is General Appliance (161 Queen's Road, Hong Kong; telephone 5-434818).

### *Furniture*

Hong Kong has the craftsmen and the beautiful woods (principally rosewood, teak, and blackwood) to make almost any style of furniture. Satisfaction is all but guaranteed—until you move back home. Variations in humidity can play havoc with pieces not constructed from fully dried wood. Your Hong Kong-made pieces will quite likely crack. Rosewood is less subject to cracking than the other woods. Check and double check your furniture maker to be sure he ages and dries his wood properly. Almost all say they do, but you cannot take this point for granted. One way to avoid this problem is to buy with the intention of reselling to another expatriate when you are ready to leave.

Rattan furniture remains a good buy in Hong Kong.

Most everything else needed to furnish your apartment can be found in Hong Kong. Don't be surprised when curtain and drapery makers come to your apartment to do their sewing. Many vendors that are supplying something that has to be made or measured for your apartment will do this at the site.

### *Daily Living*

The shopping guides already mentioned contain recommendations for items for daily living as well as luxury or tourist products. The American Women's Association puts out a periodical *Factory List,* which lists factory outlets and other lesser known but good sources for clothing, furniture, household needs, even Christmas trees. The $5 charge is a true bargain for this valuable list. The Community Advice Bureau (telephone 5-245444) includes shopping advice and sources in its excellent short Information Sheet, prepared with the help of the YWCA and available at the Bureau's office, St. John's Cathedral grounds, Garden Road, Hong Kong.

## Grocery Shopping

Virtually everything you ate at home is available in Hong Kong. Of course, there are isolated shortages of one thing and another, but there is also a variety of foods from all over the world that provide great flexibility in cooking. To help you get acquainted with the Chinese cuisine, read *Chopstick Recipes* (by Cecelia J. Au Yeung).

How you shop for food in the Territory is said to be a gauge of how long you have been living there. The newer arrivees will stick to the supermarkets with their frozen meats from the United States, Great Britain, Australia, and New Zealand. The better-known chains are Dairy Lane, Park 'n' Shop, and the Asia Provisions Company. The older residents shop more in the European manner by going to the speciality shops and large public markets.

Maintaining an account with your food supplier is a key to good service. A few of the supermarkets are leaning toward cash-and-carry only, but almost all suppliers will encourage accounts and deliver phone orders.

The big public markets are the places to go for the freshest and biggest selection of foods, with perhaps some savings. Several of them sell a really mixed variety of other items as well.

The biggest market in Hong Kong, the Central Market on Queens Road Central at Queen Victoria Street, is all food items. The daily prices are posted in the market and listed in the newspapers. You can see edibles from all over the world. As markets go, it is surprisingly clean.

In other markets—the Wanchai (Queens Road East near Kennedy Road), the Stanley Market, the Aberdeen Market, and many on Kowloon—you can buy such diverse items as marine supplies, shrines for ancestor worship, cheap rattan furniture, kitchen utensils, and fabrics, and the list goes on.

Watching the primitive but purportedly fairly accurate weighing devices of the shop owners is an entertaining lesson in the physics of weights and balances.

The best-known speciality shop for imported meat is the Colorado Meat Company (14 Wellington Street, Hong Kong; telephone 5-239139). Frozen meats at reasonable prices can be found at Sin Chung (2 Tai Wong Street, Hong Kong; telephone 5-279175).

Dairy Lane will deliver pasteurized milk, but it is expensive. Wines and liquors are available in many stores, especially the markets found in the major department stores. Some of the best bakeries are the retail stores in the leading hotels. Gourmet shops carry foods from Fortnum and Mason in London, delicatessen fare, Indian specialities, French cheeses, and other delicacies that satisfy even the most demanding appetite.

## Clothing

It is true that Hong Kong could be called the tailoring capital of the world, but there are significant gaps for the expatriate family wardrobe.

The best way to find a good tailor for both men's and women's clothing is by recommendation of other satisfied customers. There are thousands from which to choose, but the residents will usually stay away from those shops in the arcades or other places that tourists frequent.

Fabrics from all over the world are available, but Chinese silk and Hong Kong-made brocades are especially good buys. There are many cloth alleys with open stalls for both inexpensive and custom fabrics and accessories. Precise instructions for all details of the garment and very accurate measurements are a must.

Ready-made clothing is more of a problem. One of the anomalies of the Territory is that it is the world's ready-to-wear capital with more clothing exports than any other country in the world, but little finds its way into the local market. Nevertheless, there are many boutiques that carry the better-known American and European brand names.

Less expensive clothing, the Marks and Spencer brand from England, can be found at the Dodwell Chain in the Ocean Terminal (Kowloon; telephone 3-678280 or 3-673763) and in the Central Building (3 Pedder Street, Hong Kong; telephone 5-246666). Another place to look for less expensive clothing is the International Dress Shop (245 Ocean Terminal, Kowloon; telephone 3-673517), which features imported casual wear from Hawaii and California.

Moving up in style and price, you may go to the Mode Elite Ltd. (15 B On Lan Street, Hong Kong; telephone 5-227752). Two of the other leading fashion houses in the colony are the Dynasty Salon (Hong Kong Hilton Hotel, Hong Kong; telephone 5-237462) and the Dynasty Salon (Peninsula Hotel, Kowloon; telephone 3-687551).

In much of her shopping, the large Western woman may still find problems in the size and cut of her clothing. For example, many of the ready-made dresses from Europe or those made in Hong Kong will be too short-waisted. There are also problems with shoe sizes and fit, though you can select from the top European designers such as Gucci or Charles Jourdan or choose custom shoes made locally.

Jeans, sweaters, lingerie, gloves, maternity wear, leather wear, furs, and handbags are all available in good quality and variety.

Beautiful and expensive children's wear can be found at Annette's Boutique (Sheraton Hotel Shopping Mall, Kowloon; telephone 3-683828). Less expensive children's clothing and other items can be found in the larger department stores. Shoes have been a problem for children, but more are available in such stores as the Wing On department store.

Preteens have a more difficult time, and you may want to bring a good supply for this age group. But try the Crystal Company (160 Ocean Terminal, Kowloon; telephone 3-679689).

## Department Stores

There are several excellent department stores. These can be divided into those owned by the People's Republic of China and Western-style stores, some of which are branches of famous stores in Europe or Asia. But if you think more broadly in terms of a central place to buy many kinds of items, you should include the many arcades, hotels, and the spectacular Ocean Terminal/Ocean Centre complex, the largest air-conditioned and interconnected shopping center in Asia.

The Chinese stores are a fascinating contrast of cheap, simple ordinary household items and intricate or luxurious handicrafts. Silk material, linens, embroidery, decorative screens, carved ivory, and elaborate furniture all are worth your attention. A few of the better stores are:

Chinese Arts and Crafts (H.K.), Ltd.
233 Nathan Road
Kowloon
Telephone 3-670061

Lane Crawford Ltd.
70 Queen's Road C
Hong Kong
Telephone 5-266121

The Chinese Merchandise Emporium
92 Queen's Road C
Hong Kong
Telephone 5-241051

And probably the most popular store of all is:

Wing On Company Ltd.
26 Des Voeux Road Central
Hong Kong
Telephone 5-247171
It is also at several other locations.

Two others are:

Daimaru Department Store Co. Ltd.
Paterson Street
Causeway Bay
Hong Kong
Telephone 5-767321

Dragon Seed Co. Ltd.
39 Queens Road Central
Hong Kong
Telephone 5-242016

The Ocean Terminal/Ocean Centre, located adjacent to the Star Ferry Pier in Kowloon, is a multilevel, air-conditioned, enclosed mecca for shopping. It is filled with smart shops and restaurants, night clubs, a car-park, and an art gallery. It is hard to imagine anything that can't be found there—items range from a Chinese abacus to a toy zebra.

Similarly, most of the major hotels have beautiful and elaborate shopping arcades, particularly the Hong Kong Sheraton, the Furama Intercontinental, and the New World. Many of the department stores also have good food sections.

### Books

If you are a reader, be warned that books are expensive in the Territory. All are imported and marked up. Special titles can be ordered, but be prepared for a long wait. For the many publications on Hong Kong, go to the Government Publication Centre (GPO Building, Connaught Place, Hong Kong), just beside the Star Ferry Pier.

### Hardwares

The big, all-purpose hardware stores just do not exist in Hong Kong. You can find items by the trial-and-error or scavenger system through the many little alley shops. Decorating supplies can be located more easily. There are several wallpaper and decorating shops. Department stores may have some of these items, such as tools. The Evergreen stores in Admiralty Centre, Hong Kong (telephone 5-292320) and Ocean Centre, Kowloon (telephone 3-676147) handle some hardware items.

### Hairdressers, Beauty Shops, and Barbers

The major hotel shops are accustomed to foreigners and know the latest trends and techniques. In Central, barber shops are called beauty parlors and serve both sexes unless otherwise stated on the door.

### The True Bargains

Hong Kong has the biggest supply of Chinese antiques and art outside the People's Republic. *Provided* you can become knowledge-able enough or can find someone to help you, you can return home with some beautiful objets d'art to enjoy or to keep as an investment.

There is one shopping source that the old-timers know all about where some really good buys can be found: factory outlets. These lists are closely guarded, but here are a few to get you started:

The Christian Monastery (porcelain)
Tai Fo Shan Rd.
Tai Fo Shan
Shatin

Tai Wing Hong Garment Factory (leather coats)
19 Beech Street 8/F
Tai Kok Tsui
Telephone 3-940177

Tinkerbell (private residence; for children's clothing handmade
  in the Philippines)
5/A Eredine
38 Mt. Kellett Road
Hong Kong
Telephone 5-96119

Today the overnight suit is not of good quality. Jewelry, cameras, watches, hi-fi equipment, and calculators are cheaper than in Japan, but they are not the great bargains they once were. You probably will find them for less in Singapore. Often, the best arrangement is for you or your company to establish one or two shops that you patronize exclusively in return for the "bottom price."

Jewelry continues to be worth considering because precious stones can enter the Territory duty-free. Check *The Shopper's Guide to Jewelry in Hong Kong* put out by the Tourist Association. U.S. Custom's regulations make it more advantageous to bring back unset stones.

Gold is sold in Hong Kong in bar form by the *tael* (a Chinese weight of about 1.3 ounces) or as jewelry. The government makes every effort to prevent cheating by using a hallmark, the misuse of which carries severe penalties.

## Transportation

Commensurate with its size, the Territory has one of the most diverse and overcrowded transportation systems in the world, and one of the highest traffic densities. Improvements such as new tunnels, a subway, and elevated limited access roads do not seem to make a dent. Even on the Island a commute of close to an hour is not unusual.

## Private Cars

Private vehicles are a real problem for their owners. Parking is still very difficult despite the construction of new public parking facilities. Narrow, one-way streets make the statement "You can't get there from here" meaningful.

The government has adopted a policy of discouraging the import of vehicles by steadily raising the registration and license fees. This, and the right-hand drive requirement, make importation of cars by Americans unfeasible.

If you are staying in Hong Kong for 12 months or less, you can drive on your valid overseas license or international permit. Otherwise, you must have a Hong Kong license, which will be issued without a test on the strength of your valid license. You must have a Hong Kong ID card and two photos.

## Taxis

Taxis, most of which are air-conditioned, can be quite difficult to get at rush hours, weekends, holidays, when it is raining, and in the afternoon when shifts change. Radio cabs are listed in the yellow pages, but are fast disappearing.

When you wave down a cab, you may find that it is from another section, does not know your destination, and does not want to drive you. While most drivers on the Island will recognize locations given in English, many on Kowloon do not. A good way to locate yourself or to show a non-English-speaking driver your destination is to use *Hong Kong Streets and Places Guidebook,* which has addresses in Chinese and English. It is available in all bookstores.

*Pak pais,* or illegal taxis (therefore uninsured), are quite prevalent. Often, they will service particular large apartment buildings. Fares are about the same as for legal cabs.

Small change is acceptable as a tip.

## Buses

Buses, many of which are of the double-decker variety, serve the major areas on the Island and Kowloon. Fares are very cheap. Many have just one driver/collector. You pay a fixed fare for each route regardless of your destination. Remember that exact fares are required as the driver carries no change.

Public Light Buses, or minibuses, are cream and red and run more or less regular routes. Maxicabs have a green stripe and run on franchised routes. In both cases destinations and fares are in Chinese, making them difficult to utilize unless you are familiar with the route.

Trams are found on the Island, running along the main streets parallel to the harbor.

## Mass Transit Railway

The Mass Transit Railway (MTR) underground subway that opened in 1980 provides fast, comfortable service from Central on the Island across to Kowloon, and then on by two branches into the New Territories. Further extensions are now being constructed. Tickets are issued by automatic machines for the fare amount listed for different stops. These machines make no change, so you will need coins no larger than a HK$2 piece. For higher coins or bills, you will need to get in line for change at a window. The tickets are plastic cards similar to a thin credit card. You insert them as you enter a turnstile and the ticket is returned to you immediately. You keep it and insert it again at departure, at which time the machine automatically determines if you have paid the correct fare.

## Trains

The Kowloon-Canton Railway runs from the Territory to Sheung Shui across the border in China. First-class tickets can be reserved a week in advance. This is a very busy service now, and has just recently been completely electrified.

## Other Modes

There are three modes of transportation that are unique and have become famous through stories and movies about Hong Kong: the rickshaw, the Star Ferry, and the Peak Tram.

There is no hope for the survival of that epitome of individual entrepreneurship, the rickshaw man. Traffic reluctantly and barely makes room for these vehicles. The government is granting no more licenses. Yet, there are still clusters of them around the ferry piers and hotels, ready to provide a tourist with one of the world's oldest examples of transportation.

For years, the Star Ferry has been the principal transporter of people across the harbor. Service is frequent and inexpensive and provides an unsurpassed close-up view of the busy harbor and its anchored ships from all over the world. There are many other ferry services to other points and islands.

The Peak Tram is the famous cable railway that runs from the Central district to the top of Victoria Peak. It is a great tourist attraction, and residents also take advantage of its four intermediate stops to get to their homes on the Mid-Levels and on the summit.

## Communications

### *Telephone and Mail Service*

Hong Kong's success as a major business center is due in no small part to its superior communications facilities with the rest of the world. It also has very efficient internal telephone and mail services. Hong Kong had a telephone system only six years after Alexander Graham Bell registered his first telephone patent.

New telephones can be installed by the Hong Kong Telephone Company after a waiting period of a week or so. The basic charge is a monthly rental that is very reasonable and covers all calls within the Territory. There are slight additional charges for other features such as extensions, color or push-button phones, and long-distance privileges. Direct-long-distance dialing is available in most areas for a modest refundable deposit. Or you can obtain an international call code number, which allows you to make long-distance calls from any phone. There is rarely a wait for an overseas circuit.

Excellent telecommunications facilities are provided by the English firm Cable and Wireless Company, Ltd., including leased circuits, data transmissions, and facsimile and earth satellite services. A short waiting period is required for a telex installation.

Mail delivery is cheap and fast. The great majority of letters mailed before 6 p.m. are delivered the following day. Most areas have deliveries twice a day. Express mail and "speedpost" services provide guaranteed rapid delivery to major countries within 24 to 48 hours.

### *Radio and Television*

Both radio and television have one government station (Radio Television Hong Kong [RTHK]) and two or three commercial stations or channels. No license fee is required for radio or television reception. RTHK operates one AM and one FM English service, and the FM has some stereo programs. The service provides news, weather, music, discussion programs, and a 15-minute Cantonese lesson three nights a week. The one English commercial service is mostly musical (lighter than RTHK), with periodic news, weather, and stock market reports.

RTHK generally produces educational and public service television programs, which are shown on time alloted by law from commercial stations. The two private stations have an English program primarily in the evening that consists of American and English reruns as well as some locally produced shows.

American television sets are not compatible with the Hong Kong transmission system. It is not necessary to buy a set because they may be rented.

## Publications

There are four English-language daily newspapers and 63 in Chinese. The leading English-language one is the *South China Morning Post,* which has many U.S. columnists. Another is the *Hong Kong Standard.* The only English evening paper is the *Star,* which is less conservative than the morning papers. They are delivered to your door.

The *Asian Wall Street Journal* and the *International Herald Tribune* are printed in Hong Kong and can be delivered to your apartment or office in the morning. The Pacific edition of *Stars and Stripes* provides U.S. news, particularly detailed sports reports.

Papers from many of the world's major cities are flown in and may be only a day or two late. Almost all popular magazines from the United States, Britain, and Europe are found, although some may be a month or so behind. This is not the case with the international or Asian editions of the news magazines, *Reader's Digest,* and the *Far Eastern Economic Review.*

## Free Time

Leisure activity and recreation in Hong Kong is really what you and your family make of it. While the Territory is not a cultural or recreational wasteland by any means, it simply does not have the space in the urban areas and the other means to support full-time, first-rate, professional drama and music or to provide enough facilities for spectator and participatory sports. Much of your leisure time—and perhaps all, if you are so inclined—will involve mingling with others in the international expatriate community at parties, clubs, and other get-togethers.

But take heart. If you have dreaded the obligatory cocktail party at home with its banal conversation and test of stamina of feet and legs, don't isolate yourself in the Territory. Hong Kong is one of the most stimulating and important international centers of commerce and diplomacy. Conversation at a Hong Kong party, with the beautiful harbor or the South China Sea serving as a background, can be fascinating. It's the people, thrown together as in no other location, that make Hong Kong exciting.

During the holiday season it would not be unusual to have one or perhaps several social engagements each night. Spouses could very well be on the go at noon also. As many expatriates will tell you, this makes demands on your wardrobe. Often women will buy their ready-to-wear clothes in the United States on leave to avoid seeing the same outfit sitting across the table from them.

In the past, one of the most stimulating opportunities was being able to meet and mingle with people of many nationalities. Now, expatriates point out, the national groups tend to stay more to themselves, despite the fact that many clubs and organizations have a planned policy of multinational membership. Your business contacts can bring you in touch with other nationals. Many engagements are business-centered, but it is not the same as in Japan, where partying after hours is a ritual.

The Chinese usually entertain in restaurants or hotels rather than at home. Often the wives of the Chinese hosts will not be present. One American woman, whose husband has worked for a local company for four years, has never met the wife of her husband's boss. If you do get a rare invitation to a Chinese home, take a small gift to show your appreciation.

## Sports

Many of the major sports facilities—such as golf, tennis, squash, swimming, and riding—are available through private clubs. All expatriates stress that newcomers should know the sports club membership situation in Hong Kong. Waiting lists for individual memberships are very long, and you may have to wait several years to be accepted. The only way an expatriate can get prompt membership is if his company has its own membership. Such memberships are obtained by the company's purchase of very costly debentures, in effect a nonrecoverable contribution. Even these are scarce.

The Royal Hong Kong Golf Club has three 18-hole courses in the New Territories. Shek-O Country Club has a beautiful course on the Island. Public tennis courts do exist; they are on a first-come, first-served basis on weekdays and can be reserved for weekends up to seven days in advance by registering at the courts.

Both the Hong Kong International Schools and the Island School (see Education section) have pools and programs for adult and family swimming. The Hong Kong government has built several public pools, but they are very crowded, as are the public beaches.

There are 41 public beaches in Hong Kong and the New Territories, with toilets, changing facilities, snack bars, and life-guards during the summer months. Many are in beautiful natural settings that compare with those in Mexico or Hawaii. On week-ends, however, the crowds are beyond belief. It is only during the week, when the crowds have thinned out and the litter cleaned up, that they are enjoyable. Even then you may still be bothered by water pollution from the cottage industries and oil tankers.

Many expatriates find the hundreds of natural beaches on outer islands much more attractive swimming locations. These are quite crowded on weekends also. They utilize one of the most popular diversions in getting there—boating. The waters and islands of Hong Kong are ideal for boating of all kinds. One important precaution, however, is to have a good navigator to avoid straying into the waters of neighboring China.

### Boating

Almost everything about boating is probably less expensive in Hong Kong than at home. New sailboats or junks and used boats of all kinds are readily available. Imported power boats are more expensive, however. To keep expenses down, you can rent or go together with friends to buy a share of any kind of boat. Boat owners who have slaved over maintenance at home will thoroughly enjoy the services of a boat boy, who will look after everything and live on the boat for relatively little money.

Two certificates are required to pilot a boat in Hong Kong waters: a coxswains ticket and an engineer's certificate, both adminis-tered by the Marine Department. Local courses are given to qualify.

The focal point of boating in Hong Kong has been the Royal Hong Kong Yacht Club in Causeway Bay. Now the entrance to the cross harbor tunnel and new expressways are encroaching on its regal isolation, but it provides deluxe facilities for the boater who can manage a membership.

## *English Carryovers*

Being a British colony, it is natural that the traditional adjuncts to English civilization—cricket and soccer—are alive and very well played. Most other sports are not neglected. There are clubs or organizations for everything from badminton to water skiing.

## *Horse Racing*

Hong Kong's most popular spectator sport is horse racing. This is the most overt, and the only legal, sign of the Chinese dedication to gambling (except possibly for the Hong Kong stock market). Racing is sponsored and controlled by the Royal Hong Kong Jockey Club, a nonprofit organization with approximately 2,000 members. The Club has two courses: the famous Happy Valley track very near Central and a magnificent new circuit seating 37,000 in Shatin in the New Territories. Many companies have boxes at the track. Traffic on race days is abysmal.

## *American Sports*

There is an active Little League program that primarily involves American and Japanese players. The Hong Kong Softball Association has programs for men and women, as well as a clubhouse and tennis courts. Basketball and football are part of the Hong Kong International School program.

## **Entertainment and the Arts**

The two centers for the performing arts are the Hong Kong Arts Center and the City Hall. A third planned complex at Tsimshatsui (Kowloon) is in the construction stage. The City Hall is not the municipal seat of government, but rather the principal cultural center for the Territory. It contains a 1,400-seat concert hall, which is also used for theater productions; a 400-seat theater and cinema; a 120-seat recital hall; the Hong Kong Museum of Art; the main public library; and two restaurants.

The Hong Kong Arts Center on the Wanchai waterfront houses a multipurpose theater, a recital hall, an experimental studio theater, art galleries, an open-air sculpture terrace, practice rooms, and a photography studio and darkroom. Above these facilities are three floors of restaurants and offices of various cultural organizations.

The 82-player Hong Kong Philharmonic Orchestra performs a subscription series on Fridays and Saturdays at City Hall. It attracts outstanding soloists and guest conductors.

The government's Urban Council plays a major role in the recreational and cultural life of the Territory. In 1980 the Queen Elizabeth Stadium (a 3,500-seat, air-conditioned facility) was opened for all indoor sports and cultural activities. City Hall is administered by the Council for the many concerts, recitals, and performances it sponsors. In 1981 over half a million people heard artists of international repute. A typical weekly announcement of the Council's programs in the newspaper will list theater, dance, orchestral, individual recital, and jazz performances.

There are several theatrical groups in the Territory, the best known being the Hong Kong Stage Club, the Garrison Players, and the American Community Theater.

Two active choral groups are the Hong Kong Singers and the Robin Boyle Chorus, which present one or two cantatas, operettas, or musicals during the year. Free lunchtime concerts and recitals are presented by the Hong Kong Arts Center in association with St. John's Cathedral at the church on Wednesday noons.

## *Cinemas*

There are over 100 cinemas in Hong Kong and about one-third of them show U.S. or British pictures. The English-language films have Chinese subtitles and vice versa. Movies are very popular, so it is wise to reserve seats in advance by telephone. Tickets will be held until 15 minutes before performance time. The Hong Kong Board of Censors edits out much of the violence as well as the more risqué scenes from foreign movies, but leaves in much of this in the locally produced melodramas by the Shaw Brothers, who are the founders of the kung fu genre. Hong Kong distributors also contribute to the frustration of movie purists by arbitrarily cutting film to shorten the running time and thus have more showings.

If you want to see some of the scenes or movies that are not otherwise available in the public theaters, you can join Studio One (Post Office Box 5169, Hong Kong). Several of the national clubs, such as the American and French, present movies for their members and guests.

## Popular Attractions

One unique recreation facility that you will visit and probably revisit is the world's largest oceanarium, Ocean Park, located between Aberdeen and Repulse Bay. This 170-acre park is divided between a Low Lands Site near Deep Water Bay and the Head Lands Complex. These sites are connected by one of the world's largest capacity cable car systems, with six-seat cars furnishing a spectacular view of the park and the South China Sea at no extra charge.

Two newer and very popular attractions here are the dome-shaped Space Museum and Sung Dynasty Village, one looking into the future and the other commemorating the past. The museum has an exhibition hall, the Hall of Solar Science, and the Space Theater. It is located right in front of the Peninsula Hotel in Kowloon (telephone 3-7212361). The Space Theater has only one English show a day. Sung Dynasty Village in the New Territories is a re-creation of a village that existed a thousand years ago. Villagers wear the costumes of the period.

## Dining Out

Perhaps the most popular entertainment in Hong Kong is eating. If anything takes precedence over gambling, it is the appetite. Estimates are that 1.5 million people eat out daily in the Territory, the highest per capita rate in the world. The telephone directory's largest section is restaurant listings: over 5,000 entries. These include establishments that offer dishes from many countries, from Argentina to Vietnam. The Chinese have developed one of the great cuisines of the world with many regional variations. The one thing they have in common is that they all use chopsticks. Robert Elegant, author of *Dynasty* and the Time-Life book on Hong Kong, states that it would be possible to dine out every night for two years at a different restaurant without repeating a single dish. Few expatriates care to be that adventurous or esoteric in their dining, but there is no question that Hong Kong provides the ultimate contrast to the fast-food franchise monotony.

## Getting Away

Hong Kong has a country parks system that encompasses 40 percent of the total land area. There are 21 parks with 2,500 species of trees, and the Hong Kong Bird Watching Society has reached 350 bird species. One of the most popular trails for both amateur and serious hikers is the 62-mile Macklehose Trail, which is named after the governor of the Territory. It has ten segments, so you can determine the extent of your exertions quite easily. Jogging is increasing, but there are limited areas on the Island that are flat enough to attract the average runner.

## Clubs and Organizations

An invaluable organization is the Community Advice Bureau, where you can get an answer to almost any question. The service is free and run by very experienced and knowledgeable volunteers. The office is on the second floor of one of the buildings within the St. John's Cathedral compound, although it is not connected with the church. Office hours are Monday through Friday, 9:30 a.m. to 4 p.m. (telephone 5-245444). Just call or go in for an answer to your questions on shopping, classes, housing, or any other subject.

Periodically the bureau sponsors a program, "Discovering Hong Kong," that exposes the newcomer to the culture, literature, philosophy, history, and customs of the Chinese.

Other orientation programs on Chinese culture and living in Hong Kong are offered by the University of Hong Kong, the Hong Kong International School, the Hong Kong Tourist Association, and the Jewish Women's Association.

The YWCA sponsors a program called "At Home in Hong Kong" for new wives. Groups of about 12 women—ten newcomers and two more experienced hostesses—meet for eight consecutive Monday mornings to discuss all the problems of getting settled, as well as to get to know each other.

The American Club, located on the twelfth floor of the St. George's Building, 2 Ice House Street, Hong Kong (telephone 5-244013), is primarily an eating establishment not unlike the downtown eating clubs in the United States. It has several dining rooms, lounges, and private function rooms. All Americans over age 21 and living in the Territory can join. It sponsors a family bowling league and several golf outings a year. Members' children between the ages of 12 and 21 can be junior members. The Chuckwagon, serving American food, is the teenage hangout.

The American Women's Association, with over 1,000 members—51 percent American—is active in many social and philanthropic areas. It has its own welcome meetings for newcomers, "Foon Ying." Its other activities include classes, lectures, tours, luncheons, the *Factory List,* and many more that improve living in the Territory.

The American Chamber of Commerce of Hong Kong is one of the most active of the 50 chambers around the world. It helps businessmen who need information on Hong Kong or China by arranging breakfast and luncheon briefings with experts as part of its "Information, Please" program just for the price of a meal. Another important function is the Summer Youth Program, which coordinates the location of summer employment for American teenagers. The address of the chamber is Swire House 10/F, 25 Chater Road, Hong Kong (telephone 5-260165).

## Churches

Religion for the Chinese involves little formal worship, but it does play a significant part in their daily lives. The two principal religions are Buddhism and Taoism. Hong Kong has its share of old and new temples and monasteries that people may visit any time they wish. The most public expression of worship or celebration is seen during the five major festivals, with the Lunar New Year the most important.

From a more personal standpoint, there are a great number of deities, gods, and patron saints for every aspect of daily life. The most popular are those connected with the sea and the weather—Tin Hau, the Taoist Queen of Heaven and protector of seafarers, is said to be worshipped by hundreds of thousands. Almost all households and many shops have their own shrines.

Ancestor worship or respect is another fundamental of Chinese existence. This is the basis for specific and complex rules for the conduct of sons toward fathers and other intrafamily relationships.

Organized Christianity dates back almost to the beginning of Hong Kong. Today, there are nearly 600 churches and chapels, and the estimated number of Christians is 500,000, about 10 percent of the total population. These churches engage in a wide-reaching program of education, family services, health care, and social welfare.

While the great majority of Christian churches conduct their services in Chinese, there are several that are English speaking:

Protestant

    Kowloon English Baptist
      Church
    300 Junction Road
    Kowloon
    Telephone 3-372555

Church of Christ
148 Prince Edward Road,
  Fifth Floor
Kowloon
Telephone 3-819915

English Methodist Church
271 Queen's Road, East
Hong Kong
Telephone 5-741714

Interdenominational
Emmanuel Church
218 Nathan Road
Kowloon
Telephone 3-670747

Union Church
Kennedy Road
Hong Kong
Telephone 5-221515

Kowloon Union Church
4 Jordan Road
Kowloon
Telephone 3-672585

Church of Jesus Christ of the
  Latter-Day Saints
2 Cornwall Street
Kowloon Tong
Telephone 3-361261

West Point Branch
7 Castle Road
Hong Kong
Telephone 5-236925

Church of All Nations
  (Lutheran)
8 South Bay Close
Hong Kong
Telephone 5-920375

Nathan Road Lutheran
  Church
(Missouri Synod)
Truth Lutheran Church
50 Waterloo Road
Kowloon
Telephone 3-806909

Zion Lutheran Church
275 King's Road
Hong Kong
Telephone 5-705818

Pentecostal Tabernacle
71 Waterloo Road
Kowloon
Telephone 3-035455

Society of Friends
Bishop's House
1 Lower Albert Road
Hong Kong
Telephone 5-228264

Salvation Army
555 Nathan Road
Kowloon
Telephone 3-884141

First Church of Christ
  Scientist
31 MacDonald Road
Hong Kong
Telephone 5-228591

Seventh Day Adventist
  Church
40 Stubbs Road
Hong Kong
Telephone 5-746211

Roman Catholic

  Cathedral
  16 Caine Road
  Hong Kong
  Telephone 5-228212

St. Anne's Church
Stanley
Hong Kong
Telephone 5-93206

St. Joseph's Church
Garden Road
Hong Kong
Telephone 5-223992

St. Peter's Seamen's Church
11 Middle Road
Kowloon
Telephone 3-688261

St. Teresa's Church
258 Prince Edward Road
Kowloon
Telephone 3-360048

Anglican

Christ Church
132 Waterloo Road
Kowloon
Telephone 3-360848

St. Andrew's Church
138 Nathan Road
Kowloon
Telephone 3-671478

St. John's Cathedral
Garden Road
Hong Kong
Telephone 5-255111

Jewish

Synagogue Othel Leah
70 Robinson Road
Hong Kong
Telephone 5-225611

## Health Care

Expatriates are cautioned to have medical insurance when they come to Hong Kong because of the high cost of private medical treatment. Local insurance through Blue Cross or other insurance companies is available.

Medical facilities and skills are considered quite good. Government hospitals have 24-hour emergency and trauma centers. Most expatriates use the private sector, and there are several good hospitals for private patients. One, the Adventist Hospital, located at 40 Stubbs Road, Hong Kong (telephone 5-746211), has a 24-hour casualty center. 999 is the emergency number in Hong Kong for all police, fire, and health emergencies.

# Macao

With a reputation (at least for those who haven't been there) of oriental mystery and perhaps sin, one should know something about this Portuguese colony just 45 minutes from Hong Kong by jetfoil. It is the oldest continuous European settlement in the Far East, with a history going back over 400 years. Although only six square miles, it has played an important role in trade between China and the outside world. The tea ships invaded by American patriots at the Boston Tea Party sailed from Macao.

As a place where European and Asian cultures have melded, the city is a charming mixture of stately colonial buildings, oriental temples, Christian cathedrals, lovely homes, and gardens, all conveying the feeling of a great trade center that has lost its vitality and is going through a dignified old age.

What keeps Macao alive and intriguing is the gambling 24 hours a day, seven days a week. There are four casinos, all owned and operated by the same company. These range from a slightly shabby but deluxe casino at the Hotel Lisboa to Chinese casinos where fan-tan and dai-sui are played. Other gambling outlets are a jai alai fronton and a dog track.

But if gambling is not for you, Macao can serve as a good getaway from Hong Kong. Its sights and cuisine provide a nice break from the Hong Kong bustle. Try a bicycle for seeing the sights.

The unit of currency is the *pataca,* about equal to one Hong Kong dollar. Hong Kong currency is readily accepted, but do not bring *patacas* back.

A visa is required for everyone except Hong Kong residents of two months or more and a few other nationals. Macao makes it simple to obtain one on entering if you do not pick one up in Hong Kong.

## Doing Business in Hong Kong

The publication *Doing Business in Hong Kong* describes the unique character of Hong Kong that most expatriates feel sooner or later:

> The British Crown Colony of Hong Kong can best be described as an anomaly—a capitalistic enclave situated at the mouth of a communist giant; a territory populated by more than 5¹/₂ million Chinese governed by a small British minority; a thriving colony in an age when colonialism is distinctly out of favor or fashion; an outpost with a possible death sentence which attracts long term investment; a large and bustling environment which has never lost its small town atmosphere.

There are good reasons why Hong Kong has changed from a sleepy link in the opium trade to a major supplier of quality merchandise bearing internationally famous names and labels. There are more good reasons why it is rapidly becoming one of the world's top two or three international finance centers. They all add up to making Hong Kong the world's showplace and maybe the last bastion of the laissez-faire economy.

Just think! No exchange controls, no antitrust laws, no local ownership requirements, no militant unions, no governmental control or reporting (except for the barest minimum), low taxes, ample financing, and excellent infrastructure. Only business without all the outside forces that businessmen around the world point to as being the real roadblocks to success.

This does not mean that business in the colony is without rules, patterns, and customs. In fact, the lack of government interference places a greater burden on the businessman to establish a viable business morality. The result is a blend of Western (primarily British) and Chinese practices.

At the outset it is necessary to put into perspective the extent of corruption in Hong Kong. One of the government's own publications, *Hong Kong—the Facts*, admits that corruption has been widespread in both government and the private sector. In 1971 the Territory passed the Prevention of Bribery Ordinance that created new offenses and increased penalties, including prison terms. Still, there was great concern over the adequacy of the enforcement of this law. So in 1973 the Independent Commission against Corruption (ICAC) was created. By the end of the second year it had investigated 7,000 reports of corruption and attained convictions of 244 violators, including police officers and other civil servants as well as people in the private sector. The commission seems to be achieving its purpose.

The laws prohibit illicit payments to civil servants. In certain instances the private sector is covered as well. Specifically, it is against the law for a company to offer an "advantage" to an employee of another firm without the approval of the employee's superior. The exchange of traditional Christmas and Chinese New Year gifts has come under the scrutiny of the ICAC. The expatriate businessman will have to know how the local laws and customs are affected or modified by his company's own standards or code of conduct. Certainly the U.S. Foreign Corrupt Practices Act overlaps the Hong Kong laws in some respects and places restrictions on foreign subsidiaries of U.S. companies.

As in other parts of Asia, "face" and the loss of it are serious concerns to the Chinese. Always provide an avenue of honorable retreat for Chinese who may have been in error, or who may not be able to answer you or provide you with the assistance you need.

Typically, the Chinese businessman will not entertain you at his home. Functions are held in public restaurants or clubs. As in Japan, wives are seldom invited unless the host is very westernized. The traditional Chinese meal is long with at least one dish more than the number of guests. The meal is accompanied by frequent toasts.

The business card in Hong Kong, as in Japan, is an essential tool to identify and remember your business contacts.

Learning Chinese—or more accurately, Cantonese—is a task for which few foreigners will have the time and patience. Since Hong Kong is bilingual officially, most business, governmental, and social contacts will be in English. Knowing a few words or phrases will help, however, if you can achieve a pronunciation that will prevent you from sounding completely ridiculous. There are many stories of how slight variations in tone by a foreigner, thereby stating the wrong word, can result in very silly or insulting occurrences.

Any westerner doing business in Hong Kong must never forget the importance of *fung shui*, literally "wind water." The *fung shui* expert determines the most propitious circumstances for starting any project and for appeasing evil spirits. If proper deference is not paid to these spiritual laws, bad *joss* ("luck") will be the result.

Women in upper management are still not accepted completely and naturally. Women's liberation is not an intense goal in the Territory—yet. This is unusual because women in China traditionally have been a strong force commercially as well as in the family.

Getting things done is a problem voiced by many expatriates. They have found that the everyday office skills, perhaps something as simple as preparing an important presentation in a folder, are difficult for many of the local staff. Word processing and similar technical innovations have just begun to appear.

Trade with the People's Republic of China presents some special problems. Here language is critical. The mainland Chinese who are specifically assigned to duties bringing them into contact with westerners speak excellent English. But in most commercial situations, an interpreter is mandatory. This is where you can run into trouble. There are so many dialects in China that there is a high probability of error in translation of some commercial or technical terms. China realizes this and is trying to institute reforms in three areas: simplicity of written characters, popularization of one dialect (Mandarin), and use of the *pinyin* system of latinized spelling of Chinese words. Special emphasis is being given to scientific language reform.

There are many people in Hong Kong who purport to be experts in trade with the mainland, most quite legitimate and truly skilled but a few simply opportunists. The American Chamber of Commerce has prepared an excellent book, *Doing Business with China*, that will get you started down the right path.

Macao is now getting some attention as a busines site. It's biggest plus is location. Close to Hong Kong by jetfoil, it has road access to Canton. Land and labor are cheaper and more available than in the Territory. Foreign exchange transactions are unrestricted. One thing it lacks: the excellent port facilities of its larger neighbor.

There are some clouds on the horizon. Hong Kong is experiencing inflation. Some labor unrest is appearing. Businessmen may find that greater attention must be given to preserving Hong Kong's greatest national resource—its workers.

## Legal Matters

### *The Courts*

The same common law system that is the basis for U.S. and British Commonwealth jurisprudence is the foundation of Hong Kong law. English acts of Parliament are generally not in force in the colony unless specifically adopted by the Hong Kong Legislative Council, or so stated in their own terms. The fundamental laws and protections for individuals have been enacted locally.

The court system begins with the magistrates courts (primarily criminal) and the district courts (both civil and criminal). The next levels are the high court and the court of appeal. Appeals from this last court can go to the judicial committee of the Privy Council in London.

There are other special tribunals: tenancy, labour, lands, and small claims, whose jurisdictions are just as their names imply. Small claims can handle any matter under HK$3,000.

Expatriates feel that they are treated quite fairly and equally. In fact, any English-speaking person has one distinct advantage in Hong Kong courts: all proceedings are in English.

You may have a chance to participate in the system through jury service. Expatriates are called fairly frequently and may serve anywhere from three days to three weeks.

### Births

To register a birth, one of the parents must appear at the Birth and Death Registry with the parent's passport and certificate of marriage within 42 days after the birth. The U.S. Consular Service should be consulted for a State Department birth certificate that will be honored in the United States.

### Deaths

The person reporting the death, preferably a close relative or someone present at the time of death, should go to the same Birth and Death Registry within 24 hours after death with the deceased's passport and a medical death certificate. If there is any suspicion of death by other than natural causes or if there is an inquiry by the coroner, the registration of death shall await the coroner's report. The Consular Service at the embassy will handle the U.S. documentation and assist in the arrangements for transport of the body.

### Marriages

Marriages are registered in the Marriage Registry in the city hall. The parties first file their intent, and a notice is posted for 17 days. If there is no objection, the marriage is recorded. One local lawyer advised that if Hong Kong will not register a marriage (as when one of the parties had a "quickee" divorce not honored in the Territory), the best place to go to get married is Singapore.

## *Divorces*

### *Who Can File for Divorce?*

In order for a divorce to take place in Hong Kong, at least one of the two parties must be resident in the Territory. Ordinarily residence of three months will meet this requirement. In addition, the two parties must have been married for at least three years. Annulment of a marriage existing for less than three years is only possible if it has not been consummated.

### *What Constitutes Grounds for Divorce?*

Irretrievable breakdown of the marriage must be established before a court decree of divorce can be issued. Evidence of such breakdown is demonstrated by proof of any of the following conditions:

1.  Unreasonable behavior;
2.  Adultery;
3.  Separation for two years (if both parties consent to the divorce) or for five years (if the divorce is contested). The separation need not be by court decree; it is sufficient that the parties simply not be living with each other for the required length of time.

### *Is It Necessary to Hire an Attorney?*

In all but the simplest cases it is advisable to employ an attorney to handle the divorce action. As of January 1982 the minimum fee likely to be charged by private legal counsel is HK$4,000-5,000. A list of attorneys practicing in Hong Kong and handling divorce cases is available at the American consular services unit on the first floor of the consulate general. If a wife is without funds and seeks legal counsel, she may apply to the Legal Aid Department of the Hong Kong Government for assistance. No such assistance is available for husbands. Legal advice on an informal basis from the Hong Kong Law Society may be applied for through any City District Office (CDO).

*How Long Will It Take to Obtain a Divorce?*

Given the heavy backlog of cases on the dockets of the Hong Kong district courts (the courts that have jurisdiction over divorce cases), it normally takes six months to obtain a decree nisi. This decree becomes final after three months if no objection is raised. Thus, any American citizen contemplating divorce in Hong Kong must be prepared to wait nine months after the initiation of divorce action for the divorce to become final. Obviously, this period of time would be extended if the divorce were contested.

## Crime

Hong Kong is astoundingly crime-free by U.S. standards. In a Territory with a population nearly half that of New York City, murders usually run about 3 percent by comparison. Most crime centers in the Walled City of Kowloon, two-and-a-half acres of festering tenements jammed with 30,000 Chinese in the midst of Kowloon's elegant shopping and hotels. Both England and China assert sovereignty because of an anomaly in the 1898 treaty granting the 99-year lease to Britain; but neither can rule effectively. The enclave, not walled since 1943, is controlled by the Chinese groups or triads. They fill the void and make this their center for drugs, abortions, gambling, and prostitution. They also provide whatever semblance of order exists in this ghetto. Surprisingly, most tourists and many expatriates walk and live within blocks of this area without realizing its nature.

## Drugs

In a sense, opium made Hong Kong, and the Territory has been addicted to some extent ever since. Drug abuse is the greatest law enforcement problem today. Attempts by the police to break the habit should probably be measured in various degrees of failure. Now the culprit is opium's more dangerous cousin: heroin. It was not until 1946 that the importation of opium was officially prohibited. Estimates are that there were 100,000 drug addicts by the mid-1970s. Half the Territory's customs service is assigned to antinarcotics work. There are some indications that the government is making a little headway.

The Territory is funding an active program for the treatment of addicts, and there are private clinics and halfway houses. Still, the facilities can handle only a fraction of the total potential patients.

Narcotics present two problems for the expatriate family: the availability of low-price hard drugs, and more potent drugs, which can cause serious or even fatal complications for the new western user. Marijuana is not a common drug and is relatively unavailable.

A few years ago there was a drug-related death at the Hong Kong International School. Since then, this and the other international schools have had an active educational program. Certainly, the results of addiction are obvious. As a result, drugs are not a big problem nor even a frequent conversation topic. If you do have someone that gets involved with drugs, the best thing is to get help at home rather than depend on the almost nonexistent facilities on the Island for non-Chinese.

The Hong Kong Dangerous Drugs Ordinance gives the police some extraordinary powers to combat this problem. Some important points for expatriates to know:

The list of drugs subject to the ordinance includes some medicines like valium and quaaludes.

Any person caught with _any_ traceable amount of a drug is presumed to be trafficking.

Police can search individuals, cars, or homes without a warrant when they have any reason to suspect a violation.

There are severe fines and prison terms for drug-related offenses.

Some discretion in prosecution for offenders under age 16 is allowed. Expulsion from the Territory is not unknown for repeating youthful violators.

In Hong Kong any minor can buy unopened bottles of liquor or packages of cigarettes. It is considered unlawful only when someone under 18 is served liquor or offered a cigarette.

## Customs and Immigration

In keeping with the importance of tourism and commerce to Hong Kong, most foreign nationals can enter without any visa for a visit of from one to three months, depending on one's nationality (U.S. citizens are given one month). Citizens of the United Kingdom can visit for six months. This allows simple and sufficient access for trips to get acquainted. But, as a visitor, you are not permitted to enter into any employment, to establish or join a business, or to enter a school as a student. A visitor is required to have funds sufficient for the intended stay and onward transportation, although very infrequent check is made of most tourists.

When you go to Hong Kong with the intention of working, studying, or taking up residence, you must have a valid visa from any British embassy or consular office prior to arrival. While visas are seldom refused, they are not granted as a matter of course. Each application is considered on its merits, and the applicant must not be taking a job that can be filled by a national of Hong Kong. The work permit comes with the visa. The usual term for Americans is six months and multiple-entry visas can be arranged. The family has dependent status for the same period. One important point is that a dependent spouse may accept employment without any additional approval from the authorities.

Identity cards are compulsory for anyone over 11 years old. You should register within 30 days after arrival at the Registration of Persons, Causeway Bay Magistracy, Hong Kong. The government is also enforcing a requirement that all persons over 15 years old carry either the ID card, a current passport, or valid Hong Kong driver's license. A violation carries up to a HK$1000 fine.

Customs regulations are also quite simple. All but a very few items (liquor and tobacco) enter freely and without restriction. No firearms and ammunition are allowed; a very rare possession license may be granted by the commissioner of police. Drugs are prohibited, of course.

Pets can enter Hong Kong if they have their own "visa" obtained in advance from the Department of Agriculture and Fisheries, whose agents meet and check each arriving pet. Cats and dogs from the United Kingdom and Ireland are exempt from any quarantine requirement. Pets from all other countries are held for six months. There are government kennels for this purpose, which are quite adequate, but many pet owners prefer the private kennels, such as the Royal Hong Kong Jockey Club kennels.

### Taxes

A liberal tax policy has been another cornerstone in Hong Kong's development. Rates of taxation are among the lowest in the world. There is no comprehensive income tax system as in the United States. Instead, the Territory operates on a "schedular" form of taxation, levying tax on only certain classes of income: profits of business, salaries, interest, and property. There is no tax on dividends or capital gains, and there is no sales or turnover tax. About the only other direct tax that will affect most expatriates is a minor stamp tax on contracts and other official documents.

The important concepts in other tax systems of residence, domicile, and nationality are relatively insignificant in the Hong Kong format. If you have an income in one of the four categories or schedules, you are taxed regardless of your residence, domicile, or nationality. The crucial factor is whether the income was derived from activities or sources within the Territory. Foreign source income, even if remitted, is not taxable. On the other hand, Hong Kong source income is taxable wherever paid.

The salaries tax is levied on income from employment earned during a period of more than 60 days in Hong Kong. If the taxpayer has regional responsibilities outside of the Territory and has a contract of employment with a non-Hong Kong company entered into outside of Hong Kong, he may apply for assessment on the proportion of his income that relates to the actual days spent in Hong Kong.

All wages, leave pay (unless used only to procure transportation), fees, commissions, bonuses, profit sharing, living allowances, education allowances, tax reimbursements, gains on the exercise of a stock option, and any other remuneration not in kind are included as taxable income. If housing is furnished rent-free by the employer, or where an employer reimburses the employee's rent, the rental value is declared to be a percentage of the employee's total income. This percentage set for a house or apartment is 10 percent. This rental accrual can be offset by actual rent paid by an employee and not reimbursed. Thus, an employee with rent-free housing pays salaries tax on 110 percent of his earnings. If a housing allowance is granted, it is considered income and taxed accordingly.

Any income of the spouse is taxed along with the other partner's income. There is no separate return.

Expenses related to the income subject to the salaries tax, such as travel expenses and entertaining, are allowed. Another deduction is charitable donations. There are several personal allowances as well.

Salary income is taxed at graduated rates from 5 to 25 percent on amounts over HK$50,000, less personal allowances and charitable contributions (not more than 10 percent of total income). The maximum amount due, however, is limited to 15 percent of the total income less charitable deductions—without considering the personal allowances.

The tax year runs from April 1 to March 31. There is no withholding. An employee receives a report from his employer in

April listing his total income. Then the Hong Kong Island Revenue Department, which gets a copy of the employer's report, sends out a return in May or June. The taxpayer completes the form within one month and then later in the year is assessed his tax. About 75 percent is due the following January or February and the remainder by the following May.

The interest tax is a flat rate of 15 percent on any interest or annuity of Hong Kong origin. It is paid by the payor who deducts it at the source of the interest paid. The same 15 percent rate is imposed for the profits and property taxes.

An individual who is a resident of Hong Kong and has income subject to more than one of the four taxes can elect to be assessed personally. The taxes of various forms are aggregated, appropriate allowances are made, and the tax is calculated on the 15 percent salaries tax basis. Persons considering this should consult a tax expert.

Many of the world's leading public accounting firms maintain offices in Hong Kong.

# 19

# Assignment Tokyo

*D*ON'T LET TOKYO FOOL YOU! At first glance, this gargantuan
city may overwhelm you, and her flashy Western facade
may trick you into thinking she is not all that different from
hometown USA.

Tokyo *is* big. She sweeps along the western shores of Tokyo Bay
and then rushes inland across the Kanto Plain of Japan, swallowing
scores of cities and villages, dozens upon dozens of rivers and canals,
and nearly 12 million people. And the numbers game doesn't stop
there. She claims the world's largest golf driving range, the largest
night club, and the largest chorus line in existence. You can climb
mountains, sail over Pacific waters that drop to five-mile depths, and
lie on a beach without ever leaving her boundaries.

Space is tight. Canals are filled in and concrete roads are poured
on top. Freeways are elevated above the city, and restaurants and
shops are sandwiched between the girders. When the Japanese cannot
find land on top of the ground, they simply burrow underneath;
giant multilevel subterranean shopping centers offer a multitude of
services and merchandise.

In recent years, driving in Tokyo has settled down to a respect-
able adventure, but streets are still so congested and parking space is
at such a premium that you must prove you have a spot to put an
automobile before you are allowed to buy one.

Luxury homes squeeze between restaurants and hotels; stores

and raucous night clubs stand cheek to jowl with peaceful shrines. Rich live among the poor, and foreigners among the natives.

Tokyo is always changing—new shops, new restaurants, new ideas. By day she is energetic and rather gray as her concrete canyon walls cast shadows across treeless congested streets. At night she drops her dignity; and as the neon lights begin to flash, Tokyo bursts into color to become frivolous, giddy, and sometimes even naughty.

Want to learn the Charleston? Study American jazz? Be serenaded by mariachis? Buy a dirty toothpick (not the used variety but one wrapped in paper with suggestive sayings)? Visit a love hotel— only to observe, of course? It is all there for you to discover.

Woven into the Japanese language are English phrases. Commercials sing forth American products; teenagers sport U.S. university T-shirts; and mixed into a galaxy of signs are the brightly colored letters that spell McDonald's, Dunkin' Donuts, Kentucky Fried Chicken, and Shakey's Pizza. But pocketed between the new buildings and trendy spirit are touches of the old Japan, and oriental attitudes and traditions remain firmly entrenched.

Tokyo is not strictly dedicated to naughtiness and frivolity. She is the nation's capital and the economic, financial, industrial, and educational center as well. While there may be other cities in the world that can claim such combinations, it would be hard to find one that could come up with the cultural offerings of Tokyo. There are over 300 museums in the city to meet every conceivable taste and interest, 8 symphony orchestras, and more concerts and recitals each year than in any other metropolitan area in the world, including New York and London. One hundred and three universities and eighty-four junior colleges lie within her boundaries, with a student population of over 650,000.

When asked what they like most about living in Tokyo, foreigners usually answer, "Her safety." It *is* safe. Foreign children ride public transportation all over the city right along with the Japanese youngsters, and their parents do not have to worry about their being home before dark. Women can be out alone at any time. If you lose a package, wallet, or luggage, your chances of getting it back are excellent. You can leave your home without fear of someone breaking in. Around December, however, everyone is a little more cautious about locking up, as there are a few burglaries when more cash is in the home to pay all the bills before the New Year rolls around.

The *koban* (neighborhood police box) undoubtedly plays a large role in helping to keep the crime rate down. Each neighborhood is very carefully watched from the *koban,* manned 24 hours a day by one or two police who keep an eye on an area of no more than five or six city blocks. They know who lives where and watch who comes and goes. Shortly after you move in, they may come to call and to register you in their official records. If they don't, rest assured they know where you live.

The first time you try to find your way to the grocery store, you will realize that Tokyo is put together like no other city on earth. Streets start and end within a few blocks, twist and swing into multicornered intersections, and wind in such an irregular path that if you attempt to walk around the block, you will become entangled in an unending maze. Many evolved from the spider web of alleys that surrounded the old shogun palaces. Very few of the streets have names, and buildings are not numbered consecutively but in the order in which they were built. This system can put number 50 on the corner and number 1 in the middle of the block. The first rule to remember is never try to take a shortcut.

One of the main problems faced by foreigners who come to live here is the cost of living. In recent years, financial horror stories have trickled across the Pacific of $3 cups of coffee, steak dinners for $70, and bar tabs quickly escalating to over $100. All the stories are true; but once you learn your way around, you will find that while prices are far higher than in the States, there are some secrets to surviving. For example, it is possible to have dinner in one of the back alley restaurants for a few American dollars.

There are many foreign residents in Tokyo, over 117,000. Many of the Tokyoites are new to the city, too. In fact, there are not many around who can call themselves an *edokko,* a person whose family has lived in the city for more than three generations.

Living in Japan may be the closest you can come in the real world to discovering Alice's Wonderland behind the looking glass. Baffling, quixotic, yet pragmatic and efficient, Japan is a land of contradiction and fantasy. She is a beautiful country once you leave the metropolitan areas, and she offers a culture whose depths you can never reach but must try to explore.

The four principal islands of Japan—Honshu, Hokkaido, Kyushu, and Shikoku—make up 98 percent of the country's area; the other 2 percent is scattered over small islands. It all adds up to a nation just slightly smaller than the state of Montana. Over three-fourths of this land is ruggedly mountainous and virtually uninhabitable. That leaves a very small area for a population just about half that of the United States. These hardy people, compacted into several large urban areas, go through numerous earthquakes in an average year, although "just" 2 or 3 a month are noticed. But this is how it goes in Japan. You will find yourself constantly shaking your head and saying, "Unbelievable," and you will return home with a deep respect for the people who made it all turn out that way.

The people are what make living in Japan so different. It is not the fact that they look oriental. Many appear surprisingly Western because they have gone to plastic surgeons to have their noses chiseled away, sculpting them into delicate nostrils, and have erased the corner folds of their eyes, eliminating the indigenous slant-eyed appearance. Kimonos are stored carefully away and brought out only for festivals or special occasions; the people, instead, reflect an awareness of high fashion that fits the Western world, and a work force whose products are exported to nations hungry for new ideas and innovations. It is the attitudes of the Japanese that are still bound in a tradition and culture steeped in time, and they have an effect yet today on almost everything they do.

The free-wheeling, to-hell-with-formality, and to-know-us-is-to-love-us approach of Americans had best be put aside. The Japanese love, practice, and respect formality. Also bear in mind that our height can be overpowering, our voices overbearing. An arm around the shoulder of a Japanese or a pat on the back is an intrusion, not a sign of friendship. Above all, forget about using first names and get accustomed to using the word *san,* as in "Smith-san."

Individuality is not appreciated. Children are taught to conform to the group and to avoid ridicule at all costs. Japan is geared to the masses, not to the individual, and this same theory applies to foreigners who plan to settle there.

The Japanese are sensitive. They *do* care what you think of them and their country. With typical American impatience to get things done in a hurry—a repair made, a question answered—we often offend them. In this country, more than anywhere else, the foreigner must practice patience.

The language itself points up the importance of position and rank. Japan has been a democracy since after World War II, but here society is authoritarian. In speaking Japanese, you must know all the various honorific forms to use based on the position of the person with whom you are speaking. There are at least eight different ways of saying *I* and as many different words for *you*; and to err is to insult. But in spite of the complexities of the language, it is important for all members of the newly arrived family to learn at least a few phrases of polite conversation. The Japanese will appreciate your efforts.

And while we are on the subject of linguistics, we should point out that you should try to avoid putting the Japanese in the position of giving you a direct no. Saving "face" is the oriental perfection of the concept of not causing embarassment and is very important in all aspects of Japanese life.

Pronunciation may be the easiest aspect of Japanese to the foreigner, but English causes the Japanese some unique problems. When a Japanese airline attendant tells you she hopes you enjoyed the "fright," or when you buy rice and hear it called "lice," don't be startled. The Japanese have difficulty with the English *l* and *r*.

Many more of them will speak English than we can muster up on the other side of the Pacific to speak Japanese. That is not to say that everyone knows English. The majority do not. But since World War II many Japanese have been studying not only our language but all our little idiosyncrasies; you might as well resign yourself to the fact that they are going to know far more about you than you will ever know about them.

The attitudes and subtleties of Japanese society are hard for a Westerner to perceive and accept. The concepts of women's liberation, for example, have barely gained a foothold, let alone made any headway in Japan. A woman still has three bosses in her lifetime: first her father, then her husband, and last her son. By the time she is 30, she is supposed to be retired from the office and at home rearing a family.

Settling in Japan means that family members must realize that the traditions and attitudes of another culture will influence their lives. It can present a problem. The wife will probably have the greatest adjustment to make. Her husband will be king, not for a day but for the entire tour of duty. An American woman may be offended the first time her husband receives an invitation to a party and she is not included. She also may feel put down the first time a man rushes through a door before her. But these are the customs of Japan, and no rudeness is intended. Independence on the wife's part is needed, but at the same time she has to be willing to play second chair. It is a difficult road to go. One American woman put it rather wisely when she said, "I just look at my role as play acting. I know it will not last forever, and in the meantime, there is so much to learn, to see, and to do. The rewards are worth it."

Another American woman learned by trial and error how to handle the Japanese attitudes. She ordered a set of china from a local department store only to find after delivery that the wrong dishes had been sent. When she called the store to report the mix-up, the clerk at the other end of the line impatiently informed her that the mistake was impossible and then promptly hung up. The next day, the frustrated customer changed her tactics. She called the store and explained that her husband hated the dishes. This time help came immediately. The clerk apologized and assured the lady that they would be out instantly to exchange the merchandise. The American had learned two lessons: always allow the other party to save face, and the husband is always right.

The Japanese have a word for people who settle in their midst. They call them *gaijins,* and the word gives you an idea of how they will view you. Literally translated, it means *outsider.* The Japanese are gracious to foreigners, and they will welcome you to their islands. But they never fully accept you. Don't worry about it. They like you as you are; don't ever try to become one of them. They even have a word for people who put on the kimonos, sleep on the floor, and hobble around on *getas:* they call you *hen-ne-gaijin.* It all comes out as *crazy foreigner.*

Do not believe that the gifts the Japanese are quick to bestow or their courtesies, which they are masters at giving to those they deem worthy of receiving them, necessarily imply friendship. That is something you must work to achieve.

## Practical Pointers

You are sure to hear or see the word *Kanto.* The Tokyo-Yokohama area is located on the Kanto Plain. This word is used regularly in the media to refer to this area. *Kansai* refers to the geographical district comprising the Osaka-Kobe area and the surrounding suburbs.

Tipping in Japan is not customary.

There are two types of toilets—the Western and the Japanese. The latter may be a receptacle slightly rectangular on a raised floor, or in more rural areas, simply a hole in the floor. Both are straddled in a squatting position facing the flushing handle. They have the advantage of being sanitary because no part of the body comes in contact with the fixture.

Carry-out food *(o-bento),* well prepared and beautifully packaged, is readily available. One of the delights of train travel is the opportunity to eat a special type of box lunch called *eki-ben,* which are sold at stations and on the trains and may have some Western tidbits for tourists.

You can go inside the Imperial Palace grounds (without very special arrangements with the palace household), and perhaps see the emperor waving at his people, though only on two days a year—January 2 and April 29, the emperor's birthday.

Never cross chopsticks when they are put down. It is a sign of disrespect.

When taking a Japanese bath, use soap and wash outside the tub or bath and rinse before entering.

Japan is the world's most literate nation. Pick any subject and you are likely to find more books published on it in Japan than anywhere else. But the most popular mass reading material is the adult comic book found in large stacks at any public newsstand.

Booze, beer, and sake are available from automatic vending machines in the streets throughout Tokyo.

In Japan, fireworks are legal, guns are not.

Tokyo is the place for chewing gum—banana, champagne, coffee, yoghurt, and green melon.

When giving a gift, avoid groups of objects that add up to four and nine, as these symbolize death and misfortune.

Be very careful when pounding a nail or anything metal into a Tokyo wall. The electrical wiring is not shielded by a metal conduit. One man was killed when he struck a live line.

Dependents are not supposed to be employed unless, of course, they also obtained the visa that permits this. But many wives work out of their homes as "editorial assistants" for American companies. This usually entails composing English letters or other papers for them.

Some of the handicrafts still practiced in Japan are unique, such as sand casting of iron kettles. There may be only a handful of artisans left for each skill. Some have been designated "living cultural assets" by the government. Being able to learn about these traditional arts is a special advantage of a tour in Japan.

## To Bring or Not to Bring

Expatriates all acknowledge that you can find virtually any article, somewhere, and at some time, in Tokyo.

There are two major reasons for bringing things with you to Japan: the convenience of not having to hunt for the item once you are there, and the expense of any imported item (double or triple what it would be at home) once you find it. In addition to the items listed in Chapter 3, Americans in Tokyo suggest you bring:

Furniture. The Japanese furniture is scaled to smaller sizes. It is possible to have furniture made here, and some Western-type pieces are available to rent or buy. But the prices are high. Some foreigners have gone to Taiwan to have furniture made. The lower costs merit shipping it back to Japan.

Food seasonings. These can be bought here, but sometimes your grocery will be out of a particular item you need.

An ironing board and covers to fit it.

Linens for American-sized beds.

Vacuum cleaner bags.

Spare parts for any large appliances.

A dehumidifier for muggy summer months and a humidifier for dry winter ones.

Card tables and chairs; they are just beginning to appear in Japan.

Vitamins and nonprescription medicines; they are very expensive here.

Deodorants.

Dietetic foods; there are a few diet cookies, jams, and salad dressings available, but that is about it.

Government restrictions on products containing certain chemicals, such as diet colas, vary from time to time so these products can be scarce; iodized salt can also come under this category.

Current in the Tokyo area is 110 volts 50 cycles, just slightly different from the U.S. 110 volts 60 cycles. Your appliances will work in Tokyo, although the cycle difference will make them slightly less efficient. (See Chapter 4.)

Many of the Western-type housing units furnish major American or American-type appliances (negotiate with your landlord if they are not there), and used American ones can be purchased through advertisements in the English-language papers or on bulletin boards in stores frequented by foreigners. Do not bring your electric range. Few housing units have proper wiring for them; to obtain it requires special permission from the local electric company and an electrician to install it, a time-consuming and costly operation. Gas stoves are commonly used.

You will find a ready market for any of your furniture or appliances if you do not wish to ship them home.

Do not bring your television set, as it will not pick up local channels. AM radios will work, but FM radios will need an adapter.

Although the newer generations are larger in stature, Japanese sizes still are too small and out of proportion for the average or larger-sized American. This is particularly true for shoes. Most expatriates bring a full wardrobe and supplement it with buying trips to Hong Kong, Korean, and Taiwanese tailors. The Isetan department store in Shinjuku has begun carrying the larger American sizes for women. A few shops are beginning to import ready-made wear from other Asian countries.

Natural fibers are recommended for hot, humid summers. Lighter weight winter clothing and a topcoat are needed from November until February.

Dress is more formal than in the States. Men wear conservative suits and women stick to dresses, suits, or skirts and blouses. Social demands wil require a more extensive and probably a more formal wardrobe. Children and teenagers have an easier time finding clothing; they can wear what they would normally wear at home. On weekends, however, anything goes. The younger Japanese will be wearing jeans or the latest mod outfit from Europe or America.

Be sure to pick up the excellent publication of the American Chamber of Commerce in Japan, _Living in Japan,_ available at most hotel bookstores. There is a similar volume for the Kansai area (Osaka, Kobe), _Living in Kobe,_ published by the Community House and Information Center in Kobe.

## Housing

Your Tokyo dream house—the odds lean heavily toward its being an apartment instead—may be sandwiched between a pickle factory and a trendy boutique. While no one area can be considered _the_ residential district for Tokyo, there are some spots that have proved popular with the foreign community. Their desirability depends on several things: closeness to the banking area and many corporate offices, as well as availability to the city's top hotels and entertainment districts.

There are pockets of strictly residential buildings, but they are small. Shops will be just around the corner. The advantage to this arrangement is that no matter where you settle in Tokyo, the chances are good that you can walk to a meat market, a grocery, and an assortment of little shops that can meet your everyday needs. In the districts favored by foreign residents, the groceries are apt to have a high percentage of American and other imported food products.

Rents are _high,_ several thousand U.S. dollars per month, plus utilities.

The further you travel from central Tokyo (while there officially is no "city center," for practical purposes we shall use the terms "center" or "central" to refer to the area near the Imperial Palace), the greater your chances of finding a house versus an apartment. But life in these outlying districts is far from being anything like suburbia USA. These outskirts are all part of the Tokyo metropolitan district, and houses are on the small side and always crowded next to each other. Yards are minuscule or nonexistent.

Most foreigners will stay away from Japanese housing. The rooms are very small; there is no central heating; kitchens are poorly equipped; and walls are quite thin. Western housing with central heating, bathrooms like home, and kitchens equipped with the latest appliances (even microwaves in some cases) has been constructed for the expatriate. The Japanese have been very successful in providing this housing to meet almost any requirement and continue to build Western-style apartment buildings. There are some apartment hotels that are suitable for longer stays:

Kitano Arms (three months minimum)
16-15, Hirakawa-cho 2-chome
Chiyoda-ku
Telephone 265-2371

Kioicho Court
3-31 Kioi-cho
2-chome
Chiyoda-ku
Telephone 264-4511

If possible, you also should avoid being put into a spot where you can select from just three or four places. Work with one or more realtors. Several realtors are accustomed to dealing with the needs of *gaijins*. A few of these are:

Overseas Corporation
Dai San Bldg.
19-15, Ginza 1-chome
Chuo-ku
Telephone 562-2061

Plaza Homes, Ltd.
Chuo Iikura Bldg.
Plaza and Lease Bldg.
2-8-5 Higashi Azabu
Minato-ku
Telephone 583-6941

Sun Realty & Insurance Corporation
Homat Royal Bldg.
14-11, Akasaka 1-chome
Minato-ku
Telephone 584-6171

There are some terms that will be helpful in your search:

*Apato, manshon.* The word *manshon* comes from the English word *mansion;* but in Japanese, it means more luxurious than an *apato* although both refer to apartments.

*Dainingu kitchin.* A combination dining-kitchen area is common in many Japanese apartments. When for rent, they are advertised as "2DK," meaning two rooms plus a dining-kitchen area.

*Suisen toire.* This is a flush toilet.

*Tsubo.* This is used extensively in Japan to describe the area of a plot of ground or floor space of a house. One *tsubo* is the size of two standard *tatami* mats (about 180 × 360 cm).

*Shikikin.* When renting, a deposit is usually required.

*Reikin.* This is "thank you money" or "key money" given to the landlord before you move in, usually about one or two months' rent; this is in addition to any deposit.

Part of the decision in selecting your new abode depends not so much on whether you want a house rather than an apartment but if dad should be close to the office and the entertainment circuit or the kids near their school. The American School is out in Chofu-shi, one of Tokyo's outer cities and about an hour's commute from the central areas. Some Americans do live in Chofu and nearby towns; the American School even has some houses to rent. But for those who opt for the outlying districts, it means that dad, who will have many late nights of entertaining, has to catch the last train home unless he has a car.

Here is a rundown, in descending order of popularity, of the *kus* where you find the most Americans.

*Minato-ku.* The name translates to *port.* Minato-ku's eastern boundaries touch the Tokyo Bay. Home of the famous Tokyo Tower, Shiba Park for Nature Study, temples, museums, Keio University (the country's oldest). About 10 to 15 minutes to the city center by train or subway. Around 22 percent commercial, small industrial development, 64 percent residential. Several areas have personalities of their own:

Roppongi. Probably the city's most popular area for Americans. Location of the Tokyo American Club, pubs, trendy boutiques, restaurants, embassies.

Azabu. A favorite residential quarter. Many embassies, Prince Arisugawa Memorial Park, Nishimachi International School.

Akasaka. Location of the Akasaka Detached Palace, the nation's State Guesthouse. Lively, expensive, swinging entertainment area. Top hotels. Popular residential sections.

Aoyama. Exclusive boutiques. Home of the Crown Prince and the Princess. Restaurants. Residential areas.

Chiyoda-ku. Dignified. Location of the Imperial Palace, several museums, the National Theater, the giant Tokyo Station. Political center of Japan with National Diet and many government buildings in the Kasumigaeseki district. Many top hotels. Hibiya Park, a delightful combination of Western and Japanese landscaping.

Kanda. Tokyo's Latin Quarter with bookstores, commercial but elegant pockets of residential areas.

Shibuya-ku. One of the city's largest shopping and amusement centers surrounds the Shibuya Station. Location of the Meiji Shrine, one of the city's most important worship centers, and the Yoyogi Sports Center, which served as the Olympic Village in 1964.

Harajuku. Popular for shopping and once an area that housed the American occupation forces.

Shoto. An area of expensive single-family houses. Location of the International School of the Sacred Heart. About 89 percent residential.

Setagaya-ku. Quieter, less crowded than previous wards. About 97 percent residential. Approximately 30 to 40 minutes from the center. Neighborhood shopping but nearby Shibuya Station area for large shopping. Developed after the war. Seijo and Kyodo, two popular residential areas. Koshun-en Gardens. Home of Seisen International School and St. Mary's International School. Jiyugaoka Station area on the Tokyo Line, a desirable shopping district.

Meguro-ku. About 93 percent residential. Fewer bars and cabarets. More houses than apartments. Kami-meguro and Abura-men, two popular residential areas. Daiei Department Store, great for bargains, located on Mejoro Dori in this ku. Home of the American School in Japan Nursery-Kindergarten. Housing costs slightly lower than in more central kus. Management and office occupations. High percentage of home owners but rentals available. About 40 to 60 minutes to city center.

Shinjuku-ku. Jumping, busy, fast-paced area around Shinjuku

Station that is popular with Tokyo's young people. Station is city's busiest with infamous "pushers." Second only to Chuo-ku of Ginza fame in number of bars and first in number of cabarets. Movie theater center. Four major department stores. Gigantic underground shopping center. Yet, 76 percent of ward residential. Home of Meiji Olympic Park and the peaceful, extensive Shinjuku Gardens. About 20 to 45 minutes to city center, depending on exact location within ku.

*Ota-ku.* Denchofu, one of the city's most delightful residential areas, the first location to come under a city plan just after the war. Pleasant shops and many foreign bakeries. A touch of Europe in the Orient. Expensive homes under strict building codes in Denchofu. Invitation into Japanese homes comes quicker in this area than in almost any other in Tokyo. Other areas of Ota-ku highly residential. Particularly popular with German community—German School (Deutsche Schule) in this ku. Tamagawa-en Amusement Park and Senzoku Park.

*Shingawa-ku.* A busy post town on the road between old Edo and Kyoto during feudal times. Today 13 percent commercial, 30 percent industrial, the remainder residential. Takanawa a particularly desirable residential area. Several large hotels. Around 20 to 40 minutes to city.

## Domestic Help

Some foreign residents have a cleaning lady once a week, a few have live-in help. Wages run about the same as in large metropolitan areas in the United States and good help is hard to find. You are expected to give a bonus of one month's salary twice yearly, in midsummer and in December. It also is normal to allow three days off at the New Year and at least one week's holiday in the summer in addition to one day off per week. Some servants expect full board. Others provide most of their food but expect breakfast and/or staple foods such as rice and sugar. Some may expect to be provided with a uniform.

Since the selection of American-size clothing is very limited, many of the women hire dressmakers who come to the home once a week. The charge is about the same as it is for a maid.

## Education

The availability of educational facilities to foreign families is one of the big pluses of an assignment in Japan. There are approximately

40 schools in the East Asian Regional Council of Overseas Schools, and 23 of them are in this country with 11 in the Tokyo-Yokohama area. For those parents who contemplate giving their children a real cultural experience by placing them in a Japanese school, the advice from foreign residents already in Japan is, "Think carefully about it. It is a very difficult experience."

Not only is there a language problem, but the schools are run so differently from those elsewhere in the world that severe emotional problems can result. For example, the school day does not end at two or three o'clock. Instead, many Japanese youngsters are expected to go to school after school, an institution known as *ju-ku,* where they prepare for entrance examinations to the next level of education. The local children take exams even for kindergarten; if they do not meet qualifications for a specific school, they must go to one of lower stature. This all leads to the grand finale: the college entrance examination, which will determine their success in life. Entrance to Tokyo University, the most prestigious college in the nation, ensures a student a good job after graduation. Failure, once you have been admitted to a university, is almost unheard of, for this would mean that the admissions board had chosen incorrectly, and this would cause them to lose face.

Pressure is so strong all along the educational trail that suicides at the seven-year-old level are not unheard of. One American mother with whom we spoke had put her child in a Japanese nursery school and was finding the experience a pleasant one. She pointed out, though, that because of the lack of communication with the other children, her child was unable to take part in imaginative types of play; but he did participate in physical activities.

Parents of children enrolled in schools for foreign residents appear to be extremely pleased with the education their children are receiving. Quite often, the children are ahead of their class when they return to the States. Most find their educational experience in Japan a good background for college and have no trouble in being accepted at the school of their choice.

Programs for children with physical, emotional, or learning problems are very limited. The international schools are geared for the college preparatory student with no disability and who is independent and highly motivated. They do a good job for these children. They grade high on the national tests from the States and receive merit scholarships. A very high percentage go on to top universities and colleges. Students who would go into technical training or otherwise not continue on to higher education may have a difficult time.

Table 7 provides a list of schools available for American and European children. The school year in the international schools runs from September into June.

Other international schools are located in Fukuoka, Hiroshima, Kobe, Kyoto, Nagoya, Okinawa, Hokkaido, and Yokahama. Generally, they follow an American college preparatory curriculum.

With commuting, classes, extracurricular activities, and sports, the typical school day for the expatriate child is long.

## Shopping

There is probably no other city in the world that offers the shopping temptations of Tokyo. "If you can't buy it here, it isn't worth buying," say natives and foreigners alike. And with few exceptions, they are right. Nearly everything, however, is expensive, but quality merchandise crowds the stores.

The Japanese were the first to think up the idea of a department store, and these stores provide the most mind-boggling assortment of merchandise ever assembled for shoppers. The basement levels are giant grocery stores that carry not only local foods but foreign products, while the upper levels run the gamut from traditional Japanese clothing and housewares to the latest foreign fashions and gadgetry. Bargains are on the top floor, and the *Saturday Japan Times* will give the details on current sales.

The Japanese receive generous bonuses from their employer twice a year, just before the New Year and in July. At both times, gifts are presented to supervisors in the office and to the family. Department stores stock up at these two times. They are anxious to attract buyers and then just as anxious to get rid of leftover merchandise, so watch for bargains then.

Stores are open 10 a.m. to 6 p.m., including Sundays and holidays, but they close one day during the week. This day varies from store to store; so again check the *Saturday Japan Times* when in doubt.

The department stores are more than places to shop. They provide cultural centers, restaurants (one has 18 under its roof), theaters, and usually an amusement center on the rooftop. At the Mitsukoshi Nihombashi store you can even fish for your supper. Near the main entrance of most department stores you will find an

## Table 7

### Schools Available for American and European Children in Tokyo

| School | Address | Grades | Type | Type of Plant | Enrollment and Faculty | Curriculum |
|---|---|---|---|---|---|---|
| The American School in Japan (accreditation: Western Association of Schools and Colleges) | 1-1, Nomizu 1-chome, Chofu-shi Telephone 0422 31 6351 (western Tokyo) | Kinder-garten-12 | Day | A modern plant with indoor swimming pool, gymnasium, theater, two libraries, cafeteria, language lab, on 12 acres, tennis courts, train five minutes away, bus service for Tokyo students | 845; 72 faculty | College preparatory; Japanese language and cultural courses taught, modular schedule in secondary school; comprehensive sports program |
| AOBA International School | Aobadai 3-10-34 Meguro-ku Telephone 461-1442 | Nursery plus three additional levels; ages 1½ to 6 years | Day | Seven classrooms and an assembly room for music, sports, and other group activities | 163; with 15 countries represented; coed; 20 faculty | A program to give children a good foundation in music and English |
| The American School in Japan Nursery Kindergarten | 2-15-5, Aobadai, Meguro-ku Telephone 461-4523 | Nursery and day kindergarten; 2½ to 6 years | Day | Classrooms centered around a common activity area, a room for music and other activities, library of audiovisual materials, and playground | 119; coed | Classes of 15 or 20 children with one teacher and one assistant; play and work to prepare children for elementary school |

| School | Address | Grades | Type | Facilities | Enrollment | Program |
|---|---|---|---|---|---|---|
| Christian Academy in Japan (accreditation: Western Association of Schools and Colleges) | 2-14, 1-chome Shinkawa-cho Higashi-Kurume-shi Telephone 0424 71 0022 (northwestern Tokyo) | Kinder-garten–12 | Day and boarding | Modern, functional buildings and campus | 285, coed day; 26 boarding; 40 faculty | Sponsored by six Protestant evangelical missionary organizations; originally for missionary children, but today 20 percent are from other backgrounds; American educational program, college preparatory–foreign language and courses in art, music, band, choir, physical education, home economics, industrial arts, and bible |
| The International School of the Sacred Heart (accreditation: Western Association of Schools and Colleges) | 3-1, Hiroo 4-chome Shibuya-ku Telephone 400-3951 | Kinder-garten–12 | Day | Modern building; designed to give the feeling of four separate buildings for different age levels but actually one structure; library, labs, gymnasium/auditorium | 620; girls and boys accepted in kindergarten; 80 faculty | English instruction courses in Christian ethics; arts and sciences; French and Japanese college preparatory |

| School | Address | Grades | Type | Type of Plant | Enrollment and Faculty | Curriculum |
|---|---|---|---|---|---|---|
| Nishimachi International School | 14-7 Moto Azabu, 2-chome Minato-ku Telephone 451-5520 (in heart of Tokyo Azabu area) | Kindergarten-9 | Day | Four buildings, library, art, music, and multipurpose rooms; mountain campus in Gunma prefecture | 350; coed international student body including Japanese; 57 faculty | Classes are in English but emphasize learning Japanese; upon graduating, student is able to enter either Japanese or international or American school |
| St. Mary's International School (accreditation: Western Association of Schools and Colleges) | 6-19, Seta 1-chome Setagaya-ku Telephone 709-3411 | 1-12 | Day | Modern building on seven acres; indoor swimming pool, gym, tennis courts, language lab, music and art rooms, and library | 750; boys only; 60 nations represented; 60 faculty | College preparatory; participation in sports encouraged |
| Seisen International School (accreditation: Ministry of Education, Japan; Western Association of Secondary Schools and Colleges) | 12-15, Yoga 1-chome Setagaya-ku Telephone 704-2661 | Kindergarten-12 for girls; boys kindergarten only | Day | Three buildings plus gym, library, and chapel; more up-and-down structurally than spread out over a big campus | 500; boys; kindergarten only; many nationalities; 55 faculty | College preparatory; religious instruction (Catholic) but classes divided between Catholic and non-Catholic; extracurricular activities encouraged |
| Yokahama International School (accreditation: International School Association) | 258 Yamate-cho Naka-ku Yokohama Telephone 045-622 0084 | Nursery-12 | Day | Modern classrooms and labs | 360 coed; 33 faculty | Combines American, British, and Continental programs |

information desk that will tell you what is located where. If they do not have someone on duty who speaks English, they can put you in touch with someone who does.

Almost all the stores have parking facilities, so have your ticket validated when you buy something. The stores often have direct access to subway stations.

As you travel around Tokyo, you may think that the city is one giant shopping center. It isn't. But at first glance it certainly appears that way, since every subway and train station has its own shopping complex. There are many giant commercial areas with stores, offices, restaurants, and multiforms of entertainment located at the junctions of the Yamanote Line (see Transportation) with other train and subway systems. To the Japanese *downtown* is just the opposite of what it means to a Westerner: it refers to that part of the city generally to the northeast, where owners either live above their shops or very close by.

From a Westerner's point of view, *the* downtown area begins close to the Imperial Palace and spreads across several districts. The following is a list of the major shopping areas in Tokyo and some that are popular with the foreign residents.

## Major Shopping Areas

Two districts—the *Marunouchi* and *Otemachi*—contain many of the nation's leading banks and corporate offices. In addition, there are other districts famous for shopping and entertainment within this downtown area.

*Nihombashi* district. This area, located near Tokyo Station, is the old, established shopping district of the city. Through the years, it has maintained a prestigious air. Department stores like Mitsukoshi and Takashimaya, steeped in tradition, are here. Hundreds of shops carrying everything from records to clothes are located in a giant underground shopping mall beneath Tokyo Station. (Reached by Yamanote Line to Tokyo Station or Ginza and Tozai Subway Lines to Nihombashi stop.)

*Ginza* district. Just a hop, and literal skip, away from Nihombashi (the Kyabashi district is in between) is the city's most famous shopping and entertainment area. Location of many department stores and branches of the Matsuzakaya and Mitsukoshi, the area merely throbs with energy by day and then explodes with excitement at night as the expense account crowd takes over the many bars and restaurants. Wako, one of the city's most elegant stores, is definitely worth a tour to admire if not to buy the merchandise. (Reached by Yamanote Line to Yurakucho stop or the Hibiya, Ginza, or Marunouchi Subway Line to the Ginza stop.)

*Shinjuku.* You may gasp with astonishment when you step off the train or subway at this thriving subcity and see a galaxy of stores, every conceivable form of entertainment, and skyscrapers, among them the 55-story Mitsui Building, one of Japan's tallest. The Isetan, probably the most "international" store, Mitsukoshi branch store, and Odakyu and Keio department stores are connected by an underground walkway. And speaking of underground, you will find another one of those giant below-street-level shopping centers at the Shinjuku Station. This entire shopping area follows close behind the preceding districts as Tokyo's most important downtown. (Reached by Yamanote Line or private train lines to the Shinjuku Station or the Marunouchi Subway Line to the Shinjuku stop.)

*Shibuya.* This is one of Tokyo's giant city centers. The area around Shibuya Station is a conglomerate of shops, department stores, inexpensive restaurants, and entertainment. It is a favorite destination of young people out for an evening of fun who meet each other at the statue of a dog just outside the station. Seibu department store, Toyoku department store, and its parent store, Tokyu, are here. (Reached by Yamanote Line or private train lines to the Shibuya Station.)

*Ikebukuro.* It is quickly becoming one of Tokyo's major city centers with the new Sunshine Center skyscraper, Tobu and Mitsukoshi department stores, and the main Seibu department store along with a wide assortment of speciality shops. It is a little farther out than the other areas and thus is patronized more by people who live nearby. You may find prices a little lower here. (Reached by the Yamanote Line and private train lines to the Ikebukuro Station or the Marunouchi and Yurakucho Subway Lines to Ikebukuro stop.)

*Ueno.* This is Tokyo's "cultural downtown" with art museums and galleries; the Tokyo Metropolitan Festival hall for concerts, operas, recitals, and other entertainment; and many other museums. It is also the location of Matsuzakaya department store. (Reached by Yamanote Line and Hibiya and Ginza Subway Lines to Ueno Station.)

## Other Shopping Areas

*Roppongi.* "It reminds me of Manhattan's Upper Third Avenue," said one American who lived in the area. It is "city center" to many Americans because it is in close proximity to the Tokyo American Club and because so many of their countrymen live close by. The department stores are missing, but the area abounds with trendy boutiques, bakeries, discos, and restaurants. (Reached by the Hibiya Subway Line to the Roppongi stop.)

_Harajuku._ This is an extremely popular area with Americans, other foreigners, and the sophisticated Japanese younger set. During the occupation, this area was known as Washington Heights. The boutiques and shops boast an international flavor. The tree-lined streets are reminiscent of Paris. One street, Omotesanda (that's right, it actually has a name), is a particular shopping favorite. (Reached by Yamanote Line to Harajuku Station or Chiyoda Subway Line to Meiji Jinqumae stop.)

_Asakusa._ An area near the famous Asakusa Kannon Temple, it is a marvelous place in which to pick up the traditional things of Japan—fans, wigs, the bowls made of thread, and so forth. (Reached by Ginza and Tokyo Municipal Subway Line to Asakusa stop.)

_Akihabara._ Here you will find everything and anything in electrical and electronic products, and cheaper than elsewhere in the city. There is also a vast wholesale vegetable market in the area. (Reached by Yamanote Line to Akihabara Station or Hibiya Subway Line to Akihabara stop.)

_Azabu Juban._ Athough this is really just a neighborhood shopping center, it is one of the favorites with the Western community. There are many little shops, restaurants, and a bathhouse where you might like to stop not only to bathe but to listen to the entertainment. Patrons sip tea and sing after the cleansing ritual. Most of the stores are closed on Tuesdays. (Reached by Hibiya Subway Line to Roppongi stop.)

_Kanda, Hongo,_ and _Waseda._ These areas of the city have many used bookstores with many editions in English and other languages in addition to Japanese. Check with International House, Kikusai Bunkan (11-16, Roppongi 5-chome, Minato-ku; telephone 470-4611) for maps of these areas.

Recommendations of friends and your own explorations will enable you to collect a list of shops. But you may need some help at first. _Living in Japan_ has an excellent list of all types of stores and services. Newspapers and other English-language publications carry advertisements for shops catering to foreigners. An abbreviated English-language _Yellow Pages,_ available in hotels and bookstores, is a useful reference.

## Flea Markets

A few years ago Tokyo had no such markets. Now there are several where you can find old kimono fabrics, furniture, bamboo baskets, and other curios. One is the Araiyakushi Flea Market, held the first Sunday of each month near the Araiyakushi Temple; another is the Roppongi Antique Fair, held the fourth Thursday and Friday of each month in front of the Rippongi Roa Building near Rippongi Station on the Hibiya Subway Line.

## Bargain Shopping

Daiei Department Store
Megurodori Avenue
Himonya 5-chome
Meguro-ku
Telephone 710-1111
A four-star winner when it comes to bargain shopping in Tokyo. There is a giant food market in the basement with food prices among the lowest in the city and snack shops and restaurants throughout the store. You can find good bargains in clothing, particularly children's and women's if you are considered an "average" size. Pottery and ladies' boots. Not much English is spoken here. It is a popular store with the Japanese.

Oriental Bazaar
9-13, Jingumae 5-chome
Shibuya-ku
Telephone first floor, 400-3933; second floor, 407-3331
Located in the popular Harajuku area, this store has good buys in lamps and incidental household furnishings.

Okachimachi Area
Reached by the Yamanote Line to Okachimachi Station or Hibiya Subway Line to Naka Okachimachi stop.
The Matsuzakaya department store can be found here, but check out all the small shops that carry everything from watches to food and clothing. Prices will be much lower than elsewhere. It is a good idea to take along someone who speaks Japanese if you really want to take advantage of bargains.

Simmons Japan Limited
6259, Hibarigaoka
Zama
Kanagawa Pref.
Telephone (0462) 51-0833
You can buy Beautyrest, Deepsleep, and hide-a-beds from factory outlets.

Fuchu
Reached by Chuo Expressway, exit 5
This is a town near the Yakota Air Force Base where you can buy seconds in Noritake china.

Seto
A town near Nagoya that has a series of shops with all types of china at prices lower than you find in Tokyo.

Inquire about customers' clubs sponsored by the various department stores. They generally operate something like this: you pay monthly for one year into a special department store fund, and then obtain a 15 to 20 percent discount on your purchases. There is another type wherein you join a department store's customers' club through an introduction and receive a special discount without the usual savings deposits. Check with any Japanese friends you might have for possible introductions.

## *Electrical Appliances*

Go to the area around Akihabara Station where numerous shops and stalls sell most kinds of electrical goods at less-than-normal retail prices. If something goes wrong with one of your appliances, compare repair charges with the price of a new one in this district.

## *Interior Designers*

Matsumoto Designers
7-15, Roppongi, 7-chomo
Minato-ku
Telephone 401-1801/408-4355
They are quite famliar with what foreigners want and aware of the dollar problem, as well as very reliable. They handle draperies, slip covers, reupholstering, and refinishing.

456    /    Americans Abroad

## Hobby and Toy Shops

Kiddyland (on Omote Sando)
1-9, Jingumae 6-chome
Shibuya-ku
Telephone 409-3431
Here you will find toys, gifts, English books for children and adults as well as English magazines, Christmas, Halloween, and Easter decorations in season, records, and party supplies.

## Bookstores

Kinokoniya Book Store (near Isetan department store)
17-7, Shinjuku 3-chome
Shinjuku-ku
Telephone 354-0131
They carry foreign books, magazines, and maps.

Maruzen Co. Ltd. (opposite Takashimaya)
3-10, Nihonbashi 2-chome
Chuo-ku
Telephone 272-7211
They have the best stock of books in various languages, and cover most interests from light fiction to classical and technical. You'll find a supply of Penguins and Pelicans and cheap books for younger children. Foreign books are on the third floor.

Imperial Hotel Book Stall
Imperial Hall
1-1, Uchisaiwai-cho 1-chome
Chiyoda-ku
Telephone 591-3151
You'll find a good selection of English translations of Japanese books as well as books on Japan and American magazines.

The Tokyo American Club Book Shop
1-2, Azabudai 2-chome
Minato-ku
Telephone 583-6381
They carry books for children and adults. The store is open to nonmembers.

For a listing of all the English books published in Japan on and about Asia, you can subscribe to a monthly newsletter called the

*Japan Publications Guide.* This not only will give you a list of the most recent books, but it will tell you about bookstores and periodicals. Contact the Japan Publications Guide (CPO Box 971, Tokyo, Japan) or telephone 661-8373 for further information and subscription rates.

## Shoe Repairs

Any of the small local shops are good enough for ordinary shoes, as are the pavement menders who will do a fairly good quick job while you wait. There are heel bars at Seibu, Mitzukoshi, and some other department stores. The Washington Shoe Store (7-7, Ginza 5-chome, Chuo-ku; telephone 572-5911) has a reputation for good shoe repair work.

## Dry Cleaning

In each neighborhood there is at least one small cleaner and laundry. Hotels, particularly the Okura, also can accommodate you for dry-cleaning services. It is wise to mark linens well before sending them out.

## Hairdressers

Many beauty shops in the gaijin area are used to Westerners' hair, which is usually finer than Japanese hair. Most hairdressers in Tokyo do not mind setting hair that has been washed at home. They will also do a comb a few days after a set for very little, and it looks as good as new. Some shops include a scalp and shoulder massage with the price of the hairdo, a hand and arm massage with a manicure, and a foot and leg massage along with a pedicure.

## Grocery Shopping

Grocery shopping will provide you with a wide variety of choices from all over the world. International supermarkets are found in the popular gaijin residential areas, and some stock as much as 70 percent American foods, a smaller portion of European products, and a smattering of local foods.

Good quality meat, fish, fruit, and vegetables can be found in both international and Japanese supermarkets. Chickens are not as plump, and turkeys are imported frozen from the States. A wide selection of prepared, canned, and convenience foods are on the shelves. One store carries over 100 varieties of bread. Such items as rice and baking soda are found in the groceries now. Japanese food producers are beginning to put English names on their products. These often are equal to those from the States and cost less. Also, do not neglect the neighborhood shops where you will find almost every conceivable item. Try the *nashi* (pear-apple) or the *yamaimo* (a long, potato-like vegetable).

Milk is pasteurized, but with a slightly different taste. Other dairy products are good.

Imported liquors are expensive. There are adequate Japanese substitutes for whiskey and very good beers. A fledgling wine industry is beginning to produce some drinkable vintages.

If you want, however, to eat like the Japanese, you can save some money and probably shed a few pounds in the process. The local people are enviously slim and trim, and their diets, which contain large quantities of fish, are simple. Probably the best way to handle the food costs in Tokyo is to try a combination of local foods and American products. It takes a little basic knowledge to know how and what to buy and what to do with it once you get it. This know-how is best obtained through a cooking class and books, both of which are readily available. The Tokyo American Club provides cooking courses for members, and a charming Japanese lady by the name of Kiyoko Konishi teaches a course in Japanese cooking in her home. Either call or write her at 7-17 Shimomeguro, Meguro-ku; telephone 714-0085.

Here are a few cookbooks to ease the way into local food preparations:

*Buy It 'n Try It, Hints on Cooking and Living in Japan.* This is put together by the Women's Society of Tokyo Union Church and can be obtained thorugh the church (7-7, 5-chome, Jingumae, Shibuya-ku) or IMS Supermarket.

*Japanese Guide to Fish Cooking* (Shufonotomo, Tokyo). This book is available in local bookstores.

*Rice Paddy Gourmet* (*Japan Times,* Tokyo). This book is also available in local bookstores.

Before tackling any Japanese cooking and even before venturing into the little eateries down the back alleyway, there are two words that everyone should understand—*tofu* and *miso*. They play as important a role in the Japanese diet as bread and butter, meat and potatoes, and bacon and eggs, all rolled into one, play in the American's food plans. There are over 30,000 shops in Japan dedicated to the preparation of tofu and many, many tofu restaurants. Poems have been written about it; proverbs honor it. Miso has been around for well over 2,000 years and had its origins in China.

What exactly are they? Detailed books have been written about the two and how to use them. But simply put, there are seven basic forms of tofu, all made from soybean curds that are high in protein and low in calories, and it is used in everything from salads to dessert. Miso is made from fermented soybean paste and really has no equivalent in Western cooking. Some have compared its texture with peanut butter. There are a half dozen basic types, and they are used as seasonings throughout Japanese cooking. Two excellent books on the subject—with hundreds of recipes included—are available in the United States: *The Book of Tofu, Food for Mankind* and *The Book of Miso* (both published by Autumn Press, Brookline, Mass.).

The small, local food shops—meat, vegetables, bakeries—offer better prices than the large, international supermarkets. For an unlimited selection of fish as well as a fascinating excursion, visit the Tsukiji Fish Market early in the morning. It is primarily a wholesale market, but it is possible to make small personal purchases. Write the name of the fish you want to purchase in large letters on a piece of cardboard or sturdy paper and hold it up as you walk through the marketplace. Someone who can read English will spot it and direct you to the right stall.

The following is a list of some of the international markets:

Kinokuniya International
11-7, Kita-Aoyama 3-chome
Minato-ku
Telephone 409-1231

and

Todoroki Store
18-1, 7-chome
Todoroki, Setagaya-ku
Telephone 704-7515
A good selection of meat, vegetables, bread, and cooked meats and a wide variety of cheeses are stocked by this store. There is also a good selection of canned and frozen foods and a deli upstairs. There are no telephone orders, but they will deliver once you have purchased the food.

National Azabu Supermarket
5-2, Minami Azabu 4-chome
Minato-ku
Telephone 442-3181
They have a high percentage of imported foods and unusual items. It is an excellent place to buy liquor and wine.

Benten
102 Wakamatsu-cho
Shinjuku-ku
Telephone 202-2421
This store will furnish you with a catalog so that you can call in your orders. If they receive your call before 10 a.m., you will have the food that day. Prices are a little lower than some of the other supermarkets. Good for bulk items like dog food.

Hara Store
4, Azabu Juban 2-chome
Minato-ku
Telephone 451-8951
This store delivers and takes orders by telephone.

Olympia Foodliner
35-3, Jingumae 6-chome
Shibuya-ku
Telephone 400-7351
You'll find a wide selection of Japanese goods and frozen foods. The store also operates a snack bar and a self-service launderette and dry-cleaning facility.

National Azabu
5-2, Minami-Azabu 4-chome
Telephone 442-3181
This store is located behind the main Juban Street and a block back from the Hara store. It has a large selection of Japanese and Western products and a good variety store upstairs.

Yours
5-12, Kita Aoyama 3-chome
Minato-ku
Telephone 408-6101
This store stays open until 2 a.m. and has good donuts.

Shell Garden Supermarket
23-1, Jiyugaoka 2-chome
Meguro-ku
Telephone 718-6481

This store is a joint venture with Shell Oil Company and has a gas station, supermarket, and coffee shop in one location. It carries top-quality Japanese foods along with a high percentage of foreign foodstuffs. They will take orders by telephone and deliver. A small parking lot is available.

Meida-Ya Supermarket
Many locations. An excellent selection of American, European, and local foods. At the front of the Hiroo store is a coffee shop, elegant and pleasant. Grocery shopping in the States was never like this!

Seiyu
This chain is found all over Tokyo and stocks mainly Japanese items. Prices are lower than in international supermarkets. There is a store in Azabu Juban.

## Transportation

Tokyo is crossed, criss-crossed, bisected, and looped by one of the fastest and most efficient transportation systems this world has to offer. The infamous pushers, those not-too-gentle men who shove the passengers into the already full coaches and then pull them out again when they stop, are only around at certain stations during the rush hours (generally 7 a.m. to 9 a.m. and again at 5 p.m. to 7 p.m.). If you really want to experience the thrill of being pushed on board, you will have to go to the city's busiest terminal, Shinjuku, where nearly 2 million passengers pass through the portals each day.

Trains and subways are clean (no graffiti in sight), and where they can't take you, a bus will. As a last resort, take a taxi. Here is a rundown on the various forms of transportation around the city.

### *Subways*

For the most part, these underground trains travel within the inner portions of the city with a few arms stretching outward here and there. There are nine lines, three of which are operated by the government, the others privately managed. The entrances to the subways—and the major stops have many, so be careful in getting and giving directions—will be marked with a blue-and-white *S* sign or a six-spoked wheel. The subways start running at 5 a.m. and stop slightly before midnight.

There are excellent, easy to follow, English, color-coded subway maps available in the city's largest hotels and at the Japan

National Tourist Office. Fares are purchased at in-the-wall vending machines. If you are not certain as to which ticket to purchase, buy the cheapest one and hold out a fistful of change at the other end so that the ticket taker can select the balance. The ticket will be punched at the entrance to the train platform and taken at the exit, so hold on to it. The machines will make change, but there is a special pink-colored machine to change Y1,000 bills.

Children under 6 go free and up to 12 go half price. Push the buttons at the bottom of the vending machines for the children's tickets. There are also special commuter and student tickets available. Students should have their schools fill out transportation forms and then present them at the various station ticket windows near the vending machines for reduced fares.

Each stop has several signs in both Japanese and English. The name in the middle indicates that particular station, the one on the left tells the preceding stop, and the one on the right indicates the next stop down the line. There are many connecting stations where you can transfer to both subways and trains. The system is so easy to follow that within a day or two you will be feeling like a native.

## Trains

In addition to the subways, there are local electric surface trains. Tickets and discounts are purchased in the same manner as for the subway rides; but if no vending machine is available or if the fare exceeds the amount available in the machine, the ticket can be bought at a nearby window. The Japanese National Railways (JNR) operates one group of local trains in and around Tokyo. They are known as the Kokuden trains. The individual lines within this system are identified by the various colored coaches.

The Yamanote Line (green coaches) is probably the city's most famous train. It runs through Tokyo station and makes a loop around the heart of the city, connecting the major train stations and city centers surrounding these stations.

There are also dozens of private train lines that connect with subways, the Yamanote Line, and other private and JNR systems. Like tentacles of a giant monster, these various lines reach out to grasp the outer areas of Tokyo, making it possible to travel to any section within the metropolitan district as well as to its neighboring towns with ease.

Be sure to get the "Communications Network, Tokyo and Vicinity" map from the tourist office. It is excellent for showing the train routings around the area.

Traveling from city to city in Japan is made easy by the fast Shinkansen (bullet) trains. Service is frequent and the cars are clean and comfortable. Dining cars are on all trains. The fares, however, are rather steep. One tip—don't bother with first class, the second class reserved seats are just as nice. Areas not serviced by the bullet trains can be reached by the equally efficient and pleasant but slower limited express trains. Most trains have station announcements in English.

## Buses

What the subways and trains don't reach, the buses will—or almost. They are tricky, however, and it is easy to be confused by them. You need to know the number and routing of the bus, and, in addition, you have to be able to recognize the correct stop. If you can't do the latter, tell the driver your destination as you board and act puzzled, and the chances are good he will keep an eye on you and tell you when it is time to get off.

## Taxis

You can catch a taxi by flagging it down, by going to a taxi stand at a hotel or station, or by calling one by telephone. If you get a cab by phone, expect a 20 percent increase over your regular fare. You are charged both mileage and time; if you wish to go by expressway, you are expected to pay the tolls. Between 11 p.m. and 5 a.m., the taxi fee is again 20 percent higher. If you are having difficulty flagging down a cab late at night, you can wave one, two, or three fingers, indicating your willingness to pay that many times over what the meter reads. Illegal and distasteful as it is, the system enables you to get a cab. If you really need help, go to a policeman and ask for a *ta-ku-shi-i*. Taxi doors are opened and closed only by the driver, who controls them from his seat.

## To and From the Airports

### Haneda Airport

Monorail links Hamamatsu-cho Station (by the World Trade Center) with Haneda Airport, from which domestic flights leave and enter Tokyo.

### Narita Airport

This is the international airport through which you probably will enter Japan. When arriving at Narita, which is 40 miles from the center of the city, the best buy for getting into the city is a bus from the airport to the Tokyo City Air Terminal, just a short taxi ride from many of the main hotels and offices. At Narita there is a small charge per bag for the transfer from the baggage claim area to the buses. The ride is comfortable, and there are English announcements. The normal non-rush hour trip lasts a little over an hour. If expense is no object, take the taxi direct to your destination. Then, there are about three different routings involving subways and trains to various stations in the center of the city. But these involve at least one intermediate transfer, so they are not for the passenger with lots of luggage.

## Finding Your Way

In spite of the fact that streets are unnamed and buildings are not numbered consecutively, finding your way around Tokyo is not all that difficult. Have you ever tried to give directions to someone in the States only to find yourself stumbling over street names? You knew how to get from here to there, but you certainly could not give a rundown on all the names in between. You had to rely on landmarks. So it is in Tokyo.

There are addresses, but they are quite different from what you find at home. First, the country is divided into prefectures *(ken)*. Next come the cities *(shi)*, which are divided into wards *(ku)*. The ku, in turn, is subdivided into neighborhoods *(cho)*. And these are divided into blocks *(chome)*. You put it all on your envelopes and let the postman worry about it. You still find your way by landmarks.

It is customary to put a map showing directions to your home on the back of your personal card; it is wise to have your children always carry these cards with them in case they become lost. Also, have them carry some change for a phone call. (See Communications for how to use the telephones.)

It is essential to get a good map before you begin to explore Tokyo; while many are to be found in Japanese, a top-notch English one is not that easy to come by. One we highly recommend is "Falk's Plan of Tokyo, Red Series Number 1" (Falk International, Hamburg, The Hague), available in Tokyo's foreign-language bookstores.

There is at least one passable English-language map of the Kanto

Plain (the 5,000 square mile hinterland of Tokyo) that provides adequate directions for main road travel. This is the "Handy Map of Kanto for Drivers." It should, however, be regarded with caution when going off the beaten track. (See also Cars and Drivers.)

If you are lost, write your destination down (that is, print it) and show it to someone, preferably a young person who probably has studied English in school.

## Communications

### *Newspapers*

There are more English-language newspapers in Tokyo than in any city in the United States. The country as a whole has over 1,000 papers and 15,000 magazines.

In Tokyo you will find five daily English newspapers: the *Japan Times*, the *Asahi Evening News*, the *Mainichi Daily News*, the *Yomiuri*, and the *Shipping and Trade News*. In addition there is the *Asian Wall Street Journal*, which is published daily in Hong Kong and flown to Japan, and the *Pacific Stars and Stripes*, available by subscription only.

There are several weekly English papers as well:

*Tokyo Weekender*. It is a tabloid and includes classified ads covering rentals and household goods being sold by those leaving Japan. It is free and distributed at most large supermarkets and places where foreigners go frequently.

The *Japan Times Weekly*. This is tabloid size and carries news features.

*Tour Companion*. This paper keeps you abreast of what is going on in Tokyo. It is available in hotel lobbies and newsstands in the Ginza.

Several American publishers print special English additions for Japan, such as *Time* and *Newsweek*.

Daily editions of the *New York Times* can be delivered to your door in central Tokyo—but at an exorbitant price. They are also sold at newsstands in Tokyo and Osaka only. Contact the Overseas Courier Service (9-2 Shibaura, 2-chome, Minato-ku; telephone 453-8311).

*Forecasts,* available on subscription, will provide information on cultural events in advance.

## Television and Radio

Tokyo has no less than seven television channels showing high quality programs, all in Japanese. Motion pictures are shown in their original language in theaters; movies on television are dubbed.

For parents who find American television too ladened with sex and violence, Japanese television may be a shocker. Bedroom scenes, nudity (from the waist up), and violence so strong it repels the average Western viewer are not uncommon.

At a recent seminar, a professor from Keio University and two other researchers reported their theories that Japanese television violence tended to release subdued aggressiveness and had the effect of keeping the audience from initiating violent actions. At any rate, the violence is much more explicit and agonizing than on stateside television.

Channel 42 (UHF) in the Tokyo area carries a 30-minute English program entitled "World Today" Monday through Friday. In many of the hotels there is a special cable television station, channel 2, with English programs for a few hours in the morning and then resuming at 6 p.m. You can't get this in private dwellings, with some rare exceptions where the special cable has been installed.

There is a device, a multiplex adapter, that allows you to hear the original English soundtrack on American and English programs. What happens is that the local stations have both dialogues available and run the English on FM multiplex. The newspapers will indicate for which programs this feature is available.

English-language radio programs can be picked up on the Armed Forces Far East Network, 810 kHz.

## Telephones

They work beautifully! Public phones are always in order; directories are stacked neatly beside them with no missing pages; and at some public phones you may even find a notepad for your convenience.

Your home telephone will be black, but the public phones come in a rainbow of colors that indicate the type and number of coins they will take. All public phones take Y10 coins, and the yellow telephones will also take Y100 for longer calls. The Y10 coin allows you to talk three minutes on a local call; at the end of that time, you will be cut off without a warning; depositing more coins *before* the time is up will prevent this. For a long-distance call, if you don't know the exact amount, you can keep depositing coins until the connection is made. Surplus money is returned in the coin slot at the end of your call. Here is a rundown on the various telephones and the number of coins each will take:

| Telephone | Coin Used | Number of Coins Accepted |
|---|---|---|
| Blue phone (in street booths): for local and short-distance calls | Y10 | Up to ten on one call |
| Red phone (found outside stores): for same calls as the blue | Y10 | Up to six coins per call |
| Pink phone: same as red phone | Y10 | Same as the red |
| Yellow phone: for all calls | Y10 Y100 | Up to ten Y10 and nine Y100 coins |

Private telephones require a high installation charge and an even higher deposit or bond, but it is refundable after ten years and bears interest. You may be able to sell your bond to another party. Bills are issued monthly and include charges made for calls during the preceding month and rental for the month to come. Your bank may pay your bill directly from your account if you wish.

There are several English directories available, but they must be purchased in local bookstores. One is the _Yellow Pages Japan Telephone Book,_ and another is the _Japan Times Telephone Directory,_ which lists foreign residents as well as some shops. Telephone numbers stay with the house or apartment, so the foreign colony knows who has moved and when. There is the very expensive, three-volume _Japan Directory_ (published by the Japan Press, Ltd.), which has a more detailed list of businesses and stores.

## Telegrams

There are three types of services available: ordinary, urgent, and letter. These and cables may be sent either from the Kokusai Denshin Denwa Co., Ltd. (telegraph-telephone offices) or from most post offices. Hotels also have this service available in most cases.

## Mail

Post offices are open from 9 a.m. to 5 p.m. Monday through Saturday. The main post office, located in front of Tokyo Station, stays open until midnight seven days a week. Stamps can be purchased at hotels and some shops displaying an official post office sign, a red capital _T_ with a line above it.

If you think you may not be getting all your mail, you could be right. Japanese addresses are difficult for Westerners. The *Japan Times* lists undelivered mail in each edition. It's a good idea to check this daily.

## Free Time

Entertainment, yes—relaxation, maybe! Amusements in Japan are enjoyed wholeheartedly and with a fervor that many foreigners consider too intense. As with many other aspects of Japanese life, the effort in time and money to get a ticket to a popular movie on the Ginza or to get to a well-known hot spring resort outside Tokyo on a summer weekend can seem overwhelming. But there is no other country that offers you such a wide selection of ancient Eastern and modern Western entertainment.

### *Tickets*

Getting tickets is the biggest problem in enjoying theater, concerts, movies, and other performances. You are advised to obtain your tickets through various agencies known as "playguides."

The old hands at the Tokyo American Club put together a few other tips:

Seats in the eighth row and behind, even the very back, are really better for Kabuki and Bunraku.

Get to the theater early enough to buy an English program and to arrange for your meal, which you can book at a special counter. The meal will be on the table in a restaurant connected to the theater at intermission. Your name will be on that table.

Keep your eye on the time while eating, as the curtain bell does not ring in some theater restaurants.

Your coat may be rolled up in a bundle and tied with a numbered cord in the cloak room. Retrieve your coat during the last intermission. Most theaters have coin lockers.

It is quite proper to come late and leave early and to come and go from your seat during the performance.

### *Theater*

Kabuki, with its stylized acting by males only, its atonal music played on the three-stringed *shamisen,* and its pantomime, is the most famous of the Japanese classical theater arts. No theater in the world excels Kabuki in its lavish color, glamour, costuming, staging, emotion, and extraordinariness. In Tokyo, plays are staged almost every day of the year. Japan's best-known Kabuki theater is the Kabukiza Theater (12-15 Ginza Higashi, 4-chome, Minato-ku, Tokyo; telephone 541-3131), where English programs are available. (For a better understanding of Kabuki, read *The Kabuki Handbook: A Guide to the Understanding and Appreciation, with Summaries of Favorite Plays, Explanation, Notes and Illustrations* [Charles E. Tuttle Company, Tokyo].)

Kabuki developed as the theater of the common people; Nō, or Noh, for the highborn and learned. Noh can be compared with ancient Greek drama. There is no specialized scenery—only a stage setting that has been characterized as a "house within a house"—but the costumes are magnificent. The essential characteristic of Noh is its symbolism, elegant and solemn yet graceful.

A third type of classical drama of interest to foreigners is the puppet drama *(bunraku).* This form of theater was once in decline, but the government and the Japan Broadcasting System sparked a resurgence.

One of the most impressive theaters is the new, huge National Theater in "contemporary-traditional" Japanese architectural style. It has a large auditorium and a smaller one within. All the traditional theatrical forms are represented, as well as modern Japanese plays. An occasional performance will have instantaneous translation or explanation in English, and there are English programs. Performances are announced in the English-language newspapers, and reservations are accepted in English by telephone (265-2838).

For English-language theater, you must look to the amateur groups sponsored by various organizations. Many foreign clubs have them.

Musical reviews began when the famous Takarazaka All-Girl Troupe began staging Western-style performances in 1927. Today's shows at the troupe's theater near the Imperial Hotel include both revues and operettas. New performances are introduced twice a year. Staging and costumes are spectacular.

Another troupe, reminiscent of the Rockettes of New York, is the Shochiku Kagekidin. You can see its high-stepping chorus line at its own theater.

Few tourists pass up a chance to attend the Nichigeki Music Hall, which houses Japanese musical revues and festivals. Try another floor and you will find modern burlesque featuring Japanese and Western dancers.

If your interests are less eclectic, walk through the Tokyo parks on a sunny Sunday. In Yoyogi Park in Shibuya, for example, you can watch high school roller skating clubs—complete with uniforms of their own—practicing the slalom by criss-crossing through a maze of rubber cones they set up on the closed-off streets. Or watch the harajuku dancers, groups of teenagers in the most bizarre costumes dancing in a circle to the beat of a rock group from a tape player or radio. Look out for tennis and frisbee players who will be practicing their skills in any halfway vacant spot on the sidewalks or roads.

## Music

The Japanese enjoy the best of music around the world—whether it be symphonic, jazz, or country. There are eight very active orchestras in Tokyo holding their own subscription concerts. Guest artists include the great names in the music world. Other performers are shown on television and heard on radio frequently. Several leading Western groups such as the Chicago and Boston symphonies have visited Tokyo.

Chamber music, choruses, and brass bands are all very popular. Individual recitals by Japanese performers—from graduates of the 20 music schools in Japan to international artists—number in the thousands each year.

There are more than 100 opera performances annually in Tokyo. Occasional visits by ballet companies round out the classical music spectrum.

The focal point for good jazz and other popular music is the night club area of Tokyo, where there is no limit to the variety and quality of performance. (But see the section below for a few precautions.)

## Night Clubs and Night Life

The setting of the sun marks the time when thousands of cabarets, bars, restaurants, hostesses, turkish baths, pachinko parlors, hotel receptions, and other privately arranged parties all vie for the right to provide their services to the Japanese male seeking some relaxation, and perhaps some informal business arrangements, before returning home.

The Ginza and Akasaka areas are the centers for the plush, gilded night clubs with hostesses and lavish floor shows, such as the Mikado and Copa Cabana. These will have a basic cover charge, and food and drink will be served only when ordered. Hostesses are also not provided unless requested. All of this is geared to the Western patron. There are many other night life centers around Tokyo, such as Shinjuku and Shibuya. All of these areas offer a bewildering array of bars and cabarets to suit any taste. There is one where the band goes up and down on an elaborate elevator-stage and beer is delivered on a miniature railway system; another has men dressed as mummies and horror film stars mingling with the guests. There are some bars that cater exclusively to women.

All of this machinery is lubricated by the ample expense accounts Japanese industry grants to its middle- and upper-echelon employees.

In few places will a foreigner be "taken," but the many charges can add up before he realizes the total cost. Most bars and cabarets outside the areas where tourists frequent are not accustomed to foreigners. Do not be offended if you are politely refused admission. These places are simply for the Japanese and are not prepared for an alien presence to dampen the goings-on.

Hotel bars are operated as in the United States, and a number have night clubs or rooms featuring dancing. By law, all dancing ceases in Tokyo by 11 p.m.

Tokyo night life closes rather early, usually before midnight. There are some places, however, that continue until 4 or 5 a.m. under the pretext of serving food.

Another unique masculine attraction in Japan is the Turkish bathhouse. They can be quite luxurious. You are attended to by scantily clad young girls, but the reputable spas are not disguised brothels. The communal baths so famous in Japan are found in other cities.

## *Movies*

Japan is both a major producer and consumer of movies. In the past few years, imported films have gradually taken precedence over those locally produced. New American or other foreign films appear in Tokyo quite quickly after their premier in the country where produced. Normally, foreign films are shown in their original dialogue with Japanese subtitles.

The major first-run movie houses have reserved seats and long ticket lines are common.

## Museums and Galleries

There are over 300 museums and 200 galleries in Tokyo. The *Tour Companion,* the weekly publication of what's going on in Tokyo, habitually devotes two pages to exhibits in the many museums, galleries, and department stores that also present excellent exhibitions. Most are closed on Mondays.

## Restaurants

The variety is endless. One report claims that there are 80,000 in Tokyo, but they must have missed a few. The range in cost is just as great as the scope of the cuisine.

American culture in the form of its favorite franchise food emporiums has truly captured Japan. Hamburgers, donuts, pizza, fried chicken, and multiflavored ice cream have attracted loyal Japanese adherence.

Food of any type will be served with an eye toward beauty, color, and arrangement on the plate, even in the most humble restaurant (American fast-food chains are the exception).

One of Tokyo's most interesting art forms is the duplication in plastic of the dishes served in restaurants. The copies are very detailed and look good enough to eat. Most restaurants will display their dishes in a case near the door with the prices underneath. This practice helps reduce surprises for the hungry expatriate.

It is helpful to know some of the principal types of Japanese restaurants (*ya* means "shop" or "house"):

*Soba-ya.* Soba is noodles, and these restaurants serve many varieties with vegetables, meat, or fish on top.

*Koryori-ya.* These are small restaurants, but they have semiprivate tatami mat rooms. They serve a variety of seasonal fresh fish and vegetable dishes.

*Sushi-ya.* These restaurants serve seasoned rice and rolls in bowls topped with slices of raw fish.

*Kissaten.* They offer a great variety of modern and traditional tea rooms and coffee shops.

*Tempura-ya.* Here, fish, shrimp, and raw vegetables are dipped individually in a specially prepared batter and deep-fried.

*Shabu-ya.* Thin slices of beef, pork, or fish are cooked in boiling water, then dipped into a special hot sauce before eating. Vegetables are also eaten in the same manner. Boiling water, now heavily seasoned, is a delicious clear soup for the last course.

*Yakitori-ya.* Small pieces of chicken or whole chicken grilled on a skewer is eaten with a special sauce.

Western foods tend to be more expensive, expecially orange juice, steak, and imported foods of all kinds.

Many Japanese restaurants will have silverware available, but some practice with chopsticks before arriving will make you feel more comfortable.

Sake (pronounced "sa-kay") is the traditional white wine from fermented rice. It has strong religious and social ties. One of the distinctive features is warming it to body temperature before drinking, although cold sake in the summer is fashionable. When drinking, one should never pour his own sake but allow another person to fill his cup. In the process of filling the cup, it should be held above the table and not allowed to rest on it. A last word of caution: don't think that sake is a weak drink. The best quality is from 16 to 16.9 percent alcohol.

### *The Traditional Arts*

What night life is to the men, the arts are to the women. *Bonsai* (the cultivation of trees by artifical dwarfing), *ikebana* (flower arranging), *origami* (the art of folding paper into delicate designs and figures), and *chanoyou* (tea ceremony) are popular courses for expatriates. It is interesting that in Japan the masters of these arts are men, but the practitioners are women. The directory mentioned in the Sports section lists schools for the traditional arts.

## Organizations

First among the organizations for Americans is the Tokyo American Club. An oasis in the oriental world, this club—better known as the TAC—is the hub around which much of the social life of the American community revolves. A combination of superb, modern facilities, delicious American and international cuisine, and an excellent sports program make this club a favorite among expatriates and a prestige establishment that the Japanese enjoy visiting as well. The initial membership plus a refundable bond purchase add up to an amount that few individuals care or are able to contribute for a short stay. Many companies include this initiation expense as part of the expatriate's compensation package.

The Women's Group of the TAC is a social organization to

which all female club members are invited to join. It has monthly luncheons with programs and sponsors about 15 different classes on the traditional arts, cooking, bridge, needlepoint, and other such diversions. A real bargain are the trips the women sponsor in and out of Japan.

The TAC is the main club for famlies. A soda bar, Olympic-size pool, bowling, and facilities for movies and stage productions attract the children. Santa always makes an appearance at Christmas.

There are many other business, professional, cultural, social, fraternal, university alumni, and special purpose clubs for expatriates. Virtually all have both American and Japanese members and most encourage participation by all nationalities. The English-language telephone books are good sources to check for your particular interest.

## Sports and Recreation

Japanese do not play sports—they attack a variety of sports with intensity. When they participate in athletics, even on an amateur basis, they spend great amounts of time and money in equipping and providing themselves a place to play. Then they settle down to defeat the opponent (either an actual antagonist or their own record) by mastering every detail of the chosen sport.

Tickets for the major spectator sports on a day-to-day basis are almost as scarce as were tickets for the Olympic Games held in Tokyo in 1964. Baseball tops the list. This American import is the most popular crowd pleaser with the possible exception of horse racing.

For the other great spectator and television attractions you must turn from the modern games to the ancient martial arts of Japan and particularly to sumo, the ritualistic form of wrestling that is over almost before it begins. This is the only martial art that is both professional and amateur, and its origins go back 2,000 years or more.

Karate is a legitimate spectator and participant sport. It is not so old, having begun with very humble origins among the priests in Okinawa. It arrived in Japan only about 50 years ago.

Two of Japan's manias—go and pachinko—involve some participation, but also a lot of contemplation. Go, the national game of Japan, is believed to be the world's oldest game. It is a board game that takes years to master, although the fundamentals can be learned quickly. Pachinko is best described as vertical pinball. Millions of all ages are caught up in it.

The traditional sports and martial arts from *aikido* (a form of wrestling emphasizing overcoming an opponent with minimum force) to *shintaido* (a system of empty-handed fighting) have been preserved and nurtured to new heights of accomplishment. Simultaneously, Japan has made a name for herself in many modern sports, such as golf.

There are few public golf courses. Joining a club, particularly those with well-laid-out courses, is a major investment in time and money, although a club share can be sold when you leave. It usually takes up to two hours to reach most of the better clubs. Between outings, you can practice at one of Tokyo's elaborate driving ranges if you can find an open spot. Golf and your handicap are things that bridge the language and culture gap quicker than almost any other topic.

The better ski areas are nearly two—and many up to six—hours from Tokyo by train, and they are jammed. Do not count on luxury resorts or apres-ski revelry. The Japanese make excellent equipment—but not for those over six feet tall.

Reservations are necessary for the public tennis courts, and dates are made a month in advance at your local ward office. Frequently, you reserve on the fifteenth of the month.

Almost every other sport known to man is recognized and available in this country. Where and what to do can be found in the *Japan Guide and Directory to the Martial Arts and Modern Sports,* published by BAT and available at the Foreign Correspondent's Club of Japan (20th Floor, Yurakucho Denki Building, 1-chome, Chiyoda-ku; telephone 211-3161). This club is located just across from the Yurakucho Station of the Yamanote Line.

Bicycles have always been used for transportation in Japan. Even in the heart of Tokyo's business district, sidewalks are divided by a white line for pedestrians and bicyclers making deliveries. Now sports cycling is very popular. There is a public cycling path around the Imperial Palace and many at historic shrines where cars are banned.

The newest craze is jogging and running. There is a very convenient three-mile course around the moat of the Imperial Palace. Over 5 million jog twice a week or more in Japan. It all culminates in the marathon at Ome, about 60 miles west of Tokyo. Here thousands of runners, including a couple hundred gaijins, compete in races amidst a carnival atmosphere.

## *Young People's Activities*

Tokyo abounds with activities for children and teenagers. The schools have active extracurricular programs—swimming, tennis, theater—that keep them busy. But the city itself is a never-ending playground. Anything youngsters do here in the way of fun can be a learning experience. Even a visit to one of the local amusement centers will give them a glimpse of the Japanese genius for creating illusion. Try Summerland—but in the wintertime. It is an indoor park in Akikawashi, one of Tokyo's outer cities, covered by a glass dome that sweeps three stories high over an area the size of a baseball diamond. Here, youngsters can swim in a miniature ocean complete with a man-made surf, a terrifying plastic shark, and rain showers that will send them scampering for the synthetic beach that rims the water. It is reached by taking the Chuo or Keio train to Hachioji Station and then transferring to bus 12 for a 30-minute ride to the park.

There are puppet theaters, children's concerts (with explanations given in English), all types of imaginative parks (junk, tire, railroad), hundreds of museums appealing to youngsters (Tokyo Metropolitan Children's Center, Baseball Hall of Fame, Paper Museum, Sugino Gakuen Costume), recreational facilities, factory tours, hobby shops, and classes (origami, crafts, music, ballet). For a complete listing, we highly recommend *A Parent's Guide to Tokyo* (Shufunotomo, Tokyo). It is available in bookstores patronized by Westerners in Tokyo. If you wish to obtain a copy before leaving the States, write to the Kinokuniya Book Store of America Co., Ltd. (1581 Webster Street, San Francisco, California 94115). It is more than a guide for parents. It provides a rundown on what to do in Tokyo for people of all ages.

Children's friends will probably not live close by. But it is quite easy for children to take public transportation. Teenagers, in fact, told us they enjoyed the freedom they had in using subways and trains. They did not have to wait for mom and dad to give them permission to drive the car. Few have licenses in this country, and few seem to mind. Even younger children, once they can read, are able to get around on public transportation.

The Amercial Chamber of Commerce, in conjunction with the Tokyo American Club and the American embassy, helps find summer employment for teenagers. Contact the American Chamber of Commerce in Tokyo for further information and job availability.

There is also an active scouting program in the Tokyo area. Inquire through your school or the Tokyo American Club about troop membership.

Summer camping programs are available in Japan. Inquire through your school about these programs also. Youth hostels offer an excellent, inexpensive way for teenagers to see the country. For more information, contact the Japan Youth Hostel (Hoken Kaikan, 1-2, Sadohara-cho, Ichigaya, Shinjuku-ku; telephone 268-8101).

There is another great plus about living among the Japanese. Parents say that the local attitudes involving great respect toward parents and schools appear to rub off on foreign young people.

While there is no problem with clothes for young children, teenagers may find the sizes in Japan too small. Just as with adults, dress tends to be a little more on the formal side. However, don't leave the blue jeans behind. There will be many occasions to wear them. At the American School, where uniforms are not required, students wear jeans to class.

## Religion

The two major religions in Japan are Shinto and Buddhism. Christianity was brought to Japan in the sixteenth century, but it suffered a setback when, in the last year or so of that century, all the missionaries were expelled and the religion went underground. The doors were opened again in the middle of the nineteenth century. Although there are no restraints put on Christianity today, less than 2 percent of the nation are followers.

There are several churches in the Tokyo-Yokohama area that have English services and function as a religious home as well as social and cultural centers for the expatriate. These are listed in *Living in Japan*. The congregations include people from all walks of life— missionaries to company presidents—and from countries all over the world. They provide help in cultural adaptation and in answering questions on any facet of life in Tokyo.

## Health Care

The sanitary conditions in Japan are the best in all Asia. The water and milk, generally, are considered safe throughout the country. However, if you should be traveling through some rural areas where water comes from wells and is not chlorinated, you should boil it for at least 20 minutes. The pasteurized milk is safe, but check on deliveries during the hot summer months. Improperly refrigerated products can spoil. Raw meat and the popular raw fish should be eaten only in quality restaurants where you are assured that the meat was inspected and the fish were not caught in a sewage area.

## Doctors and Hospitals

There are a number of English-speaking doctors in Tokyo, many of whom have had some training in the States. And there are several Western-type hospitals in the city. *Living in Japan* not only lists these but provides maps on their locations. Foreigners are usually more comfortable in these than in strictly Japanese hospitals where they are required to feed and bathe themselves as well as make their own beds. If they are too ill to do so, their families have to lend a hand.

Hospitals generally have a staff of their own doctors, and other physicians are not allowed to treat patients there. This means if you require hospitalization, your doctor may have to refer you to someone else who is on the staff of the particular hospital you enter. However, there is one hospital in Tokyo, Seibo, that has a semiopen staff and allows some outside doctors to use the institution. Medical treatment can be complicated by a shortage of beds, even in an emergency situation.

Some doctors have their own small—around 20 beds—hospitals. Major surgery normally is not performed here.

Paramedic training and services as found in the United States are not yet in Tokyo. The Fire Department runs the ambulance service, but you have to summon them in Japanese. The attendants are equipped to provide only first aid. They will not take women in labor.

Medical insurance policies such as Blue Cross/Blue Shield can be used in Japan. Check to make sure your policy is honored before leaving.

## Medication and Physicals

Most basic medications are available in Japan—but not all the mixtures. If you bring long-term medication, also bring a letter from your doctor and there will be no problem with customs. It is possible to have medication imported. See a local doctor for the procedure.

Birth control pills can theoretically be given only for medical problems, but it is not uncommon for them to be prescribed for contraceptive use only. Other types of contraception are available, and condoms may be bought from public vending machines.

All help should have yearly examinations that include a chest X ray, a blood test for venereal disease, a urinalysis, and a stool examination. Tokyo Sanitarium Hospital and St. Luke's International Hospital have this service available.

## Help Groups

There are several social agencies in Tokyo that help foreign residents with many kinds of problems.

Tokyo English Life Line (TELL). This organization helps with emotional and social problems. Dial 264-4347 from 9:00 a.m. to 1:00 p.m. and from 7:00 p.m. to 11:00 p.m. every day, including holidays. This group not only handles problems, but it is a great source of information on all types of questions concerning living in Tokyo.

International Social Service (ISS). This is the local branch of a worldwide organization with headquarters in Geneva. The organization counsels individuals on sociolegal problems, divorce, status of foreigners, migration, and repatriation; handles adoptions; and helps in locating lost family members (711-5551).

# Yokohama

Many foreigners have located in the port city of Yokohama, so the amenities found in Tokyo for the expatriate are also available in this city. You will find Western-style housing, food stores that cater to foreigners (such as Meida-Ya), and Motomachi, a quaint international quarter with charming boutiques. Isezohi-cho is the central shopping area for day-to-day items. Prices tend to be a little lower than in Tokyo.

There are good recreation facilities. The Yokohama Country and Athletic Club is one of the more popular clubs, as is the Yokohama International Tennis Club.

One unique facility in this city is the only hospital established by foreigners for foreigners: Bluff Hospital (telephone [045] 641-6961), which is administered U.S. style.

There are at least two good international schools, St. Joseph College (elementary through high school) and Yokohama International School.

# The Kansai Area

The Kansai area embraces Kyoto, Osaka, and Kobe. It is about 300 miles southwest of Tokyo. While often treated as one unit, each of the three cities has its own personality.

Osaka, sometimes compared with Chicago, is a financial and commercial center.

The international expatriate community is not located in Osaka where many gaijins work but in Kobe, just a few miles away. Kobe is an important port city dating back to the fourth century. It may have its greatest reputation in the West for its high-quality beef. The cultural and historical treasures, old world ambience and charm, and less frantic pace are aspects foreign inhabitants prize. They point out that having a car here is much easier and you actually can drive into the countryside without spending hours in urban traffic.

Other differences from Tokyo are:

The electric current in the Kansai area is 100 volt/60 cycle so U.S. appliances will operate, even clocks, but with slightly reduced efficiency. Some Kobe houses have 200-volt lines as well.

Gas equipment from the United States or that purchased in Tokyo should be checked by the Osaka Gas Company for possible modifications required before use.

The Osaka/Kobe airport in Itami is not an international port. A new international facility is still in the talking stage.

While the Osaka/Kobe area does not have clubs that compare with the Tokyo American Club, there are organizations for different nationalities. The International Committee of the Kansai (ICKAN) (telephone 221-8161), a group for foreigners, acts as an effective liaison with the Japanese authorities.

The Community House and Information Center (6-12 Ikuta-cho, 4-chome, Chua-ku; telephone 078-2421043) is a great help to newly arrived expatriates. It publishes the book *Living in Kobe,* runs an orientation series for wives called "Bloom Where You're Planted," workshops on various topics such as cultural adjustment and the Japanese language, and an up-to-date information service.

Social life revolves around three clubs: the Kobe Club, Shioya Country Club, and the downtown Kobe Regatta and Athletic Club. All three provide dining and various sports facilities; the first two have swimming pools. Generally, club membership is easier to arrange than in Tokyo.

Some of the most well-regarded international schools, such as the Canadian Academy and St. Michael's International School, are found in this area.

American and European food products can be found in several stores, although you may have to go to more places to complete your shopping than in Tokyo.

Western-style housing is increasing, and there have been a number of larger (by Japanese standards) apartments built with more than one bath and with appliances.

The Kyoto City Subway began operating in the middle of 1981.

## Doing Business in Japan

When you try to do business with the Japanese, you sometimes wonder how a system so alien and ritualistic can be so successful. To work with them is to have patience and appreciation for the little things that can mean success or failure. Don't take anything for granted.

A tired, hungry businessman ordered a cheeseburger at a Tokyo McDonald's and requested that the sauce and pickles be left off. He thought the "contract" was completed when he said, "A cheese-burger plain, please." The Japanese girl at the counter nodded in understanding. What he received was plain all right—it had no cheese. But, of course, since he had asked for a cheeseburger, that was what he was charged for.

Most American businessmen have heard something about the ingredients in the Japanese recipe for its burgeoning gross national product: great loyalty to the company and the company's guarantee of a job in return; the decisions by consensus; the importance of position as evidenced by that key to all opportunities, the business card; the reluctance to express a pure no; the after-hours conferences in restaurants and bars in the Ginza or Shinjuku; and the list goes on.

You start with the language. Our State Department sends its future Japanese and Asia/Pacific experts to a branch of the Foreign Service Institute in Yokohama for up to 18 months to master spoken Japanese and acquire a lesser expertise in reading, along with doses of history and culture. Writing is left to the scholars. American busi-nessmen, however, have mixed emotions about tackling this difficult language. Some feel it is a waste of time for a short-term expatriate to try to learn a language limited to the islands of Japan. Many others consider some speaking ability essential to establish rapport with their business associates and ease the day-to-day task of living.

Using interpreters results in the already hard-to-fathom thought processes of the Japanese going through another filter in the Western-ization of the idea. Many Japanese concepts don't make it to the American listener's ear.

There is another problem with interpreters. Often, the English-speaking Japanese you rely on is at a relatively high level. Using a lot of his time as a translator wastes his other talents and may lower him in the esteem of his fellow workers.

Many transactions can be negotiated successfully with the modern English-speaking Japanese. Remember, though, that in few other countries is what is said and how it is expressed as important as the written contract. Make sure you speak distinctly, use no idioms, and repeat if necessary to get across your idea.

If you are going to learn Japanese, many suggest that you start before you leave home and do not postpone lessons when you first arrive on the excuse that the press of a new job demands it. You may never get started again.

The basic preliminary in all new contacts is the exchange of business cards *(meishi)*. Do not take this ritual lightly. It is as important in Japan as the tea ceremony. Hand your card and receive the other's as if they were very valuable documents because they *are* worth money. The business card and the title on it are better than a charge card for entertaining.

To the Japanese your card is the simplest and best indicator of your status. Make sure your position is understood by having one side in Japanese. There are many printers who can do this, either in the United States or Japan.

A couple of tips on handing out cards: give your card to each member of the opposite group and hold your card with the appropriate side up.

Now, how about the facts and myths of business entertaining and that exotic, shadowy presence in the background—the geisha? All of this is changing, but slowly. Many expatriates spend a whole tour in Japan without ever having an opportunity to attend a genuine dinner with geishas in waiting. The cost is too high (maybe $100 to $300 per person) even for the generous expense accounts of the top Japanese executive except for very special occasions. Besides, once is usually enough for Westerners. The ability of the geisha to make her guest feel like a combination of Paul Getty and Robert Redford is unique and unsurpassed—even when there is a language barrier, as there usually is. But the variety of music and silly games the geishas play for their partners quickly becomes old hat to the Western businessman.

Night clubs, restaurants, bars, and hotel receptions thrive on the business trade after office hours. The reasons that the Japanese began this practice are buried in the whole mystique of personal interrelationships in the company. For expatriates there are reasons why they, too, must plan on devoting time to these functions:

Attendance is a sign of recognition and respect for the host company or person.

Being together with your associates on an informal basis, which translates into having some drinks with the boys, gives everyone the chance to say what they really think (with the help of sake or Suntory Scotch) with the understanding that all is forgiven and forgotten the following day.

Expatriates report that the amount of time required for these nocturnal functions each week varies considerably. If you work in a Japanese company, have a large number of Japanese associates or subordinates, or your position requires you to deal with Japanese customers or suppliers, you can expect to have frequent social obligations from formal receptions to drinks. Other American businessmen whose positions are more isolated resist successfully all but the most command performances. In any case, some moderation by Americans is accepted.

Invitations for the expatriate family to a Japanese home are rare—usually extended only by the younger, internationally experienced Japanese. A Japanese executive who encountered and liked the idea of inviting business friends to the home tried to introduce this practice in Tokyo. He invited his associates and their wives. The responses fell into four categories. The first, smallest group accepted and came. The second group of husbands discussed the whole idea with their wives and went over all the possibilities and implications, and then the couple came. The third group of husbands, the largest, told their wives of the invitation but left them home. The fourth group did not even discuss it with their wives and turned down the invitation for their wives immediately.

Business negotiations will customarily involve a group on the Japanese side. The difference in approach to these meetings is well expressed in the excellent publication, *Business in Japan,* by Japan Air Lines. "The trouble with foreign businessmen is that they try to negotiate a contract while Japanese try to negotiate a relationship." In cementing this relationship, the Japanese are interested in conveying a positive note of understanding and encouragement but not necessarily agreement in the legal sense. This explains the oft-cited misunderstanding by foreigners of the use of the word *hai;* it usually is translated as "yes," but in discussions it may simply indicate polite encouragement.

Be prepared to work most of Saturday, as most businesses operate on at least a five-and-a-half-day week.

Gift giving in business is still customary, but be sure that you are not violating any law governing commercial bribes.

There are many books that have been published these last few years analyzing and reanalyzing the unique Japanese economic system, management methods, and overall success story. A few have tried to put the Japanese "magic" in proper perspective. Read at least a couple.

## Legal Matters

Japan's history and cultural background have always emphasized respect and obedience to superior authority. Its present-day adherence to the law is second nature. Even driving in Tokyo, once ceded as near the top in risk taking with its kamikaze taxi drivers, has taken on a somewhat orderly flow as traffic laws become more sophisticated.

### *Banking and Foreign Exchange*

It is advisable to establish a relationship with a U.S. bank that has one or more Japanese branches for up-to-date advice on foreign exchange regulations and the mechanics of transfers of funds. As Japan's trade balances are high with most major industrial countries, particularly the United States, there are hardly any restrictions on remittance of dollars or the currencies of other countries from Japan. There is no currency black market, as the yen is allowed to float freely against other major currencies.

Payments by check are not nearly as accepted as in the United States for several reasons. Banks screen those who open checking accounts carefully. Penalties for overdrafts are severe. Stop-payment orders are difficult to obtain. Endorsements are not required to be authenticated by banks. Canceled checks are not normally returned by banks. Americans report that they carry more cash than they did back home.

Credit and charge cards are more widely used. Often the credit card may serve only as identification for later-billing at the holder's office if the holder or his company is known to the establishment.

A new development is the increase of the on-line system by which terminals in department stores are connected to banks, recurring payments are made directly by banks, and customers can make and withdraw deposits at any time from any branch office. Japan is proceeding rapidly toward the cashless society.

Invoices from company creditors have instructions for the transfer of payment through the banking system from one account to another.

There are many types of savings and time deposits with varying interest rates.

## Legal System

Japan has an independent professional judiciary. There is a single, national system of courts headed by a supreme court, then 8 appellate courts, 49 district courts, and some specialized courts for the family, traffic violations, and small claims (under Y100,000). Judges begin their training in an advanced legal institution and are appointed, thereby forming a career judicial civil service.

The common law system of the United States and England, which emphasizes interpretation of the law by past decisions, is not followed. Instead, Japan has several major codes (civil, penal, commercial, and so forth) that are the foundation for the myriad of interpretive rules, regulations, and special statutes that fill in the gaps and explain the basic codes. Japan, then, follows the civil law tradition that the applicable law, not past precedent, is controlling.

No juries exist in Japan. If a dispute gets to the trial stage, the judge or a panel of judges hears the evidence, often in a series of court dates separated by daily or monthly intervals. These procedures can string out a complex case over years. A losing party can appeal, and in civil matters the appellate court hears the whole case from the beginning.

Most disputes do not reach the litigation stage, however. Settlement, conciliation, and arbitration are much more common methods of resolution.

There are several international lawyers or firms in Tokyo. The firms consist of foreign (primarily American) lawyers who are thoroughly familiar with Japanese law but may not be able to appear in court, and Japanese lawyers with excellent language capability and substantial training or experience in the United States or other countries.

## Relations With Police

The police assigned to your local police box *(koban)* can be a source of help in many ways. They can advise you about the many regulations, and they are a good source of security.

One important point to remember: No person in Japan need answer any question that may incriminate him.

Another point is the emphasis upon maintaining law and order and not disrupting society. Thus graffiti, littering, and disorderly conduct are hardly seen. One exception to this rule is drunkenness. You will surely see many inebriated Japanese businessmen (never a woman) on the streets or subways. But few are shocked by this. If he is loud or stumbles, he can't help it.

## Customs

For arrival by air, no declaration is required for accompanied baggage. All unaccompanied baggage must be declared. For arrival by sea, a written declaration is required for all baggage. Be sure you get the proper forms and explicit instructions on this procedure to avoid any problem when your unaccompanied baggage arrives later.

There is a duty on new, unused appliances.

Pets do not have to go into a long quarantine, but they will be detained for two to three weeks. They must have been inoculated against rabies not less than 30 days and not more than 180 days prior to entry. There are other documentary requirements that will take some time to complete before you leave; check with the Japanese embassy or consulate for the latest regulations before departing.

There is no restriction on the amount of money you may bring into Japan.

## Cars and Driving

As is the case with so many other institutions in Japan, the car—particularly the business car—seems to have a ritual all its own. Like the attire of its passenger, the car is almost always a dark color. It will be relieved and accented by plain white seat covers and white curtains at the windows. Chauffeurs are common for business cars. The reason is simple: parking is almost impossible. For the expatriate who can possibly manage one, a driver will prove an invaluable time-saver and guide in finding locations in the Tokyo maze. It is also a prestige factor and so may be important from that standpoint alone.

Driving is on the left. There is an elaborate system of penalty points and fines for violations. Drunken driving or driving under the influence of drugs brings 15 penalty points, resulting in license revocation. A few other violations, such as driving without a learner's permit, carry six to nine points. Most involve one to two points and reasonable fines. If you have your license suspended, you cannot drive on an international license.

A great emphasis is placed on business responsibility for the safe driving of its cars. As of April 1978 there were almost three million business cars.

The Traffic Code devotes considerable attention to the regulation of two-wheeled vehicles and bicycles.

If you have a valid foreign license (one issued at maximum three months before), you can get a Japanese license without too much trouble. And you need a local license right away. The procedure includes an eye exam but no written test. If you don't have a valid foreign license, you will have to take all the tests—and they are tough.

International traffic signs are used. Direction and other signs on expressways are frequently in Japanese only.

The Japanese Automobile Federation has published a 112-page English booklet, *Rules of the Road*. It also puts out a *Driver's Map of Japan,* with names of major cities and towns in both Japanese and English. Both can be purchased at the Federation office (5-8 Shiba Koen, 3-chome, Minato-ku; telephone 436-2811).

Importation of one automobile duty- and tax-free with your household effects is allowed, provided you meet some stringent requirements on emission control. Be sure you have these requirements and the car's documentation straight before shipping your car.

Inspection of cars every two years is a necessary evil in Japan. No one argues with the purpose, only the method. Americans report that authorized garages are ingenious in finding problems that result in repair bills far beyond that anticipated for a routine inspection.

Periodic maintenance checks every six months are required. A record of these must be in the car at all times and submitted at the inspection.

Third-party liability insurance is compulsory, and the policy must be carried in the car. The coverage must be obtained locally. There are several foreign companies represented in Japan. Liability for injury or death caused by a driver or owner is considerable. Insurance rates are not excessive.

## Death

Japanese funeral customs have some aspects that most Americans will find quite unfamiliar and undesirable, such as compulsory cremation in most areas and family members washing and dressing the deceased body. Therefore, you will probably arrange for the return of the body home through consular officials who can give you the details on preparation and transport. A few points to keep in mind are:

Under Japanese law, a corpse can be transported only by an authorized undertaker.

Only certain locations can perform embalming to meet U.S. airlift standards, and most of these are at major hospitals.

Only a few firms make caskets that meet U.S. airlift standards.

Check with your lawyer on any inheritance and tax matters. Generally, inheritance is governed by the laws of the deceased's country.

## Marriage and Divorce

Marriages are conducted according to Japanese law—that is, a civil registration at a government office. This is recognized throughout the United States as a valid marriage. Religious ceremonies are not legal marriages, although they may be conducted in addition to the civil portion. Some aliens go through the religious ceremony but do not register right away, thereby allowing for a change of heart.

For two aliens marrying, there are some preliminary forms that must be completed at the embassy. If minors are involved (under 21 for males and 16 for females), a notarized letter of consent from parents or guardians is required.

There are different documents necessary for the marriage of a Japanese national to an alien and for American citizens of Japanese ancestry.

A divorce obtained under the laws of Japan is usually recognized in the United States. There are three types: by mutual agreement, through the services of the family court, and by judicial divorce in the civil courts. The civil court procedure by mutual consent is the one used by most aliens, but mutual consent is difficult to document for recognition purposes at home. The family court procedure involves conciliation procedures with Japanese that may not be appropriate.

## Immigration, Visas, and Resident Permits

The U.S. embassy advises that one of the biggest problems for the consular service is Americans arriving in Japan with faulty visas or other documentation. This is surprising because there are ample sources of information on these requirements.

Generally, a visa is required for anyone planning to engage in any activity for remuneration. On arrival the "status of residence" and the "period of stay" are stamped in the passport. The status will be abbreviated by the numerals 4-1-__ (the first two numbers refer to the actual article and paragraph number of the immigration law; the third, for the exact status under that law). The period normally is that specified for the status granted. The scope of activities in which an expatriate can engage is defined by the status category. For example, status 4-1-5 is for persons engaging in the management of business, foreign trade, or capital investment activities, and the period of stay is three years. If you engage in activities not included in your status, you may be subject to deportation.

Family members have a special status with the same period of stay. Spouses of the primary holder who wish to work must apply for a special visa.

For visas other than tourist status, there are several documents required in addition to the application, such as a letter from the firm or association with which the applicant will be working in Japan.

A stop in Japan of more than 90 days requires registration at the municipal office of the city, ward, town, or village where you reside. You will receive a Certificate of Alien Registration, which is required to be carried at all times by aliens 14 years of age or older. For aliens granted a stay of one year or more, a fingerprint is taken.

There are a number of procedures and forms for amending and correcting the data submitted for residency and registration, change of status, exit and reentry, extension of stay, and the like.

Recent changes in the immigration laws have eased certain requirements, at least in theory. Now it is possible to change your visa status without going out of Japan and then returning. Practically, it is still hard to change from a tourist visa to a work visa. Certain minor changes in your status, such as issuance of a new passport, need not be reported to the alien registration authorities immediately, but can wait until the next renewal of your card. An alien leaving Japan with a reentry permit no longer has to leave his registration card with the authorities—he can take it with him.

The child of an alien family must be registered within 30 days and application made for residency status. Such a child does not have an option to become a Japanese citizen.

On death or divorce, the status of the wife does not change, but she may be required to state reasons for remaining in Japan when the period of stay expires.

## *Taxes*

Japan has a very sophisticated tax system, so doing anything but following the letter of its code is not only illegal but also foolhardy. All expatriates need the advice of a good international tax expert to explain the interrelationship of the Japanese and U.S. tax laws. Many international auditing firms have branches in Japan.

Japan has a national income tax and local inhabitant's taxes, prefectural and municipal. The responsibility for compliance with the tax laws lies with the individual expatriate. The collection system is v .y similar to the U.S. system: annual returns, withholding, estimated payments, and frequent audits for foreigners. There are special forms in English and an English-speaking service for help. A tax treaty to avoid double taxation exists between the two countries.

Both the national and local taxes are graduated with some basic exemptions, deductions, and allowances. The current rate for the national tax runs from  0 to 75 percent; for the local, from 2 to 14 percent. The tax on income in the $50,000 to $70,000 range is higher than in the United States.

A few points to know are:

There is no capital gains tax on the sale of stock;
Necessary business travel expenses, including reasonable home leave, are exempt from tax;
Taxable income includes reimbursement for housing, overseas living allowances, children's school allowance, and other similar benefits; and
A resident departing from Japan before March 15 must file his return before departure or else have someone appointed his representative to file before that deadline.

An expatriate is assumed to have a domicile in Japan if he has an occupation, profession, or assignment that normally requires him to stay in Japan continuously for a period of one year or more. He is then considered a "resident" taxpayer. For the first five years of his stay, he is usually considered a "nonpermanent" resident. As such, he is liable for the income from sources in Japan or for foreign income paid in or remitted to Japan. Once you become a "permanent" resident, you are liable for tax on your income from all sources.

# 20

# Assignment Manila

MANILA IS A STUDY IN CONTRASTS—a strange potpourri of old and new, rich and poor, East and West. For the expatriate, life in Manila will be exciting, rewarding, and strangely beautiful, but at times frustrating and filled with puzzles that will not unravel.

The culture is diverse and interesting, the people intelligent. Official statistics show a literacy rate of 85.7 percent—reportedly the highest of any Asian country.[1] The population is young; 55 percent are under 20 years of age.[2] Physically, they are a race of unusual beauty—basically Malay, with blends of Chinese, Indian, Arabic, and Caucasian.

About 83 percent of the country's 44 million people are Roman Catholic. The rest are Muslim, Protestant, or adherents to folk religions.[3] They speak a total of 88 dialects, all belonging to the Malayo-Polynesian family of languages. Pilipino, which is based primarily on the Tagalog dialect, is the national language. However, English is almost universally understood, making the Philippines the third largest English-speaking country in the world.[4]

Filipinos are noted for their hospitality; they are friendly and outgoing and often draw the expatriate into their fiesta syndrome of life. Yet, some Americans indicate that they never really get to know them as neighbors or companions. The high privacy fences surrounding their homes, the extended family living, and the *compadre* system all work together to eliminate the need for outside interests.

Family ties are a consuming responsibility from which the Filipino never resigns; there is strong pressure to conform to the norms of the family and to suppress individual desires. Rank, status, and family position are important aspects of life, and the Filipino depends heavily on them for his own recognition—trading on this influence whenever possible. Big homes, expensive cars, imported objects, and white-collar jobs are revered status symbols.

The oriental concept of *machoism* remains strong. Until the recent campaign for birth control, large families, which were considered proof of virility, were prevalent, and after-hours socializing with the beautiful hospitality girls, or mistresses on the side, was the norm. Surprisingly, even under these conditions the woman's position is very secure. She not only plays the wife and mother roles, she is the financial manager of the family—spending and investing the family's money. (The fact that women now own one-third of the businesses in the country attests to their success.[5])

The emphasis on education (70 percent of the college graduates are women)[6], the ready availability of household help, and extended-family situations have enabled women to widen their sphere of influence into the business and professional world, and with considerable success. Women are now doctors, lawyers, engineers, bankers, and diplomats—a group with considerable status.

The American will find much to approve about the Filipino way of life. Politeness, consideration, and sensitivity to the needs of others are carefully cultivated characteristics. However, those unaccustomed to the Filipino code of conduct may have difficulty in accepting the extremes to which the Filipino will go to maintain *pakikisama* (smooth relationships).

According to those who have made a study of the culture, relationships often take on dimensions that Americans may not understand, and thus may stifle in their early stages. They may not perceive that real friendships can mean prying questions and a desire to know all about each other—How many children do you have? Why don't you have more? Weren't you able to, or did you not want them? How much money do you make? Americans, offended by these questions, may skirt around them and then find that a relationship with the Filipino goes no further. The Filipino will not be insulted by the lack of response; he most likely will interpret it is a lack of desire on the part of the American to become really good friends.

The incoming American, in particular, may not be sensitive to the obligations that relationships normally entail, whether they are personal, friendly associations, or those of employer–employee. They may not be aware, for example, that it is customary to assist employees with all types of problems and to make sure that families are taken care of, and that in return the employee will feel dedicated to serve beyond the job itself. Filipinos refer to this as *utang na loob*. It implies a sense of duty or gratitude to one who extends a favor, and it is an important element in a system based on reciprocal obligations.

American expatriates who find themselves drawn into this system of life may feel unsure how to react. For example, is an invitation to serve as a sponsor for a wedding or baptism a simple honor, or is one being asked to assume a lifelong relationship and the responsibilities of a *compadre* (social, economic, and political assistance)? If religious convictions or business responsibilities make it impossible to serve, how does one say no without offending the *amor propio* (self-esteem) of the parties involved?

As with most oriental practices, there is a prescribed game plan. First of all, the invitation is meant to confer honor on the expatriate (although being seen as a foreigner and as an individual with business acumen brings honor to the family of the celebrants, and it is expected that the invitation will be accepted). Since expatriate postings are usually fairly temporary, their sponsorships are generally regarded as implying participation in the ceremony only. If expatriates are unwilling or unable to accept the honor, they should not reply immediately but rather indicate that they will let the parties making the request know soon. They can then compose a tactful note, or else relay their inability to serve through a go-between. In this way there is no embarrassment or loss of face.

It is this code of conduct, so inherent in the Filipino way of life, that causes Americans the most difficulty. Accustomed to evaluating situations and then taking quick and direct action, Americans are uneasy with the seemingly endless letters and the go-betweens that may be necessary to consummate a deal. Many Filipinos are accustomed to American attitudes and practices; after all, the Philippines was an American colony from the Spanish-American War of 1898 until its independence in 1946; and there remains a subtle American influence. However, there is strong emphasis on nationalism and "doing things the Filipino way."

Americans heading for the Philippines should take time to read and research the historical background of our complicated relationships. George Guthrie's *Six Perspectives on the Philippines* (Manila: Bookmark, 1968) is on the "must-read" list for Peace Corps workers, and is highly recommended for everyone. *Four Readings on*

*Philippine Values* (Quezon City: Ateneo de Manila University Press, 1973) is also suggested reading. In *Making It in the United States* (Quezon City: Phoenix Press, 1974), Roger Goulet and Rosalina Morales-Goulet provide a comparison of the American and Filipino cultures. An even more in-depth description of the Filipino culture is made in *The Philippine Experience: A Newcomer's Introduction* (Manila: World Fellowship Committees of the Young Women's Christian Association, 1975). However, it is available only in Manila.

Renato Constantino's *History of the Philippines from the Spanish Colonization to the Second World War* (New York: Monthly Review Press, 1976, 1981) provides a somewhat critical analysis of Spanish and American colonialism, as well as pertinent insight into how many young Filipinos view the past. George Taylor's *The Philippines and the United States: Problems of Partnership* (New York: Praeger, 1964) explores the new nationalism and the Philippines' role in Southeast Asia.

*But Not In Shame* by John Toland (New York: Random House, 1961) covers the period following World War II. *Noli Me Tangere (The Social Cancer)* and *El Filibusterismo* are the writings of Jose Rizal, who is considered to be the foremost Filipino writer, as well as the "Father of His Country." Both books were written in Spanish and were published in Europe to expose the Spanish tyranny in the Philippines. The Spanish government in Manila felt that Rizal's writings incited the Philippine Revolution, and Rizal was arrested and executed on the spot where his statue now stands in Rizal Park. After Rizal's death, both books were translated and reprinted—*El Filibusterismo* in London (Longmans, Green and Company, 1965); and *Noli Me Tangere,* first in New York (World Book Company, 1921), and later in Manila (Philippine Education Agency, 1926, 1961). *The First Filipino,* by Leon M. Guerro (Manila: National Historical Commission, 1969), details the life of Jose Rizal.

An excellent source for books on the Philippines is the Cellar Book Shop (18090 Wyoming, Detroit, Michigan 48221; telephone [313] 861-1776). The owners, the Morton Netzorgs, were once in business in the Philippines, and are well informed on subjects related to the islands.

## Asia—With a Difference

The Philippines is an archipelago of some 7,100 islands stretched out between the Pacific Ocean on the east and the China Sea on the west. Only a third of the islands are named, and less than 900 are occupied.

Two islands, Luzon in the north and Mindanao in the south, comprise about 68 percent of the total land of the archipelago. Another nine islands—Samar, Negros, Palawan, Panay, Mindoro, Leyte, Cebu, Bohol, and Masbate (chiefly in the Visayan group)— compose another 27 percent.

The land area is not great; its 116,000 square miles equal about the size of Arizona. Its coastline is calculated to be nearly 22,000 miles long, some 9,000 miles longer than that of the continental United States. As a result, it has a wealth of natural harbors, as perfect for scuba diving and water skiing as for shipping.

Rivers cut through mountain ranges, creating rich valleys and providing a contrast to the central plains and rolling uplands. Tropical rain forests ordinarily cover the lowlands and the wetter mountain slopes, although much of the original forest has been cleared to make way for agriculture and grazing. Its natural beauty, varied topography, and many climates make it as much a source of wonder and delight for the expatriate as its history and its culture.

"The Islands," as they are so often called, present a picture of an Asian country with a difference. Primitive tribes occupy its hinterlands and outlying islands, with heretofore undiscovered groups coming to light from time to time. On the other hand, the Islands comprise the outer reaches of Christianity in Asia, as well as being the furthest outpost of Islam.

Even before Ferdinand Magellan planted the cross of Catholicism and claimed the archipelago for Spain in the sixteenth century, waves of immigrants from nearby Indonesia and Malaysia had established colonies, pushing the native Negritos inland. Fourteenth-century immigrants established Islam as the official religion and the dominating force in the Sulu and Mindanao islands.

Under the Spanish rule, tribal groups that were converted to Roman Catholicism reached a high degree of westernization. However, in 1898 the Spanish-American War broke out and the Philippines was lost to America.

In a presentation given to the General Assembly of the United Nations in September 1977, Imelda Marcos, head of the Philippine delegation to the United Nations General Assembly and wife of President Marcos, summarized this period in Philippine history:

American policy rapidly developed a system of public education which, before long, extended from the primary barrio school to the university—a lay missionary effort that covered the archipelago and not only taught the usual subjects, but also inculcated the American spirit. As early as the 1920s, more than a third of the population of school age was enrolled. Politically, the Americans encouraged self-government, introducing representative institutions of the Anglo-Saxon type and a large degree of autonomy under a commonwealth inaugurated in 1935.

World War II brought Japanese occupation and interrupted the building of a nation. In 1946 full independence was given to the Philippines. The next three decades were a political and economic stalemate. Communism gained a foothold, and a "New People's Army" was founded. In the midst of countryside ambushes and urban terrorism, martial law was ordered in 1972. President Ferdinand Marcos, a controversial figure who has operated as chief executive without benefit of a functioning legislative body, has managed to bring a large degree of order out of chaos. In theory, martial law no longer exists. In actuality, conditions are much the same as they were when it was in effect.

## Manila Today

Manila has been gradually rebuilt. Tall buildings of cement and glass line the eastern shores of Manila Bay and stretch out along the shores of the Pasig River. As the capital city, it has become the center of the country's government, trade, and culture. Luxury hotels, restaurants, and night clubs catering to the growing tourist population line its broad Roxas Boulevard. Shopping and banking establishments crowd into Escolta Street, while the Chinese shops, restaurants, and theaters line Ongpin Street in Binondo, one of the city's oldest districts.

The Tondo-Foreshore area, a cramped tract of reclaimed land north of Manila Bay, contains the country's biggest slum colony with a density of over 2,000 persons per hectare. It reflects the country's inability to provide adequate housing or employment for the ever-increasing number of people who have flocked in, seeking a better way of life, but who often exchange the poverty of the countryside for a more extreme poverty in the city. In direct contrast to it is Makati, a planned community located eight miles from downtown Manila. Ultramodern buildings, elegant branches of downtown stores, restaurants, hotels, boutiques, and supermarkets constitute the downtown district; while beautiful homes, each individually designed and carefully kept, and prestigious private golf and yacht clubs compose the outlying areas.

In all, a total of four cities and 13 municipalities—Manila, Quezon City, Pasay City, Caloocan City, Makati, San Juan, Mandaluyong, Las Piñas, Malabon, Marikina, Muntinlupa, Navotas, Paranaque, Pasig, Pateros, Taguig, and Valenzuela—all individually distinctive, make up the bustling metropolis known as Metro Manila. Some 7.5 million people reside in this area.

## Practical Pointers

The climate of the Philippines is tropical. There are two pronounced seasons: the dry summer months from November to May, and the rainy—with risk of typhoons—from June to October. The weather in Manila generally ranges from a low of about 69° Fahrenheit in January to a high of about 93° Fahrenheit in May.

All money (bills) should have the *bagong lipunan* (new society) seal on them. Bills without this seal have been demonetized. A 24-hour banking service is available for the convenience of incoming and departing passengers at Manila International Airport.

Conventional tipping (around 15 percent) is expected in the large hotels and international restaurants, but in the small family-type operations only a small tip—10 percent or less—is customary.

Gifts are very much a part of the Philippine way of life. They are presented on birthdays, for Christmas, at weddings, anniversaries, baptisms, and confirmations, as well as to the hostess at a dinner party. However, Filipinos seldom write thank you letters.

There are ten designated holidays: New Year's Day, Bataan Day (April 9), Maundy Thursday, Good Friday, Labor Day (May 1), Independence Day (June 12), Philippine-American Friendship Day (July 4), National Heroes Day (November 30), Christmas, and Rizal Day. However, it is not unusual for declared holidays and typhoon days to bring the total of holidays around 25 to 28.

Do not be surprised if you are asked to perform—sing, dance, or tell jokes—at a celebration, or to make a speech at a ceremony. The longer you talk, the more honor you bring to the event. If you are caught unaware, don't worry; the guests will continue with their conversations.

A mixed system of weights and measures is used. Distances and weights are metric; capacities are pint, quart, and gallon; dry measures are Filipino standard—chupa, ganta, cavan: eight chupas equal one ganta or three liters, and 25 gantas equal one cavan or 75 liters.

Do not hesitate to ask questions. Filipinos consider your interest a compliment. Even at dinner parties, if you like the dish being served, ask the hostess what it is and how to prepare it.

# To Bring or Not to Bring

In planning your shipment for the Philippines, it may be helpful to know the following.

Houses are generally large and airy. Windows have decorative wrought-iron grills, and may or may not be screened. Unless the house has been rented previously by someone who has air-conditioned it, it probably will not have glass in the windows. A few expatriates have found centrally air-conditioned apartments.

The high heat and humidity, the mildew, and the dust from open windows make heavy velours and satins in overstuffed furniture and draperies impractical. It is also unwise to bring antique or veneer furniture. Light, airy draperies and washable upholstery fabrics win the vote of those living here.

Utilities are quite expensive, and it is common to air-condition just the bedrooms and perhaps a family room. Some international companies storehouse air-conditioners for loan to expatriates, but those without this option should consider bringing some window units.

Appliances may be purchased locally, but they may be smaller in size, as well as two to four times the U.S. price. Housing customarily has or can easily be adapted for both 220 and 110 voltage.

"Wash girls" are readily available, but most expatriates prefer automatic washing machines. Dryers are especially important during the rainy season. The cost of operation is less with the bottled buta gas, so appliances that can be operated on gas and have a convertible natural gas–buta gas orifice are a good choice.

Many expatriates consider a freezer or second refrigerator (some purchase locally an older secondhand type) indispensable for the large number of dry products they try to protect from bugs and humidity.

Dishwashers are considered a plus, but the low water pressure in some areas may handicap their use.

At least two irons are recommended, as the casualty rate on terrazo floors is quite high. A floor polisher–rug cleaner combination is useful for the large stretches of terrazo floors and area rugs; however, carpet-cleaning solution is sometimes difficult to find.

Expensive radio, hi-fi, and tape recorder equipment should be protected by a voltage control.

Fires are sometimes started by termites eating through electrical wiring. Smoke detectors and a good supply of batteries kept in a close-fitting plastic Tupperware-type container are a good precaution.

Burglaries of homes and cars are not uncommon. A proximity-type battery-operated burglar alarm system for the house (which can be easily installed and maintained) and an electronic burglar prevention system for a car might be wise investments.

Bath and bed linens and the lightweight blankets used in the tropics are expensive; pillows, in particular, are of poor quality. Specialty items, such as traverse rods, which are imported, are also expensive.

Dehumidifying crystals are a great boon. Most expatriates bring salt shakers and canisters topped with crystals, as well as bags of various sizes for use in drawers and closets. It is well to be aware that some crystals can be revived by oven heat—others simply melt away.

Tupperware-type containers in various sizes and shapes are handy for the storage of dry ingredients and lentils.

Three-way light bulbs are reported to be generally unavailable.

Hobby and sports equipment, including playing cards and bridge tables, are prized items. Include all sewing items, as relatively inexpensive "sew girls" will come to the house. Many can duplicate designs from pictures, so catalogs and pattern books are much used.

Mothers with babies who use disposable nursers and refills should bring a supply. Disposable diapers are sometimes available, but do include a supply of cotton diapers as well as plastic pants in all sizes.

Bathing suits and a couple of wading pools—one for the yard, and one for the shower to bathe the children in (there are few bathtubs)—are also suggested.

Educational and building toys, puzzles, record players, and records are much appreciated bring-alongs, as are birthday and Christmas gifts for the babies and young children.

Women who wear narrow or wide shoe sizes, or larger than size 7½, will want to bring a good supply of shoes, as will men who wear a large shoe size. Socks of all types and stockings should be included, as well as special sports shoes.

Toilet articles (and for the women, cosmetics), which sell locally at two to four times U.S. prices, are considered a plus. Most women bring their own birth control needs, as well as a supply of tampons.

Bras for the slight Asian figure do not accommodate the size or provide the comfort of a good American or an English Marks and Spencer brand.

Cotton rates high for both outer wear and underwear; and while dry-cleaning is available, washable clothing is definitely preferable. Most women dress modestly, out of respect for the customs of the

Islands, choosing simple cotton dresses or slack suits for daily wear and more elegant cottons for luncheons and teas. Shorts are worn in public only for sports; attire length often drops to the floor for evening, with women wearing long dresses and skirts in gay and colorful patterns.

Work wardrobes for men often include short-sleeved safari suits or washable slacks combined with a barong Tagalog or other short-sleeved shirt. Suits are seldom seen, although some men do wear dinner jackets for formal occasions. Most seem to prefer the style of the Islands—the long-sleeved, elegantly embroidered Filipino shirt, the barong Tagalog, combined with tuxedo pants.

The "No Uniform Rule" allows school-agers a wide range in attire. Most choose jeans or slacks with cotton knit shirts; or for the girls, sun dresses and other simple clothing.

Travel clothing, particularly for flights arriving in or departing from Manila International Airport, should be chosen with coolness in mind. However, travel wardrobes should include some warmer clothing for trips to nearby Baguio or to Tokyo and Hong Kong.

## Housing

Compared with many parts of the world, housing in the Philippines is expensive. However, it is reasonable in relation to other Asian countries, and it has imagination and style, which provides a background for a comfortable expatriate life-style. Architecturally designed and individually styled, each facility, whether it is one of the many recently completed hotels, apartment buildings, or one of the older (but built since World War II) houses, is constructed with consideration for the tropical climate and the beautiful lush greenery of the area.

There are many fine hotels in Manila; however, a hotel in Makati is considered to be the most convenient for an initial stay. Housing, shopping, and schools are nearby. A partial listing of hotels expatriates should consider includes:

Intercontinental Hotel
Ayala Avenue
Makati, Rizal
Telephone 89-40-11

Mandarin Hotel
Makati Avenue
Paseo de Roxas
Makati, Rizal
Telephone 85-78-11

Manila Peninsula Hotel
Makati and Ayala Avenue
Makati, Rizal
Telephone 85-77-11

## Interim Living

Some families move into a furnished apartment or town house almost immediately upon arrival, while others seek leave houses for the interim between arrival and establishment of their own homes. The Gilarmi, Monterrey, Tuscani, and Urdaneta apartments in tall modernistic buildings across and down from the Intercontinental Hotel on Ayala Avenue in Makati have been popular temporary and sometimes permanent choices of incoming expatriates. Many apartments have been constructed, and more are going up all the time in nearby Legaspi Village. Some, on a condominium basis, allow purchase by expatriates if at least 60 percent of the condos are Filipino owned.

Notice of the availability of leave residences, which are the fully furnished and equipped (including maids) homes of vacationing expatriates, are usually posted on bulletin boards at clubs, supermarkets, and churches. The Union Church, which is a center for many expatriate activities, is commonly used for such postings. Leave housing can provide a pleasant, almost painless, introduction to Philippine living. During the customary six weeks to three months in which houses are sublet, it is usually possible for furniture to be transported, permanent housing to be found, and the necessary paper work relative to renting to be completed.

## Permanent Housing

Finding permanent housing is much like finding temporary accommodation. Acquaintances, bulletin board notices, and the classified ads are the best sources. Some newcomers have had luck placing their own advertisements describing their needs and requesting that landlords call them. Others have dealt solely with real estate agents who have been successful in finding desirable rentals. Long-term expatriates advise, however, that newcomers really should survey the general area and, based upon their own needs, determine the priorities of housing. Is there a need to be near the school? Does traffic hassle you? If not, perhaps a house that is farther out, and thus cheaper, would fill the bill.

Village associations often have a list of available houses for rent. The inquiry should be a personal one, however, as the information may not be given to drivers. Within the village there may also be "for rent" or "for sale" signs or partially constructed houses that may be possible rentals. Unoccupied houses generally have a caretaker living in them and thus can be seen without appointment.

In terms of desirable village areas in which to live, the recommendations of long-term residents will usually vary. In terms of the larger area—the city—the recommendation will almost certainly be the same: Makati.

Areas in and around Makati are, for the most part, planned communities. Village associations are responsible, and charge property owners accordingly, for security, street maintenance and repair, sanitation, health, and recreational facilities. In line with these responsibilities, guards are maintained at entrances and drivers are requested to have a permit or sticker to enter; trash is picked up, and mosquito spraying is done. In some associations, a doctor, a dentist, and a nurse are on duty at the association (primarily for health care for servants, but they are available for emergencies). They also provide and maintain central play areas (basketball courts, volleyball courts, and the like) and do such mundane things as keeping lists of unsatisfactory servants.

One resident, a recent transferee from Singapore, put it this way:

> Living here is marvelous! Houses are large, airy, and attractive; and the Village system makes it possible for the children to play outdoors and the adults to bicycle, walk, or jog in privacy and safety, something we could not do in other places we have lived.

## *Tips on Housing in Manila*

Vacant lots beside a house may mean potential construction with noise, dirt, and congestion. In some areas without strict enforcement of regulations, there may be squatters and their animals and no sewage.

Individual villages may have water problems—including low water pressure.

Termites often are a problem here. A pre-rental termite inspection and a routine extermination plan is good advice.

Telephones are difficult to obtain. Having a telephone installed is expensive.

## Residential Areas

Some of the more popular areas for Americans to live are:

*Forbes Park and North Forbes.* The "Beverly Hills" area; elite, distinguished. Many residences of ambassadors; some local managers of long-established American firms also here. Some rentals. Owing to age of homes, there may be electrical and plumbing problems. Excellent security. From 5 to 10 minutes to Makati.

*Dasmarinas.* Second most distinguished area; many embassies. Homes large and attractive, much newer than Forbes Park area. Excellent place to live. Excellent security. From 5 to 10 minutes to Makati.

*Urdaneta.* Older area, smaller houses; some condominiums for rent or for sale to expatriates on 60/40 basis (60 percent Philippine holdings, 40 percent expatriates). Good security. From 1 to 5 minutes to Makati.

*Magallanes—Sections I, II, III, and IV.* Nice houses; relatively inexpensive for comparable areas. Largely Filipino. Some flooding. Inadequate security. From 10 to 15 minutes to Makati.

*San Lorenzo.* Smaller homes; often poorly maintained; less expensive. Inadequate security. Two minutes to Makati.

*Bel Air.* Smaller homes; some very nice. Home of the International School. Inadequate security. From 5 to 10 minutes to Makati.

*Paranaque.* Some lovely homes. Many vacant lots with squatters and no sewage. Little security. Commuting may be a problem during the monsoon season. From 35 to 45 minutes to Makati.

*Green Hills—East, West, and North.* Relatively new residential area. Houses large but less expensive than Forbes-Dasmarinas. Excellent shopping in nearby Vera Mall. Excellent security. From 25 to 35 minutes to Makati.

*Quezon City.* Many lovely homes. Location of the beautiful University of Philippines as well as the United States Information Service Library. From 45 to 60 minutes to Makati. No city security.

There are, of course, many other areas in which expatriates have found comfortable homes. Outside Manila there are small expatriate colonies in:

*Baguio.* A modern mountain community 155 miles from Manila. Pleasant hotels, elegant summer homes, and rolling golf courses contribute to its resort reputation. It is the location of the Brent School, an Episcopalian boarding and day school; Maryknoll Day School (grades 1 through 6); and the John Hays American Air Base (military rest and recreation resort).

The climate varies between the dry and wet season, with the dry season running from December to June. Temperatures vary from 50° Fahrenheit at night to 80° Fahrenheit during the day.

Notre Dame de Lourdes Hospital and Pine City Doctors Hospital are recommended for use.

*Cebu City.* Located 350 air miles from Manila on the Island of Cebu in the Visayan group. It has a population of 450,000, including a small European-American business community. It is also an outlying base for Protestant and Catholic missionaries, and Peace Corps workers.

The climate is hot and humid.

Cebu International School, an American-oriented school, provides acceptable education from grades 1 to 7. There are a number of U.S.-trained physicians; Cebu Doctors Hospital is relatively new and considered adequate.

*Davao.* Located 600 air miles south of Manila on the Island of Mindanao. It has a population of 750,000. The climate is hot and humid, and the temperature ranges from 73° Fahrenheit to 89° Fahrenheit. The small American community includes missionaries and private industry personnel.

There is no American-style education. However, instruction in English can be obtained in kindergarten through grade 2. For higher grades, expatriates use the Calvert Home Study System or the boarding school in Baguio.

# Education

In a random survey, 20 students who had averaged more than five years apiece in overseas residence, and who, in addition, were citizens of five different countries, rated the schools in the Philippines as outstanding. Interestingly, only two would rather have been back home going to school. All felt that the opportunity to learn about a different culture and to meet people from different parts of the world had made a significant impact on their lives. As one boy put it:

> Geography—and history, for that matter—has just got to be more interesting when in a class of 22 kids, 18 are from different countries. We hardly discuss a place in the world that someone in the class hasn't lived in, or at least been to. Oh, sure, they're not experts; but they can talk about it, and that makes it interesting.

The students agreed that one of the surprising aspects of life in the Philippines was the emphasis put on educational achievement. Teachers are also highly regarded; and expatriate students, like Filipino students, are expected to show respect toward the teaching staffs of their schools.

Besides the interscholastic programs at the schools, there are active Boy Scout and Girl Scout Troops (Cubs and Brownies; Sea Scouts), both at the schools and at the American embassy. The embassy also sponsors 20 to 30 softball teams for the age group 6 to 16, as well as a limited program of driver education for the 16-plus teens. The International School has a beginning after-school work experience program for teens, as well as plans for a summer work program. Most English-speaking expatriate students attend the schools listed in Table 8.

Some English-speaking expatriate children have attended the following Filipino schools, which operate on a June-April, six-year junior school, four-year high school plan. However, college-bound students should be aware that the ten-year curriculum may not provide the background needed to be competitive on the college entrance exams.

*Retarded Children*

Learning Center
4566 Quintos
Makati
Telephone 87-53-61

**Table 8**

## Schools Attended by English-Speaking Expatriates in the Philippines

| School | Address | Grade | School Year | Curriculum | Description |
|---|---|---|---|---|---|
| International School Village of Bel Air | P.O. Box 323 Makati Metro Manila Philippines 3117 Telephone 88-89-91 88-89-92, 88-89-93, 88-89-96 | Kindergarten through 12; day school | Early August through late May | American; college preparatory and general academic with full diploma; International Baccalaureate program available (for students seeking admittance to European-type universities or advanced placement in American universities) | A private, independent school established in 1920 as the American School; name changed to reflect the increasing internationality of students. Enrollment in 1978: 2,358; largest fully accredited American-type school outside United States; large, modern plant, with extensive enrichment facilities and comprehensive, extended-day, extracurricular activities; international faculty with high academic qualifications |
| The British School Village of Parañaque | Merville Park Subdivision, Parañaque Metro Manila Philippines 3117 Telephone 828-2261 | Kindergarten through junior-middle (ages 5-12); day school | Early August through late May | British preparatory | A private, independent school providing British-type education |

| Faith Academy | Valley Golf Subdivision Cainta Metro Manila Philippines 3117 Telephone 695-0640, 695-0641 | Kindergarten through 12; day school | Early August through late May | American; college preparatory and general academic | A private, independent school established for the children of missionaries; other students admitted on space-available basis |
| --- | --- | --- | --- | --- | --- |
| Brent School | Baguio City Baguio Philippines | Kindergarten through 12; boarding and day school and junior college | Early August through late May | American; college preparatory, as well as freshman-sophomore-level college courses; seminar approach to learning with pupil-teacher ratio of 8:1 | A private, independent school established in 1909 under the auspices of the Episcopal church; presently, the only double-accredited coeducational, nonsectarian, day and boarding school in Southeast Asia; also, first American-curriculum junior college |

## Schools for Girls

Maryknoll College
Katipunan Parkway
Quezon City
Telephone 98-85-81
Primary through college

Assumption College
San Lorenzo Drive
Makati
Telephone 817-2375
Preprimary through college

## Schools for Boys

Don Bosco Technical Institute
Pasay Road and Pasong Tamo
Makati
Telephone 87-78-31
Primary through high school; Salasians

Ateneo de Manila
Loyola Heights
Quezon City
Telephone 99-87-21
Primary through high school; Jesuits

LaSalle Green Hills
Ortigas Avenue
Mandaluyong
Telephone 70-18-91
Primary through high school; Christian Brothers

Colegio San Augustin
Palm Avenue
Dasmarinas Village
Makati
Telephone 89-25-16
Kindergarten through third grade

Montessori Casa International
17 Palm Avenue
Makati
Telephone 817-3221

San Lorenzo School
Zuleta Circle
San Lorenzo Village
Makati
Telephone 817-0653

Some high school graduates wanting that last year in the Philippines, and some wives attempting to finish a college degree, have taken university-level courses at the following schools:

Brent School
Baguio City
American curriculum Junior College; credits fully transferable to United States colleges.

University of the Philippines
Quezon City
Telephone 99-83-69
Elementary through postgraduate studies; medical school

University of Santo Tomas
Espana Street
Manila
Telephone 742-3101
Undergraduate, graduate, medical school; Dominicans

Ateneo de Manila
Loyola Heights
Quezon City
Telephone 99-87-21
Undergraduate and graduate; Jesuits (American and Filipino)

## Domestic Help

The desirability of having domestic help is a debatable issue. However, most expatriates living in the Philippines agree that there are certain advantages.

The heat is debilitating; the houses open and dusty; water has to be boiled; vegetables scrubbed; and washing and ironing done every day. Besides, Philippine domestics are quite affordable and usually very pleasant.

In hiring it is well to remember that 88 dialects are spoken in the Philippines. While a domestic may be multilingual, his or her comprehension of English may be limited. By the same token, an individual may have no knowledge of the dialect spoken in a different province. If more than one domestic is to be hired, a common dialect should be a factor of consideration.

Dealings with help can also be complicated by the very great differences in background from the employer. Unless an employee has had extensive domestic experience, he or she may have no understanding of the difference between a piece of Melamac and a piece of Meissen, a stem of Waterford crystal and a jelly glass; or why they should not plug a 110-volt radio into a 220-volt dryer outlet while they iron. Communication can be further complicated by the oriental concept of *hiya* (saving face), which makes it difficult for the employees to admit that they do not understand what is being said to them, and by *pakikisama*—the need for smooth interpersonal relationships.

The Civil Code specifies that the workday should not exceed 10 hours and that time off should include at least one full day a week. Two weeks' vacation with pay is customary after a full year's service.

Salaries vary from position to position, and often from area to area. Factors that influence salaries include experience, recommendations, and ability to understand and speak English. Salaries may include a food allowance or a rice allowance, or the employer may provide the food. Day employees receive food as well as daily payment. Full-time employees are usually paid on the fifteenth and final day of the month. Christmas bonuses are customary—two weeks' salary for one full year of service or a pro-rated amount for less time served.

Uniforms are furnished by the employer; usually three, sometimes five, are provided. These remain the property of the employer.

## Shopping

Most expatriates agree that almost anything is available in Manila for a price. Imported items are almost certain to be expensive—much more so than the "made in the Philippines" products or those from nearby Asian countries. "Buy local" is good advice. Do note country of origin, contents, and directions or care instructions, as well as price. Many brands with which you may be familiar are made locally.

The stores and shops in Manila are many and varied. Most needs can be easily met. If home furnishings are an immediate must, you are in luck. Locally made furniture is of excellent quality (do be sure it is kiln-dried) and comparatively inexpensive. Rattan furniture is a specialty; however, local furniture makers using your designs and your size specifications will make-to-order wood, overstuffed, or wrought-iron furniture. Labor-involved services such as made-to-order lamp shades, draperies, or custom framing are good buys. There are also beautiful oil paintings by local artists.

While clothing for the larger-than-Asian figure may be hard to obtain on a general retail basis, top French, Italian, and U.S. designers have franchise arrangements permitting lower-than-U.S. prices. There are many "sew girls" who will work in your home, or theirs, as well as an abundance of ladies' and men's tailors.

Fabric shops for clothing, upholstery, and draperies are numerous. Shoes can be ordered custom-made. Babies' and children's clothes are made so beautifully and with such imagination that they are hard to resist.

Barbering and beauty salon services are numerous and all seem to have standards that are high. Rates are usually posted, and a small tip to each person providing a service is customary. Many are in large hotels and some, of course, are more luxurious than others.

In prestige stores, prices are fixed; but a 10 percent discount is often given to encourage goodwill. In the Philippines, in general, a system of bargaining exists that can be a pleasure or a pain, as the expatriate must take care not to offend the amor propio of the salesperson. Regular (frequent) customers are usually afforded a *suki* relationship, and the shopkeeper will go to any effort to please as long as the *suki* is treated with respect.

There are many quaint, out-of-the-way shops in Manila; but there are also modern, multistoried, air-conditioned department stores with branches in the suburban shopping centers. No list would be complete, as change is an everyday occurrence; however, the following expatriate suggestions may help in getting settled.

### *Appliance Repairs*

Aircon
South Super Highway
Parañaque
Telephone 828-0061

Handyman Electric
1791A Mabini
Ermita
Telephone 59-97-89

Macondray & Co., Inc.
Filipinas Life Building
Makati
Telephone 79-04-85

Reserco (Carrier repair)
308 Buendia Avenue Extension
Makati
Telephone 88-94-41

Ace House of Services
153 Libertad
Pasay
Telephone 80-96-59

*Appliance Rental*

Crison's Appliance
811 E. de los Santos Avenue
Makati
Telephone 89-46-76
(Appliances rented by the week or month; prices established by
bargaining)

*Exterminating and Pest Control*

Manila Pest and Termite Control
2533 Madre Perla
Manila
Telephone 50-92-71

Pheta Pest Control
8 Magsaysay
Manila
Telephone 34-14-22

Pest Control Services
745 Aurora Boulevard
Quezon City
Telephone 79-45-67

Rentokil
575 Atlanta
Port Area
Telephone 40-98-84

*Furniture*

Arte Espanol
1128 Canonigo
Paco
Telephone 59-63-05
(Wrought iron)

Designs Ligna
Makati Commercial Center & Harrison Plaza
Makati
Telephone 85-31-20
(Wooden, upholstered, custom made)

Dave Harvey, Inc.
686 Quirino Avenue
Parañaque
Telephone 832-210
(Interior decorators)

Rattan Creations, Inc.
7909 Makati Avenue
Makati
Telephone 88-29-82
(Rattan)

*Gardening Supplies and Plants*

Bulacan Garden
51 Greenland
Pasay
Telephone 831-6147

Cartimar Market
Taft Avenue between Buendia and Libertad
Manila

Makati Garden Club (across from Urdaneta Apartments)
Makati
Telephone 817-2738

Gertrude Stewart
340 Callejon Flores
Pasay
Telephone 59-32-53
(Landscaping, house plants, also rents plants)

## *Lamps, Lampshades, and Repair*

Henry's Art Lamps and Shades
1223 A. Mabini
Ermita

Lising Crafts
1130 A. Mabini
Ermita

Moremci Lamps and Shades
1202 A. Mabini
Ermita
(Lamp repair)

Palayan
1550 A. Mabini
Ermita
(Makes lamps and shades)

## *Plumbing*

A-1 Plumbing Service
34 Rosa Roxas
Quezon City
Telephone 61-37-12

A.B.S. Plumbing Service
1013 Aurora Boulevard
Quezon City
Telephone 98-75-24

Jervis Plumbing and Service
No. 6 12th Street
New Manila
Quezon City

Ortiz Plumbing
21 Gen Tinio
Caloocan City
Telephone 35-12-70

## *Rugs and Carpets*

Carpetmasters
Makati Commercial Center
Makati

House of Rugs
1677 A. Mabini
Ermita

Nagar Rugs and Carpets
176 Salcedo Street
Makati

Tai Ping Rugs
Anson Arcade, Pasay Road
Makati

*Upholstery, Slipcovers, and Drapes*

Cancio Associates
2240 Pasong Tamo
Makati
Telephone 87-85-91
(Upholstering)

House of Decor
1872 Taft
Manila
Telephone 59-55-92
(Draperies)

The Shader
6092 Dimatimbangan Street
Parañaque
Telephone 831-8691
(Draperies, blinds)

Mrs. Julia Unas
2332 Garrido
Santa Ana
Telephone 59-87-45
(Slip covers)

## Grocery Shopping

Philippine processed foods are excellent. Fresh vegetables, primarily grown in Baguio, are often delivered straight to your door by a Baguio vegetable man. The same is true for fruits. Lamb is imported from New Zealand and Australia; beef, from New Zealand, Australia, and Argentina. Local beef from Batangas and

Cebu is also available. Local pork, veal, chicken and turkey (Tenderbird Victoria Farms, Mandaluyong) are highly rated. Many varieties of fish and seafood are available, either fresh or frozen, and the price is right—less than half of the stateside cost.

## Open Markets

The open markets that offer fruits, vegetables, fish, and a wide array of goods—ranging from exotic birds and plants to shoes and baby clothes—are a real challenge to most expatriates. The newly arrived often take their maids as a walking reference about the products for sale. As they later note that their maids are charged less than they, many resort to allowing her to do the weekly open market shopping.

Some of the open markets are: Cartimar (Taft Avenue, Pasay), Libertad (Pasay), San Andress (Malate), Quiapo (Arangue Market, morning shopping), Guadalupe (E. de los Santos Avenue, shop around 2:00 p.m.), Cubao Farmer's Market (shop around 4:00 p.m.), and Greater Manila Terminal Market.

## Supermarkets

Fruits, vegetables, meats, and breads as well as the usual processed foods are also available at: A.B. Green Farm Best Buys (7838 Makati, Makati), Makati Supermarket (Makati Commercial Center, Makati), Rustan's (Makati Commercial Center, Makati), Unimar (Greenhills, Ortigas Avenue, Mandaluyong), and United Supermarket (Makati Commercial Center and Forbes Park).

## Bakeries

Philippine bread is delicious and is available from supermarkets, as well as many bakeries. Bake shops used by expatriates include: Dulcinea (Makati Arcada, Makati), Goldilocks (2152 Pasong Ramo, Makati), Rolling Pin (Angela Arcade, Makati), and Sunny Bake Shop (7850-B Makati Avenue, Makati).

## Other Products

Locally processed milk products are of good quality and are completely safe. These may be purchased in supermarkets, or arrangements for home delivery may be made by contacting Magnolia

Milk Products (Soriamont Marketing; telephone 88-20-11). Locally made ice cream is delicious, the flavors are many and exotic, and they are available at the 33-flavors-type of establishment around Manila.

San Miguel's dry yeast as well as its beer is excellent. Home delivery by the case of beer and soft drinks may be arranged by contacting the San Miguel Corporation (telephone 882-0561).

### *Other Produce*

Fruits and vegetables differ from those with which Americans are familiar. A beginning guide to adventure in the market place includes:

*Gulay*—Vegetables

| | |
|---|---|
| Agar agar | Boiled seaweed |
| *Beno* | Purple water hyacinth buds, referred to as "sea peanuts" (inner white resembles shelled peanuts; eat with salt) |
| *Gabi* | Taro root |
| *Kang kong* | Swamp cabbage |
| *Kamias* | Filipino pickle—sour when eaten raw (use in salads, as seasoning for *sinagog,* or make into candy) |
| *Kalabasa* | Squash (boil with other vegetables to make *bulanglang)* |
| *Kulitis* | Spinachlike, wild plant |
| *Luya* | Fresh ginger (use as seasoning) |
| *Patola* (plain) | Long, smooth squash (saute and use in *pancit)* |
| *Patola* (ribbed) | Long squash with sharp ridges (peel, slice, and saute with garlic and onion; add water and noodles—*misura)* |
| *Pechay Tagalog* | Chinese cabbage (use boiled, sauteed, in salad and in *lumpia)* |
| *Tamarind* | Souring ingredient; spice |
| *Trepang* | Sea cucumber |

*Prutas*—Fruit

| | |
|---|---|
| Breadfruit | Green, knobby fruit, with mildewed appearance (peel, chop, and boil) |
| *Chico* | Brown, medium-sized fruit, tastes like pear |

| | |
|---|---|
| *Durian* | Large, spikey fruit from Davao; has unpleasant odor, but a delicious taste; said to be an aphrodisiac |
| *Guayabano* | Green, irregular, warty outside; white, sticky, sweet inside |
| Jackfruit | Long, yellow green fruit; considered expensive; portions for sale (dip in honey) |
| *Lanzones* | Small yellow fruit; flavor of grapes |
| *Macopa* | Pink, smooth fruit |
| Mango | Ripe—sweet and juicy |
| | Green—popular, eaten like a pickle |
| Mangosteen | Thick, brown rind; delicious |
| *Rambutan* | Red, spiney exterior (break open to eat inside); sweeter than grapes |
| *Saging* | Banana—there are many different types for eating and frying |

## Food Preparation

Do buy a good Filipino cookbook and become familiar with local produce and methods of preparation. Cookbooks popular with expatriates include: *From Baguio Kitchens* (Monday Afternoon Club, Baguio City, Philippines), *Cuisine Around the World* (Le Gourmet Internationale, Philippines), *Mini Cookbook* (Union Church of Manila, Philippines), Manila Cook Book (Evening News, Manila), and *The Plain and Fancy Cookbook* (Summer Institute of Linguistics, Philippines).

## Transportation

The Philippines operate on a left-hand drive basis; however, traffic is highly congested, and there is not great knowledge of, nor appreciation for, the commonly followed rules of the road. Parking is a problem, and pilferage or theft is a common occurrence. Although there is an increasing tendency, particularly among the younger expatriates, to drive yourself, many still employ full-time chauffeurs.

Shipping costs, insurance, and the 100 percent export duties make it more economical to buy a car in the Philippines. Air-conditioning is a definite plus. Six-cylinder, four-door cars reportedly have better resale value.

For-hire cars with a driver are available on a short-term basis through the major hotels. Cars with or without a driver also may be obtained from car rental agencies.

Taxis are plentiful; between 5,000 and 10,000 cruise the streets of Manila. However, some are antiquated and have drivers who appear to double as kamikaze pilots. Nonetheless, expatriates who are centrally located often use taxis in preference to assuming the problems of owning cars.

Some expatriates take jeepneys—colorful adaptations of World War II jeeps featuring extended bodies, chrome trim, folk art, and all manner of mirrors, statuettes, and streamers. Jeepneys charge nominal fees but often do not follow regular routes.

Bus service is also available both in Manila and the provinces. Routes are regular, the service frequent, and the fees are low; however, the buses are often old, poorly maintained, and very crowded. Their hard wooden benches, unglassed windows, or (in some instances) open sides are so different from what most expatriates are used to that they tend to avoid them. The Philippine Department of Tourism does have a fleet of modern air-conditioned buses that are available for interisland tours as well as regularly scheduled runs between Manila and the mountain resort of Baguio.

The Philippine National Railway operates nearly 700 miles of roadways within the archipelago. However, it is not considered a viable means of transportation by most expatriates. Most tend to prefer the regularly scheduled flights of Philippine Air Lines to towns and cities throughout the Philippines or—for a taste of the exotic—the interisland ships that sail almost daily for ports of call at major port cities.

## Communications

### *Newspapers and Magazines*

Although Pilipino is the official language, English is widely understood. There are four English daily newspapers: the *Philippine Daily Express, Bulletin Today, Times Journal,* and *Business Day.* The *American Stars and Strips* and the *Asian Wall Street Journal,* as well as *Time* and *Newsweek,* are also available at local newsstands. The Filipino bookstores are quite good and well stocked with the latest American books. A wide selection of American magazines can be found in department stores, such as the Shoe-Mart, or bookstores, such as Alemars; however, they will probably be several months old as well as expensive.

## Radio and Television

Radio and television are similar to that found in the United States with programs offered either in Pilipino or English. Many of the popular U.S. series and movie reruns are carried in English, as are the local news and public affairs programs. Locally produced shows are generally in English. There are, at present, 36 radio programs in Manila with eight broadcasting FM stereo with pop and light classics. There are five television channels in Manila, all being color equipped and having the same channel allocations as those used in the United States. (Thus American-designed television sets can be used.)

## Telephones

There is excellent long-distance service to the United States and to other parts of the world—providing the local phone is in working order. Unfortunately, phones are sometimes in disrepair for long periods of time. Single lines are almost impossible to obtain, and new phones have a six-week to two-year waiting period for installation. (It is unwise to consider renting a house that does not have a phone already installed.) Phone bells seem to ring incessantly (often with no one on the line), and there are many wrong numbers and nuisance calls.

## Postal Service

Postal service also has a reputation for unreliability. Even mail to the immediate areas may take up to three weeks for delivery and, in some instances, never arrives. There are a number of private companies that provide reliable delivery service locally, for less than the price of a U.S. postage stamp.

There are also reports of pilferage in the international mail. Packages to be mailed abroad may be taken to the Makati Commercial Center Post Office or to the Hilton Hotel Branch Office to be inspected and rewrapped there. (Take paper, tape, pen, and scissors with you.) Incoming packages are usually subject to high import duties.

Worldwide telegraph and cable service is also available and is apparently totally dependable.

## Free Time

Any time is fiesta time! And there is always something to celebrate—births, baptisms, confirmations, weddings, harvest time,

May time, or the birthday of a saint. Where else could you devote a month to fiestas honoring the Virgin Mary and extend Christmas to the longest Yuletide season in the world—a record-breaking three weeks of early dawn masses and marathon giving?

There are, however, a few things to be aware of: arriving "Filipino time" may mean any time; host country guests may arrive very late and may bring an extra guest or two—and perhaps a driver, a *ya ya* (children's nurse), and the children.

Filipinos consider eating proper reason for a fete; they prepare abundantly and would be offended if their guests did not respond to their hospitality by sampling every dish. However, no Filipino would consider making his way to the buffet table until he had been invited at least three times, and no Filipina would move through the lines unless she was properly escorted.

Business occasions many socials often in the form of cocktails or dinner; however, Filipinos often do not drink alcoholic beverages, and they may not bring their wives. Westernization is fast changing these two aspects, but reflections of the macho spirit live on in the after-hours entertainment; the beautiful "hospitality girls" are ever available, and still very acceptable.

## Entertainment

One of the more swinging spots is Manila's maritime casino— the MV Philippine Tourist—a sleek white ship lying in anchor in Manila Bay. Besides its three floors of casinos, the Manila Bay Casino operates an elegant dining room and several lounges in which top pop singers serenade the passengers. Passage is by way of the tourist ferry, operating at 15-minute intervals from the grandstand landing in Rizal Park.

Entertainment, in the best Philippine tradition, may also be found in the sophisticated supper clubs of the big hotels—the Manila, Inter-Continental, Philippine Plaza—or in one of the many bars, night clubs, or restaurants along the broad Roxas Boulevard. Disco dancing is "in" and the for-free shows in one of the many discos in Makati and Manila may be almost as good as the professional.

Filipino folk dancing is also enjoying a wave of popularity. Among the best is the internationally renowned Bayanihan Dance Troupe, which performs Saturdays at 4:30 p.m. (when they are in Manila) at the Bayanihan Folk Arts Center (Philippine Women's University Social Hall, Taft Avenue, Manila; telephone 58-31-87.)

Modern dance is presented under the auspices of the Cultural

Dance Workshop Committee, and ballet by the Manila Symphony Society. The Manila Symphony Society also presents opera, and the Manila Symphony Orchestra presents concerts. Opera in a different vein is presented by the Chinese Opera Guilde of the Philippines and should be tried by everyone at least once. While there is no legitimate theater, there are a number of drama groups that are open to international participation. One of the more outstanding is the Philippine Educational Theater Association (PETA), whose performances are considered quite professional.

Visiting concert and dance artists also perform regularly in the Philamlife or the Meralco auditoriums or in the imposing Cultural Center of the Philippines on Roxas Boulevard.

## *Movies*

Movies are another popular and very inexpensive form of entertainment. Top-run American and European films as well as Chinese, Japanese, and Filipino films are shown. The restricted and parental-guidance-suggested rated films are usually cut to conform with a "general audience" rating.

Theaters are air-conditioned and, for the most part, comfortable; but they often are crowded, as many of the local residents who arrive for the 9:00 a.m. showing have a tendency to spend the day.

The theater fires that have occurred in recent years have caused expatriates to be choosey about the theaters they patronize. They recommend:

Rizal Theatre
Makati
Excellent. But with a tendency to oversell.
May be crowded.

Quad Theatre
Quad Shopping Center
Excellent. But with a tendency to oversell.
May be crowded.

Green Hills Theatre
Vira Mall Shopping Center
Vira I and Vira II. Very good. Usually not crowded. Far out.

## *Sports*

The tropical climate, physical attributes of the islands, and a wide range of sporting facilities make the Philippines a sportsman's paradise. Golf, tennis, swimming, bowling, riding, scuba diving, and boating are all popular sports. Hunting—for the wild carabao (water buffalo) and pigs, deer, or a wide range of migratory birds, including partridge, quail, and doves—intrigues some expatriates. Other expatriates become avid fishermen, trying for the huge marlins, barracuda, tuna, leather jackets, and swordfish in saltwater; and giant eels, murrel, tilapia and catfish in freshwater; or they simply become collectors of the beautiful shells that are indigenous to this area.

Some expatriates become inveterate sightseers—hiking, backpacking, driving through the accessible areas, taking interisland steamers, or flying to others. In the Manila Guide Series, "Sightseeing in and Around Manila," written for the United States Embassy Women's Club, Frances Engel—a dedicated student, and a fine author, of Philippine history and culture—outlines a series of tours in and about Manila. She also guides longer tours into the outer regions and around the islands and lectures on the history of the areas visited. She can be reached through the U.S. Embassy Historical Library.

## *Entertainment for Children*

Entertainment is limited only by the imagination and ingenuity of parents. While there are not the large Disneyland-type entertainment centers that many expatriates are used to patronizing, there are a variety of cultural and zoological exhibits that make interesting family outings. Just a trip to one of the large, open markets—Cartimar and Libertad in Pasay, or San Andres in Makati—can be a source of delight, as well as a very real educational experience for children. At Cartimar, for example, there is a wide range of goods: everything from tropical plants to tropical pets, including a huge selection of puppies, rabbits, guinea pigs, exotic birds, and fish—even monkeys.

Of course, there is the "for real" aquarium, with tropical fishes, turtles, and eels on Palacio Street just outside Intramuros, Manila; and the Oceanarium (1340 Quirino Avenue), in Parañaque. These are good prologues to a skin-diving trip to view the fish in their natural habitat.

Children will also be delighted with the Manila Zoo (M.

Adriatico Street, just off President Quirino Boulevard, Manila), where they can view the wild animals, visit the small natural history museum, or rent a boat and sail around the minilake.

The Botanical Garden at the same spot has a wide range of native herbs, flowers, and ornamental plants. Those who really enjoy this type of outing will also want to visit the National Botanical Gardens (Real, Quezon City), the Paco Botanical Gardens (San Marcelino Street, Paco, Manila), and the Parks and Wildlife Nature Center (Quezon Memorial Park, Diliman, Quezon City).

The Rizal Park at the end of Roxas Boulevard in Manila is a favorite of most Manilans and many expatriates. Besides beautiful oriental gardens, both Japanese and Chinese, there is a special playground for blind children, a coffeehouse operated by the deaf, and an outdoor rollerskating rink. Children also love to watch the changing of the guard at the Rizal Monument, tomb of Jose Rizal, the national hero, and attend the open-air concerts given by the Manila Symphony Orchestra and other groups.

The Nayong Pilipino (Philippine Village) on the Manila International Airport Avenue in Pasay City is an exciting place to visit. There on 30 hectares is a collection of the cultural aspects of Philippine life. Miniature villages portray the life-styles of the different minority groups, while replicas of the Banaue rice terraces, Mayon volcano, and many other scenes point up the diversity of the islands, fascinating the would-be explorer. Village shops exhibit and sell crafts from the different regions; and on weekends folk dances and other cultural festivities are presented.

There are a number of museums of special interest to children and one especially designed for them, the Children's Museum and Library (East Avenue, Quezon City).

Horseback riding taught by the D-Rossa School of Horsemanship (3904 Quingua Road at Harvard, Makati; telephone 88-99-62) is an all-time favorite pastime.

Children enjoy the Fish Fun Restaurant (6 Litre, Malabon, Rizal; telephone 23-77-20), where they can catch their own fish and have it cooked to their specifications. A ferry boat ride up to Pasig River is also marvelous fun. Children also enjoy a trip to Baguio or the Island of Cebu to purchase a guitar from one of the native artisans—and then guitar lessons, Filipino style, from one of the Guitar Masters (385 E. de los Santos, Makati; telephone 89-83-10).

# Organizations

Official statistics compiled by the U.S. government list 55,000 Americans as residents of the Philippines in 1982. A comparable number of military men and dependents are also posted in the Philippines. Thousands of young servicemen who gave their lives during World War II are interned in the beautiful Manila-American Cemetery at Fort Bonifacio.

There is an extensive U.S. Mission, which includes an active Peace Corps program; and there is an ambitious American missionary program. The result has been such a pervasive American influence that there appears to be no need for either an American Club, with its umbrella of concern for American problems, or an American Women's Club to promote friendship among American women.

One group that felt there was a void and organized to draw Americans together is Hospitality International, sponsored by the Union Church of Manila (Legaspi-Rada Streets, Makati; telephone 88-99-81 or 86-38-09). Their concern for the frustrations and loneliness of the newcomer led to the publication of an informative handbook on life in the Philippines, as well as to monthly open houses and general assistance to newcomers.

Social and social-service-type organizations to which expatriates often belong include:

All Nations Women's Group
Telephone 60-12-51 or 62-14-80
(Promotion of international friendship)

Association of International College Women
(Previously Association of American College Women)
MCCPO Box 311
(Lectures on understanding of the Philippines, as well as a scholarship program)

Family Life Workshop of the Philippines
1729 J.P. Laurel Street
San Miguel
Manila
Telephone 48-32-85
(Family life and international relations)

Foster Parents Wanted
Telephone 70-49-62 or 86-67-29
(Care of children awaiting adoption in the United States; all
expenses paid)

International School P.T.A.
Bel Air
Telephone 88-98-91
(Assist with trips, plays, parties, scouting)

Manila Theater Guild—Army and Navy Club
Telephone 40-25-91
(Amateur dramatics)

Women's Board of Manila Symphony Society
Telephone 40-80-41
(General promotion of symphony)

Women's Board of St. Luke's Society
Telephone 87-97-98
(Hospital and thrift shop volunteers)

Y.W.C.A.
Telephone 50-19-26
(World fellowship and other special interest groups

Youth organizations include:

Boy Scouts of America
International School
Telephone 88-98-91

Girl Scouts of America
International School
Telephone 88-98-91

Children's Choir—Union Church
Telephone 88-99-81
(Interdenominational choir for ages 8-12)

Little League Soft Ball—American Embassy sponsored)
Telephone 59-80-11
(Ages 6-16)

Candy Stripers
Makati Medical Center
Telephone 87-60-11 or 85-33-11
(Ages 13-20)

Business clubs and fraternal organizations include:

Elks Club
Amapola Street
Makati
Telephone 88-32-08
(Dining and sports complex)

Kiwanis Club of Manila
The Medical Center
Taft Avenue
Telephone 58-25-66

Knights of Columbus
Admiral Beaterio Building
Telephone 47-61-62

Lions International
Fernandez Building
Telephone 521-5413

Manila Overseas Press Club
Roxas Boulevard
Pasay City
Telephone 831-3258

Masonic Lodge
Plaridel Temple
1440 San Marcelino
Telephone 522-1743
(Scottish rite temple)

Petroleum Club
1034 Pasay Road
Makati
Telephone 85-73-61
(Social, business; with wives' auxiliary)

Rotary International
208 Taft Avenue
Telephone 521-4859

University Club
400 Remedios
Makati
Telephone 59-34-77
(Exclusive)

Y.M.C.A.
1068 Concepcion
Manila
Telephone 47-14-61

## *Clubs*

Except for the more exclusive clubs where high membership costs and long waiting lists make them less desirable for the expatriate, memberships in private clubs provide recreational facilities at modest cost. Memberships, of course, must be sponsored by a member in good standing.

Army and Navy Club of Manila (next to American embassy). Swimming, tennis, billiards, air-conditioned dining; open to retired or ex-officers of any nation. Associate memberships to businessmen and diplomats.
Telephone 521-5161

Casino Espanol (663 T.M. Kalaw, Ermita). Chiefly Spanish, but open to others; bowling, jai alai courts, lending library, air-conditioned dining.
Telephone 522-2350

Filipino Golf Club (San Pedro). 18-hole course; dining facilities
Telephone 842-2276

Manila Boat Club (on Pasig River, 103 Havana Street). Single and double schulls, light and heavy pairs, light and heavy fours.
Telephone 58-74-31

Manila Club (1461 Colorado, Ermita). Chiefly British with associate membership to other nationals; bowling alleys, tennis courts, air-conditioned dining, popular for businessmen at lunch.
Telephone 50-10-07

Manila Golf Club (Forbes Park, Makati). 18-hole course, snack bar; membership by share purchases (seldom available).
Telephone 88-02-66

## *Churches*

Churches that are frequented by expatriates include:

Interdenominational—Union Church of Manila
Legaspi-Rada Streets
Legaspi Village
Makati
Telephone 88-99-81

Episcopalian—Church of the Holy Trinity
48 McKinley Road
Forbes Park
Makati
Telephone 817-9440

Church of Jesus Christ of Latter Day Saints
320 Buendia Avenue
Makati
Telephone 82-62-92

Jewish—Temple Emil
1963 Taft Avenue
Pasay
Telephone 59-34-31

Roman Catholic—San Antonio Church
McKinley Road
Forbes Park
Makati
Telephone 817-0411

## Health Care

Medical care in the Philippines is considered good and comparatively inexpensive. In a survey of expatriates here, most preferred to return home for major surgery; however, all agreed that emergency treatment, routine medical and prenatal care, as well as delivery were good. A number of American-trained and U.S. Specialty Board-certified doctors have offices in Manila. Plastic surgery and orthodontia, in particular, are considered noteworthy and inexpensive by U.S. standards.

The Makati Medical Center is the usual choice for hospital treatment. Expatriates who are very ill prefer the privacy afforded by a private room. It may also be necessary to have a special private-duty nurse to obtain the nursing care usually obtained from a floor nurse, or a relative or household helper in attendance to provide some of the care and to call the doctor or nurse when needed. Filipino hospital care is usually provided by a series of relatives who are in and out for various reasons and who may not have high regard for "Do Not Disturb" signs.

Makati Hospital does provide 24-hour-a-day emergency room care, but emergency ambulance service has a reputation for unreliability. It is suggested that patients be transported by private means, using whatever first-aid information and equipment may be available at the scene of the incident.

Medicines and vitamins are generally available and less expensive than in the United States. There are occasional voids, however; and incoming expatriates should bring all prescriptions and regularly used medicines for at least six months, as well as any other particular needs such as contact lens solution. Imported medical items are expensive.

Tuberculosis and intestinal parasites are common in the Philippines, and malaria is found in the rural areas. Annual physical examinations should include chest X-rays, stool examination, and blood serology. Immunizations for smallpox, typhoid, paratyphoid, tetanus, diphtheria, polio, cholera, and hepatitis should be kept up-to-date, and persons traveling into the rural areas should take a malaria prophylaxis (usually chloroquine) prior to the journey and for the prescribed number of weeks afterwards.

## Health Care of Domestics

Pre-employment physical examinations are considered imperative. Stool tests and chest X-rays should be repeated annually. Complete examinations at reasonable cost are available from the Associated Medical Specialists (third floor, Kalayaan Building, Dela Rosa and Salcedo Streets, Makati; telephone 85-59-06/7/8) and the Manila Sanitarium (1975 Donada Street, Pasay City; telephone 57-40-87).

## Health Care of Pets

The expatriate pet, like its family, must adjust to the high heat and humidity of the tropics and the diseases that go along with it. Intestinal parasites are common; the incidence of rabies is high, and there is danger of bacterial, fungal, parasitic, and allergic skin diseases. Pets should be checked regularly for the mites, lice, ticks, and fleas that cause most parasitic conditions. Open wounds should be treated carefully; blood analysis should be made periodically; immunizations should be given regularly. All puppies should be vaccinated for canine distemper, hepatitis, and leptospirosis at three to four months, and then receive booster shots annually. Cats should receive feline distemper shots at ten to 12 weeks of age, with a booster shot annually. Grooming, clipping, and boarding facilities are available at the following clinics, which also have well-qualified veterinarians:

Dr. Enrique P. Carlos
Dog and Cat Hospital
Amapola Street
Makati
Telephone 88-63-86 or 87-68-66

Dr. Francisco Cortez
Cortez Animal Hospital
153 E. de los Santos
Mandaluyong
Telephone 79-27-50

## Doing Business in the Philippines

One American businessman in the Philippines summed up his feelings in this short statement: "As long as the company keeps sending my check, I hope that the home office forgets I'm here." For many foreign businessmen, this statement says it all. The business climate is excellent in the Philippines, and living conditions are among the best in the Far East.

Philippine business runs in much the same manner as U.S. business. This is probably the result of associations before, during, and after World War II. The Philippine community has a mini-stock market patterned after Wall Street; but the investor had best be wary and keep his chips ready for a fast break. A word of caution: don't play with more than you can afford to lose. As a matter of fact, one of the few negative comments on Philippine business relates to a wicked combination of news reporting and its effect on the wild fluctuations in the stock market. As in most small countries, news travels fast; if there is a slight manipulation of the facts to affect the market—why not? The oil fever that has gripped the Philippines in the past few years has resulted in a large number of oil ventures; this group seems to be particularly vulnerable to wild market fluctuations.

The modern Philippine businessman has basically evolved from the small mother-father entrepreneurship such as the corner grocery and the handicraft shop. World War II provided an opportunity for the keen-minded Philippine businessman to expand into greater fields. An excellent example is the thriving jeepney business. When surplus supplies of jeeps were exhausted, almost anything with wheels began to look like a jeep. Even special stainless and chrome bodies can be obtained to fit almost any chassis, and the resultant jeep is hard to tell from the real thing. Body shops are adept at repairs and provide good-as-new jobs with the magic of Philippine mechanics with body solder and an acetylene torch. Philippine mechanics can make almost anything run with a modicum of parts. This mechanical ability has gained them jobs with the ship owners of the world; their aircraft mechanics are among the best anywhere. This mechanical aptitude has been a Philippine export for years, and Philippine expatriates may be found plying their mechanical skills in the far corners of the world.

Although few Filipino businessmen are the result of years of corporate training, they learn fast and soon become good "company" men. The trick is to have a planned training schedule that will allow orderly learning and testing of skills and to recycle slower learners without requiring those who are faster to waste their time repeating an already learned process. The expatriate businessman will do well to remember that much of the training done in high schools and colleges in the United States must be done by company personnel in an overseas post. The expatriate businessman not only must be a professional himself, but he must be able to teach his skills to subordinates. Knowledge without the ability to pass it on is not enough.

In some ways, doing business in the Philippines can be downright fun. For example, as in many smaller countries, the government people are accessible; and it is little wonder that with a president such as Marcos, who enjoys golf, that many ministers and deputy ministers also find the game to their liking. In the Philippines a lot of business finds its way to the fairways and greens of the lovely golf clubs in and around the capital city.

The Philippine government has tried very hard to provide a climate for attracting and keeping foreign business interests. The government rcalizes that free enterprise will do for it many of the things necessary for the development of young nations without the necessity of spending their very short supply of hard currency to do these things for themselves. This has worked out very well for the Philippine economy and provided the excellent climate for investment that exists today. Most, if not all, government policies reflect this feeling, and the expatriate businessman feels welcome in the Philippines.

A few words of caution are in order. The Philippine businessman and government officials are proud and sensitive. They do not want to offend or to be offended; so if you have asked for something or tried to do something and encounter the slightest reluctance from your Philippine associate, heed the warning signals and don't push the point. He is trying to say no or slow down or wait, but he is very sensitive and does not want to offend by saying *No*. Let it keep for awhile, and chances are that you will get most of what you need and your Filipino friend will still have kept face. Diplomacy is the keynote. Know when to slack off, and always leave your friend an out.

While there are exceptions to every rule, the wife of the American businessman in the Philippines will find herself in a position somewhere between the "left-out-of-it" in Japan and the "constant hostess" bit in some of the European countries. Philippine business treats the woman as important in social business relationships; however, she has little, if any, participation in business discussions. Unlike the Middle East, there are no social restrictions on the movement of expatriate wives. Of course, care should be taken that dress is socially acceptable.

If your business requires movements along the many islands of the Philippines, you are in luck. Most islands have modern airstrips, and even those not served by internal airlines can be reached by private aircraft. General aviation flourishes in the Philippines owing to the very favorable and realistic policies of the Civil Aviation Authority. Private charter aircraft, fixed wing, and helicopters are available at reasonable rates, flown by excellent pilots, and serviced by well-trained and qualified mechanics. Movement is not restricted, but flight plans are required. As in most countries, flights over military areas require special plans, but your charter pilots will keep you on the safe track here.

One does meet with some frustrations in doing business in the Philippines, however:

Most firms require payment on delivery, and some require down payments. Credit can be established, but this requires completion and approval of credit applications. The lack of credit facilities can be maddening.

Presidential decrees requiring withholding of taxes on payments have created a nightmare for major company accounts.

Associates are extremely sensitive to and conscious of making a mistake, thus presenting problems in obtaining true opinions and feelings in matters of mutual concern.

Labor relations are a world unto themselves, and special care must be taken by the expatriate businessman not to run afoul of the myriad rules relating to union organizing, membership, and the like.

There are some limitations on the leasing and owning of lands by foreign persons and businesses, but they are not severely restrictive and can be handled by competent Philippine lawyers and accountants.

All in all, the climate is favorable for the American expatriate to do business in the Philippines. All he needs is the will and understanding to fulfill his job and to maintain an easy grace with his Philippine counterpart. At least one expatriate has done that—the one whose quotation began this section. Try his formula.

## Legal Matters

### *Automobiles*

Persons coming to work in the Philippines are entitled to bring in one car duty-free and tax-free (unless sold locally thereafter). An international driver's license is recommended.

### *Purchase and Lease of Property*

Foreigners cannot buy land in the Philippines—not even a multinational company can unless a substantial majority of its shares are owned by Filipinos. A multinational company may own buildings and apartments, however, provided they are constructed on land leased under an agreement that has a term not exceeding 50 years in total. There are also restrictions upon foreign ownership of condominiums. It probably is just as well that these restrictions are in effect since getting clear title to property is often very difficult.

## Foreign Exchange

All foreign exchange transactions are subject to control and regulation by the Central Bank.

## Visas, Permits, and Registration

The Philippine government has authorized special incentives for the establishment of regional or area headquarters of multinational companies. Among these are relaxed visa and work permit requirements for executives of the parent company and their families. If you are assigned to such headquarters and your company issues a letter confirming your status, you will not need a work permit and you and your family will be issued multiple-entry visas. These usually are good for one year, but they can be extended annually upon proof that the qualifying conditions still exist.

Any other foreign national will need a visa and work permit secured prior to entry through application at a Philippine embassy or consulate. Foreigners already with jobs are admitted as "prearranged employees." Generally, the visas are for two years. Immigration officers at the port of entry in the Philippines have wide discretion to determine the length of stay.

All aliens except multinational headquarters executives must register and obtain a certificate for stays over 59 days. Tourists can remain in the country for up to six months without registration.

You may go to the Philippines for a get-acquainted visit or other purpose (except to work) for up to 59 days on a relatively easily obtained, no-charge visa.

## Taxes

Residency status is the key to determining tax liability in the Philippines. Most expatriates will fall into one of the nonresident alien categories. Those who are employed by a regional or area headquarters of a multinational corporation are taxed on their gross compensation received from such headquarters at a flat rate of 15 percent. Their other net income from Philippine sources is taxed at regular graduated rates. Other nonresident aliens who are engaged in a trade or business (that is, who stay in the country for an aggregate period of more than 180 days in any calendar year) are taxed on their Philippine source income at the same graduated rates applicable to residents. Nonresidents not engaged in a trade or business are levied a flat rate of 30 pecent on their gross local income. There is no separate capital gains tax. The gain or loss from the sale of capital assets is included within ordinary income.

Income is defined and deductions and exemptions allowed in a manner not unlike the U.S. system. Individual returns are filed on a calendar year basis on or before March 15 of the year following the tax year. Payment is made with the return, but it can be divided into two payments if the tax due is over a certain amount.

All persons leaving the Philippines, except regional headquarters employees, must obtain a tax clearance from the Bureau of Internal Revenue.

Other taxes of which to be aware are the stamp tax, which is levied on various documents, instruments, and transactions, including a 4 cent tax on *every* bank check; and the residence tax, which is an annual tax based on income and property that does not exceed P3,000 for individuals.

## Notes

1. As reported in "From the Philippines to the United Nations General Assembly—An Invitation to the Frontiers of the Third World" (Manila: National Media Production Center, 1977), p. 4.

2. "Five years of the New Society—Statistics and Indicators" (Manila: National Media Production Center, 1977).

3. "From the Philippines to the United Nations General Assembly."

4. Ibid.

5. "Creating New Communities in the Philippines," *Fortune,* April 23, 1979, p. 35.

6. Ibid.

# Appendix

# Appendix

It is impossible to give exact size comparisons, as clothing designs vary greatly from one country to another (for example, French clothes for women tend to be narrow in the shoulders, and the arms are shorter). These numbers will put you into the approximate size range, and you can start your search there.

## Clothing—Comparative Sizes

Women's Dresses and Suits

| | | | | | | | |
|---|---|---|---|---|---|---|---|
| Japanese | 9 | 11 | 13 | 15 | 17 | 19 | 21 |
| American | 10 | 12 | 14 | 16 | 18 | 20 | 22 |
| English | 32 | 34 | 36 | 38 | 40 | 42 | 44 |
| Continental | 38 | 40 | 42 | 44 | 46 | 48 | 50 |

Men's Suits, Overcoats and Sweaters

| | | | | | | | |
|---|---|---|---|---|---|---|---|
| Japanese | S | | M | L | | LL | |
| American | 34 | 36 | 38 | 40 | 42 | 44 | 46 |
| English | 34 | 36 | 38 | 40 | 42 | 44 | 46 |
| Continental | 44 | 46 | 48 | 50 | 52 | 54 | 56 |

Shirts: Sleeves

| | | | | | | | |
|---|---|---|---|---|---|---|---|
| Japanese | 36 | 37 | 38 | 39 | 40 | 41 | 42 |
| American | 34 | 36 | 38 | 40 | 42 | 44 | 46 |
| English | 34 | 36 | 38 | 40 | 42 | 44 | 46 |
| Continental | 44 | 46 | 48 | 50 | 52 | 54 | 56 |

Shirts: Collars

| | | | | | | | |
|---|---|---|---|---|---|---|---|
| Japanese | 36 | 37 | 38 | 39 | 40 | 41 | 42 |
| American | 14 | $14^{1}/_{2}$ | 15 | $15^{1}/_{2}$ | 16 | $16^{1}/_{2}$ | 17 |
| English | 14 | $14^{1}/_{2}$ | 15 | $15^{1}/_{2}$ | 16 | $16^{1}/_{2}$ | 17 |
| Continental | 36 | 37 | 38 | 39 | 40 | 41 | 42 |

Women's Shoes

| | | | | | | | |
|---|---|---|---|---|---|---|---|
| Japanese | 23 | $23^{3}/_{4}$ | 24 | $24^{1}/_{2}$ | 25 | $25^{1}/_{2}$ | $25^{3}/_{4}$ |
| American | 6 | $6^{1}/_{2}$ | 7 | $7^{1}/_{2}$ | 8 | $8^{1}/_{2}$ | 9 |
| English | $4^{1}/_{2}$ | 5 | $5^{1}/_{2}$ | 6 | $6^{1}/_{2}$ | 7 | $7^{1}/_{2}$ |
| Continental | 36 | 37 | 38 | 38 | 38 | 39 | 40 |

Men's Shoes

| | | | | | | | |
|---|---|---|---|---|---|---|---|
| Japanese | $24^{1}/_{2}$ | $25^{3}/_{4}$ | 26 | $26^{3}/_{4}$ | $27^{1}/_{2}$ | 28 | 29 |
| American | $5^{1}/_{2}$ | $6^{1}/_{2}$ | $7^{1}/_{2}$ | $8^{1}/_{2}$ | $9^{1}/_{2}$ | $10^{1}/_{2}$ | $11^{1}/_{2}$ |
| English | 5 | 6 | 7 | 8 | 9 | 10 | 11 |
| Continental | 39 | 40 | 41 | 42 | 43 | 44 | 45 |

# Units of Capacity

| Unit | Liquid Equivalent | Dry Equivalent |
|---|---|---|
| Milliliter (ml) | .0338 fluid ounces | .0018 pint |
| Centiliter (cl) | .3381 fluid ounces | .0182 pint |
| Deciliter (dl) | 3.3815 fluid ounces | .1816 pint |
| Liter (l) | 1.0567 quarts | .9081 quart |
| Dekaliter (dkl) | 2.6418 gallons | 1.1351 pecks |
| Hectoliter (hl) | 26.4178 gallons | 2.8378 bushels |

## WEIGHT
*(1 pound = 0.454 kilogram)*

| Kilograms | Pounds | Kilograms | Pounds |
|---|---|---|---|
| 1 | 2.2046 | 7 | 15.43 |
| 2 | 4.4 | 8 | 17.64 |
| 3 | 6.6 | 9 | 19.84 |
| 4 | 8.8 | 10 | 22.05 |
| 5 | 11.0 | 50 | 110.23 |
| 6 | 13.2 | 100 | 220.46 |

| Metric Units | Avoirdupois |
|---|---|
| Milligram (mg) | .0154 grains |
| Centigram (cg) | .1543 grains |
| Decigram (dg) | 1.5432 grains |
| Gram (g) | .0353 ounce |
| Dekagram (dkg) | .3527 ounce |
| Hectogram (hg) | 3.5274 ounces |
| Kilogram (kg) | 2.2046 pounds |
| Metric ton (t) | 1.1023 short tons |

# Lengths and Distances

*(1 foot = 0.3048 meter; 1 meter = 39 inches)*
*(1 mile = 1.609 kilometers. Roughly speaking, 1 kilometer is ²/₃ mile)*

| Meters | Feet | Meters | Feet |
|---|---|---|---|
| 1 | 3.3 | 7 | 23.0 |
| 2 | 6.6 | 8 | 26.2 |
| 3 | 9.8 | 9 | 29.5 |
| 4 | 13.1 | 10 | 32.8 |
| 5 | 16.4 | 50 | 164.0 |
| 6 | 19.7 | 100 | 328.1 |

| Kilometers | to | Miles | Miles | to | Kilometers |
|---|---|---|---|---|---|
| 1 | | 0.62 | 1 | | 1.60 |
| 2 | | 1.24 | 2 | | 3.21 |
| 3 | | 1.86 | 3 | | 4.82 |
| 4 | | 2.48 | 4 | | 6.43 |
| 5 | | 3.10 | 5 | | 8.04 |
| 6 | | 3.72 | 6 | | 9.65 |
| 7 | | 4.34 | 7 | | 11.26 |
| 8 | | 4.97 | 8 | | 12.87 |
| 9 | | 5.59 | 9 | | 14.48 |
| 10 | | 6.21 | 10 | | 16.09 |
| 20 | | 12.42 | 20 | | 32.18 |
| 30 | | 18.64 | 30 | | 48.27 |
| 40 | | 24.85 | 40 | | 64.37 |
| 50 | | 31.07 | 50 | | 80.46 |
| 60 | | 37.28 | 60 | | 96.55 |
| 70 | | 43.49 | 70 | | 112.65 |
| 80 | | 49.71 | 80 | | 128.74 |
| 90 | | 55.92 | 90 | | 144.83 |
| 100 | | 62.14 | 100 | | 160.94 |
| 200 | | 124.18 | 200 | | 321.86 |
| 300 | | 186.42 | 300 | | 482.79 |
| 400 | | 248.56 | 400 | | 643.72 |
| 500 | | 310.70 | 500 | | 804.65 |

## Converting Foreign Measurements

| To change | To | Multiply by |
|---|---|---|
| centimeters | inches | .3937 |
| feet | meters | .3048 |
| gallons (U.S.) | liters | 3.7853 |
| grains | grams | .0648 |
| grams | ounces | .0353 |
| hectares | acres | 2.4710 |
| inches | centimeters | 2.5400 |
| kilograms | pounds | 2.2046 |
| kilometers | miles | .6214 |
| liters | pints (liquid) | 2.1134 |
| liters | quarts (liquid) | 1.0567 |
| meters | feet | 3.2808 |
| meters | yards | 1.0936 |
| miles | kilometers | 1.6093 |
| millimeters | inches | .0394 |
| ounces | grams | 28.3495 |
| pints (liquid) | liters | .4732 |
| pounds | kilograms | .4536 |
| quarts (liquid) | liters | .9463 |
| yards | meters | .9144 |

## Automobile Tire Pressure Table

*(Instead of measuring tire pressure by pounds per square inch, European countries measure it in atmospheres or in kilograms per square centimeter.)*

| American (psi) | European (atmos) | European ($kg/cm^2$) |
|---|---|---|
| 16 | 1.08 | 1.12 |
| 18 | 1.22 | 1.26 |
| 20 | 1.36 | 1.40 |
| 22 | 1.49 | 1.54 |
| 24 | 1.63 | 1.68 |
| 26 | 1.76 | 1.82 |
| 28 | 1.90 | 1.96 |
| 30 | 2.04 | 2.10 |
| 32 | 2.16 | 2.24 |
| 36 | 2.44 | 2.52 |
| 40 | 2.72 | 2.80 |
| 50 | 3.40 | 3.50 |
| 55 | 3.74 | 3.85 |
| 60 | 4.08 | 4.20 |

# Weights and Measures

| *Liquid Measures* | *(1 quart = 0.946 liter; 1 gallon = 3.785 liters)* <br> *(1 imperial gallon = 1.2 U.S. gallons or 4.5 liters)* | | |
|---|---|---|---|

| *Liters* | *U.S. Quarts* | *Liters* | *U.S. Gallons* |
|---|---|---|---|
| 1 | 1.06 | 1 | 0.264 |
| 2 | 2.11 | 2 | 0.53 |
| 3 | 3.17 | 3 | 0.79 |
| 4 | 4.23 | 4 | 1.06 |
| 5 | 5.28 | 5 | 1.32 |
| 6 | 6.34 | 6 | 1.58 |
| 7 | 7.40 | 7 | 1.85 |
| 8 | 8.45 | 8 | 2.11 |
| 9 | 9.51 | 9 | 2.38 |
| 10 | 10.6 | 10 | 2.64 |
| | | 50 | 13.20 |
| | | 100 | 26.40 |

| *U.S. Quarts* | *Liters* | *U.S. Gallons* | *Liters* |
|---|---|---|---|
| 1 | 0.946 | 1 | 3.78 |
| 2 | 1.89 | 2 | 7.57 |
| 3 | 2.84 | 3 | 11.36 |
| 4 | 3.79 | 4 | 15.14 |
| 5 | 4.73 | 5 | 18.93 |
| 6 | 5.68 | 6 | 22.71 |
| 7 | 6.62 | 7 | 26.50 |
| 8 | 7.57 | 8 | 30.28 |
| 9 | 8.52 | 9 | 34.07 |
| 10 | 9.50 | 10 | 37.85 |
| | | 15 | 56.79 |
| | | 20 | 75.71 |

# Temperatures

*(To Convert Fahrenheit to Centigrade, subtract 32 and multiply by $5/9$.*
*To convert Centigrade to Fahrenheit, multiply by $9/5$ and add 32.)*

| Centigrade (Celsius) | Fahrenheit | Centigrade (Celsius) | | Fahrenheit |
|---|---|---|---|---|
| 40 | 104.0 | 17 | | 62.6 |
| 39 | 102.2 | 16 | | 60.8 |
| 38 | 100.4 | 15 | | 59.0 |
| 37 | 98.6 | 14 | | 57.2 |
| 36 | 96.8 | 13 | | 55.4 |
| 35 | 95.0 | 12 | | 53.6 |
| 34 | 93.2 | 11 | | 51.8 |
| 33 | 91.4 | 10 | | 50.0 |
| 32 | 89.6 | 9 | | 48.2 |
| 31 | 87.8 | 8 | | 46.4 |
| 30 | 86.0 | 7 | | 44.6 |
| 29 | 84.2 | 6 | | 42.8 |
| 28 | 82.4 | 5 | | 41.0 |
| 27 | 80.6 | 4 | | 39.2 |
| 26 | 78.8 | 3 | | 37.4 |
| 25 | 77.0 | 2 | | 35.6 |
| 24 | 75.2 | 1 | | 33.8 |
| 23 | 73.4 | 0 | (Freezing) | 32.0 |
| 22 | 71.6 | −1 | | 30.2 |
| 21 | 69.8 | −2 | | 28.4 |
| 20 | 68.0 | −3 | | 26.6 |
| 19 | 66.2 | −4 | | 24.8 |
| 18 | 64.4 | −5 | | 23.0 |

# Furniture Dimensions
## For use in designing custom-made furniture

*Living Room*

| | |
|---|---|
| Chairs and sofas | 14" to 18" from surface of seat to floor |
| Coffee tables | Comparable to height of sofa or 1" or 2" less |
| Lamp table | 17½" to 20½" high for large to average lamp tables; 28" high for small lamps |
| Game tables | 32" square; 27" to 30" high |
| Game chair | 16" to 18" from surface of seat to floor |
| Desk | Writing surface 29" from floor |
| Desk chair | 18" from surface of seat to floor |
| Bookcase | Shelves at least 10" deep; 10" to 14" in height |

*Dining Room*

| | |
|---|---|
| Dining table | 27½" to 29½" high |
| Dining chairs | 18" from seat surface to floor |
| Sideboard | 18" deep; serving surface 36" from floor |

*Bedroom*

| | |
|---|---|
| Beds | 6" to 8" from bottom of box spring |
| Highboy | 20" deep; 45" to 60" high |
| Dresser | 20" to 22" deep; 34½" to 36½" high |
| Dressing table | 16" to 22" deep; 30" high |
| Dressing table stool | 16" to 18" high |
| Nightstands | 28" high |

*Kitchen*

| | |
|---|---|
| Table | 27½" to 29½" |
| Work counters | 36" from floor (average—may also be based on individual sizes) |

# Weight Chart

| Article | Estimated Weight (pounds) | Article | Estimated Weight (pounds) |
|---|---|---|---|
| *Bedroom* | | Spinet | 350 |
| Bed, spring, and mattress | | Upright | 650 |
|   Bunk—2 | 275 | Bench | 35 |
|   Double | 150 | Rack, magazine | 10 |
|   King size | 230 | Radio | |
|   Single | 120 |   Portable | 10 |
| Chair | |   Table | 15 |
|   Rocker | 25 | Rug | |
|   Straight | 20 |   Large | 75 |
| Chest of drawers | 180 |   Small | 20 |
|   Dresser | 200 | Pad | |
|   Dresser, vanity | 150 |   Large | 35 |
| | |   Small | 15 |
| *Dining room* | | Sofa | |
| Bar, portable | 120 |   Two-cushion | 150 |
| Buffet or breakfront | 200-300 |   Three-cushion | 200 |
| Cart, tea | 40 |   Hide-a-bed | 230-250 |
| Chair, straight | 30 | Stereo equipment | |
| Chinaware (packed per | |   Speaker | 40 |
|   cubic foot) | 12 |   Tuner and amplifier | 45 |
| Server | 110 |   Turntable | 25 |
| Table and extensions | 210 |   Tape deck, | |
| | |     reel-to-reel | 35 |
| *Living room and family room* | |   Tape deck, cassette | 20 |
| Bookcase | 100 | Table | |
| Bookshelves, sectional | 25 |   End, coffee or nest | 40 |
| Chair | |   Library | 100 |
|   Arm | 50 |   Occasional | 90 |
|   Occasional | 50 | Television | |
|   Rocker | 40 |   Console | 160 |
|   Straight | 25 |   Portable | 40 |
| Clock, grandfather | 100 |   Table model | 65 |
| Desk | | | |
|   Small | 100 | *Nursery* | |
|   Secretary | 200 | Bassinet | 35 |
| Fireplace equipment | 35 | Bed, youth | 110 |
| Lamp, floor | 20 | Chair | |
| Piano | |   Child's | 20 |
|   Baby grand | 500 |   High- | 25 |
|   Concert grand | 1,000 | Chest of drawers | 80 |

| Article | Estimated Weight (pounds) | Article | Estimated Weight (pounds) |
|---|---|---|---|
| Chest, toy | 20 | Sewing machine, | |
| Crib, baby | 80 | portable | 50 |
| Playpen | 35 | Washing machine | 200 |
| Table, child's | 35 | | |
| | | *Miscellaneous* | |
| | | Grill or barbecue | 40 |
| *Kitchen* | | Gym Set, outdoor, | |
| Ironing board | 15 | child's | 140 |
| Cabinet | | Outdoor furniture | |
| Kitchen | 210 | Lawn chair | 20 |
| Utility | 75 | Rocker, swing | 80 |
| Chair, breakfast | 25 | Settee | 100 |
| Roaster | 35 | Swing, outdoor | 220 |
| Stool | 10 | Filing cabinet | 140 |
| Table, breakfast | 90 | Can, trash | 15 |
| | | Carriage, baby | 75 |
| | | Carton, books per | |
| *Appliances* | | cubic foot | 25 |
| Air-conditioner, | | Clothing | 40 |
| window | 210 | Linen | 65 |
| Dehumidifier | 60 | Cleaner, vacuum | 30 |
| Dishwasher | 150 | Clothes hamper | 10 |
| Dryer, electric or gas | 175 | Fan, electric | 30 |
| Freezer | | Golf balls and clubs | 40 |
| 10 cubic feet or less | 210 | Heater, gas or electric | 35 |
| 11 to 15 cubic feet | 315 | Hose, garden, and tools | 80 |
| 16 cubic feet and | | Ladder | |
| over | 420 | Extension | 45 |
| Range, electric or gas | 220 | Step | 25 |
| Refrigerator | | Mower | 35 |
| 6 cubic feet or less | 210 | Hand | 75 |
| 7 to 10 cubic feet | 315 | Tool chest | 100 |
| 11 cubic feet or over | 420 | Tricycle | 25 |
| Sewing machine | 100 | Wagon, child's | 35 |

# Index

# About the Authors

JOHN KEPLER, President of Kepler Associates Ltd., an international relocation firm, has been an international lawyer for over twenty years. He was a member of the Foreign Service of the State Department and a special agent in the U.S. Army Counter Intelligence Corps. He was graduated from George Washington University Law School and received his undergraduate degree from Northwestern University. He also did graduate work at the University of Chicago, London School of Economics and the Institute of Advanced Legal Studies of the University of London, and New York University. Mr. Kepler has been a guest lecturer on international matters at several World Trade Institute seminars and before other organizations.

ORVILLE GAITHER is Vice-President, Africa and Middle East Region, for Amoco Production Co. (International). He has a total of 34 years of professional experience, 16 of which have been directly related to the international field. Mr. Gaither is the author of a number of professional papers, and holds a Master's degree in Petroleum Engineering from the University of Houston, and a Bachelor's degree in Engineering from Rice University. He is also a graduate of Stanford University's Executive Program.

PHYLLIS KEPLER was a reporter and home furnishings editor on the *Indianapolis News* and at present is a free-lance journalist. Her articles on travel have appeared in the *Ladies Home Journal, Women's World, New York Times, Chicago Tribune, Los Angeles Times,* and other publications. She has traveled extensively throughout the world to interview children, their parents, and teachers for a series of articles that appeared in the many Scholastic publications, distributed in schools throughout the United States. She taught school both here and abroad and served in U.S. Army intelligence. She was graduated from Northwestern University with a degree in journalism.

MARGARET GAITHER is a psychiatric social worker with Bachelor's and Master's degrees from the University of Texas. She has served on the staff of both the University of Texas—M.D. Anderson Hospital, and Baylor University—Jefferson Davis Hospital, as well as holding the position of Consulting Social Worker, Visiting Nurses Association, in Houston. She has been associated with Clearbrook Center, which provides services to the mentally handicapped youth of Northwest Chicago, and was instrumental in establishing the early education program for the infant retarded.